A Lumbertown Tale
Volume I
They All Fall

K. Wallin

authorHOUSE™

1663 LIBERTY DRIVE, SUITE 200
BLOOMINGTON, INDIANA 47403
(800) 839-8640
WWW.AUTHORHOUSE.COM

First published by AuthorHouse 11/05/04

ISBN: 1-4184-9809-2 (sc)

Printed in the United States of America
Bloomington, Indiana

This book is printed on acid-free paper.

For Elizabeth, the love of my life,
my steadfast companion and devoted friend

The First Chapter

A Most Peculiar Fellow

The winds of October blow cool and indifferent through the muddy streets of St. Paul. They gust and swirl down the alleyways, chasing smoke from the chimneys and causing passersby to clutch their clothes tightly about them as they hurry on their way. Those that know of such things can sense the hand of winter on these October winds and see snow in the heavy gray clouds of the northern sky. There are others, however, that refuse to entertain such gloomy thoughts, thinking fondly of Indian summers they have known, sure that the weather will warm to pleasant days once more. October, she just laughs and winter comes when it will.

At the railway depot in St. Anthony Park of St. Paul, the nightly 4:15 was running late, though not so unusual this time of year. Trains were the necessary course of business and travel these days, and St. Paul fairly bustled with both, expanding its boundaries almost daily, or so it seemed.

The ominous gray clouds that had moved in from the Dakotas last night, now sat low and dark on the shoulders of the tall buildings, a stark contrast to the fiery colors of autumn found throughout the city. Seeded by northerly winds they soon began to cast a fine drizzle, occasionally punctuated by mumbles and grumbles of thunder lost deep within. It was a most miserable bit of weather to those that had to be out of doors this day.

Most everyone that was waiting for the 4:15 going north were dry and comfortable in the depot, staring out of the rain soaked glass at the shifting

1

clouds or involved in the simple chatter of weather or politics or similar fare. Mothers whispered softly to their children, telling stories or singing sweet songs to pass the time. Businessmen, gathered under the lights to read their newspapers and smoke, compared the time on their watches now and again, mumbling under their breath about schedules and trains. Young lovers milled about slowly, clutching each other's hands as a symbol of embrace, pressing tightly to initiate an intimate glance and warm knowing smile. There was some comfort in the stifling warmth of this crowd, some bond that moved them closer together with each grumble of the darkening sky.

But there was one waiting passenger who would not suffer this close association, choosing instead the hostility of the night. He stood in the dark shadows of the train yard, midst the cold gray bulk of idle machinery, withdrawn into a narrow alcove nearly invisible to the depot platform. His coat was pulled tight with the collar up against the wind, his hat pulled down snug against the rain. Once or twice he gave an involuntary shiver and cursed through clenched teeth, the 4:15.

If he shifted his head to peer about in the gathering gloom of the late afternoon sky as he often did, the rain trickled down his neck, a cold intrusion on what little warmth he still maintained against the night, bringing yet another shiver and curse.

In spite of his discomfiture he made no move when the mournful whistle of the 4:15 turned his attention again to the south. From his cold and miserable perch, he watched nervously as the lumbering engine began a slow chug and clang into the train yard, the smoke from its stack bullied about by the wind in playful swirls until it settled in low along the ground in stifling clouds of sulfur and soot. It made him cough weakly, the sound quickly muffled by the wet wool of his rain soaked sleeve.

As the engine slowed to a stop near the depot in a cacophony of squeaks, squeals and groans, a sigh of steam escaped from the black machine and suddenly the dusk was illuminated with lanterns and alive with people scurrying about.

Still he did not move. Passengers leaving the train appeared in the doorways, pausing to squint awkwardly into the wet night, and then hurrying off to meet family and friends in the shelter of the depot platform. Almost as quickly the waiting passengers inside filed out of the lighted warmth and made stumbling dashes through the mud for the cars, women holding on to their skirts and hats and the men lumbering behind them with bag and baggage.

This scene was watched from his dark corner for some time, until most movement around the train cars had ceased and the depot agent, again checking his watch, readied to signal the engineer. Then he picked up his small valise and stumbled out of the misty dusk.

The depot agent, a rather rotund fellow with huge jowls, was startled at first, to see this wet bedraggled man appear from out of the shadows. He lifted his lantern high and stared at the ragged form thinking it a miserable wretch of unfortunate circumstance come to beg for warmth and food.

"Train to Pratt?" the young man queried through wet bluish lips.

The agent looked him over for a few seconds, briefly reassessing his first impression, deciding it was not far off in spite of the query. He scratched absently at his many chins while pondering the situation. "Now where in blazes did you come from? Soakin' wet ya are." The depot agent shook his head at the thought of it.

"I need to get to Pratt. Pratt, Wisconsin," he said again in that hoarse whisper that had become his speaking voice of late, and then cast his head about nervously to see if anyone else had heard. Curious, the agent followed his looks to either side wondering what it was they were looking for, then peered at him closely and watched another shiver wrack his frame.

"Right ya are," said the agent deciding to waste no more time on the matter, "this one's heading north to Ashland and Bayfield and Pratt's in there somewhere between or so they say, never been there myself." The man nodded and a small stream of water rolled off his hat.

"She's ready to get going now, though she's a bit late at that," added the agent. He pulled out his pocket watch as if to confirm that fact, his thick chubby fingers fumbling with the cover. He peered at it closely in the dismal light that remained of the day while a low grumble of thunder moved across the sky. Then nodding his head in affirmation, he slowly held the lantern out again, his mouth open as if to speak. But the pathetic young man had disappeared.

"Well, now!" He shrugged his shoulders and shook his head at such foolishness. Then feeling the chill of the drizzle begin to penetrate his clothes, he hurriedly signaled the engineer with long sweeping arcs of the lantern and retreated to the light and warmth of the depot.

The Pratt bound passenger had carefully selected the rear most car of the train, just forward of the caboose, in which to settle in. There were few others in the car; a family or two, a young couple slumped close as if for warmth, a few rather large and crude looking men in heavy woolen clothes.

He sat near the back, the valise stashed between his feet, avoiding the curious gaze of his fellow passengers by appearing to stare out the window

3

at the mist-shrouded buildings of brown and gray. In mute silence they passed, all bundled up against the rain behind sturdy doors and shutters. But the buildings held no interest for him. In the dim kerosene light of the moving car, he watched the reflections of the passengers in the rainy glass, watched them shuffling and sliding and peering about until at last they lost interest in all but their own little affairs.

As the train continued on, slowly gaining speed in bumps and jerks, he allowed a barely audible sigh to escape his lips, the tightness in chest beginning to ease. It made him cough ever so lightly and quickly stifled once more. He removed his sodden hat, brushed what water he could out of it, then replaced it snugly on his head, low over his eyes nearly covering his face. In spite of his present condition; wet, cold and just a little bit hungry, he allowed himself a weak smile as he watched the last of the lights of St. Paul fade into the darkness behind him.

And as the musty odor of soggy wool slowly seeped into his senses, sharpened now by days of constant watch and worry, he found himself beginning to ease into the naturally relaxing rhythm of the rails, rocking him gently, letting the weariness of the last few days slowly overtake him like a drug.

How long the train had been rumbling on to the north, he didn't know. He hadn't slept but had been lost in the myriad of thoughts that had taken hold of his mind and quickly cut him off from time and travel.

He re-focused on the present now as a conversation in the front of the car began to get loud. He couldn't quite make out the words of the men but could sense some heat to them. It made him settle deeper into his seat and pull his hat down further over his face, as if it would make him disappear.

Each stop along the railway brought a little of this anxiety to the surface, quickening his pulse if only briefly and forcing him to peer out from under his hat in sinister fashion at those that came into the car. Until finally, far north into this rainy October evening, it no longer seemed important and his fears were set aside, allowing the weariness once again to show through and casting him into a light fitful sleep.

When the train stopped at Spooner, the men who had been in heated discussion from time to time got off and stumbled along into the night. The young man was roused from a restless slumber long enough to peer out on the bustling town, noting even on this dismal evening, the noise and lights of the barrooms and bawdy houses down the muddy streets.

4

There were other short whistle stops along the way, lumber towns all, snatches of light and life in the dark wilderness of the north through which they passed. He watched as if in a trance, unmoving, his two dark eyes peering out from under his sodden hat at the events surrounding him.

On into the night the engine rumbled, the names of the little towns forgotten by this weary traveler before the lights of their warm buildings had even faded behind them. Until at last a signboard made him sit up in his seat and take notice. It was the bustling little mill town of "Drummond", deep in the piney woods of Wisconsin. No bigger than the others, no more special, but he had been told that Pratt was the next village up the line. Like a statue come to life, he was suddenly animated once more, nervously pulling on his eyebrows, his eyes dancing about while he was in thought, his weariness set aside.

So, the journey was almost over... and what then?

The depot at Pratt was fairly deserted as the train pulled in. Julius Halprin, the depot agent, gently set his lantern down and pulled a watch from his vest pocket. He peered at it closely, bringing it near to the depot window and raising his glasses a little. Then he shook his head.

"Late again, Mr. Cooper," he said. "Third time this week. Might as well change the schedule."

John Cooper, a well dressed gentleman leaning against the depot wall in the shadows and almost out of the rainy drizzle, reached into his coat pocket and pulled out a cigar. His face was briefly lit in a soft orange glow as he touched a match to the end of it.

"Now, Julius," he said between puffs, "might be there was a reason." He shook the match out and tossed it aside.

"Well, there's always a reason," came the reply. "Weather's too wet, weather's too dry, cows on the track or the engineers got indigestion. I know'em all. But there's something about this night, I'd say, the way the winds been mussing about, the rain switching directions so a person don't know which way to turn to keep dry. Seems like the night is even darker than usual, course that could just be October and the rain. Nights just seem to get darker in October, don't know why. But I don't like it, I don't like it at all.

"But she's here. Hey! Bert!" yelled the agent suddenly, and off he strode toward the engine mumbling to himself about late trains and October nights.

There was only one passenger getting off at Pratt that Cooper could see: Mrs. Muggsley, a middle aged woman of great charm and beauty, splendidly dressed as if she was on her way to the theater instead of stepping down into this crude little lumber town. Cooper's eyes followed her as she moved gracefully across the depot platform, a low sigh barely escaping his lips as he appreciated the simple elegance she brought to a dark rainy night.

Mrs. Muggsley was soon met by a huge gruff looking man, a stark contrast to what one would expect for such a woman. They hugged briefly, her small frame being swallowed up by his bear like arms around her. It made Cooper wince a little, though he didn't know why, exactly. Mr. Muggsley was a sociable man. Then slipping her delicate hand into his huge paw, they walked off to a wagon waiting behind the depot. As Cooper wondered about this odd pairing, he could hear them rattling off slowly into the night. Most of the other passengers had been dropped off at the many other whistle stops along the way or were heading north to the Lake Superior country, to the cities of Ashland and Bayfield on Chequamagon Bay.

Soon, the agent was back, carrying a brown satchel under his arm and still mumbling, then laughing to himself. "Hah! Says Roosevelt's train come first down in St. Paul and he had to wait at the switching station. I bet Roosevelt never even been to St. Paul.

"But she's here, finally. Not startin' up a camp this soon, are ya, Mr. Cooper? Got some 'jacks' on this one? There's snow in them skies alright", he observed, squinting up into the night, "but the grounds as soft as swamp water, I'd say."

"No Julius," he replied, "just meeting a friend from the cities." They both looked around for this mysterious passenger but the platform was empty and most of the cars were dark. When the train was ready to move on, Cooper was still leaning against the wall quietly.

"Appears he missed this one, Mr. Cooper," said the agent. "She's ready to go. 'Course she won't make up much time on the schedule tonight, but might as well send'er on, I 'spose." He held up the lantern toward the engine and waved it back and forth a few times until the whistle sounded and the big machine, belching smoke and steam, began to move.

As the last car was passing the depot, a figure suddenly appeared in the doorway, looked around quickly, then jumped awkwardly down onto the platform, startling the men already there.

"For goodness sakes!" exclaimed the agent.

"Well, damn my bones!" muttered Cooper.

John Cooper warily approached this dark apparition at the edge of the platform, with Julias just slightly behind him. As they drew near, Julias held the lantern outstretched, illuminating him in eerie patterns of shadow and form, distorting his size and appearance and muddling his features.

"Well, what the.... where'd.... how come you..." stuttered the agent.

Cooper remained quiet, staring at the young man, looking him up and down with a piercing gaze and sensing the nervous energy lying within. Even in the false shadows of the light, he noted dark eyes in a pale and handsome face, unable to hold steady under his scrutiny, and clothes more akin to city streets. He watched, unspeaking still, until the lad coughed weakly and shivered, his eyes blinking against the light.

"Perhaps you'd like to follow me back to my office," said Cooper calmly, puffing lightly on his cigar.

The young man looked him over nervously before responding. Cooper seemed like the kind of man he was told to look for; neatly dressed in coat and vest with an air of respectability about him. There was a broad brimmed white hat gracing a head of silver hair. A distinguished mustache rode above the protruding cigar, which danced about in his lips as he waited for an answer. But the more intimate features of the gentlemen's face remained indistinguishable against the light.

"That your friend, Mr. Cooper?" asked the depot agent while trying to rub the rain off his glasses with his forefinger.

"I don't know, Julias," Cooper replied cryptically. "Are you?" he asked of the young man.

He nodded silently. And with that little bit of commitment and without another word spoken, Cooper turned his back and began to disappear into the darkness, his new 'friend' at first hesitant, then struggling to keep up.

And as he followed the dark shape ahead of him, up a rough climb and over the bluff, led by a near invisible trail of cigar smoke and smell, it occurred to the young man that he may have made a mistake. It made him weak in the knees and the hill hard to climb.

Julias Halprin could only shake his head and mumble to himself, about train schedules, rainy nights, and peculiar visitors that don't have nothing to say.

He turned the lantern down and entered the depot, still mumbling while he went about his business, sorting the incoming papers and logging the nights work in his ledger. But the whole thing made him jumpy, what with the weather and all to boot. So much so, that he nearly fell out of his chair when the night telegraph operator came in sometime later, disturbing him in the middle of these ponderous thoughts and the wind, taking hold of the door, pushed it open with a sudden bang. It started Julias to mumbling all over again.

"What's that you say, Julias?" asked "Nightowl" Bill after he had closed the door again and began to remove his coat. "What's got you so skittish, anyway?"

"Well, the train was late again... always late...ain't cause of Roosevelt, I'd say... and that stranger... most peculiar fellow... nothing good will come of it... nothing good... jumpin' off trains in the middle of the night. You mark my words, Bill... nothing good comes out of a night like this, nothing good at all."

The Second Chapter

Pratt, Wisconsin

Late into the night the wind lost some of its playfulness, allowing a cool autumn drizzle to find its way to the ground unhindered. If you looked closely about the skies, you could see fine flecks of snow nearly hidden in the mist, occasionally caught in whatever light was yet to be found along the streets and alleyways, a most encouraging portent to the lumber towns along the Chicago, Minneapolis, St. Paul and Omaha line.

Pratt was indeed one such town, whose fragile economy for the most part relied on the pine and hardwood forests to the south, supplemented by the small farms taken up where the lumberman had already reaped a fine harvest with axe and saw. The 'easy' wood had been taken some years before, that along the main railroad line, spurred on by Charles Pratt who would not only prosper well by this first harvest of virgin pine, but would lend his name to this little village often called the "sightliest" town on the Omaha Road.

To the south lie the wooded hills, a rise of nearly 500 feet of gradual inclines reaching to the great watershed divide; water on the south side running eventually to the Mississippi and down to the gulf of Mexico, while water on the north finding it's way through the low country of marsh and swamp and on to Lake Superior. Two fine trout streams wandering down from the hills touch the town on the right and left, and these empty into Long Lake streams a mile below in the marshy swampland of White River, a light brown ribbon meandering its way northeast to the great lake.

The view from the railroad, running east to west at least 80 feet above this rich loam country, is full of beauty, embracing the wide wooded valley of the White River and the pine covered hills to the northwest, almost to the source of the Long Lake streams.

Nearly 400 people make their permanent home here, in the village and the farms surrounding, with a number of lumberjacks coming and going according to the season. And for the most part, Pratt is a quiet little town of modest means.

The Straddle Creek Lumber Company, an organization born of the Cooper brothers of New Richmond, moved into Pratt sometime after the recovery from the great bank panic of 1893, it's eye on the less accessible wooded lands to the south and southeast. The company owns the Mercantile, runs the area logging operations and services the remote camps with a standard gauge railroad called the Pratt & Southeastern, with tracks connecting to the main railroad in the village. Though the lumber business in Pratt makes up only a small part of the Cooper organization, brother John has taken it up as his own personal affair, sometimes from his office in New Richmond, but more often than not from an office in the village, up along the bluff strategically overlooking the splendid view of the lowlands to the north.

At this time of night there are few lights still burning, save for the depot where Nightowl Bill stands his lonely vigil. Even the saloons have surrendered to the evening, waking those that had stayed too long and shooing them home. The smell of woodsmoke is in the air, early fires for the early cold of October.

The light in the office of the Straddle Creek Lumber Co. still burns brightly though the business day has come and gone. John Cooper, sitting behind his desk, watches intently as the young man before him removes wet layers of clothing, working clumsily with shivering hands. Now and again Cooper would grunt or cough lightly, just to remind him that he was not alone.

"Pretty wet aren't ya," he started finally. "That Omaha car must of sprung a leak along the way... or have you been swimming? No matter, I guess... it's your business. Hope you have some dry clothes in that bag." There was no response from the mysterious visitor, as if he were deaf to the world about him. He glanced briefly down at the valise near his feet then shifted his gaze slowly along the floor of the room deliberately avoiding Cooper.

"In case you haven't guessed by now, my name is John Cooper," he continued. "Ed Harding said you were coming tonight, but he was a little cryptic in the details. Didn't even mention your name, come to think of it." He watched for a reaction from his guest but he didn't even look up from taking off his wet boots. "Is there a reason that I shouldn't know your name?"

The young man stopped suddenly and slowly sat up straight, eyeing Cooper warily. His thick brown hair was in disarray and wet and his face was shiny from the rain. But he didn't answer. He sat there trembling lightly, no thoughts able to form themselves into words.

John Cooper leaned back in his chair and puffed thoughtfully on his cigar while his guest shifted about nervously. "Harding seems to think I owe him something," he continued suddenly, "and maybe I do. He's calling in his marker. Says to merely offer you comfort and hospitality without the burden of explanation." The two men looked eye to eye for the first time, until the younger man once more had to look away.

"I am probably going to help my good friend... and that means helping you," continued Cooper in the one sided conversation. "But let me tell you something, mister, this is a small town and people will want to know all about you; who you are and why you are here. It's their nature."

Cooper paused for effect then, his lips shifting around the cigar to allow for a stream of smoke to spiral upwards. The silence played on both men's nerves.

"Well, assuming you can speak when you want to, they are going to be asking you a lot of questions or questions of me, and it would be helpful to know some answers. Don't get me wrong son, your business, such that it is, can be held as close as you want, make no mistake about that. But you are going to have to get your act together. And mister, an act it is."

Cooper stood up then and pulled his coat straight. He forcefully put out the stub of his cigar in a big glass ashtray on the desk where it continued to smolder miserably.

"In the back you'll find a cot and a small stove already lit and warm. I suspect you'd rather not put up at the Pratt Hotel just yet," he said as he moved toward the door.

"Thanks, Mr. Cooper," said the young man finally, "I appreciate your kindness, under the circumstances."

"Hrrmmph," grunted Cooper ominously. "Could be your thanks is a little premature. I'll be back in the morning after you've had a chance to think things out. Could be you'll feel a bit more like talking after a good night's sleep."

Cooper left the room in an obviously unpleasant mood, the door shutting a little harder than it was used to, rattling the pictures on the wall and startling the half-dressed, shivering young man.

In a back room off to the side of Cooper's office he found his lodgings. A small pot bellied stove in the corner radiating a comfortable warmth, a small cot up against the wall and a little table with a wash bowel and pitcher, were the extent of the furnishings. He took notice of a door leading to the back of the building and poked his head out once to have a look-see. Through the cold misty rain he could still make out the dim glow of the light at the depot down along the tracks and oddly, he found it some comfort. He noticed also that there was a pile of hardwood chunks for the stove stacked along the north wall under a protective lean-to.

Shivering, he pulled the door in tight behind him and huddled briefly in front of the stove. As the warmth began to penetrate he shed the rest of his wet clothes down to his underwear and moving the table closer he replaced the pitcher and bowl with his wet things draped over the side nearest the heat. When he felt warm and dry enough he crawled into the cot and pulled the good wool blankets up close. If this wasn't sanctuary, he reasoned while listening to the pop & crackle of the wood burning in the stove and feeling its warmth, it was close enough for tonight.

The morning dawned cool and bright on the northland. The kind of day that brings the partridges to sit on grassy banks to warm themselves in the sun and starts the geese to winging south high up in the bright blue October sky. The small woodstove was long cold by the time the young man began to stir. He gathered the few blankets tight around him in a circle of warmth and tried to recapture the lost moments of sleep, but it was no use. Images of the last few weeks darkly clouded his mind, making him toss and turn in restless angst, until finally admitting defeat, he sat up in bed and rubbed the sleep from puffy reddened eyes. He could hear some stirring in the outer office; the moving of chairs, the clink of an ashtray and some occasional barely stifled coughing. When cigar smoke eventually found its way to the back room, he figured it was time to rise.

"Good morning, Mr. Cooper," he said with an attempt at cheerfulness. It was the first time he saw his benefactor in good light, noting the lively blue eyes, the graying hair and well trimmed mustache, and the fine cut of his clothes, truly a gentleman of business.

"Yes it is," answered John. He was leaning back in his great chair behind the desk, holding a copy of the Bayfield County Press, one of the local newspapers. "I trust you slept well. It's a beautiful day today, just beautiful. I think I smell a bit of snow in the wind."

"Warmer than yesterday, I think," added the young man. "And I don't hear that damnable rain. Snow? It's gonna snow already?"

"Well, the smell isn't that strong...just a whiff...but there could be snow soon...there should be snow soon." Cooper took on a wistful look, as if trying to conjure up a snowstorm.

"Anything is possible, I guess."

"Well that should do for a weather report," said Cooper suddenly coming forward in his chair and giving over to an icy stare, his blue eyes suddenly turning dark and penetrating. "Suppose we establish a playing field here. You tell me all that you figure you can, and I'll decide if I am able to help you. Or want to for that matter."

"Sounds fair," said the other, pulling up a chair in front of the desk.

"Fine, but no lies, no games. You tell me what you can and leave out the rest if you have to. I have enough business sense to know deception when I hear it and it's seldom made me an agreeable man."

Mr. Cooper seemed to be larger than life sitting behind the desk and Leon suddenly felt like a schoolboy called to task by the teacher. As he started to talk he found his mouth had gone dry.

"I'm a friend of Mr. Harding of St. Paul... or my father was. The Harding Mill & Paper Co.?"

"Of course."

"Well it seems Mr. Harding has been plagued by a bit of trouble lately... a missing payroll or two taken off the train down south of here. He thinks that it may involve a few of the lumberjacks in this area. Of course it's not certain yet, but that's primarily why I'm here in Pratt; to find out more information... get a lead on the perpetrators."

"I see. And that's your line of work is it? This detective thing?"

"Well... my father was a Pinkerton man."

"I don't see your father here."

"No... I.. I'm on my own. Mr. Harding thought I might be of some use in finding something out."

"Well, I will admit that it can be a bit primitive up in this part of the country, son", injected Mr. Cooper, "but we do have the law up here. As a matter of fact I know the sheriff of this county personally. He's a very capable man."

"Yes, well, Mr. Harding did not want to get the law involved just yet. He felt that a bit more information was needed on the whole affair before going to the authorities."

There was silence as Cooper sat puffing on a cigar and the young man sat across from him fidgeting.

"Well," he started again, "it seems that the information on the suspects came from a well known harlot down in St. Paul. Perhaps you have heard of her; Swede Annie?" Mr. Cooper's face betrayed no emotion.

"Swede Annie, uh... in the course of business, was privy to some careless discussion by a few lumberjacks that she believes are from this area. In a fit of bordello bragging they indicated to the girls that they had come into some money lately, and while there was no direct reference to the robbery in question, Miss Annie seemed inclined to believe the information could be to Mr. Harding's advantage."

"I think," said Cooper calmly after a few thoughtful minutes, "that you should take the next train out of here." The young man's face suddenly turned white.

"Wwwhat? Why?" he sputtered.

"I'm not some lumber town hick, you know. You can spin your yarns all day long if you want to... but get someone else to listen to 'em, I got work to do."

"But Mr. Harding... Mr. Harding said you'd help me!" The voice was whiny and scared and caught Cooper a bit by surprise.

"You want to start over, son? You want to try this again? I got the patience of Job for the truth." The young man stared at Cooper, for the first time holding his gaze. But the look went right through the man, the focus on some distant event past, the eyes clouded over with a troubling mist. Truth to tell, it unnerved Cooper just a bit as a few minutes went by and the face remained the same.

"I... I've had a bit of trouble," he stuttered nervously, finding it hard to say. His face warmed as he spoke and Mr. Cooper watched the color rise up the white of his neck. If truth had a color, he reckoned this was it.

"And Mr. Harding has been kind enough to suggest that a visit to the north woods would do me some good. He thought... well... I thought... that I could do something out here in the wilderness and lay low for a while.

"What kind of trouble?"

The young man lowered his head, his hands clenched tightly together, the chair suddenly becoming uncomfortable. When he looked up again, his mouth opened but nothing came out.

"Trouble with the law?" prompted Cooper.

"Oh...no..no...not exactly. I... I've done nothing wrong, really. But there are some people looking for me... they... they probably want to do me some harm. A lot of harm."

"That so?"

The young man nodded silently.

Mr. Cooper leaned forward in his chair then and cleared his throat with a slight grunting sound. "Well now, why didn't you say so? Some people think they're the only ones who ever trifled with trouble... or that they got to do a little dance with words and wander in and out of the truth to save a little face. Hah! When all is said and done it's your friends that'll pull your bacon out of the fire. Say, just where is this trouble you're talking about? You're being awful careful about your self here, though I doubt anyone up this way has ever heard of you. Or am I wrong about that? Are you from St. Paul?"

"No... no, I don't know anyone here. I don't want to know anyone. I just want to lay low for awhile... forget about things."

"Chicago then, I'd guess. There's city about you."

The young man shifted uneasily in his chair, coloring slightly once more. "I won't deny that it's convenient for me to remain somewhat... uhh vague, as to my identity at this time. Let's just say it's caution."

"Let's just say it's foolish," said Cooper, puffing on his cigar and studying the young man, reading his character with sharp blue eyes gone steely gray. There was much untold, he decided, but nothing he felt threatened by just yet. In fact, against good judgment, a fatherly feeling started to envelop him as he watched the lad wrestling with his troubles and fears, watching his lower lip tremble when he occasionally lost control over it. The weak smiles and attempts at humor were painfully transparent.

"Well, sir, I think that's good enough for now," he said finally after his purposeful silence failed to produce any further revelations. "But whatever is bothering you is clouding your judgment. You can't walk around this town nameless. Have to have a name attached to your face or the people won't stand for it, won't stand for it at all."

"I'll stay out of everyone's way. They won't even know I'm about, really."

"There's got to be a better plan than that! Why if you want to bring attention to yourself, you just lay low, low as you can get. Everyone in the county will want to know who the mysterious stranger is, why he's here and where he came from.

"What do you suggest?"

"Well, the thing is, you've got to get into one of the camps, the lumber camps... we got three going in probably this month. We got lumberjacks coming and going most of the season. It's not important 'what' camp exactly... not at first. They all mix around, anyway." He was lost in

15

thought for a minute, scratching behind his ear while taking a thoughtful puff on his much shorter cigar. "Stand up," he said suddenly.

"What?"

"Stand up. Just stand up right there and let me take a good look at you." The young man slowly got up and stood restlessly in a slightly stooped posture, his hands shoved into his pockets as Mr. Cooper studied him closely.

"Show me your hands", he said gruffly, coming out from behind the desk.

"What?"

"Your hands, let me see your hands," he said again. When the lad stuck out his hands, Mr. Cooper grabbed them in his own and turned them over. "Nope," he said. "You're near big enough, I suppose, but none too solid and your hands would never make it a week. You'd never pass as a Lumberjack."

"Hah", exclaimed the other. "I've handled an axe often enough and I'm no stranger to work. With a change of clothes and ..."

"Work! Say, Mr. Chicagoan, being a lumberman is no evening stroll in the park. These boys work everyday from daylight to dark. Hard work. Grueling work!" He threw the young man's hands down and walked casually to the window, almost as if he had suddenly become disinterested in the whole affair.

Mr. Cooper stared out of the dusty glass at the swampland lying North in the White River valley. The sun, low in the East, highlighted the autumn colors of Maples and Poples and Elms that surrounded the large tracts of farmer's fields in the rich loam soil of the low country. Peering intently, he tried to find White River beyond the trees, but it was much too far and far too low beneath the tangled growth of alders and brush in the heart of the swamp. He liked to try though.

But back to the problem at hand. He stifled a low sigh, hoping that the other didn't notice, then grabbed at the remaining stub of the cigar stuck between his brown stained teeth and put it out on the window sill in a smudge of ash and tobacco.

"My secretary, Mr. Jacobs, hates when I do that," he said as he turned around. "Nasty habit, I guess, but that's the nice thing about being boss." He walked over and smiling gently he took hold of the young man's arm at the elbow.

"Look, son," he said, "obviously there's something working on your mind just now. Keep it to yourself if you want to, that's your business. But with my promise to Ed and all... well, I guess I'd like to try to find a way to help if I can. If you'd let me."

The young man started to say something, but it stumbled low and thick in his throat, collapsing as a mumble not quite understood by either party.

"You give it some thought, son," said Cooper releasing his arm then and retreating back behind his desk, shuffling through the papers he found there, as if he was unable to find whatever it was he was looking for. "It's a fine morning along the bluff," he said without looking up. "You go ahead now and clean up a bit and we'll talk over breakfast."

K. Wallin

The Third Chapter

The Story

The young man squinted when he stepped into the bright sunshine outside the office of the Straddle Creek Lumber Company.

"I told you it was a fine morning," said Cooper from behind him. "Puts a person in a whole new frame of mind, doesn't it, much better than that gloomy precipitation of last night. Rain this time of year isn't good for a thing, not a damn thing... just makes mud."

"Still a bit brisk out," observed the other, pulling up his collar and looking about. There was a light sheen of frost on most things not yet hit by the warming rays of the sun.

"Brisk? My boy, this is Northern Wisconsin! That's snow in the air you feel, and it feels great, believe me." He inhaled deeply and patted his chest for effect. "Snow before long, yes sir."

"Well these damp clothes don't help any," the other grumbled.

"Yes, we'd better take care of that pretty soon, I suppose. But let's get some breakfast first and I'll show you around this little burg. It's quite pretty you know," said Cooper stepping down from the porch onto Superior Avenue. He looked about for a moment, as if caught by the beauty of the day, and then abruptly started off down the street to the west at a brisk pace.

Across the way from the Pratt Hotel there was a trail leading down the bluff towards the depot and the shops and saloons that lined the railway. Mr. Cooper led them along, stumbling and sliding at times on muddy paths until over the rails and down the line they came to the front of the restaurant. It was a primitive wooden structure with a high false front, weathered rough from the harsh Northern Wisconsin winters. Two mongrel dogs were sprawled out in the sun near the stoop, enjoying the warmth and disinterested in the rest of the world around them.

Mrs. Williams, a handsome woman of later years, was just stepping out the front door over the dogs as the men approached. She peered intently at them through wire frame glasses, brushing back a strand of gray-black hair that hung in her face, trying to anchor it with the rest of her hair tied back in a bun, but it fell loosely once more.

"Good morning Mrs. Williams. I brought you some nice sunshine today," greeted Cooper cheerfully.

"Indeed," she huffed. "I've always thought the good Lord took care of providing our weather, Mr. Cooper." She began to gently sweep the porch stoop. "And quite good at it, He is."

"So true, Mrs. Williams, so true. And I wouldn't want it any other way," smiled Cooper. "Say, I thought I smelled some of your hotcakes and bacon from up there on the bluff. Woke me right up from a sound sleep! I swear, one of these days I'm going to make you my chief cook, give you the pick of the camps to cook for, and make all the lumbermen wear bow ties so as to set the proper mood. What do you think of that?"

"Just foolishness," she laughed. Then finding the dogs in the way of her sweeping, she gave them a halfhearted swat. "Git, you Brownie... there's sunshine all over the place, you don't need to git it here."

"Well, I got some good fresh eggs from the Anderson farm this morning," she said turning back to the men. "And Dotty should have the skillet on by now. I suppose you and your friend had more on your minds this morning than jibber jabber."

"Brown eggs? You know I can't eat them white ones, give me indigestion," kidded Cooper. "I need'em brown and tender."

"That so? Well, they come from brown chickens, I'm told. That suit you?" She smiled then winked at the younger man. "More foolishness." The wink gave Cooper inspiration.

"Have you met my companion Mrs. Williams? This fine young gentleman is, ah..ah.." Cooper stumbled over the words, leaving plenty of time for the young man to fill in the gaps or think of something else on his own rather quickly.

"LL..Leon Mancheski," he stuttered hesitantly, then offered his hand. Cooper noted that it shook just a little.

"Yes... Leon, a nephew of mine from Ohio," added Cooper. "Says he's interested in the logging business, but I suspect it's only because his Pa pushed him this way. Of course we may never get the chance to learn one way or the other if he starves to death within three feet of the finest breakfast place this side of St. Paul."

Mrs. Williams stepped aside and waved her arm toward the door. "Please come right in gentlemen," she said, but as Mr. Cooper passed her she swatted him gently with the broom. "More foolishness," she mumbled.

"What do you recommend?" asked Leon when they were seated at a table. "I don't see a menu around here anywhere."

"You don't need a menu in a place like this, son. Eggs, bacon, hotcakes, hash...you name it and they have it and it's good. Simple as that," replied Cooper. "Something about this October air, I think... my stomach wants it all."

When the girl arrived and stood before them expectantly, without pad or paper, Leon became distracted, suddenly finding interest in the tablecloth design.

"Dotty, I'll have the works... hotcakes, bacon, eggs and a barrel of coffee. If you have a little bit of beef back there, fry it in with the eggs would ya?"

"Are you sure your belt can stand it?" prodded Dotty good-naturedly.

"Well, hrmphhh," mumbled Cooper. "It's good leather."

"And you sir?" she asked of Leon.

"You get sirred and I get harangued," mumbled Cooper, "age ought to buy you something these days."

"Well, I don't know him yet," said Dotty.

"I guess I'll have an egg... over easy, and a small glass of orange juice if you have it," said Leon cautiously.

Both Dotty and Cooper stared at the young man in disbelief.

"Oh, and two strips of bacon, lean, and padded dry," he added.

Dotty continued to stare at him, thinking perhaps it was a joke. But when he didn't smile and made no attempt to add to the order, she curtsied and said, "yes sir." Then she disappeared quickly. In moments there was laughter in the kitchen, and Leon shifted uncomfortably in his chair, thinking he may have said something funny, but not knowing what it was.

"I think that's the first curtsy I've ever seen in William's Restaurant," marveled Cooper. "Don't take it wrong, son. They are just used to serving a heartier fare, here. I've never heard of someone ordering just one egg in all my born life."

"I'm not much of a breakfast person, I guess. I just don't feel that hungry."

"That's quite alright, son, quite alright. And if you can't finish what you've ordered, I may just be able to help you out with it."

Leon wasn't amused. "Pretty clever with the introductions there," he said soberly, "... caught me by surprise. And what's all this nephew business?"

"Keep your voice down, son... people kinda like to listen around here," said Cooper calmly. "I was on the spot too, you know. I had to make some kind of introduction and you weren't giving me much to go by. That wasn't your real name was it?"

"Why? Why must I be introduced at all? I told you I'd rather not... well... I just think... maybe you don't understand."

"Could be, son. Like I said, I don't have much to go by. But if you think you can walk around this burg a stranger, you're foolin' yourself. That may work all right in Chicago, but things are a little different up here in the woods. Give me a chance, son... I think I may have a few ideas about this situation of yours. For now though, being a relative of mine just might buy you a little time... and allow people to adjust to your presence."

Leon grew quiet then, thinking of things he'd really like to say, thinking that already he'd grown tired of Pratt and this old gentleman. But he simmered instead, waiting for breakfast to come and lighten his mood.

As they ate, others arrived and were greeted with the same homespun hospitality. Leon noted that there was "much foolishness" all around, but it was a breakfast fare equal, at least, to many of the fine places of Chicago and surpassing most in portions and pleasantness. He took another sip of the strong simmering coffee and stared absently out the window, while Mr. Cooper watched with interest the faraway look in the young man's eyes.

After breakfast Cooper led the way on a walking tour of the little logging town up on the bluff. From Blake Street on the West side to Senover Street on the East, the town covered only about six blocks. From Superior Avenue on the North running parallel with the railway to 3rd avenue on the South, another three blocks wide. Most of the residences in the village were in this area, as well as the hotel, a few stores and the school. The rest of the small businesses were along the north side of the track just down the hill, across from the depot. There one could find William's Restaurant, the Blacksmith shop, another store and the saloons. There too, were a few small bunkhouses for the Omaha section crew when they were in town.

Cooper would stop and introduce his "nephew" to each and every person they met in the street. He pointed out each house as they strode by, naming its occupants and any odd gossip he found amusing. Leon thought he did so with a child's fascination, as if he found the size of the town and the knowledge he held about it as some great wonder. In the end though, Leon decided that Pratt was much the same as a neighborhood in Chicago, the people, the personalities, the odd bits of notion about this or that. Except when the block ended on Blake Street, there was only wilderness beyond, though ragged and barren of old growth trees.

"There's hardly a tree in town," observed the newcomer as they strolled back down Superior Ave. "I would have expected it to be quite wooded this far north."

Cooper stopped and removed his hat and scratched his head curiously, eyeing up the boy. "Why, son...it's called the lumbering business. That's what we do here mostly, cut trees. When they finally pushed the railroad up this way... oh about 25 years ago, there were plenty of trees... thick stands of virgin pine, hemlock and hardwoods... huge yellow birches, perfect for hardwood floors. There's Pratt yellow birch in the Hayward Roller Rink floor... and Mason's. Have you ever been roller skating?"

"Nope."

"Well, you oughta. It's fine sport if you can keep your feet." Cooper rubbed his backside as a recent memory entered his mind. It also made him smile. "Yes, sir," he began again, "Charlie Pratt knew a good thing when it come his way. He bought up most of the land around here and harvested most of the timber within a mile or two of the railroad line. You see, they didn't have their own railroad then, like I do, so everything came into town by horse and sleigh. Or sometimes they'd dam up a creek and push'em down. Either way they couldn't get too far from the Omaha road without the work eating up all the profit.

"That left a lot for my brothers and I, but we got to go a little farther and work a little harder and settle for a little less. Not so much White Pine anymore...some... but not like the old days. So we take the hemlock and hardwoods and whatever pine we can find. There is still plenty of money to be made... you just have to work at it more."

"Looks kinda barren to me," said Leon without emotion.

"Well, I figure you'll see all the trees you want by the time you leave here," mused Cooper.

"What do you mean by that?"

Cooper let the question go unanswered and walked over to the edge of the bluff, looking north over the valley.

"I'll tell you one thing," he said looking back over his shoulder, "Mr. Pratt sure picked a grand spot for this old one horse town. Just look at that view, son...just look at it. Down there in the valley is the Long Lake Branch of the White River... that and a dozen other spring fed creeks flowing into it. You see there..." he pointed to a thin dark wavy line barely visible in the tangled growth of colors and mist. "And down near Wheelers farm... down that road there, there's a little bit of a creek... Straddle Creek we call it, cause you can stand astride it in most places, and just teeming with Brook Trout... trout firm and tasty and so hungry and game, you're apt to find them digging their own worms and catching their own flys. They'd just jump into your basket if you'd give 'em half a chance."

"Trout?"

"Hmrph... well, some people like 'em. Probably do you a little bit of good. Anyway... just look at that view. Just look at it! Why it just sort of sucks you in," Cooper added wistfully.

"Kinda makes you wish you could fly, doesn't it." said Leon, not nearly as moved by the grand scene before him.

"That's exactly right son, exactly right," sighed Cooper. "In fact, it almost convinces you that you can."

Cooper led them on after a few moments, occasionally casting his eyes north, as if the view would just not let him go. At the east end of the town stood the Pratt Mercantile, the "company store" of the Straddle Creek Lumber Co., and he led them there, slow and wandering.

It was a huge building, built into the upper side of the eastern slope of the bluff, with a walkout basement and icehouse in the back leading to a short spur of Southeastern track. Along the front ran a muddy road that after a little jag at the top of the street, stretched south up the great divide all the way to the Namakagon Lake country and beyond. To the north it continued down the slope of the hill, across the tracks and further down still toward the farm country, reaching pasture land where it split left and right to outlying farms.

Inside the store there were three long rows with goods hanging or stacked on either side. Leon marveled at the wide variety of goods; pots, pans, washtubs, rakes, shovels, dishes, clothes, farm implements...an endless accumulation in orderly fashion. Everything a family would need in the Northern Wisconsin wilderness and more.

While Leon continued to wander around the aisles of merchandise, Mr. Cooper was busy chatting up the manager, a Mr. William Farley.

"I think I have it all here, Mr. Cooper," said Farley. "There's a few things I'll have to order but they should be along in a week or so. Nothing they'll need right away."

"Very good Bill," nodded Mr. Cooper. Just then Leon stumbled into the merchandise and a resounding clanging and banging was heard as things fell willy-nilly about his feet.

"Sorry!" yelled Leon sheepishly from across the room. Mr. Cooper turned back to Bill Farley and smiled.

"Might need an extra pair of caulked boots and some Malone trousers," he said.

"What ever you say, Mr. Cooper," answered Bill. "And this stuff should be ready by the end of the day, so you just send Jake to tell me when and where you want it."

"Thanks Bill, that'd be just fine. I'll send word. There's snow in the air you know." He turned to spot Leon coming up the aisle to him.

"That right?"

"And say, Bill, if my ...uh... nephew should need anything... well you just go ahead and throw it on account."

"Sure thing Mr. Cooper."

As they walked back down the street to the Straddle Creek offices, Cooper seemed deep in thought, disappearing from view as soon as they had gained the front porch. He was out and about most of the day, while Leon sat in his room mulling over the events that had led him to this small lumbering town in the north. And sitting there now, while the October sunshine fell warmly through the window, his trouble back in Chicago seemed all the more just a trifle, a distasteful inconvenience. It might even be an opportunity. Oh, Pratt seemed a nice enough town, what there was of it... and the people were friendly enough, but it was certainly not someplace he imagined staying the winter. No, not at all. He had to think a few things out... see if trouble was following him up the line or had forgotten all about him. Then get out of Pratt before the winter snow and cold set in. Slowly but surely, daylight courage was bucking up his spirits.

Mr. Cooper returned to the office around 2 pm, making no mention of where he had spent his time, offering no clue as to what he had been up to.

Of Course he was a businessman, a lumberman, Leon reasoned. He must have had business with the new lumber camps they were forming somewhere up in the woods. Anyway, he was too much a gentleman (and Chicagoan) to ask, if the man made no offer to discuss it.

When finally Mr. Cooper asked him into his office to talk, he felt an air of confidence returning.

"So, do you think everyone is convinced that I am your nephew from Ohio here to learn the lumber business? I'm sure it seems plausible enough to them," he continued without waiting for a reply to his question, "though I can't see as how it's any of their business to begin with."

"Oh you don't do you," answered Cooper somewhat crossly. "For your information mister, these people have a vested interest in this town." He leaned forward in his chair behind the desk, affixing Leon a stare that made his new found confidence go up in cigar smoke. "They work very hard to make this little whistle stop a home, a place they can be proud of," he continued soberly. "And if you haven't figured it out yet, life here is not always easy. It matters very much to them what goes on here; who visits, who stays, who leaves, who dies." Cooper, feeling the blood rushing to his neck and face, suddenly sat back and took a deep breath.

"But it doesn't matter anyway," he continued after his calm had returned, "because it won't work. I forgot about Mrs. Gillis."

"Who?"

"Mrs. Gillis. Mrs. Gillis has one of those supernatural instincts for gossip. If there's a secret in town, you can bet it won't be long before Mrs. Gillis knows it, abuses it and passes it along. God, that woman is something! And in a few days, the questions will come; what part of Ohio are you from, which side of the family, what does your father do, how old is he, where, what, how, when... she'll want to know everything and that will get others to wondering. Pretty soon there will be questions a plenty. Questions that will be increasingly harder to answer to, you see. And you'll have to remember each lie in turn to make sure you tell it exactly the same way to the next person."

"I told you I should've just laid low. I could've held up nice and quiet for a few weeks and nobody would've known the difference. Now... now, I guess I've met half the people in town, of course they're going to be curious. I should've just laid low... I told you."

"Well, it wouldn't have done you any good to hide out in here... that woman could find out everything there is to know about an egg without cracking the shell. These four walls wouldn't have stopped her for an instant. I'm telling you son, you just can't hide from Mrs. Gillis once she's on the scent of scandal or gossip."

Leon moaned a little in exasperation, throwing his hands up in the air. "Now what?"

"Well, if you'll settle down a little bit, I'll explain an idea I've been working on. Pull up that chair there and sit." Cooper began fumbling in his inner coat pocket obviously seeking a fresh cigar. When he found none, he searched the desk and still had no luck. "Damn it Jake, get in here," he yelled. When there was no answer he yelled again. Slowly the door to the office opened and Jake shuffled in with a box of cigars. He was older than Leon, but not nearly as old as Mr. Cooper, tall and erect with a neat and clean appearance. His face had a slight flaw around the mouth, giving it an odd character of being forever in a grin, in spite of whatever true nature lay behind the mood. It was not an unpleasant smile until, like Cooper, you discovered that it did not betray any real emotion or sincerity.

"How did you know I wanted cigars?"

"Well, what else would you be yelling your damn fool head off for," replied Jake carelessly. "And if you took a little more care about where the ashes were apt to fall, you'd find your secretary a little more sympathetic to your nasty habit. Might even be a fresh box nearby when you are apt to be needing one. As it is, you're more likely to burn the place down one of these days."

"Aww you're right Jake, the point is well taken. I'll try to do better," said Cooper a bit sheepishly. "Now git out." Jake looked at him doubtfully, but none-the-less retreated through the office door without so much as a side-glance at Leon.

When the cigar was lit and the blue haze began to fill the small room, Mr. Cooper looked back to the matter at hand with his composure fully restored.

"Look, I've given this no little thought since I remembered about Mrs. Gillis. What we need is some insurance."

"I should've just laid low," moaned Leon, his head held in his hands.

"Perhaps you were right son... but it doesn't matter now. We've got to get on with another plan."

"Well, what's this insurance you're talking about?" asked Leon coming to grips with the truth of the matter.

"Mrs. Gillis," Cooper said calmly.

"Mrs. Gillis? But I thought... I thought she was the problem."

"Sure she is... but she's also the solution. Mrs. Gillis is our best insurance, bless her little heart."

"I'm not sure I understand yet," admitted Leon.

"Well, the more I thought about it, the clearer it became. We let on to Mrs. Gillis, in confidentiality of course, what your real purpose is up here. That is, to write an article for ...uh, oh... say, Harper's Weekly... sort of a secret article, on the life of the lumberman in northern Wisconsin. That's plausible enough. Everyone will know the secret but no one will ask you much, afraid to let on that your secret is out...not wanting to jeopardize your mission. And if anyone asks about family or Ohio, you can tell them any damn thing you please, because sooner or later everyone will know "the secret".

"Sounds kinda complicated. Suppose Mrs. Gillis acts in good faith and keeps the secret, telling no one."

"My boy, there are few things of certainty in life, but Mrs. Gillis sharing a secret is one of them."

"Are you sure this is all necessary? I mean, this whole writer thing, it seems like it would be even more likely to draw attention to me."

"That's the beauty of it. We'll let on that it's all supposed to be on the QT, research in confidentiality in order get the real story and not some would-be Paul Bunyans telling tall tales. We'll let'em know, that if your cover is blown, you might as well go home. Everyone will be in on this most important secret, everyone will think they know exactly who you are and what you are up to... and they will also know that it can never be discussed. Oh, they may ask you half-heartedly about Ohio, just to be polite, but I'm sure they won't be listening to the answers."

Leon shook his head in wonderment. "I just don't understand why it's so important for everyone to know all about me... whether it's the truth or not it's nobody's business."

Cooper was unmoved, though he said nothing. Sometimes his silence was worse than the raised voice and it made Leon a little edgy. "Very well," he agreed reluctantly. "If you think that's the best way to be on with this, so be it. It's only for a few weeks anyway. By then.... well..."

"I'm sure," smiled Cooper patronizingly. Then rising from his chair as if in a sudden hurry, he continued, "Well, let's pay an impromptu visit to Mrs. Gillis, because I have an important train to catch this afternoon."

"Leaving?"

"Yes, for a few days, I've some business to attend to. And look, I have a few men in my employ that I could ask to keep an eye on you, if you want, sort of guardian angels as it were."

Leon stiffened in his chair. "I don't need anyone looking after me. I'll be alright. I've been on my own for many years now and do right fine taking care of myself."

Mr. Cooper did not push the matter. "Suit yourself, son. It never hurts to have a friend or two when you have to be looking over your shoulder from time to time. But as I say, that's your business. In any event, should you need anything, Bill at the store will put you on account. You may want to get yourself some good warm clothes from the looks of it."

"Thanks," Leon said sincerely. "I think you're right about that... if even for a few weeks."

"Yes, well, we'll settle up one of these days when this is all over. Meanwhile, I suspect that we may be able to bump into Mrs. Gillis at the store."

"Are you sure this is absolutely necessary?" whined Leon as Cooper guided him out the door.

K. Wallin

The Fourth Chapter

Mrs. Gillis

Mrs. Gillis was indeed at the store, as she was most every day around 2 pm. She was a short gray haired woman with sparkling eyes and a frame that was slightly stooped with age. The Gillis' had come to Pratt in the early years, her mister supervising one of the sawmills of the day, and now since retired on a modest pension.

The Gillis residence was an older two-story structure on the northwest side of town, on Blake Street. Every day at a quarter to two, Mr. Gillis would go upstairs to take a nap, or so he would say. Many suspect that he goes upstairs to take a nip before his nap for his moods seem to brighten toward late afternoon. In any event, that leaves Mrs. Gillis with no one to talk to save ol' Blackie, their ancient Labrador. And he never has much to say that hasn't been said before according to Mrs. Gillis. Blackie retired from active life about the same time the mister did.

So it's off on a round about town, visiting each store on the bluff, to compare prices or give unwelcome advice on a checker game, or re-distribute the latest gossip as the case may be. She generally arrives at the company store between 2 and 2:30, weather permitting.

"I suppose you've got no ice," she said to Bill Farley after browsing a bit.

"No maam," he replied politely. "Not til the lakes freeze again. Run out just last week."

"Poor plannin'," she said.

"Well, Maam, we put up all we got room for, but it was an awfully hot summer and we lost alot."

"Poor plannin'," she muttered and took short steps down the aisle. In moments she paused and picked up a canning jar looking it up and down carefully. "These are bout half this price over in the town of Mason, you know," she said. "Course they're Mason jars."

"Maam, the Mason jars aren't made in Mason, that's just the company that makes'em."

"I know that. Just thought it was peculiar though. They're cheaper in Mason. At least a nickel."

"Yes, Maam." Bill gave in. Normally he didn't have time for this kind of exchange with Mrs. Gillis, but the store was empty save for her. Bill secretly hoped someone would come in; anyone.

In moments, he got his wish. Mrs. Smith came in, then George Bent and Henry Croft. After greeting the storekeeper the men went directly to the farming tools, while Mrs. Smith went directly for Mrs. Gillis. Mrs. Smith was the second best secret sharer in town, but unfortunately, the secret she wished most to share, she didn't dare share with Mrs. Gillis; that Mr. Gillis went to the bottle every afternoon. Of course Mrs. Gillis had known this for years and this too was the one secret she chose not to share with the rest of the town.

"Why Margaret Gillis, just the person I was hoping to meet," greeted the portly Mrs. Smith.

"Yes, well I have already heard; nephew from Ohio. I'll just bet he is. There's more to that story or it won't snow this winter."

"What have you heard, Margaret?" She leaned closer and whispered, "I won't tell a soul."

"Well, it's a secret I suppose," answered Mrs. Gillis, "though I shouldn't wonder if he wasn't in some sort of trouble. I won't say what, mind you, I'm not one to talk, but some sort of woman trouble probably. When they're young, it's women, when they're old, it's whiskey."

"So true, so true." murmured Mrs. Smith.

"Thank heavens I've not had to put up with that sort of thing. The mister and me have been quite happy all these years with no trouble at all."

"Yes, you've been blessed, Margaret," nodded Mrs. Smith. She thought she would just burst for want of exposing Mr. Gillis and his whiskey afternoons, but changed the subject instead.

"Did you hear about Ellen's daughter, Barbara?" She whispered.

"A soldier, no less! Been to Mexico or so they say." No one scoops Mrs. Gillis.

"And Elmer Rose has the indigestion almost all the time now... some say on account of that time he got pushed around by Wheeler's bull down along 18 mile creek, but..."

"More likely it's them onions he eats. Never saw a man so fond of onions. A person can't stand to talk to him but a few moments, unless you put a handkerchief over your nose."

And so they continued sparring, a jab here, a poke there, comparing notes on people and places and events. Even a few pets were slandered before they were through. All to no harm of course, or so they were apt to think, and great fun for the ladies. Bill Farley stayed as far away from them as possible.

Mr. Cooper, with Leon in tow, came into the store after Mrs. Smith and Mrs. Gillis had run out of new gossip and had wandered off down different aisles. Mrs. Smith went to see what the farmers were talking about and Mrs. Gillis went to harry Bill Farley about the price of something or another. The men waited until Bill was able to shake loose of Mrs. Gillis and she had drifted off down the aisle once again to the crates of Mason jars.

Mr. Cooper led the way to an area just opposite the jars, within hearing, but the view blocked by some merchandise on display.

"So when did you say they wanted the first draft?" he said loudly to Leon.

"Huh?"

Cooper elbowed him in the ribs and tried again. "The draft manuscript, when did you say they had to have it? They'll give you time to talk to everybody, won't they?"

"Uh, yes. The manuscript. Gee, I don't know," said Leon searching for words. Though he had the general idea of what Cooper was trying to do, the conversation had caught him by surprise.

"A special issue! Imagine Pratt being featured in a special issue of Harper's Weekly," said Mr. Cooper just a little bit lower in voice. He could see Mrs. Gillis working her way around the store goods to get closer and identify the talkers. He waited until he caught her eyes peeking through a small hole in the stacked goods near the end of the aisle, before he reeled her in.

"Well, good morning Mrs. Gillis, you're looking fine today," started Mr. Cooper. Mrs. Gillis edged around to their side of the aisle, turning her head slightly toward the men and nodding politely.

"Yes, I suppose," she said absently while checking out Leon. She gave him a good once over without trying to hide her interest.

33

"Oh, and have you met my nephew from Ohio?"

"No I don't believe I've had the pleasure," she said coming closer and extending her hand daintily to Leon. "Nephew you say, from Ohio?"

"Yes, indeed. Leon Mancheski," replied Cooper. "Leon, this is Mrs. Gillis, one of the finer ladies in town."

"Happy to meet you," said Leon smiling and taking her hand gently.

"Yes, ...well..."

"Leon is interested in being a lumberman someday," interrupted Mr. Cooper. "Thought I'd bring him up here and teach him a few things about the business."

"I see," said Mrs. Gillis skeptically. "Doesn't look much like the lumberman type, if you'll pardon me saying so. Hands are pretty soft, too. Course that's your business, I suppose. Now take that Ed Ginty fellow, couldn't cut a piece of kindling without he'd cut his arm off or something. No, Mr. Leon, you don't seem the lumberman type. Hands too soft, your nature too dignified. More like gentry. Perhaps you should take up something more respectable, like... uh journalism, perhaps."

"See, I told you we would never be able to fool Mrs. Gillis," interjected Mr. Cooper. "We may as well come clean on it." Mrs. Gillis beamed brightly.

"Do you think so?" said Leon soberly. "Can we trust her?"

"Impeccably," said Cooper. "Is that not so, Mrs. Gillis. We need your word on this, now. It's kinda important."

"You know me, John Cooper, I'd never tell a soul. I'm not a gossip like..." she looked around the store for a moment and spotted Mrs. Smith down at the other end chatting with the farmers. "Like that Mrs. Smith there. Can't keep her tongue still for a moment, that woman. Nice though, bakes a great cherry cobbler and ..."

"I knew we could trust you," interrupted Cooper. "Come closer now, so no one else will hear. This is for your information only, because there is no one else we would trust." She moved closer and turned her head so that her best ear was within inches of John Cooper, her eyes focused down the aisle.

"Leon, here, is a writer," he whispered. She nodded. "He writes for a prestigious New York magazine and he's come here to do a story on the lumber industry, sort of a first hand account, naming people and places and such."

"No!" she whispered back.

"Yes indeed. It's just the mention that this town could use, you know. Put us a step above Drummond or Mason for sure."

"But why not just talk to people? Why, my mister could tell you..."

"Why, Mrs. Gillis, you of all people should know how some people act when they think they're gonna be famous. It's hard enough to get the truth out of some of these fellows, what with trying to live up to that Paul Bunyan reputation. Just look at the story of Buck Johnson's deer, now, it's grown to be bigger than an ox with more antlers on its noggin that you'd find on a full grown elk. Mamm, Leon just wants the truth, with no show or bravado, and the only way he can get that is, if people don't know the real reason he's asking. The truth should be interesting enough for that million readers or so. Its got to be kept a secret, or Leon might as well pack up and go home."

"Yes, yes of course," she nodded again. "I'd forgotten how some people can be. A million you say?"

"Or so," replied Leon. He was still in awe of the whole matter.

"So you see, Mrs. Gillis, this must be kept a secret at all costs. No one is to know, save for the three of us," said Cooper.

"Just the three of us," repeated Mrs. Gillis. "And you must talk to my mister...he was a legend in the logging days a few years back. Knows a dozen stories...all true, I swear."

"Well Leon will probably keep him for last...a place of importance in a magazine like this." He pulled back from her then and pulled out his pocket watch. "Yes sir, Mr. Gillis would be the last man, I'd talk to," said Cooper playfully. "My, look at the time. I gotta pack and catch that next southbound this afternoon. Going to St. Paul on business, you know." He grabbed Leon by the elbow and steered him toward the door.

"Good day, Mrs. Gillis," said Mr. Cooper.

"Good day, Mrs. Gillis," said Leon, tipping his hat.

Mrs. Gillis was still pondering that last remark about Mr. Gillis and her gossip good fortune and only waved at them weakly as the door was closing on them. In moments she was focused on the bobbing head of Mrs. Smith coming up the far aisle of the store. The truth about Leon was a plum, she thought, and Cooper's travel plans just the much better.

John Cooper was already standing on the depot platform when the afternoon train came in from the east. He had heard the warning sound of the whistle as it passed over 20 mile creek, and spotted the plume of smoke and steam moments later, rising above the brush and small popples that blinded a gentle curve in the line.

He took his unlit cigar out of his mouth and spat over toward the tracks. "Not bad for this time of year," he said to no one in particular, while checking his watch. Besides Cooper there were only 3 other people on the platform; a woman with a small toddler in tow and Leon, hands shoved in his pockets, leaning against the depot wall.

At the second sound of the train whistle, Julius came out of the depot carrying a leather briefcase full of papers. He stopped and tied the string around it tight and then peered off toward the east where the train was slowing. The wind was biting a bit from the north, but the night absorbed it well and it was not uncomfortable to be out.

"I've got 6:39, Julius," said Cooper again peering at his watch. He shook it a few times, then banged it on his heel. "But it could be later. I haven't seen this thing move in awhile."

Julius shook his head. "Its 6:31 by the depot clock, not bad for this time of year, I'd say."

"Hah," spat Cooper, "never been on time since the tracks were laid." Julius just grinned. In moments the huge machine was creeping along in front of them and as it came to a stop, steam was released with a whistle, groan and screech, startling the toddler to tears.

Cooper turned to Leon, still leaning against the building. "I'll see you in a few days," he said. Leon nodded but remained silent. He couldn't explain it entirely, but Cooper leaving even for a few days gave him an uneasy feeling.

Julius handed the briefcase to the conductor and carried away a few more bundles that had been handed to him. Cooper and the others were on board shortly and before long the train was moving again. Leon glimpsed Mr. Cooper in the dimly lit car re-lighting his cigar as the train pulled out of the station, wondering to himself just what it was that made this man such an imposing figure.

The train whistle sounded again as it passed over 18-mile creek, here heading west but on its way south to St. Paul and all stops between.

When Leon was the only one left on the platform, he stood up straight and brought up his collar against the cool breeze. He knew he should just return to his room in back of the office but he felt restless. And the feeling would not leave him alone, in spite of his new surroundings.

As he stepped off the platform, he could hear talking and laughing coming from one of the saloons on the north side of the tracks. It was "Charley's" just on the other side of the bunkhouse from Mrs. Williams restaurant.

Ahh… the restaurant. There was a slight aching in his stomach that needed tending to. He had enough money in his pockets to see to a good meal and now his feet were leading him in that direction. He was almost surprised when his wandering steps brought him to the door of the Saloon instead of the eating establishment. He hadn't really meant to go there... or had he? There was an ache in his mind that needed tending to as well. He mused on it a moment, looking for an excuse to go in. When he could think of none, he went in anyway.

As he entered he was surprised to see a heavy ornate bar and stylishly done interior, where he had expected no more than a wooden plank and a few tables. Charley Halverson, a tall skinny man with a studious quality, was stooped behind the bar reading a newspaper and didn't look up. Three men were at a table playing cards, the source of the strong voices he had heard in the darkness.

"Deal the cards, Poppy, for Chris' sakes," bawled the oldest looking man. He was dressed in plain working clothes, neat but worn, and his beard was down to his chest, trimmed to a rounded fullness.

"Well I don't deal so damn good since I cut off those fingers, you know." He held up his left hand to reveal stubs where his index and middle fingers had once been. "God, I miss'em," he lamented.

"Yeez, Poppy, everyvun knows yew can get along yust as vell vith eight," said the youngest man. He was strongly built, square shouldered and straight with big calloused hands. His handsome face was clean shaven but sported one small scar across the chin, which he stroked every now and then as he talked. "Now toes... ya need'em all, every single von of dem, or yew'll not valk so goot."

Everyone grinned, including Leon, who at first was appalled at the stubs of the missing fingers.

"You want somethin'?" muttered the bartender so that Leon barely heard him. He casually ordered a beer and turned his attention back to the card game.

Poppy, middle in age to the other two, was dealing. He too sported a few whiskers but not near as neat as Jack Bender, the other bearded man.

"It's true, you know," said Jack. "I knew this guy over Marengo way that cut off a few toes while limbing one day. Well, of course he didn't think nothing of it, ceptin' he was sorry to ruin his boot and stocking like that. He just packed some flannel in there to stop the bleeding and finished the day."

"Didn't bother him none?" asked Poppy.

"Well, not so's you'd notice, not right away. Limped a little though. But that night when he went to walk out of the woods he nearly ended up down at Mellen. His right foot come up short every time and kept heading him off in the 'tother direction."

The men guffawed at this, none so much as Jack Bender. All three men set their cards on the table and picked up beer mugs to wash down the laughter.

"And if he would've kept going long enough," Leon added suddenly with a silly grin, "he would have come around back to where he started; full circle." He made an imaginary circle in the air with his index finger.

The men stopped laughing then and looked up at this stranger. Charley was just pouring him his second beer. There was some hoarse whispering at the card table between Poppy and Jack Bender, but the younger man just stared hard at Leon. The look made him uncomfortable and so he turned away and read bottle labels off the bar stock. A few moments later he was startled to find the young man at the bar next to him. He noted that he must be at least 6" taller than him and at least that much wider besides. It made the beer sour in his throat.

"I didn't mean nothing by it," Leon said softly.

"Ay spose not," said the larger man. "Buck Yohnson." he held out his huge hand to Leon and shook hands roughly.

"Ahh, Leon Mancheski," returned Leon. "I'm a nephew of John Cooper."

The others all nodded knowingly. Buck downed his beer and slammed the mug on the bar making Leon jump.

"'nother, Charley. Might'en be a long venter. Give us all von an ay'll pay yew next veek," said Buck. Charley grunted a little but filled all the glasses from a big metal pitcher, even Leon's.

"Thanks," said Leon holding up his mug.

"Certally," said Buck as he sat back down to the game. He eyed Leon for a few moments, then when Leon looked away back to the labels he motioned for Charley to come over. He whispered briefly in his ear, and then Charley, as emotionless as ever, returned to the back of the bar. Leon hadn't even noticed.

As the night wore on, more men wandered by, some joining in the card game, others merely milling about talking, drinking, joking, laughing. Leon's glass always seemed to be full whenever he went to drink from it, a fact lost on him in the first hour. As the warmth of the people and the saloon began to embrace him, he stopped trying to figure out who was buying him drinks. That he was greeted warmly by all who entered totally amazed him.

At one point a thought had struck him out of the clear blue. It was Mrs. Gillis! Her gossip had made him popular; people grateful for a mention in his imaginary magazine article. He grinned like a fool at the absurdity of it.

But no, not even Mrs. Gillis was that good. Most people were still thinking of the first story they had heard, if they had heard anything at all, and were still a little bit suspicious of this lad from Ohio.

And then the toasts began. "Drink to a mild winter and an early spring," said one man. "To a stout axe and sharp saw," cried another in turn. "To Swede Annie," said Jack Bender and all the men cheered and laughed.

"To Mrs. Gillis," said Leon lifting his mug. The room grew quiet for a moment as the men looked at Leon in wonder.

"Hell, ay'd drink to da debil hisself," shouted Buck Johnson tipping his mug back for a long swallow. The others laughed again and joined in the toast.

"Could be she's related," said Poppy, and more laughter erupted. Leon could not remember when he had felt better.

It was around midnight that Leon noticed that the bar had cleared out again. Buck was still at the table with Poppy but Jack Bender was sleeping peacefully in the corner. Two other men that Leon didn't remember meeting were at the bar, well dressed and city mannered. He could feel himself beginning to reel a bit and he thought of that climb up the hill to his room. He thought he had better leave and get started but his foot seemed to be caught between the bar railing and the spittoon.

When the door to the back room opened, he turned suddenly to have a look and with his foot still caught, lost his balance. The floor felt pretty comfortable at the time though, so he made no effort to get up as he watched a young lad come in the door dressed in worn working clothes a trifle too big, and a floppy felt hat nearly covering his face.

"I've finished, Mr. Halverson," said he in slender voice.

"Oh?"

"Everything's cleaned up & washed & swept... just as you said."

"That's good, Andy, you do a fine job. Now let's see," said Charley, suddenly deep in thought. "That's two hours a day for a week," he mumbled.

"Three on Thursday," reminded the boy.

Charley nodded then went to the cash register to get some change. The lad eyed Leon on the floor then quickly looked away.

Though Leon's view was a bit tilted from his floor position, he noticed the boy was rather slight built, with a smooth delicate face.

"That about right, Andy?" asked Charley as he poured a handful of change into the boy's hand.

"Thanks, Mr. Halverson."

When the boy was gone, Leon got back wearily to his feet. "Kinda soft looking wasn't he?" he blurted out. He looked around the room smiling at his own remark. "A real pretty boy, eh? I seen some of them pretty boys in Chicago." He held on to the bar railing with both hands mumbling about those funny pretty boys and various other matters wandering through his mind until he felt a tap on the shoulder. He turned to meet Buck with his arm drawn back and a surly look on his face. The last thing he remembered was the hammer-like fist coming at him and the feeling of being unable to move out of its way. He flew backwards from the blow and fell to the floor.

"Dat fellar vas startin' to git on my nerves," sighed Buck. No one said anything for awhile, and Buck poured down the last of his beer.

"I've got to close up pretty soon, Buck. Can you get'em out of here," pleaded Charley. He rubbed his thin fingers through his hair a couple of times nervously. "I hope Mr. Cooper doesn't take offense to this. What'd you have to hit'em for anyway?"

"He said Andy vas pretty boy. He ain't got no call to be saying dat," explained Buck to his own satisfaction.

"Maybe," said Charley, "but get'em out of here would ya?"

"Certally," Buck answered and picked up Leon's prostrate form by the belt and dragged him out the door. Poppy started to follow.

"Poppy, you go and wake Jack, now... get'em up and moving. I want to close up now."

"Aw right, aw right." said Poppy and stumbled over to Jack Bender to begin shaking him. Jack made no noticeable response, so when Charley went into the back room for a second, Poppy ambled out without him.

Charley came back to find Poppy gone, Jack still in the corner and the two gentlemen still at the bar. "Jeez," was all he could say.

"Say, bartender, you have many fights like that around here?" asked one of the men.

"Nah," returned Charley, "not more'n two or three a week, now. But you wait till Spring, hoo boy. After them jacks been in the woods all winter and got some gold in their pockets. They'll all be for letting off a little steam."

"That so?"

"Said so, didn't I. Now you two scoot along too, I want to lock up and get some sleep."

"What about the guy in the corner?"

"Well," pondered Charley, "It wouldn't be the first time he slept in that chair. Guess he won't freeze to death."

Outside Buck sat on a tree stump between the saloon and the bunkhouse, a weighty issue on his mind. Leon was sprawled out cold at his feet, his face in the wet leaves.

"You hit'em didn't you," said a gentle voice from behind him.

"Yust a little, Andy," conceded Buck, "must of ban the beer dragged him down so fast."

"I suppose," smiled Andy. "Break his nose?"

"Nah, yust bent it a little. Gonna have a sore spot dere though."

Andy shivered a little as the wind peeked in between the buildings. "I got to get home, Buck. You take care of him, now, its too cold to just leave'em lie."

"Vell, it ain't dat cold maybe," said Buck.

"Buck Johnson, you laid him out, you got to take care of him. Take him back to the company office. I heard he's been staying in the back room there."

"O.K. Andy. Ay spose ay vill. Ay didn't hit'em dat hard, yew know. Must of ban the beer dat dragged'em down."

Andy smiled at Buck through the dim light, but sensing that he might not have seen it, ruffled his hair.

"He called yew a "pretty boy", yew know," explained Buck.

"Well, I suppose I look so, in these old clothes," she said as she started off between the two buildings, heading up along the tracks.

"Ay'll catch up vit ya, in a little bit," Buck shouted after her. An arm waved briefly and then the form was swallowed up by the darkness.

Buck picked up Leon and threw him across his shoulder like a sack of potatoes, his arms dangling behind, and started across the tracks and up the hill to the company house. When he got there he noticed a light on in the front office and peered in the window. Fred Jacobs was sitting at his desk, leaning back in his chair with his feet propped up, smoking a big cigar and holding a generous glass of brandy in smiling contentment.

When Buck knocked on the door, Fred nearly fell over backward in his chair and while he was still trying to extinguish the stogey, Buck walked in with Leon slung over his shoulder.

"Oh, it's you Buck," he said somewhat relieved.

"Yake," nodded Buck. "Gotta lay dis fellar down sumplace."

"Sure, Buck." Jake led the way to the back room through Cooper's office to the bunk where Leon was laid gently down with his head at the foot of the bed.

"Maybe we should turn'em," observed Jake.

"Nah, he von't know the difference til he vakes up and den it don't matter. Got any more of dat sipping stuff?" asked Buck.

It was a long lonely walk back to the Johnson farm. It was easy to find, being along the railway of the Pratt & Southeastern, but late at night during the autumn of the year it was a very dark and dreary two miles. The logging railroad had tracks leaving Pratt on the east side of town, heading out in a southeasterly direction to various camps and sidings in the timber lands. Areas closer to town that had been logged off years before had been sold as farmland, such that many small homesteads followed the railway in the wake of the timber harvest.

The Johnson farm was located near an old landing across 20-Mile Creek and not far from the track run. It was as productive as any farm in the area, running about half a dozen cows, some chickens and long fields of corn and grain. The house was a large frame structure with a stuffy upstairs that served as bedrooms for the Johnson children. There were five of those at present time, Buck being the oldest. Two girls followed, being Martha and Andrea. Then young Joe, at eleven wizened years, and Emma at five.

Andrea was walking under quarter moon light which adequately lit up the track way, the rails catching the moonshine in shiny parallel lines. Sometimes she walked on a rail, balancing carefully and imagining a tightrope in the circus. When bored of that she made careful to step only on ties, sometimes counting them. She was almost to the bridge on the creek by the time she heard Buck clomping down the tracks. He didn't see her at first and almost ran into her before he caught himself.

"Did you take good care of him, Buck? You didn't just dump him someplace did you?" She said accusingly.

"Put hem to bed like baby," he replied picking up a pace beside her.

"Imagine, a writer for Harper's Weekly," she sighed. "Read by millions. Millions! What could be better than that?"

"Vell, it ain't de Svenska Post, certally. Ay don't know much about dis Happer's Veekly. Vhat vould yew say to a million peoples, ay don't know," shrugged Buck.

"I could think of a few things, maybe," laughed Andrea.

As they approached the middle of the bridge, Andrea stopped and went carefully to the edge, feeling the way with her foot tentatively. She could hear the peaceful bump and gurgle of the water below them as it wandered its way north to find the larger streams and on to Lake Superior.

"Vhat is it," asked Buck.

"Nothing, Buck, nothing at all, I just like to listen to the water sometimes. You can go on."

Buck sat down on a rail and brought out a snuff box. He pinched a generous portion between thumb and forefinger and slipped it between cheek and gum. "Big money yew got tonight, eh Andy?"

"Not so big, I guess," she sighed. "But little money adds up to big money someday."

"Ya" murmured Buck spitting a copious amount of snoose juice between the ties. They both listened for a second or two for the sound it made hitting the water, then smiled at each other. Clouds obscured the moon momentarily and both were afraid to move along the trestle in the darkness so they sat quietly and still. When the moon again appeared, a wolf howled suddenly and they were startled by its closeness. Without saying a word they both arose and began walking briskly along the tracks toward home.

K. Wallin

The Fifth Chapter

The Morning After

The morning brought a new chill to the wind. Leaves that still clung tenaciously to the trees in the clearing around the Johnson house, hung stiff and bounced clumsily in the breeze. The look of warmth in the sunshine was a cheery deception.

Emil Johnson and Buck were in the barn finishing the milking when Joe burst in with news of breakfast.

"Yas, ve'll be along dere soon, Yoseph. The chickens are fed, eh?"

"Well, mostly, Pa," stammered Joe.

"Yew feed'em more dan mostly, dan vee haf breakfast, yah? Me and Buck vill finish by den tu."

"Ok, Pa."

Emil moved his three-legged stool under the spotted cow affectionately called Molly by the children. With strong hands he applied the milking strokes to her teats, reaching a rhythm that allowed for the greatest production with the least amount of effort. Buck was dumping frothy pails of milk into a ten gallon can.

"Chickens' all fed Pa," yelled Joe from the yard after a bit. "And Ma says don't worry about the smoke, it's just the hotcakes burning."

"Vhat yew say!" grunted Emil. "Buck, vee go to breakfast now, ay tink."

The warmth and smells of the kitchen wrapped around them as they entered from the cool autumn morning. Alma Johnson was at the stove, flipping hotcakes on a sizzling griddle, and did not even acknowledge their presence. Martha and Andrea finished setting the dishes on the table while Buck grabbed the big coffee pot off the stove and poured himself and Emil cups of the strong dark liquid. Moments later, the entire Johnson clan converged on the kitchen and chatter and confusion reigned until all were seated and Emil raised his hand, signaling the time for grace.

They each bowed their heads then, nearly in one motion and Alma spoke calmly, the grace they said at each meal.

"I Jesu namn till bords vi ga, Valsigna Gud den mat vi fa. (In Jesus' name we go to the table, May God bless the food we eat). Amen," she added, then Martha, Andrea and Joe added their own amen, Buck said 'Ya' and Emil reached for the platter of eggs and hotcakes.

"Martha, is that coffee you have in cup?" asked Alma causally after the meal had begun in earnest. The children all exchanged nervous glances except Buck who continued to work at his plate. Emil appeared disinterested in the subject.

"Yes, Mama.... I'm old enough now, don't you think. Amy Stewart drinks it all the time and she's 4 months younger than me. And Mary Muggsley... why she's been drinking coffee for years."

"Miss Amy and Miss Mary do not sit at Papa's table. But Martha Yohnson does," Alma answered calmly.

"But Mama..."

"One cup, I think..." offered Emil. "One cup... today, with sugar and milk." Martha immediately beamed brightly, sitting up straighter and nudging Andrea ever so slightly so no one else noticed.

"How about me, Papa?" asked Joe with a grin.

"Yew...," replied Emil sharing the grin, "yew drink your milk and grow up big like Buck... den yew drink all the coffee yew vant... ya?

"Vell, vell... a new day for Martha," sighed Alma, "she is all grown up now... so maybe she vill do laundry now vhile vee still haf clothes to wear."

"Oh, Mama!"

"Dat Molly cow..." injected Emil, "not so much milk as before. Sometimes gude... but sometimes not so gude. I tink maybe she gonna take a valk one of these days." He never admitted to killing a farm animal, even for food, just that they 'took a walk.'

"Could be she's just a bit skittish of that wind, Pa," spoke up Andrea. "Most times she gives good milk."

"Ya," jumped in Buck with a mouthful of hotcakes, "da vind."

"Bah, da vind," grunted Emil.

"I heard there's going to be a dance on Saturday night," said Martha.

"Dance?" asked Alma.

"Well, music and all. They are going to play in the Modern Woodmen Hall again. Jack Bender with his banjo, Mrs. Humphries and her piano. Amy says everyone's invited and they are going to have punch and things to eat."

"Who do dis?" asked Emil.

"The Royal Neighbors are putting it on. The money is to fix up the new school with a few things," added Andrea. "They'll want you to play, papa, I'm sure of it."

"Do yew tink the Hanson boys vill sing," asked Alma. "They haf such lovely voices."

"Pa's got a lovely voice," added Joe. "You should hear him sing to the cows, huh Buck?" Buck cleared his throat and tried to hide a little smile.

"Hah," sneered Emil.

"It's true, Pa. And no one can play the violin like you. Everyone says so," added Andrea.

"Vell, vee may go. For avhile ay think," allowed Emil. Sam Hackett tell me to come und play. Vee go if all vork is done and Yoseph don't starve the chickens."

"Ah, Pa," laughed Joe.

When Leon first opened his eyes he was at a momentary loss as to where he was. He couldn't hear the normal hustle and bustle of the Chicago streets, and he couldn't place the barren four walls around him. His breathing was nasal and wheezy forcing him to cough occasionally. In a sudden convulsive fit, he coughed up a gob of mucus and spit it carelessly over the side of the bed. A throbbing soon came to his head reminding him of his alcohol consumption from the night before and slowly images started to come back to him. He smiled at drinking a toast to Mrs. Gillis. Then the image of a huge hairy fist coming at his face startled him. Slowly his hand went to his nose and he winced in pain.

"My God, my nose is broke," he said aloud to no one. His head hurt even more when he rose to seek out a mirror. On his way to the far wall where the mirror hung above the basin he stepped on the gob he had just spit and nearly lost his balance.

At first he didn't recognize the face in the mirror. The hair was disheveled, his eyes barely squinted in the morning light. And in the middle of his face was a large reddish purple tomato that used to be his nose.

"Oh my God!" was all he could say.

The other thing he noticed in the mirror was that he was still dressed, save for his shoes and socks. He wandered out into the office, softly feeling his tender nose, forgetting that Cooper was gone.

Jake was sitting at his desk writing in a ledger when Leon stumbled into the outer office. He jumped a bit when he saw this awesome figure.

"Good day, sir," said Jake politely, then thoughtfully added, "you look just awful."

"Mr. Jacobs, isn't it? I think I need a doctor. Can you get me a doctor? It's my face... and my head. Somebody beat me up! Is there a doctor in this God forsaken village?" raved Leon.

"Oh, I think you'll be alright, Mr. Mancheski," smiled Jake. "I don't think it's broke or anything. Just a might bruised. Want some coffee?"

"I want a doctor!" insisted Leon. "My God, do you see what somebody did to my face?"

"Have a cup of coffee and relax. I can go find Doc Parker if you like, but I'll tell you what he would say. He'd say, 'have a cup of coffee and relax, the swelling will go down eventually.' That's what the doc would say."

Leon groaned and staggered to a chair near the desk while Jake poured him some coffee from a pot sitting atop the wood stove and put it in front of him.

"How did I get here, anyway? The last thing I remember is some huge guy swinging a club at me."

"A club?"

"See this nose?!?" argued Leon pointing at his own face. "Must of been a club. A big club. So how did I get here? Would you know?"

"Oh, Buck dropped you by. Laid you on the bed nice and gentle like. God, that man is strong. Carried you like a small sack of potatoes."

"Buck?"

"Buck Johnson, one of Cooper's lumberjacks. At least he is when the season starts."

"By God, I think he's the one that hit me," exclaimed Leon.

"Well, that may be. That certainly would explain your face this morning. Wasn't quite as swelled up last night. I took off your shoes you know. I never could sleep in shoes myself, so I figured maybe you felt the same way."

"Thanks, but I doubt if I would have known the difference." Leon tipped the cup up to drink and winced as his nose got in the way. "Got any aspirin, Mr. Jacobs? My face sure hurts."

In St. Paul there was a light October drizzle, enough to make the streets muddy and cold and discourage any outside activity. Mr. Harding, of the Harding Mill & Paper Co. stood at the window in his office watching the streets below, the people scurrying about, coats clutched tightly. It made him appreciate the glow of his small stove about four feet away.

"Well, Coop, I'm sorry you had to make the trip all the way down here just to learn that I've already told you all that I could about the matter. A phone call might have saved you the trip."

"I thought of that, Ed. But we only got a couple of phones in the village, and them in business establishments. The way it is, a fellow has to holler on those things pretty good just to be heard a little... didn't seem like a good way to talk about confidential matters."

"Well, I don't think we should blow things out of proportion here. I just want you to look after him for awhile... until things kinda settle down... that's all."

"I know, I know," nodded Cooper. "I just don't feel that he's being honest with me. He started out telling me a story about a missing payroll of yours and... something to do with Swede Annie. Not that I believed him for a second, mind you... but the fact that he was inclined to play games didn't sit too well with me. You know how I feel about the truth."

"As I recall, you're in favor of it," mocked Harding.

"Awww Ed.... "

"Must of overheard us talking about that payroll while he was here," mused Ed. "He's inventive isn't he?"

"You mean it's the truth after all?"

"Well... there was a payroll for Benning's crew that got lifted off the Omaha a couple of weeks ago. I got a few of my men tracking it down in Chippewa Falls as we speak. Don't recall talking to the boy about it though."

"And Swede Annie?"

"Ahh the Swede..." he murmured in soothing tones, taking on a thoughtful look. "You know her Coop? Seems to me she'd be your type."

"Ahhem!" coughed Cooper. "Well... I'll do what I can for the boy, I guess, as a favor to you."

"I'd appreciate that," smiled Harding turning back to the window. "You know, I hadn't seen him in a long time, that boy, since he was in short pants, really, but his father was a good friend of mine. A Pinkerton man. We go back a long ways... to when St. Paul was an open city and thugs had the run of the place. A decent woman wasn't safe on the streets... you remember what it was like, don't you, John? Why if it wasn't for guys like

49

Art Mancheski…" he paused without finishing the sentence and stared off again out the window into the streets below.

"Let's just say, I owe that family a lot and let it go at that. He's a good lad, Coop, basically. I know he's made some mistakes... probably make a few more before he's through. But not all this trouble is his own making. He was just in the wrong place at the wrong time... and made an error in judgment, perhaps." Cooper said nothing, hoping Harding would continue.

"He wandered into my office one day out of the blue, stuttering, shaking. I didn't recognize him at all... nearly threw him out. But then he mentioned Art... and all those memories came flooding back. I was going to just keep him here for awhile, buck up his spirits, look after him. But after a few days I knew it was no use. He sat around here like a nervous cat, jumping every time the door opened, hanging onto that valise like it was his last bit of comfort. Well, I just figured he'd feel safer a bit farther into the woods."

Harding faced him again. "These folks he's running from... that's the best answer for you. They're the folks who make things happen, usually bad things, to those who don't play ball or get in their way. The kind of people that used to run St. Paul. I'm afraid Leon stumbled into something ugly that stuck to him like glue."

"Well, we're getting a little old to be playing nurse maid," grunted Cooper.

"Oh, Leon should be able to take care of himself in a pinch, if he's Art's son. Let's just hope it doesn't come to that. What he needs is some God forsaken wilderness to take his mind off the whole Chicago affair. That's what'll really do him some good. Too much city in him! Too much city in me."

"Well, there's no fool like an old fool, I always say. We got plenty of wilderness for him, that's for sure," said Cooper. "And some for you, if you've a mind."

"Yes..." murmured Harding almost to himself, "the woods..."

"I won't pull any punches, Ed. I'm going to put him to work."

"Oh? Well, he's no woodsman, John. You know that. Kind of slight built in fact."

"Perhaps. But it just so happens I need a chore boy at one of the camps."

"Chore boy? I don't know, John... he might not go for that. Kind of high strung, too."

"It's honorable work, why shouldn't he go for it? Besides it's the most he deserves until he trusts me and comes clean on the whole deal. Or you do."

"I'm sorry Coop, but I made him a promise. I'm sure he'll get around to telling you sooner or later."

"Fine," grunted Cooper as he lit a cigar. "I'm going to work on making it sooner. And in the meantime he can go to work, high strung or not. But don't worry, I'll have Buck keep an eye on him."

"Don't know if he would be a chore boy, Coop."

"Oh, I think he will."

"I 'spose you're right," conceded Harding. "I shouldn't doubt that you'd soon have him thinking it was his idea besides." Both men chuckled at that.

Ed Harding turned back to look out the window while Cooper puffed thoughtfully on his cigar. He peered through the misty gray weather to a shadowy spot along the street near the alley. The man was still there, leaning against the building under a balcony ledge, hat drawn close down over his face. Occasionally he would glance around the street or peer up at the Harding office building, then pull his coat tighter and retreat under his rain soaked hat.

"Do me a favor, Coop," said Harding quietly. "Keep this whole thing close to the vest would you?"

"Certainly," said Cooper through the blue haze of cigar smoke. "Anything else you may want to tell me before I go on to New Richmond?"

"Could be some trouble coming your way yet over this. Just be careful."

"Ed, I'll do what I can for the boy, you know I will. And if trouble comes of it, that's ok too. Might be just what I need in my life right now... a little of somebody else's trouble. It was a struggle for so many years... now that life's kinda smooth... I'm starting to feel old and unuseful. Not as old as you, of course... but I could definitely use some excitement."

"Thanks, Coop," said Harding from the window. "Snow pretty soon, I think."

"Damn right."

K. Wallin

The Sixth Chapter

Leon hears the music

Towards the end of the week some people in town had begun to wonder if Mr. Cooper's nephew had left the country. Of course the ever stoic Jake would never let on one way or another.

Leon, in fact, wished he had left town. Every day he would examine his face in the mirror and groan, his initial pain and suffering soon followed by a growing embarrassment. And Leon's way of dealing with these feelings was to retreat into the privacy of the Straddle Creek office building, with only Jake intruding on his privacy from time to time, with meals and light chatter. When alone, he would lie on his bunk and stare at the ceiling for hours, pondering in depth the course his life had taken. And with this self-reflection came mild depression and a growing desire to leave this miserable little village and its emotional contradictions behind him.

The third day brought a change, however.

Mrs. Gillis made a point of being in all the right places, at all the right times, but no one knew a thing about Pratt's new edition. Well, desperate times called for desperate measures!

"It's banana cream, Mr. Jacobs," she said, holding up the pie. "I had these bananas to use up before they spoiled and I thought; wouldn't Mr. Jacobs like a pie like this, him being a bachelor and not always able to indulge himself in bakery goods."

"It looks delicious, Mrs. Gillis," said Jake with a charming smile. "I'll have some after supper tonight. That was very thoughtful of you."

"Oh, not at all, not at all," she demurred gaily. "But... it's a lot of pie for one man... I thought you might like to share it with... ah... someone."

"Well, that's a fine idea, Mrs. Gillis. Mr. Cooper should be back this afternoon and I know he would just love a piece of this banana cream pie."

"I shouldn't wonder but the cream would sour by then," cautioned Mrs. Gillis. "Perhaps his nephew.... if he were still around... would care to share some with you."

"Well, perhaps... if he likes banana cream..."

It was an interesting game. Jake knew exactly what Mrs. Gillis was fishing for and Mrs. Gillis knew that he knew. Yet neither party would give the other the satisfaction. It would have gone on even longer had not Leon begun to stir. Hearing voices in the outer office he thought that Cooper had returned.

He opened the door expecting cigar smoke and the stocky form of John Cooper to fill his view. Instead, he saw the smiling face of a very persistent woman.

"Mmm Mrs. Gillis," he stammered, "how nice to see you again."

"Why, Mr. Mancheski, have you been ill? We haven't had the pleasure of seeing you about town lately. A cold perhaps? Your nose is a little red."

"Ah... yes, a cold. Terrible cold, sneezing, coughing. I've been in bed for days."

"Well, you certainly seem alright now... your voice is clear. And just in time, too!"

"In time?"

"For the dance, of course," she replied. "The Royal Neighbors are setting it up, and everyone will be there. It's at the Modern Woodmen Hall, you know, just down the street. I'm anxious to introduce you to Mr. Gillis. I'm sure you two would have lots to talk about," she added with a wink. "I'm sure you'll want to be there."

"Well, I don't know, I...."

"You must come. It may be the last dance before the men are all in the woods," pleaded Mrs. Gillis.

"I've gotta lay down again, ma'am. Perhaps I'll stop over if I'm feeling better." And with that, Leon withdrew to the safety of the inner office.

Jake had watched the whole thing with a broad grin, having no sympathy for either of them. Mrs. Gillis turned back to him soon enough to catch the grin before it began to fade. Saying nothing she picked up the pie and began to open the door to the street.

"Mrs. Gillis, the pie!" cried Jake.

"Yes," she said as she turned to him, "the mister shall have it with his supper... providing the cream doesn't sour. Good day Mr. Jacobs." And with that she was out the door.

Mr. Cooper arrived later that afternoon, but didn't show up at the office until near evening.

"There's business to be done here, too, ya know," said Jake just after he came in the door.

"Hrrumph," grunted Cooper. "Things you can't handle, Mr. Jacobs? Or did you just miss my smiling face."

"Snow by Saturday, some say," mused Jake. "Wouldn't be surprised if we were in the woods in a week or two."

Cooper smiled and walked near the stove to take his overcoat off. "That last section of track in, Jake? We ready to go on Camp #9?"

"Still need some supplies and a few ax men, unless you brought some back with you."

"Well, I got three strong husky fellas that oughta do. Let Bill know that they'll be at the store tomorrow to draw the proper clothes and such. We'll send'em out with the supplies, so give him a list while you're over there; what ever they need. Anything else?"

"As a matter of fact, there is. Ox Pete says he needs a good cook and chore boy as soon as you can get'em."

"Well, who did we have last year?"

"The only thing I remember is that last year's cook couldn't keep up with the crew and ran out of food during the second meal. I think the boys ate 'em! All's we found was their clothes."

"Indeed!" grinned Cooper. "Mr. Jacobs, you may save such colorful stories for around the winter fire when they'll be more appreciated." Cooper returned to his overcoat and rifled through the pockets until he found a cigar. Holding it up to his nose he drew in it's aroma with a smile. "Now this is a cigar! Bought it in St. Paul. Its imported from someplace."

"I thought you went to New Richmond," said Jake.

"Speaking of chore boys," returned Cooper, changing the subject, "how's our guest doing?"

"Close to flight, I'd say, and nervous as a cat. Had a little fracas at Charley's the other night that didn't help none," replied Jake. Cooper started into a broad grin again. "And you sure been smiling since you walked in. Could be you know a bit more than you're telling."

"Could be. Could be I'm just glad to be back in this part of God's country. Kinda muddy in St. Paul." Cooper opened the door to his office then paused halfway through the entrance. "You know, Jake. Sometimes I'm not sure who's working for who around here."

"Well, that's ok Mr. Cooper, if you forget, just ask me."

John Cooper made enough noise in his office to ensure that Leon knew that someone was about. Then he settled in his chair behind the desk and puffed thoughtfully on his new cigar. The gray light of day was dimming fast in the window behind him making the cigar end glow increasingly bright in comparison.

In a few moments Leon peeked out from the back room, comforted by the sudden smell of cigar smoke that hit his senses.

"Oh, you're back," he mumbled sheepishly peering about the darkening room. "Did you have a nice trip?"

"Splendid, just splendid," said Cooper. "How about you? Enjoying this little piece of God's country that you've stumbled into?"

"Well, sir. Truth to tell, there's some odd fellows wandering about here."

"Oh," said Cooper suddenly deciding to light the lamp. Leon said nothing further until the warm glow filled the room and the older man had settled back into his chair.

"Yes, sir. I been thinking about it some and I think that under the circumstances, I may be just as safe in St. Paul as here. Safer, perhaps."

"Safe? Safe from what?"

"Well... ah... just safe in general. Just safe to go about my business. You know... business as usual."

"Well, I suppose that's important," said Cooper studying the nervous young man before him. Jake was right. He was close to flight.

"I'll talk to Mr. Harding when I get to St. Paul, I'm sure he'll understand."

"Perhaps," mused Cooper in a strangely calm voice. "Perhaps. Well, son, it's your life, and of course you're allowed to screw it up anyway you like. But my advice to you is, if you are going to run, don't stop at St. Paul. There's plenty of odd fellows down there you won't like either. No sir, keep running and running. That way you may never have to face whatever it is you are trying so hard not to."

John Cooper's words had pretty much the effect that he anticipated. Leon's face reddened, first because of the element of truth in the sharp words, and then with the swelling of anger that began to creep up his spine. But he couldn't think of anything to say. Cooper waited, meeting Leon's gaze until the young man's anger began to subside and the shame once again took over. Leon's eyes then found the floor.

"The morning train will be by about 8:15, give or take an hour or so," said Cooper softly. That's just information, mind you, you're welcome to stay here as long as you like."

They let the matter stand there for the night.

It was a splendid evening in Northern Wisconsin. One of those rare autumn nights; warm with a wisp of a wind to rustle the leaves, the sky brilliant with stars. The dampness from previous days had disappeared into a crisp dryness that made the leaves swish and crackle along your feet as you walked. Darkness settled in comfortably around 5 pm.

Leon decided right off, after talking with Mrs. Gillis in the morning and Mr. Cooper in the afternoon, that he wouldn't attend the dance. He didn't really know anyone anyway, he reasoned. And dancing was never his strong suit. No, it was just better to stay safe in his room, perhaps read a bit, or play solitaire. The morning train seemed like such a clear choice in his mind in spite of Cooper's biting words. Still, the thought of it cast him into a gloomy despair.

He wrestled with these thoughts, lying on the bed staring at the ceiling, imagining brave solutions to fearsome problems that were unable to stand the light of day or the burden of reality. He wondered if life could ever again be the light-hearted institution it once was not many months before. And in the darkest corner of his mind, he contemplated his own death as a matter of small consequence and easily done. Such was his mood on this October evening; beyond effort and energy, beyond reason.

But the wind rustling by the open window was up to the challenge. It fluttered the leaves in playful puffs and whirls, rattled branches against the roof in a fitful rhythm and sang to him softly in sweet sighs and whispers. And soon, he was spending more and more time listening to the leaves and sampling the warm southerly breeze, and less with dark thoughts. The music from down the street began to waft in through the trees, surging and fading, matching the natural rhythm of the night. It was more than Leon could stand. Before he even realized what he was doing, he found himself out on the street in front of the office.

At first he fought the magnetic pull of the Modern Woodman Hall and its festive music and chatter. He strolled along Superior avenue, past the Pratt Hotel, past the dim lighted houses of the McCleary's, Larson's and Olszewski's, further down the road toward the west end of town where the Gillis' lived. In three short blocks he had reached the end of the street and angled south. Without much thought, he started back down 2nd avenue, the music drawing him, luring him, leading him on until he neared the hall, the doors wide open and the people milling about inside and out.

He stayed in the shadows at first, watching the light-hearted crowd and trying to identify the music and instruments. He was sure of a guitar or two, a banjo, certainly a fiddle. He heard someone talking about Bob and his mandolin, how a string had broken but Tom had another.

He didn't recognize many people, but he caught a glimpse now and then of Mrs. Gillis bustling about, sharing secrets, inquiring into this and that. And he picked out a few of the men he had met at Charley's saloon, standing near the side door sipping from a few bottles and shuffling their feet. Occasionally couples or individuals, overheated from the dancing and the warm autumn evening would exit the hall and sit in the grass or on the wagons nearby, within the circle of light given off by the kerosene lamps.

Children, many who normally would have been in bed by this time, were running in and out and all around the hall, gaining a momentum from the music and neatly staying out of the way of most folks that would have been able to stifle their activities.

Young Joe Johnson was the self proclaimed leader of one such pack of roustabouts, whose main goal in life at this time was the tormenting of young girls with crude verbal taunts and any slimy reptiles that could be found on short notice. Under his guidance the group was quite successful in their endeavors, and frequently, above the music, could be heard the involuntary screams and giggles of their victims.

Leon watched in amusement, their antics. And safe within the shadows, his mood began to brighten and his feet took on a movement of their own. The whole town must be here, he thought, laughing, singing, dancing.

Of course young Joe's activities were leading him on a collision course with trouble. Even Joe knew that. It didn't slow him down any, but he knew it was inevitable. And if it hadn't been for that trouble, Leon would have been content to spend the rest of the evening in the shadows.

Up to near the end, Robert Walden was a member of the troublemakers, enjoying the teasing and frisky play about the outside of the hall. Robert was fairly new in Pratt, his family homesteading a farm just to the South of town, but the familiarity of young boys everywhere allowed him to fall in quickly with this band of rogues. And it was fun, the music in the background just making it all the more lively.

Young Joe's calculated mistake came in picking out a new target from among the young girls sitting along the Walden's wagon. Becky Walden was just sitting there minding her own business, her dangling legs swinging to the music and her ponytail bouncing rhythmically on her shoulders, an inviting target. The gang silently descended upon her.

In the dark, Robert didn't know at first that his sister was the new victim. There were many others on the wagon whom he didn't even know. It wasn't until the familiar high-pitched squeal erupted that it suddenly dawned on him.

"Hey! That's my sister!" he exclaimed.

"So?" said Joe. "Let's cut her tail off and pin it to a tree." The other boys laughed.

"I'm gonna tell mama," whined Becky.

On impulse, Joe suddenly tossed a handful of wet leaves in her face. "Hah!" he yelled.

"Mamma, mamma," cried Becky and started picking the sticky leaves from her hair and clothes. That was it for Robert. Before Joe knew what hit him, he was down on the ground with Robert on top of him, fists flying in determination. But Joe was no slouch in a fight either. You can't be the leader of this bunch without a knack for getting the upper hand. Robert's blows were falling short of Joe's face, deflected by his arms. In fact, Joe was laughing about the whole thing until Robert landed a lucky punch on his chin.

"Hey!" yelled Joe. And soon the intensity of the conflict increased, with the two of them rolling back and forth and trying to get in that "lucky" punch.

Leon didn't really notice what was going on until the noise of the fight exceeded that of the music. The children were gathered around them, some cheering for a favorite, some just yelling for the fun of it. Becky, no longer crying, was oddly enough cheering for Joe. A group of men nearby who were passing the bottle around just stood and watched; a bit amused but not at all concerned. Those inside the hall could not yet hear the struggle and were busy enjoying the night. Leon, too, tried to ignore the tussle, but he saw the horses nearby getting a bit nervous; shifting in their traces, stamping their feet, so, against his better judgment, he decided he had better step in.

It wasn't easy. A gaggle of children were soon drawn to the struggle as bears to honey. Joe was a year older than Robert, and bigger, but the younger boy thrashed about like a wildcat and Joe had trouble trying to hold him off and evade the flying fists. Finally, Joe had him on the ground and sat on him, pinning his arms back. If Joe tried to let one arm go to take a swing at him, Robert would swing the free arm wildly until Joe had to once again restrain him in self-defense. The fight simmered then, in an uneasy draw.

"Give up, runt?" taunted Joe.

"Who you calling runt," sneered Robert. "Let me up and I'll runt you one right in the head."

"Hit'em one, Joe," yelled one of the Andrews boys.

"Right on the noggin, Joe. Hit'em a good one," said a voice that Robert could have sworn was Becky's. But suddenly another voice was heard.

"Hey! That's Bob! You can't hit my brother!" cried young Henry Walden. Henry, though even younger than Robert, squeezed through the crowd and fell upon Joe, his fists flying. And then the Andrew's boys joined in and it became a general melee.

Leon rushed over as the kids began rolling toward the buggys and wagons.

"Here, here," he said loudly. "Stop that! Stop fighting!" They almost listened to him, for a second there, but the fight had taken on a momentum of its own and continued in spite of his best efforts.

So he stepped into the fracas, pulling boys apart and dodging the swinging arms the best he could. The men passing the bottle around laughed and slapped their legs in delight at the scene, but still made no move to offer assistance. Leon was slowly losing ground, as boys, separated, were soon joined again in combat. If anything, his thoughtful interference was beginning to intensify the struggle.

By accident, or fate, Andrea Johnson had picked that moment to step out of the hall for some fresh air, and she immediately sized up the situation.

"Alright boys, that's enough. That's enough, I say!" She clapped her hands a few times to get their attention. Her voice was hardly the booming sort, but perhaps it was the female timbre that caught their ears. All the boys stopped in mid-swing, some thinking it was their mothers who had called out. Leon was nearly thrown off balance by the sudden stop to hostilities, but quickly gathering his wits, he grabbed Bob and Joe under the collars and held on. As Andrea drew near, the rest of the boys scrambled to various areas of retreat, most on the shadow side of the circle of light.

"Well, I'm not surprised to see you in the middle of this struggle, Joe Johnson. Aren't you a sight," remarked Andrea. Joe looked down at his feet in feigned remorse and a drop of blood from his nose followed his gaze to land on the toe of his shoe. "And you, Bob Walden, well, I thought you boys were friends."

"I guess we are. Ain't we Joe?" Said Bob rubbing his chin. The area around his left eye was already beginning to color.

"Well, sure we are. That wasn't much of a squabble, really. We hardly got started having fun."

"Yeah," nodded Bob, "we were having fun, really."

"Fun? You boys were apt to wake the cows down in Wheeler's barn, for heaven's sake. Do you think you could have some quiet fun for a change? There are some girls in there who could use some dancing, just waiting for a handsome pair like you two."

"Ahh, Andy," Joe sniffed. Andrea lifted up his chin to inspect the bloody nose. "It's almost stopped," he added. Andrea just shook her head and put her handkerchief in his hand.

"Go," she said. And in an instant the boys were gone.

Up to that time she had not bothered to look at Leon, more or less treating him as invisible, but as the boys disappeared she looked at him squarely, smiling pleasantly.

"It was nice of you to break up this little trouble, Mr. Mancheski. It is Mr. Mancheski, isn't it?"

"Why, yes it is. Leon... Leon Mancheski. And I'm afraid you had more to do with it than I did, miss... uh.. You look familiar, but I can't seem to recall your name."

"Andrea... Andrea Johnson. No, I don't believe we've met. But of course I have heard all about you... from... well... from the talk that's been going around. It's so nice to have you in Pratt, Mr. Mancheski. Are you enjoying your stay?" She smiled at him pleasantly, warming him, easing his burdens of the night.

"Please... my name is Leon." He returned the smile, suddenly feeling a bit awkward. "And... yes, my stay here has been most interesting." After all, he thought, that was certainly true.

"Well, that's splendid," she replied clasping her hands together. "Pratt can be a little intimidating to outside folks sometimes, but there are some really wonderful people here. It would be a shame if you didn't get a chance to meet everyone. Are you a dancer, Leon? The music is quite lively tonight and not apt to be repeated for some time, with the men going into the woods soon. Will you escort me in?"

"Well, I hadn't planned on... uh, I mean I wasn't really going to..."

"Step over here in the light," interrupted Andrea suddenly. Leon was alarmed as she took his arm and pulled him closer to the lighted doorway. "Why, I believe you've been injured, Mr. Mancheski. Your nose looks a bit sore. Is it?"

"Somewhat," said Leon awkwardly. "It's OK, really."

But Andrea stepped up on the little stone step of the hall doorway and pulled him closer. As she had done with Joe, she put her hand under his chin and tilted his head up for a look. Her eyes focused on his nose only briefly before locking on his sheepish eyes. She held his gaze only for a moment, but Leon felt her looking deep inside and it made him uneasy.

"I guess you'll live," she said softly, as if she felt the same uneasiness. "In fact, I'd say you were well enough to dance!"

And dance they did. Leon started with Andrea and learned a few steps, made up a few of his own, and then really got into the rhythm of the music. Andrea was light on her feet, moving with a graceful energy, flowing easily across the dance floor. Not so, Mr. Mancheski. After several spirited dances, Andrea was spending much of her energy and concentration dodging his feet, too polite to tell him that he was downright dangerous.

But he was getting better. And as the night wore on, he found there were many willing partners, all lovely ladies, and all gay and light on their feet. By the time the musicians were taking a break he had worked up quite a heat. During the pause he looked around the room at the milling crowd; the weatherworn faces of a hardworking people, the wide variety of dress and style. He didn't realize it at the time, but he was looking for Andrea. It came to him later as he began rubbing his chin and thinking of the soft touch of her hand as she had inspected his injury, and gazed into his eyes.

With the music stopped, the hall began to fill with the friendly babble of chatter, the sound of more than a 100 voices talking as one, though in a wonderful tapestry of language and accents. Recipes were exchanged, jokes were passed, politics and the latest gossip were discussed.

On more than one occasion, Leon was cornered by Mrs. Gillis, with the "mister" in tow, or a few others with "lumbering" stories to tell. Only with the greatest amount of maneuvering did he find his way out of those situations, usually on the pretense of dancing. During the break, it was near impossible to slip away.

"Tell'em, Harvey, about the real days of lumbering," said Mrs. Gillis with her husband clutched tightly by the arm. He was a smaller man, gone gray and hardly the sort that Leon would have figured for the "lumbering" type. "Tell'em about when Charles Pratt, himself, put you in charge of the whole sawmill. Cut over 250,000 feet a week, sometimes," she emphasized leaning closer. "Sometimes more. Tell'em, Harvey! And they brought in the wood by sleigh then, not by a fancy engine like they use now...

or brought'em down 18 Mile Creek when the dam wasn't washed out, tell'em Harvey. Harvey practically had to run everything, when Mr. Pratt was off on some other venture."

But Harvey was saying nothing, clearing his throat a little and looking around nervously.

"Of course, Mr. Soekland helped out a little... you probably never met Mr. Soekland... but Mr. Pratt really counted on... Oh!... there's Mrs. Vaughn's second cousin from St. Louis," she said suddenly interrupting herself and staring across the room. "I've been kinda wondering about him... something ailing him that ain't normal. You two keep talking now," she commanded, "I just got to see into this a little... " And off she went, shuffling across the room.

"Whew!" gasped Leon. "That woman... enough to drive you to..." he suddenly remembered Harvey Gillis standing next to him and drew up awkwardly. "Sorry," he stammered to Harvey.

"Sorry? How do think I feel?" Replied Harvey, his eyes following Mrs. Gillis across the room. "Say, where's them fellows with the whiskey, do you know?" With that, Mr. Gillis shuffled off in an opposite direction from his Mrs.

Standing on his tiptoes, Leon spotted Andrea's head near the stage talking to one of the fiddlers, an older gentleman. Trying to seem as if he was wandering with no specific destination in mind, he made his way toward her. It was difficult. The people all wanted to talk to this new man in town, all with a story or two about the best lumberjack in Wisconsin, or the best camp foreman, or the best scaler. But little by little he made his way until he was standing behind her, and gently bumping into her.

"Well, pardon me, Miss Johnson. Sure is crowded in here," he mumbled weakly. Andrea smiled.

"Pa," she said to the fiddler, "this is John Cooper's nephew from Ohio, Leon Mancheski."

"Vell, hello du. Ban dancing som haf yew?" said the older man.

"Yes, sir. Andrea was nice enough to help me out a little bit and teach me a few steps. As she says, the music is quite lively tonight."

"Yah, lively, dat's right. But vee slow it down now, I think. Yew vait," and the fiddler went back to testing his strings.

With the music starting up, there was little time to talk and Leon and Andrea moved off to the corner, trying to avoid the milling crowd.

"Where did all these folks come from?" he asked. "I guess I just didn't notice that the town was this full of people." He spoke quietly, almost as if to himself, but Andrea heard him and was amused.

"Why, Mr. Mancheski, it seems that you think you should have met everyone in such a short time as you've been here." She was smiling at him and it warmed him in an unexpected way.

"Of course a lot of these people are from farms a little out of town and around, some are from Drummond and Mason, and the town of Little Sweden, just down the road from here. Mr. Singleton, there, I believe is from Birch Lake. Some are lumberjacks here for the winter's cut, soon to start. A few I am not as familiar with may be guests at the Hotel." As she went on about the people in the room, Leon became more aware of Andrea herself, studying the gentle line of her face and features as her words wandered in and out of his mind.

"There's the Olsons, they have a farm near ours, and the Campbells, the Davis's from south of here... of course you have already met the Gillis's, there's the Anderson's, also from out the south way, the Bjorks from Little Sweden, and the Larsens, the Muggsleys... though I don't see Mary, perhaps she stayed in Hudson this trip... Mr. Sago, the Hackets. There's Mrs. Hatch and some of her kids... and another one on the way. Oh my, but she's quite large, isn't she." Andrea brought her hand up to her mouth, embarrassed that she would make such an observation. "That big fellow is her husband, Martin," she added after.

Leon wondered what it was that was touching his heart; the long brown curly hair lying neatly about her shoulders, the pretty blue eyes so sparkling and quick, the delicate lines of her face? He watched her hands nervously playing with a pretty yellow ribbon on her dress, rolling it around in her fingers.

She caught his gaze then and her hands stopped. "I'm afraid I've torn this ribbon right off my dress tonight, I don't know how really, but I'm afraid I'll lose it if I don't keep it in my hands."

"It's very pretty. Uh... the dress I mean. Lovely." The moment was becoming awkward but was saved by a particularly beautiful song that was started. As people began moving about them, changing places and retiring from the dance floor, Andrea ended up in front of him and he could no longer see her face. He did notice, however, that she declined several offers to dance from likely fellows.

Then the music caught him. It was the violin, in a beautiful melody, sad, but somehow uplifting at the same time. It continued for some time without words, quieting the hall and catching the attention of even Joe

Johnson and the ragtag bunch of pirates courting mischief outside. It brought Joe to the side doorway peering in at the orchestra.

And when the singing started, in Swedish, it carried the same melodic appeal. It was Andrea's father that was singing. Leon leaned as far forward as he dared and whispered to Andrea.

"Do you understand the words? What is he singing?" She turned around to face him.

"It's a song about someone who is missing his home and wishes that he could return there, but he cannot so he talks to a little swallow. It's called 'Halsa dem darhemma'." She then began to repeat the words in English, as they were sung, quietly so that Leon could hear but that the audience would not be disturbed. The normal chatter of the hall had ceased.

"Efter lang och strav - sam dag,"
"After a long and weary day," repeated Andrea in English.
"hor jag fjar - ran vin - ge - slag,"
"The sound of birds winging on their way,"
"Sva - lors flock, som a - ter gar mot nord"
To the northern lights and Spring, they say,"
"mot ljus mot var."
"We are lonesome for our homeland."

And so it continued, with emotion starting to be reflected in Andrea's voice.

Little swallow, though you are very small
Through day and night you follow your call
To wing your way home, you give your all
But swallow, think of me.

I wish that I could fly with you
To where grass is green and sky's are blue
Where love and friendship all are true
Swallow, hear my plea.

Greet all those at home still,
greet my dad and mother.
Greet the pretty green hillside,
greet my little kid brother.

If I had wings, like the swallow

I'd fly back home to thee
Swallow fly on homeward
And greet them all for me.

When the song was done there was much applause, none so vigorous as Mr. Mancheski. He noticed a twinkle of a tear in Andrea's eyes, and others as well, and it reached deep inside him, a foreign feeling for a man of his temperament. As the band began again to play a lively tune to restore the festive mood, the people surged to the dance floor, jostling about and suddenly pitching Andrea forward into Leon's arms. She immediately colored but was slow to withdraw.

"I'm sorry, Mr. Mancheski, I...I..."

"That's ok," he said quickly. "It was nice... I... I mean I, well uh... shall we dance?" Andrea just nodded, the color in her cheeks remaining.

And they danced. They danced forever, lightly and elegantly, the music following their movements, the light of the kerosene night shining only on them. And Leon, for a time was swept away from all his problems. Chicago, though only 500 railroad miles away, was far more distant in his mind.

The night ended so quickly for Mr. Mancheski that he swore someone must have turned his watch ahead. But soon wagons were disappearing into the night in a myriad of directions, the occupants still singing and laughing, while someone with a lamp led the way over paths the horses already knew quite well.

Through a twist of fate, Leon missed being able to say goodbye to his new friend. At the last moment, Mrs. Gillis cornered him with a question or two and a wink and a smile at their shared secret. Her bony hand clung to his sleeve as she babbled on and on and before Leon could disengage himself, the Johnson wagon was gone.

Still he smiled, and whistled a sprightly tune as he walked the block back to the Straddle Creek Lumber Co. office, a different soul than that which had been lured out into the evening by the spirited sounds of nature and music.

The Seventh Chapter

ℑhoughtful Ponderings

Leon may have slept well, if he slept at all. It would be fair to say that his thoughts had taken a different turn than the previous day's concerns. And he woke up early, hugging his pillow.

John Cooper came into work at the usual time, making the usual noise, smoking the usual cigar. When he at last grew impatient at being unable to rouse the young Mr. Mancheski, he banged impolitely on the back room door and soon discovered an empty room.

His first thought of course was that Leon had taken flight. It bothered him some that he had lost the lad, unable to help him, unable to guide him down the path of wisdom and its ways. Then, in thinking further, he realized that Leon would have had no place to go until the morning train pulled in. He must be around the village somewhere.

Cooper sat in his chair by the window drawing heavily on his cigar until the room was filled with a blue haze. It surprised him sometime later when he discovered how short the cigar had become in his ponderings. He coughed once and waved away some of the smoke, instantly deciding that the matter was not as important as all that. It was occupying too much space in his mind. He had at least 3 camps going into the woods, possibly as early as Monday, and there were many arrangements to make, many concerns to see to. Surely this one man and his problems did not warrant so much of his valuable time.

With little work getting done, he opted for breakfast and headed down to the restaurant below the hill. It was a brilliant day of sunshine and blue sky, certainly a gift from God this time of year, he thought. There was not even a breeze to rustle the few remaining leaves in the trees. He would have been more grateful had he not been praying for snow these last few days, snow for the heavily laden sleighs of logs soon to be working their way down to the railway landings throughout the forested domain of the Pratt & Southeastern.

Walking along the trail he could hear geese, distant in the sky and high, but making wild music that made him feel restless, frisky and alive. He paused, as he usually did, along the tracks, to peer west in the direction from which the train would eventually come. Expecting to see nothing but the sun glinting along the rails, he was surprised to see a small form bending close over the tracks just down the line. He walked over to see what Joe Johnson could possibly be up to at this time of the morning.

"Oh, hello," said Joe looking up.

"What's up, Joe? You look mighty serious."

"Nothing much."

"Did you get your share of dancing in last night?"

"Well, some... with Emma mostly... and Andrea. I'm not that much for dancing, though."

"What's that in your hand?" asked Cooper noticing that Joe was carefully hiding something in his left hand.

"Just a nickel."

"And what are you doing with the nickel?"

"Nothing much."

"I don't suppose you were going to put it on the tracks for the train to run over, were you?"

"I heard it was a way to get good luck. If you get a good flattened one, and rub it now and then, it's supposed to be real lucky. Sometimes I could use some luck."

"Well, I heard that too, once, so it must be true."

"You don't suppose it'll make the train roll off the tracks do ya? Pa would whip me good if I wrecked a train."

"No, I don't think so," smiled Cooper. "But I heard that the better the coin, the more the luck. Seems like you are only going to get a nickel's worth."

"Yeah... Billy Brown's got a lucky penny, but it don't seem to bring him much luck. I thought maybe I could afford a nickel's worth."

"I see... well, just as an experiment," Cooper reached into his pocket and pulled out a shiny coin, "let's make it a quarter's worth." He flipped the coin neatly in the air and Joe caught it.

"Really, Mr. Cooper?"

"You tell me if it works, Joe. I could use a little luck now and again, myself." Just then, he caught sight of another bigger form coming down the tracks from the west, tall and burly and in farmer overalls. "Say, who do you suppose that is?"

But before the lad could reply, Cooper moved off to meet the man. "Thanks, Mr. Cooper," Joe called after him. "Thanks a lot." Cooper waved his hand without turning around.

"Well, good morning Mr. Muggsley," opened Cooper when he got close enough to recognize the man coming his way. "Out for a stroll on such a fine day?"

"A stroll?" grunted Muggsley, "not hardly. I was 'sposed to be in Mason this morning."

"Mason? Well, you know the train won't be along for some time here, Muggs. You got a ways to go."

"Don't I know it? I was gonna get there early, too. I got a job there maybe, if they don't give it to someone else. The White River Company is hiring a few men. I was gonna get there real early," continued Muggsley putting his hands in his pockets, "and get one of them jobs, but..."

"You overslept?" offered Cooper.

"Overslept? Me and some of the boys got into a little of Poppy's homemade stuff at the dance last night. Musta had more than my share, though, cause I never made it ta home. Woke up under 18 mile bridge with a knot on my head. Musta missed a step."

"Mr. Muggsley, I think I can help you out," said Cooper suppressing a chuckle. "Can you cook?"

Over breakfast, which Cooper treated to, Muggsley allowed as how he could cook better than most lumberjacks and keep a cookhouse in proper running order even if he had to thump a few miscreants in the process.

Well, thought Cooper watching the man polish off his second plate of hotcakes, camp 9 got a cook, if I can afford to feed him.

"And ya know," muttered Muggsley between mouthfuls, "when I clumb the hill to the top of the bridge, there's this dude sitting there, and...(Muggsley paused to wipe his mouth on his sleeve) and when I asked him what he was doing sitting there like that, he says he's pondering. Hah, I says...aint no man ought to be pondering on a day like this. But he stayed a pondering as pretty as you please."

Leon was pretty much as Muggsley had left him when John Cooper found him sitting on the bridge dangling his legs. He was facing north looking out over White River valley, where a wispery layer of fog spread over the marsh like frosting. If he noticed Cooper approaching, he didn't show it. As silently as his heavy breathing would allow, Cooper sat down beside him and for several minutes neither one spoke.

"Kinda pretty country," said Leon finally.

"Yep," said Cooper. "I've been trying to tell you that. I've been admiring this view since '01... in fact I was thinking that the name of this village is all wrong. Now, what it should be... well I've been giving that some thought too. Now how does this sound... don't jump into conclusions right away... but let this just sit in your mind awhile, while you admire the scenery. I always thought maybe the town should be called..."

"I've been counting flocks of geese," interrupted Leon rudely. "There's almost always a flock within sight this morning."

"Yep," retreated Cooper. He decided now was not the time to be discussing names for towns, with Leon so absorbed in his own thoughts. "Yep," he said again, "good day for flying."

"Yes, I guess it is," Leon said quietly while scanning the clear sky.

"You figure on flying today, Mr. Mancheski?" asked Cooper casually.

"Well, I pondered on it some, I guess," he admitted.

"And?"

"And I don't think it'd do me much good."

"Good boy," said Cooper almost to himself, but patting Leon on the back warmly. "Stay here for awhile, let things run their course. It's not such a bad place... Pratt."

And then they sat there awhile, again in silence, watching the day develop, watching the geese wing overhead, each lost in his own thoughts. After awhile Cooper began to shift uneasily. He cleared his throat a few times.

"Well, son... do you still want my help, or do you have it in your head to do this all by yourself?"

He didn't answer at first, merely sitting there staring out over the valley, as if he had nothing to do but to scan the distant sky for the small V shaped flecks of geese dancing about the wild blue.

"Mr. Cooper," he started slowly and solemnly, "I need more help than you can possibly imagine."

"My boy, that's what I have been waiting to hear. And I think I know a way we can help each other." Mr. Cooper stood up on the bridge and stretched his limbs, feeling his legs as if looking for something. In the distance the whistle of the Chicago, Minneapolis, St. Paul & Omaha could be heard as it passed Tank Lake a mile or so down the line.

"Have you ever met Mr. Muggsley?" Cooper smiled. He took out his watch and opening it, found the time not to his liking. He banged the thing on the rail a few times, peered at it again, then closed it up and put it back in his vest pocket.

"Can't say that I have," replied Leon.

"Well, you meet me at the office at 10:00 am and we'll go over a few details."

"What kind of details?"

"I don't have time to discuss things just now," said the older man starting down the tracks back to town. "Just be on time."

When Cooper reached Joe Johnson carefully guarding his quarter on the rail, he asked him to send Buck on up to the office at 10:00 as well. Things just might work out after all, he thought.

It was a Saturday morning and the day of Halloween night, filling many of Pratt's younger citizens with restless anticipation. Young Joe Johnson was certainly no exception. Even after his trip to town he was unusually active, monkeying with this and that, chasing the chickens around, teasing the cat. Emma was following him around, trying to keep up and giggling at his antics.

"Joey... will you take me trick'er treatin' tonight? But not when it's too dark. I don't like it so much when it's so dark. Kinda spooky."

"Aww Emmy...me and the boys are going... when it's real dark... and real scary... with ghosts and goblins and witches flying through the air. Not the place for little girls." Joe separated two strands of the barbed wire fence at the edge of the pasture and ducked through. "We may stay out all night even... or sleep in the graveyard to guard Uncle Enar's grave. We might even have to kill a few spooks!"

"Jooooey....." called Emma quietly. She had tried to duck through the fence in the same manner and a barb had caught her dress and hung her up. She was literally hanging by the barb.

"Joooooey....." she called again a little bit louder. Joe turned and grinned when he saw her.

"Aw Emma... what am I going to do with you. See! That's why you can't come with us tonight."

"I couldn't help it," she said sweetly.

"Well, it's a good thing you got me around to take care of you, that's all I can say." Joe lifted her gently and unhooked the barb while Emma wiggled through. "I'll tell ya what, Emmy. I'll go out tonight and brave all the dangers and fight all the witches and ghosts... and I'll give you half of the booty I get."

"I don't want no bootys, I want candy!" said Emma.

"Well, that's what booty is... it's candy and cookies and such."

"Oh, boy," she said gaily.

"But, when Mamma asks me to take you out, you tell her you don't want to go, O.K.? I'll make sure you get plenty of candy and you don't have to fight no goblins or kill nobody, O.K.?"

"Uh huh." she nodded.

"But you tell Mamma you don't want to go... 'member now."

"Uh huh." she nodded again.

By the time Andrea went looking for Joe, he was off at the far end of the pasture walking atop a log pile, balancing carefully on the top log in his bare feet. Emma was seated nearby, contentedly watching. Andrea sensed that Joe was 'performing' for her, to some extent.

"They do this in the circus, ya know," he said, his arms stretched wide for balance. "On a long wire... high up... with lions underneath to eat you when you fall. So you can't fall."

"Really?"

"Sure... that's why you don't see no old guys up there... with gray hair. They all fell off and got eaten."

"Hi, Andrea," greeted Emma when the older girl got close. Joe jerked around to see and lost his balance, falling on his rump and sliding down a log or two.

"You be careful, Joe!" Andrea said sternly.

"Awww, that was nothing. I never get hurt."

"No lions," added Emma. "I'm glad there were no lions, Joe."

Andrea smiled at the little girl and sat down on one of the lower logs that was situated firmly on the ground, then pulled up a grass stem and stuck it in her mouth. She stretched out her legs and leaned back to look at a blue, cloudless sky, quickly falling into thoughts of things she was not likely to share with her two companions.

Just then the sound of geese reached their ears from high up in the northern sky, a V shaped form of hundreds of the big birds, winging, singing on their journey.

"Ohh... just listen to them," murmured Andrea, "it's like music to my ears."

"It's just a bunch of geese," said Joe trying to pretend he didn't feel the wild surge of spirit.

"No," said Andrea, "it's music plain and simple."

"I know," joined in Emma. "And this apple is like music to my nose. Smell it, Andrea," she said as she held out the small fruit, "smells just like apple jelly." Andrea sniffed it gently and smiled.

"Music to your nose?" Laughed Joe.

"Well, it smells awful good, don't it. And it makes me happy... like when Papa plays the fiddle. So it's kinda like music, ain't it?"

"Isn't it.... you say isn't.... good children do not say ain't," corrected Andrea.

"Oh... is it a bad word?"

"Well...it's... never mind, you'll learn all about it in school someday, ok?" Emma nodded, easily satisfied with the non-answer.

Andrea leaned back against the log again, watching the trailing end of the geese formation fade into the south, their call barely audible above the swish of the trees and fallen leaves in the light bit of air. The grass stem twisted in her mouth, bouncing with the rhythm of her thoughts... dancing once more.

"What ya thinking about Andy?" said Joe interrupting her self-reflection as he slid down beside her.

"Oh... nothing, really. I guess I was thinking that it was Halloween night tonight, and wondering if we'll all live through it again. And where in earth are your shoes?"

"Me and the boys are going to be out there tonight, Andy... we'll protect ya and kill any spooks or goblins coming this way. You just wait and see."

"Oh, Joe... how you talk. Don't let mamma hear you talking about killing things… even spooks and goblins." Joe just smiled. "And where are your shoes?

"I don't really need shoes yet," replied Joe examining his feet, noting each scar, blemish and callous. They were brown from the sun and a little from the dirt, but you could hardly tell which was which. Between his wiggling toes flashes of white skin could be seen. "What do we have to wear shoes for anyway? My feet don't like'em much... they're too crowded and too hot."

"How about in winter? Some warm shoes might be kinda nice in winter, don't you think?"

"It ain't winter yet... my feet ain't even cold. He picked a grass stem with his toes and dangled it toward her. She batted his foot away half-heartedly.

"You'll be lucky if those feet even fit into shoes anymore."

"Awww... Andy? What do you think I ought to be, this year? For Halloween, I mean. I can't be a ghost again like last year. I wanna be something dangerous and scary. Something downright spooky and horrible."

"Why don't you go as yourself then," kidded Andrea. It produced a giggle out of Emma.

"Aww Andy, this is serious. Help me find a costume, would ya?"

"Well, leave it to you to wait until Halloween day to finally get around to thinking about a costume."

"Would ya, Andy?"

"Well, I guess I'd better because Mamma will tan your hide if one of her sheets is ruined again this year. C'mon," she said standing up, "we'll check through some of my books and see if we can find something."

"Books!?! You can't find nothing scary for Halloween in no books."

"Just you come on," insisted Andrea.

They walked back to the house, across the golden field of flowers and plants long since gone to seed and withered under autumn's cold hand. Andrea lifted Emma over the fence this time, giggling and squirming in her hands. Up to the bedroom they went, the one that Andrea and Martha shared. It was dimly lit, just now only by daylight, so Andrea dragged a chest near the window and sat on the bed. Inside the chest were about a dozen books, novels of adventure and romance, all carefully arranged. Picking one up instantly brought Andrea back to its familiar tale, showering her with images of distant lands and heros and heroines.

"How about this one?" she offered. It was a book about King Arthur and the Knights of the Round Table. Joe looked at a faceplate image of a knight in armor.

"Nawww," he wrinkled up his nose. "What's so scary about a guy dressed in tin cans?" Images of damsels in distress and gallant knights faded as Andrea replaced the book in its proper place.

"How about this one?" she asked again. It was Treasure Island, by Robert Louis Stevenson. Joe was instantly caught by the word 'treasure'.

"What's it about anyways, treasure?" he asked half curious.

"Oh, pirates and treasure, hidden gold and sailing ships," she replied casually. Noticing the spark of interest she stood up and caressed an invisible mustache. "Avast ye mateys, let's scuttle this ship and hide the gold." She could tell that Joe was not yet sold on this so she continued in a more horriffic vein.

"We'll draw our swords and cut out the tongue of any land lubber who gets in our way. We'll run'em through, then make'm walk the plank, the sharks to feed on their bodies, their ugly ghosts to wander the land, looking for blood and bones." And she stuck her imaginary sword into an imaginary opponent.

"Say, now there's somethin'. I'd make a damn fine pirate, I would."

"Joe!" scolded Andrea.

"Well, I would. And so would the rest of the guys. They could be my pirate crew and me the captain. The Pirates of Pratt."

"What's a lubber?" asked Emma.

And so it was decided, and Mrs. Johnson's sheets were safe for another year, and perhaps the sheets of half dozen other families in the area who would now be tasked with outfitting a pirate venture.

"Will you help me, Andy? A costume and a sword and everything? Will ya?" he pleaded.

"What's a lubber?" asked Emma again.

"It's someone that's never been to sea. A land lover, only they call them lubbers," replied Andrea patiently.

"Will ya, Andy?" persisted Joe.

Andrea just nodded. Joe hadn't noticed that she was just a bit moved that he had gone along with her idea. She hugged the book to her chest. "I've got lots of ideas, Joe, and there's pictures, see!" She opened the book to the faceplate.

"Swell. I'm gonna go tell the rest of my gang what pirates they are," he shouted as he hurriedly left the room, trusting Andrea to come up with his costume on her own. He thought he was getting away with something. Andrea was secretly delighted.

"Oh mygosh," said Emma suddenly. "I'm a lubber!" It was enough for Andrea to burst out laughing and hug her little sister.

The weather held warm during the day, though sudden gusts of colder air were felt from time to time. Everyone knew that at this time of year, the warm weather was just a temporary gift and was soon replaced by the unpredictable weather of November. But for now, the populace of the Pratt area enjoyed the day to the fullest; young couples out for a walk, lines of laundry waving in the breeze, last minute pre-winter chores around the homesteads and in town. Any and every excuse to be out and about.

Buck was out and about. He was out of money and about to go see Mr. Cooper to discuss his future employment. He knew Cooper would hire him for one of the camps, and that was alright with him, but he could use a little of the 'needful' as an advance on his future wages to hold him over. As it turned out, he hadn't yet heard that Cooper wanted him at the office at 10:00 am and showed up about 9:45 anyway.

John Cooper and Jake were in the outer office when Buck came strolling in. Cooper glanced up at him briefly, then at the clock.

"You're a bit early, Buck," he said.

"I am?"

"But that's ok, we're about through here aren't we Jake?"

"Wouldn't surprise me a bit," said Jake. Cooper straightened up and gave Jake a smirk, raising a bushy eyebrow over one eye.

"Well, c'mon Buck, there's a few things we need to talk over before our other guest arrives."

"Other guest?" wondered Buck. Cooper motioned with a sweep of his arm toward the back office.

They had been talking for a few minutes when Leon strolled in. He heard voices behind the closed door so he knocked politely and entered when told to do so. He was smiling until he saw Buck sitting quietly like a chastised schoolboy near the desk.

"Whhhh...why, that's the guy who hit me," exclaimed Leon and slowly backed toward the door.

"Yes, so I've heard," smiled Mr. Cooper. "Leon Mancheski, meet Mr. Buck Johnson, logger and farmer and general roustabout." Buck stood up and offered his huge calloused hand to Leon, but Leon made no move to take it. After a few seconds of awkward silence, Cooper put his hand on Leon's shoulder.

"Look, son, Buck didn't mean you no harm. I had kinda asked him to look out for you awhile, while I was gone, especially if you ended up down at Charley's Saloon.

"Look out for me?"

"Yes, in case you got into a misunderstanding or something. And after talking with Buck, I was thinking that perhaps it was a good idea after all."

"A good idea?" whined Leon.

"Yes, yes. Now what is this nonsense about drinking a toast to Mrs. Gillis? Good Lord, man, what got into you?"

"What got into me?"

Cooper gave an audible sigh and moved back behind his desk where he felt more in control.

"That's all in the past now boys. I got a feeling you two will hit it off pretty good after all. Leon, did you know that this is Andrea Johnson's older brother?"

"Annn...." stuttered Leon.

"Oh sit down and stop repeating everything I say, you sound like a damn fool. And shake hands you two, so we can get on with business," said Cooper sternly. Buck turned again to Leon and offered his hand, Leon reluctantly taking it.

"I'm sorry, Mr. Mancheski. I vouldn't a hit ya so hard if I knowed yew vasn't use to it," said Buck sincerely. He even smiled.

"Awww, it's ok, I guess I didn't realize I was talking so much," allowed Leon, and he, too forced a little smile. It was a beginning, thought Cooper.

"Now that we're all friends again," he said, "let me tell you what we got going here." He spread a map of the area out over the desk, one with pencil marks all over it. There were three areas circled and lines representing railroad tracks leading to each one.

"The Company has three camps going in this year, all good timber lands. Here, here and here," he pointed. "Now the first two camps are all set, good boss's, good crews, etc. Not a worry there. Now this last camp, well, I've a haywire crew in this one. Some old hands that you will know, Buck, but some new boys and a few I didn't really want to hire, but needed them anyway. I've got Ox Pete for boss, and he'll keep them in line and working, you know he will, Buck, but he could use some help. And Lord help me, I've got Muggsley as a cook, best I could do at this time of year. Time's running out, you know. It'll snow soon, any day now, might even be snowing now." They all looked out the window where bright sunshine and cloudless skies were still the order of the day. Cooper sat back and studied Buck's face for a reaction, but he found it placid and unusually serene. Suddenly he sat up straight again.

"Sure wish Emil hadn't hurt his leg so bad," he mused. "I really could have used him this year. In fact I could have used you a lot sooner, Buck, if you hadn't had to play farmer this summer. But that's water under the bridge, I guess. You ready to go to work anytime now?"

"Yaa."

"Well I'm sending Leon, here, out as chore boy and cookie for Muggs," added Cooper. "Been thinking about it for bit and it seems like the thing to do. Joe Kinder will be there too, for Muggs and to help Ox Pete with the books."

As Leon's face began to sour, he turned to him and continued, "that will give you a chance to get some of your own chores done, to get around a bit and talk to people." He could tell that Leon still wasn't sold so he added, "Of course, you'll be living at the camp in the middle of the woods... so friends aren't apt to call... but I think you will find it accommodating." Leon, pondering only seconds, found this arrangement suddenly appealing.

"Well that's it in a nutshell then. We've been setting up the camps of late, the tracks were run this summer and should be in pretty good shape. In fact I'm going to take a ride out to the camps tomorrow on the 2 spot and I thought the two of you might like to ride along, kinda take a look around. We've got to haul in supplies anyway, as things are about ready to go." Both men nodded. "So are there any questions?"

"Mr. Cooper," started Buck suddenly, "I don't spose yew vould, vould ya?"

"Would what?"

"Let me have a dollar till I pay yew back?"

The Eighth Chapter

Of Landlubbers & Pirate Ships

It was a night for bewitching! The moon was full and bright lighting up the stark ground like pale blue daylight, save for the occasional murky cloud passing before it, sheathing the land in the temporary black of where mischief is born. The wind gusted about aimlessly, making bare tree branches rattle and clack one moment and seemingly whisper the next; making leaves dart and swirl, chasing each other across the sky or bouncing gaily at your feet. Loose gates and shutters would creak and groan to the thrust and parry of the October breezes. It was a night of noises, of earthy smells, of sights not always to be believed, truly a night for the unexpected, truly a night for imaginations to take wing.

Even before the sun was close to settling down for the evening, Joe was restless. Andrea and Martha were busy in the upstairs bedroom sewing Joe's costume and Joe was a bit worried at what they would come up with, without him up there supervising. Pirate business is not a pretty sight according to most accounts and he didn't want to end up with a pretty costume. He could hear them talking and laughing behind the closed door which didn't make him feel any better. He didn't want a 'funny' costume either. But the girls had made it quite plain that he would only interfere with the work at hand. And Andrea had promised him a pirate costume to make the peasants tremble. He liked that!

Earlier in the day Joe had made the rounds to the houses of the other would-be pirates and put the finishing touches on some plans that had been fermenting in his mind ever since the pirate idea had begun to take form.

It had taken up most of the afternoon, but then he had been much too edgy to stay at home even if his chores were not quite done.

It was all settled though. They would meet in town near the Modern Woodmen Hall, every one a pirate rogue and evil to the core. They would make the rounds about town, gathering what candy goods they could and spreading fear and panic throughout the village. And Joe, leader that he was, promised them a particularly glorious surprise toward the end of the evening. If nothing else, that alone had his crew locked in.

After his roundup he had been walking down the track line past the Pratt & Southeastern roundhouse on his way out of town when Cooper spotted him. Cooper had always enjoyed hearing what was on Joe's mind, for he was aware of the young lad's penchant for adventure and his empathy for this spirit knew no bounds.

"Hey, Joe!" he called, stopping the boy in mid-stride. He motioned with his arm for him to come over.

"The 2-Spot is ready for tomorrow, Mr. Cooper," said Sam Fieldstone, interrupting Cooper's thoughts for a moment. "Alfred will have 'er back of the store tomorrow for the load up, and the track's in good shape far as I know."

"Fine, Sam," he replied. "We're bringing the 4-Spot up from down south the day after tomorrow... she'll need a little work, I'm told."

"Whatever you say, Mr. Cooper."

He gave Sam a nod, more or less indicating the conversation was over, and turned his attention back to Joe who was in front of him by then.

"I was wondering, Joe, did you get much luck outa that flattened piece of silver?"

"The quarter? Well, I don't know...yet."

"Oh?"

"I guess I'll see some tonight, though... what with it being Halloween and all. I guy could use a little luck on Halloween."

"I suppose so."

"Especially being a pirate. I don't know if that was a good idea or not. It was Andrea's. The guys say there weren't no pirates around here, so some of them think it's kinda dumb. To have a pirate gang in Pratt, I mean."

Cooper listened intently while paring an apple to munch on. He offered Joe a slice, gratefully taken.

"Well, now... I guess maybe there weren't any pirates in Pratt, exactly. But not too far from here."

"What do you mean?"

"Lake Superior, of course. Why there were pirates all over the place in the early days. Back when they were trading goods with the Indians for furs."

"Really?"

"Well, sure. That was back in the days of sailing ships, of course... not like the good steam ships we have today. And the worst bunch of pirates there ever was... was a group up there in Chequamagon Bay. There were 12 of them, 12 rather gruesome and horrible pirates, so some people started calling them the Apostles... why I believe the Apostle Islands are named after them. I think they used one of the islands as a hideout, though I don't recall just which one it was."

"Gosh."

"Seems to me I read that some place. Yep, they sure raised hel... heck with the shipping of furs and goods in those days. A real ruthless band of pirates as ever there was."

"Well, that's different then. Wait'll I tell the guys. What else did the pirates do around here? Did they kill anybody? Bury any treasure?"

"Oh, lots of things," smiled Cooper. But just then Sam returned.

"Say, Mr. Cooper... If the 4-Spot is coming soon, I need you to..." Sam started to say.

"I'll be right with you, Sam." He carved off another big slice of the apple for Joe, then one for himself. "Well, Joe... I guess I'd better get back to business. But I hope that good luck charm works for you tonight. You let me know... alright?"

Joe nodded and as Mr. Cooper turned to go, broke into a run down the tracks.

So now he sat in the living room near the fire, letting the reins loose on his active imagination and fidgeting something awful, or so noted his mother, smiling in spite of herself.

Up in the bedroom the talk and giggles that Joe had overheard had more to do with romance than with his costume. Martha was somewhat partial to Bill Gustavel, "Night owl Bill" as he was called in respect to his position as the night telegraph operator at the depot. And Bill, in his own awkward way, had made it known that he was indeed interested in Miss Martha Johnson.

"It seems like Mr. Gustavel has finally found a little bit of courage," said Andrea. "I think he carted you around for every dance, pumping your arm like Mrs. Gillis' rusty well pump and stumbling over most everybody else's feet. Of course, seems to me, it was courage from the same bottle as Ben Wellstone and Seth Hackett were drinking from."

"Bill has lots of courage," sniffed Martha. It's just that... well he's much more courageous when we're alone. When there are lots of people around, he doesn't have much to say... and he's not so sure about things."

"Well.... if the whiskey didn't go to his head, it surely went to his feet," mused Andrea.

"Don't be silly... it wasn't the whiskey at all. Bill is just a natural born stumbler," returned Martha. Then they both burst out laughing at what she had said. "Besides... we did have a nice talk that night. Afterwards... when we went for a walk outside to cool off a bit."

"In the dark? Under that big full moon and so close to Haloween? Martha Johnson, just where is your head? You are never supposed to let a man walk you out into a night like that. Especially in October! Supposing he tried to kiss you behind a tree or something."

"Well, he didn't. We just had a nice talk, that's all. A nice talk," she emphasized. "Bill has a lot of plans... he wants to save some money... and you know that Bailey farm is for sale just North of town along the creek."

"But what if he had tried to kiss you? You wouldn't let him, would you? Not in the dark when he's barely said how'd-you-do in the daylight?" Asked Andrea.

Martha stared off into space for a few seconds, her face beginning to blush, then nodded her head, saying, "Well, maybe a little." Both of them broke out into giggles and laughter.

"Bill is just very shy. I know he's fond of me. He just doesn't know how fond, until I show him."

"That could be dangerous, Martha," said Andrea soberly.

"You should talk, Andrea Johnson," Martha said, steering a new course. "Just who is this mysterious stranger you've taken up with? He looks dangerous enough."

"Mr. Mancheski? You haven't heard about Mr. Mancheski?"

"Oh, I've heard plenty... Mr. Cooper's nephew, working for some unknown magazine or newspaper, writing a story on the life of a lumberman... I've heard it all from Amy Stewart. What I want to know is why he was following you around like a lost puppy."

"Why Martha Johnson, I have no idea what you are talking about. Certainly we danced a few times... he stumbles a lot like Bill Gusteval you know, but not for the same reason. He's kind of handsome though, in an off-hand sort of way."

"Oh, he's cute enough to be dangerous, I'd say," said Martha glad that the conversation was off of her Bill. "Did he meet Mama?"

"I guess so," said Andrea suddenly taking renewed interest in the garment she was working on.

"Well... what did mother say?"

"Oh the usual," sighed Andrea. "She thought there was something heavy in his spirit. For goodness sakes Martha, everyone has a heavy spirit now and again."

"Just the same... you be careful. He seemed to get too interested, too fast. You have to look out for fast characters."

"Oh...he's not that fast," mused Andrea thoughtfully. "But there is something about him. Something unsettling... something you feel but can't quite put your finger on. Sort of like passing a cemetery at night and it makes you shiver, even in July." She paused in that thought a few moments, then said, "Well... just look at us... the Johnson sisters... caught up with two dangerous characters. What will people say!"

"Plenty, you can be sure of that!", laughed Martha.

"I'm almost done with the shirt," announced Andrea suddenly, holding it up for inspection. "How about the pants?"

Martha nodded. "Just a few more stitches," she said.

From the Treasure Island book, Andrea had decided that both the pants and the shirt must be blousy and big, then with a big black belt to hold it in, around the waist. They had some old worn clothes of Buck's they had cut down to size, which fit the description, and had added a belt and sash. For his head they had fashioned one of Papa's handkerchiefs, and he was to wear his father's big boots, stuffed with rags to fit.

"With a little makeup for scars and such he should be the most fearsome pirate this side of Devil's Island," commented Andrea.

When, during supper, Alma suggested that Joe take Emma with him to the village and bring her safely back at an early hour, it was to everyone's amazement that Emma, herself, declined. Everyone except Joe, who sat strangely quiet, his eyes on the plate of food before him. No amount of persuading could change her mind, however, so after supper, the family gathered in the living room to get Joe dressed for the evening. With no one else going out, Joe had the attention of the entire family as they got him ready to raid and pillage the village.

Joe had expected something just a bit more vulgar and gaudy than Buck's old clothes, but he seemed pleased with the belt and bright sash. And the handkerchief, though at first giving him a comical air, looked splendidly dreadful when the makeup was applied.

"Lots of scars, Andy, lots of scars. I'm quite a horrible pirate," he said. When the costuming was complete he stood in the middle of the room to model for the family. Emma laughed and pulled on his sash. His mother stood quietly studying him and trying hard not to grin.

"Someting's missing," she said, hand on her chin as if deep in thought. "Ahhh...maybe dis vill help." She pulled a leather thong out of her apron pocket and gave it to Andrea. It was fashioned into an eye patch and Joe was delighted. Now he really felt like a pirate, and again modeled for approval.

"Still someting missing," said Papa from his comfortable chair by the window. "Vhat yu tink, Buck, yah?"

"Yah," returned Buck.

"Vell, don't yust stand dere like the Molly cow, Buck, go out and git it."

"Yah," said Buck and shuffled out the door returning quickly with something held behind his back.

"Me and Pa thought yew'd be a vorser pirate vith a sword," said Buck awkwardly.

"Pirates gotta have a sword," admitted Andrea, taken by the gesture.

"Vell, don't yust stand dere, Buck, give him the stick... I mean sword." Buck surrendered the sword from behind his back and grinned. It was about two feet long, graduating to a dull point and sanded smooth (pirates don't like slivers, they had figured), and had a cross piece near the handle. To Joe, it was glorious.

He took it and looked it over carefully. "Thanks Pa, thanks Buck," he said and Buck rubbed his head gently. Joe fitted the sword through the sash where it hung impressively by his side.

"Glorious" was all he could say. "Just glorious."

Joe lit out into the darkness, his sword by his side, hitting the tracks of the Pratt & Southeastern where they passed at the edge of the pasture. As he walked, every once and awhile he would draw the sword and swing it back and forth, fighting off other pirates or plundering ships. He kept the eye patch up as it was dark enough trying to see with both eyes, but he envisioned meeting the boys with the patch in place and sword drawn, the thought of which hastened his movements along the tracks.

John Cooper struggled up the trail leading from the Saloon and depot area to the bluff, a huffing and a puffing most of the way. It seemed that nearly all of Pratt was up hill from somewhere else. He thought of the south road leading in from the Namakagon Lake country, through the Davis hills and down into town. His camps would be out that way, though the railroad necessarily ran to the southeast and back across the hills to get to them. From the valley to the top of Davis hill was one hell of a climb, thought Cooper as he entered the office. And he didn't have quite as much steam as the 2-Spot engine.

Jake was still at his desk making marks in ledgers and muttering to himself about this thing and that. Though he heard the door open he didn't bother looking up, knowing from the heavy breathing and a slight whiff of cigar smoke that it was the boss.

"Well, don't look up, Mr. Jacobs, though I may be a thief or vagrant and up to no good," said Cooper sarcastically.

"Yep," said Jake, briefly looking up. "Vagrant." And then he returned to his work.

"Remind me to fire you come Spring Mr. Jacobs, for insolence and abuse. Now if you'll just make a note of that, we can get some work done here, and maybe, just maybe... we'll get some logs cut this winter."

"I suppose we do have a few things yet to consider. And I'll take your threat somewhat more seriously this time, knowing what you did with Mr. Mancheski." John Cooper pulled up a chair to Jake's desk where ledgers and papers were scattered about. He smiled at the comment on Leon, who presently was in the gracious company of Mrs. Gillis for the evening.

Mr. Cooper glanced at a few of the papers and then returned them to the clutter on the desk. "You understand this mess?" he asked skeptically.

"Haven't a clue," replied Jake.

"Well... I guess we better figure it out and get it right or my brother George will have us both fired."

There were several of the Pratt pirates wrestling around in the grass within the shadows of the darkened Modern Woodman Hall as Joe drew near. He recognized the voices of Billy Stamp and Carl Barksky right off as they were arguing about the toughest pirate that ever was. He noticed Robert Walden and his younger brother, Henry, as they passed through a patch of bright moonlight chasing each other. All were in a consortium of cast off clothing recently converted to pirate use.

Joe drew his sword and began to creep up on his crew, keeping to the dark patches and skirting the moonlight as much as possible. He was nearly among them when the moon fell behind a cloud and cast the country in darkness for a few moments, just what he needed. He lowered the patch over his eye and could hardly contain himself with anticipation. Slowly now he snuck up on the others until but a few feet away, and when the moonlight returned, he gave a whoop and a yell and swung the sword above his head. To Joe's delight it resulted in screams and cries of quite a clamor.

"Crimeny, Joe, you bout scared me half to death," complained Carl when he regained his composure.

"No foolin? Geez, that's great," answered Joe.

"Where'd ya get the swell sword," asked Robert trying to examine it in the pale light.

"Pa and Buck made it for me special," beamed Joe. "It's for lopping off heads and running through varmints." He pulled it out of Robert's hands and lunged it toward Carl.

"Hey! Watch it, Joe. Ya nearly stuck me," he said.

"Aww, I was just foolin'" returned Joe. "Say, where's Pete and Ryan, anyway?"

"Right here, oh mighty Captain of the seas," called out Pete as they approached. "We got a neat pirate flag and everything. My brother got it at the fair in Iron River a couple of months ago." He held up a Jolly Roger flag attached to a small stick, waving it back and forth. "And we've already been collecting treasure. Look!" He held out a canvas bag that had some penny candy in the bottom and they all gathered around to look. It was a rallying cry for the pirates of Pratt.

"Follow me, men," cried Joe and raised his sword high in the air. "We're off to murder and plunder the village!" He led the procession of oddly dressed pirates down Second Street, heading for the far side of town for to work their way back. "Take no prisoners, show no mercy," someone yelled in the darkness.

"I couldv'e had a sword too," whispered Billy to Ryan Andrews, "but Ma said I'd have found trouble with it." Ryan only smirked and quickened his steps to keep up with the rest of the crew.

The Pirates of Pratt made the rounds that night and for the most part they were satisfied with the booty they found. There were candies and gumdrops, great hoards of sugar cookies or molasses cookies, homemade taffy and fudge and sourballs and licorice sticks. From house to house they went, raising the pirate cry for pillage and plunder and no mercy for those that did not ante up some treasure. Bemused faces in the warm glow of the doorways slowly began to bulge their bags with goods.

Joe could tell that the folks were amused by the pirate theme, and made sure to avoid the other roving groups of made-up boys and girls so that the Pratt pirates could present the desired effect of one horrible crew. They even managed to fend off a few of the older boys, trouble makers too old for knocking on doors and asking for candy, who none-the-less took an interest in their treasure sacks. Two of the older Walden boys were members of this disruptive gang, Oscar and Carl, and it took a group rock throwing effort to finally dissuade them, a modest victory for the Pirates of Pratt.

They almost lost Henry Walden in that fracas, him catching a smaller rock along side his head. Henry would have folded up right then and there if Joe hadn't pronounced the wound the most glorious an aspiring pirate could ever hope for.

They arrived at Muff Brown's house on the eastern edge of town, near the end of their journey, most of the other houses with lights still on having been accounted for. Muff had a couple of children of his own; Billy and Emily, which the boys knew well. When the door was opened they could see two piles of candy and cookies heaped up on the table. Joe took in this scene and immediately had high hopes for topping off his treasure sack, already nearly bulging with goods. But all Mrs. Brown could come up with so late in the night was an apple a piece, small and bruised. Plunder hardly worth their effort. The pirates had hit a low point so close to the end of the night. As the door closed and darkness once more surrounded them, Joe hauled the apple up from out of his sack.

"An apple!" he said disgustedly. "They dare give the king of the pirates an apple for plunder?"

"Mine's even got a bite out of it," said Pete. And in the darkness, a rain of apples fell upon the house of Muff Brown, bumping and rattling as they rolled off the roof to the ground. But if Muff had looked out the door he would not have found the pirates anywhere near, and eternally innocent being absolved by the rite of Halloween passage that says, 'trick or treat'.

"And an apple is not a treat," claimed Joe. "Why we could get a hundred apples if we wanted." And all the boys agreed.

The pirates had run south as far as 3rd street, farther from the railway and with fewer houses. And there they stopped at the bottom of the wagon road grade that led up the hill and on for miles into the Namakagon Lake country. A few of the boys plopped down in a pile of leaves that had blown up against the fence, kinda pleased with themselves. Joe sat nearby on a stump near the old Campbell barn. There was relative silence for a while as each crew member investigated his sack of loot, oohing and aahing over various items, comparing quantity and quality with the others and sampling this and that. When they were all pretty much satisfied with the accounting of their share of the treasure, they settled in comfortably with the night.

"Me & Pete seen a dead body once," said Ryan.

"Really?" asked one of the others in awe.

"Yeah... it was one of the Porter boys from Mason. He fell through the ice on White River when he was skating... they didn't find his body till this Spring."

"He looked just awful," said Pete in a whisper. An awful looking thing all pale and stiff." He gave an involuntary shiver.

"Wonder if he's a ghost now," asked Henry, looking around nervously. "He'd probably be out and about on a night like this, huh, Joe?"

"Yeah... but he's probably ghosting around Mason mostly. We got our own ghosts around here, though." Joe liked the look on Henry's face at the mention of Pratt ghosts. So he continued on the subject.

"Maybe you and Bob ain't heard about Horrible Hannah... you ain't been here that long. But we all seen her once or twice, ain't we boys?" Most of the boys grunted positive sounds to that comment, some without knowing what Joe was talking about.

"Really?!? gulped Henry.

"Aww... their just pulling your leg," said Robert. Nobody ain't never seen a ghost around here."

"Ohh..." said Henry looking around carefully.

"Hannah was the daughter of a woodchopper," continued Joe. "Kinda pretty but kinda strange. She had her own axe, like her Pa's and liked to cut the heads off chickens. That's all they ate, her and her Pa, headless chickens.

"No vegetables?" asked Carl. But Joe ignored him.

"There used to be a lot of boys that wanted to go and see Hannah... her being pretty. And some say Hannah would let the boys see her naked sometimes, as long as they didn't tell."

"Woww! Naked!" mused the boys, most of which were already knee-deep into puberty. Joe wasn't sure where he was heading with this story, but liked the fact that he had their rapt attention.

"Then one day, one of the boys must have told... cause word got around. And Hannah was mad. And pretty soon they were finding all these boys with no heads... laying all over the place. Kilt every one of them that ever looked at her naked. Dead... all of them. The sherriff had to do her in for those horrible crimes."

"Aww Joe," said Robert, "there ain't..."

"And now she walks as a ghost down along the White River... down by Wheeler's pasture, through the Bibon Swamp and the Long Lake Branch... and shes naked... a naked ghost!"

There were more oohs and aahs at the thought of a naked ghost roaming the country-side.

"But you can't look... you mustn't never look... cause if'n you do... whack! off comes your head," said Joe drawing his rigid hand across his throat. The sudden image of an axe coming out of no where to lop their heads, drained the naked excitement from the boys, who all took on a nervous sober look.

"Aww Joe, that can't be, can it?" Asked Ryan.

"Well... alls I know is... ya better not be lookin' at naked women."

"Well, I'm never gonna," avowed Henry.

"If you don't really look, can you imagine them naked, or is that... well..." Pete said, suddenly feeling like there was a joke there somewhere and he wasn't in on it.

"Aww that don't work," said Billy, "every time I imagine a girl naked, they still got clothes on." It brought nervous laughter from the others.

And there the conversation sort of died; with vague images of drownings and beheadings and a nervous bunch of boys who were not altogether convinced they could actually avoid looking, if a naked ghost should chance to come their way. This vulnerability made them a little uneasy, much to Joe's delight.

So they decided to reinvest their interest in their treasure sacks, their spirits mollified by candy and sweets until they were once more comfortable with the night.

"So, Joe, oh pirate king. What about this glorious surprise you promised us," mumbled Pete while munching on some of their hard won booty. He was the picture of serenity, laid back nearly covered with leaves.

"Yeah Joe," joined in Billy, "you said it would be really glorious." He threw some leaves into Carl's face.

"He ain't got no surprise," claimed Carl picking the debris from his hair. "He was just fooling ya so he could be king of the pirates."

"Was not," defended Joe. "I got a surprise, kinda. And it is glorious. But..." He looked around as if expecting to see a crowd of people trying to horn in on his conversation, then whispered.

"But ya gotta be brave. It's a dangerous thing, real dangerous and daring." All the boys surrendered their attention once again to Joe.

"It doesn't have anything to do with ghosts does it, Joe. I think we're supposed to be home now, Bob," whispered Henry.

"Shhhh" answered Robert without looking at him. "What ya got, Joe. What's the surprise?"

"Well... ya see that ship up there on the hill?" He pointed south up the grade to an old haywagon sitting along the side of the road. "Well, matey's, we're gonna take that ship. We'll kill the crew, slit their throats...

those that we don't kill will walk the plank and go screaming to the sharks. Then all the treasure will be ours."

"Ya mean that old haywagon of Sam Campbell's?" whined Pete. "That's been there all summer since he broke the tongue on it. It's practically falling apart anyway... that's no surprise."

"Well, stay here then, if you're afraid," said Robert. "It looks like a great ship, Joe, can I be first mate?"

"I didn't say I was afraid... can I be second mate?" added Pete.

Joe just took off running up the grade lugging his sack of treasure with him, the rest of the boys scrambling to follow, leaves flying everywhere from their efforts. In a few minutes they were all aboard the wagon (safely out of the water, Joe claimed). They set up the Jolly Roger on a long stick and propped it up near the front, wedging it into a crack in the floorboards and then began setting up the pecking order of command. Joe was captain but was having a hard time deciding if Pete or Robert should be first mate. Pete was older, in fact older than Joe, but Robert had supported him when the crew was turning mutinous. The rest of the crew were beginning to raid their own plunder again and cared more about gumdrops than making prisoners walk the plank.

Poor little Henry rubbed his sore head now and again, but the magic medicine of molasses cookies was beginning to rid him of the ache. He supported Robert's bid for 1st mate, of course, but was a little afraid of Pete when his temper flew. So he sat and watched in silence, munching sweet cookies and feeling somewhat safe and content.

When it was decided that a 'plank' was needed, for prisoners or any mutinous member of the crew, Henry allowed as how he knew where there was one that would be perfect, figuring that it would buy him a little good grace if things turned ugly later on. So he climbed off the wagon and into the darkness, shuffling some rocks and removing a large plank that was bracing up the front wheels of the wagon, oblivious to its strategic importance in keeping the wagon in place. With considerable help, the plank was installed and finding somebody to walk it was the only task that remained. That, in itself, would lead to disaster.

The fight started a few minutes later when no plank walking volunteers could be found. And strangely enough, Joe was about the only person not involved. As captain (or king) of the pirates, he was exempt. The other boys were being pushed and tumbled about, each taking sides in the argument, while Joe watched in amusement from the wagon seat.

Suddenly, before any of them realized what was happening, the wagon was in motion. It moved slowly at first and when the boys stopped their fighting long enough to realize what was happening, they were merely amused. That had been the time to abandon ship, had anyone thought of it. But as the wagon got more into the steeper part of the hill and picked up speed, they could only hang on to whatever was handy, and in some cases, each other, and watch in mute silence the trees and rocks pass by in the pale light of the moon.

Faster they went, with one wheel rattling terribly, and the frame nearly shaking apart. Joe sat wide-eyed in the front, thrilled, chilled and in a mild state of panic. Occasionally, the boat would rock from stones under the wheels or dip into the ditches precariously, or weave from side to side as if at any moment the entire vessel would break into splinters. Yet, on they rode, the pirate flag fluttering gaily in the breeze, and still in silence.

Joe was trying to picture what was ahead of them, what was in store for them at the inevitable end of this wild ride. As they passed the Nelson's residence, and then quickly the Straddle Creek company store, his mild panic turned into a horrible cold fear. The others were too busy hanging on to worry about it, but Joe knew the end was probably not going to be a pleasant one. He reached into his pocket and clutched tightly a flattened piece of silver, silently calling for all the good luck it could bring.

Jake and Mr. Cooper had been hard at work most of the night, grumbling at each other like a couple of old bears now and again, but generally making some progress. Jake was one fine bookkeeper and secretary, of that Cooper had no doubt. And it was for that reason alone he tolerated the verbal abuse tossed his way and let Jake have his rein. A mutual respect held the relationship in place.

And after hours of work, Jake even felt a bit kindly toward the older man and suggested that they might relieve a bit of their stress with a little of the needful.

"Well, sad to say, Mr. Jacobs, but I've not a drop in the place. Gave my last bottle of good stuff to Buck Johnson out of pity," explained Cooper. Jake only smiled and opened a drawer in his desk, removing a pint sized Atlas canning jar that was filled with a clear liquid.

"Mr. Poppy was kind enough to share some of his homebrew with us this week," said Jake removing the top. He wrinkled up his nose at the smell, but sipped generously and smacked his lips. "Bibon Brandy," he said in a hoarse whisper, "smooth as silk."

Cooper brought a tin cup from near the stove and pretty much filled it with the stuff. He, too, made faces at the smell, but just as avidly slid some down his throat.

"Whooeeeeee!" he coughed. "Did he bother to age it at all? Feels like it's full of thistle weed."

"Nearly a week," replied Jake.

"Musta strained it through his flannels, Mr. Jacobs. It seems to have a little odor akin to last winter's sweat."

"Want to pour some of that bad stuff back into this jar?" asked Jake. Cooper just smiled. He got up from his chair and wandered around a bit, finally finding himself in the back office looking out the window at the starry night. He thought he could see some dim lights over across the valley, but couldn't be sure. That would have been the town of Mason, about four miles distant. A few more sips found him in a warm and friendly mood. He admired the dark reaches of the starry sky. He admired the happy glow of the full moon falling about the countryside. He admired the Jolly Roger fluttering from the speeding hay wagon careening down the north road, full of pirates. "Pirates?" he muttered aloud. He promptly returned the unused portion of Poppy's home brew to Jake's container.

Joe knew they were on the last leg of the journey, rolling down the north part of the road, down toward the fork. He wanted to tell everyone to jump but the words wouldn't leave his mouth. He wanted to implore them to hang on for dear life, but a quick glance back at his silent partners proved it unnecessary. As they bounced across the tracks and rumbled down the final grade, the only thing that Joe could think of to do, was to close his eyes.

The wagon bore them well, for its condition. Where the road veered right and left at the bottom of the hill, the wagon continued on straight until it hit the barbed wire fence marking the pasture of the Frank Wheeler farm. It was new barbed wire, and strong, and at that point the old wagon surrendered completely, nearly dismantling itself in a heap due to the sudden stop. Not so the pirates of Pratt. They were more or less flung in seven different directions about the pasture, and though none of them witnessed it, they were followed by a rain of cookies, candies and gumdrops.

Silence pervaded the pasture in the first few minutes after the crash. Then a few moans and groans were heard, and a few mild oaths.

Peter was the first one up, having hit a particularly marshy spot. Aside from being bruised and wet, he was ok.

Joe came to his senses with a bit of dirt in his mouth. He coughed and spit for a spell, and finally, in feeling around with his tongue discovered a tooth was missing. His face was bruised and scratched, yet he too was ok all in all.

Carl had lost his breath upon hitting the ground and was walking about trying to breathe again, tears in his eyes. When he finally was successful, he sat down beside Peter and Joe, moaning softly.

Billy's only complaint upon joining the others, besides the minor cuts and scrapes, was that he had slid across a relatively fresh cow pile and could barely stand the smell of himself. Robert's side hurt tremendously. He held his arm close to it and walked a bit hunched over to where the boys were gathering. Suddenly remembering Henry, he became frantic and started yelling his name, feeling the hurt in his side every time he shouted. Henry was not far from them, of all things laughing. He tried to stop, but couldn't. His old head wound throbbed. His new aches and pains made him weak, but yet he laid there and laughed and laughed, the others too, looking about at each other began to laugh.

And so ended the wild ride of the wild pirates of Pratt. The more they talked about it, the more they laughed. Each little scratch became a glorious wound, a drop of blood; a badge of honor. They were already back to the north road before they remembered Ryan. So back they went to call and search. And still no answer. So they spread out and searched across the pasture and if it wasn't for Peter falling over the prostrate form of his brother, they might have missed him altogether. He was out cold.

At first they were concerned. Joe was convinced that Ryan was dead and it was his fault. Peter was in tears as he wondered how he could explain this to their mother and father. The joy of the evening was drained from them. Henry, too, was next to tears. But as Robert splashed a little marsh water on Ryan's face and shook him gently, he came to.

"What happened?" he asked incredulously. And they all burst out laughing again, Robert painfully holding his side through each guffaw. In sudden inspiration, Joe suddenly demanded their undivided attention, having to threaten Henry with further bodily harm in order for the laughter to subside.

"This is to remain a secret of the pirates of Pratt," he whispered just above the sounds of the night. "We all have to take a blood pledge, never to reveal what happened tonight. Do we all agree?"

"Blood pledge?" asked Billy.

"Blood pledge," asserted Joe. "It's the only way. We'll cut ourselves and hold the wounds together to make the pledge. It's the way pirates do it. Anyone who violates the pledge gets his throat slit at midnight. Agreed?"

"But Joe," whined Henry. "I'm bleeding already. I got glorious wounds all over."

But in the end, Joe won out. The blood pledge of silence left each of them with a small cut on the thumb and a feeling of true pirate camaraderie. And true to their pledge no one ever heard from their lips what happened to Sam Campbell's old hay wagon on that Halloween night.

Joe showed up at the Johnson farm a full hour later than he was expected, so that most of the Johnson clan (save Emma) were waiting when the door opened. At first Mama was startled at Joe's face, the scratches and blood, but then thinking it was makeup, held back a smile and tried to scold him seriously about being late. Andrea and Martha knew better, and even in the dim light saw that Joe's face had had a time of it.

"Vell," said Pa standing before Joe at the bottom of the stairs. "A gude time?"

"Glorious," said Joe smiling, a gap showing where a tooth once was.

The next day, no one was sure where Emma had gotten a handful of strangely sodden candy, but the contented looks about both younger children caused no further inquiries into the night's activities.

The Ninth Chapter

The Road to Camp 9

Autumn was still flirting with the warmth of an Indian summer as the days moved into November. The day dawned with a light dusting of snow while sunlight continued to filter through the clouds, as if nature wasn't sure just which path to follow. The north wind, however, had a bite to it that was not mistaken.

Yesterday one of the boxcars of the Pratt and Southeastern line had been moved to the sidetrack behind the company store and various supplies were today being loaded for which to complete the outfit of the camps. The open door of the car was situated at close to the basement level of the store, the store being built into the side of the hill. There were a couple of planks bridging the gap between the two and it was there that Jake stood, clipboard in hand, ticking off the supplies as Bill Farley moved them laboriously aboard with a hand cart.

The Pratt & Southeastern actually kept four engines on hand at the round house during the logging season, but several were still in the southern area to be brought up later as the cutting harvest began to hit its stride. Alfred Hayworth, engineer of the 2 spot, had instructions to back onto the side track to pick up the supply car after the engine was loaded up with coal and water and then wait for Cooper to appear.

Cooper had invited Buck and Leon for breakfast that morning; that is, he insisted. As Buck sat across from him devouring load after load of flapjacks and great draughts of black coffee, Leon watched in amazement.

"Where does he put it all?" he asked Cooper incredulously.

"This," said Cooper jerking a thumb at the core of Buck's body, "is a great machine. And a machine must have fuel. Why, I wouldn't be a bit surprised if you didn't put on a few pounds yourself when you get to working with this crew."

"I thought that I was just the cook's helper?"

"No, that's not what I said. You are the chore boy, which means you will help the cook, but you'll have plenty other stuff to keep you busy, so that you'd think there weren't enough hours in the day. Right Buck?" Buck just made a guttural sound between bites and tried to nod without losing his eating rhythm.

"Now that you mention it, what are my duties, exactly? You weren't too clear on that."

"Don't worry, I'm going to let the camp boss fill you in. You'll really be working for him, anyway. And what he leaves out, Muggsley will be glad to illuminate you on."

"Muggsley?"

"The camp cook. And a damn fine one, I hear. Wouldn't you say so, Buck?" Another guttural sound slipped out between bites.

"Now, today, we'll make a little round about to the three camps we've set up through the summer months. We've got good track to all of 'em, so starting out should be an easy time of it. I've already started a few men at your camp, Buck, to help put the camp together and chop some firewood, and maybe take some easy timber. I guess they need some help so you can start today, if you want. And Muggs went out to set up the kitchen, so you might as well start today too," he said to Leon. "Unless you have something better to do."

"Well, I guess...."

"Good. Now, today we should hit camp 9 around lunch time, so we should have a chance to try out Mugg's good cooking. Jake's been down helping Bill with the supplies and so we'll be dropping some off at the other camps, too, as we go along. The oxen and horses will probably head out next week or so along with the rest of the crews.

Cooper had been all business this morning, a fact not lost on Leon. He had been wise to sit quietly and listen for the most part. Now he could see Cooper eyeing up Buck's empty plate and starting to smile.

"You about had enough, buck, or should I have Mrs. Williams butcher a steer for dessert?" Buck returned the smile. He didn't always know when Cooper was serious, but always found him generous and fair. He knew a smile was a sufficient answer in this case.

"You boys get what gear you think you need and meet me behind the store as soon as you can," said Cooper getting up from the table. "But make it soon," he added and disappeared quickly in business like preoccupation.

By coincidence, the three of them gained the back of the store around the same time. The supplies had all been loaded and Alfred had connected to the car with the 2-Spot engine, now idling in a low hiss. Cooper immediately observed Bill Farley in a heavy sweat, resting by the doorway and Jake in calm repose nearby as prim and proper as a school teacher on the first day of school.

"We got it all loaded," said Jake motioning to his clipboard.

"You did indeed," answered Cooper. "And you did so well that I'm going to bring you along and let you unload it."

"Now wait a minute, I've got plenty of work to do at the...."

"Sure you do, Jake," interrupted Cooper, "sure you do. But it can wait. I need your so-called expertise for this unloading operation."

Turning to the storekeeper, he said, "Thanks for your help, Bill. I appreciate it. You had better stay here and mind the store in case Mrs. Gillis needs a canning jar or something." Everyone smiled but Jake.

"Now if you boys will join me, we'll get this journey started," he said, moving Jake toward the open door of the car.

"What about those Jacks you brought up from St. Paul the other day," stalled Jake. "I'd better go find'em or they'll miss their ride."

"I kept stumbling over them, so I sent'em out on foot yesterday," said Cooper, "but if they mean that much to you, Jake, you can talk to them at Elmer's camp in an hour or so." Pausing at the doorway he kicked the walkway planks down and waved at the engineer. "Wind'er up, Alfred!"

In moments there was a shrill whistle of steam from the 2-Spot and a slight jerk as the engine puffed noisily to life. Almost immediately they were switched back onto the Pratt & Southeastern track heading slowly by the roundhouse, then picking up speed as they headed out of town toward the timber country.

Leon was far more delighted at this trip than he expected to be. He thought perhaps it was because all this activity was taking his mind off his real problems, now far distant in more ways than one. As the train rumbled and shook down the line he tried to stay at the opening of the car, peering this way and that about the country-side.

The trail was quite wide open at first, with the cluster of houses starting to thin in a short time. The virgin timber, once so prevalent everywhere about, was long gone, harvested years before and leaving a desolate country of scrub brush and small popples. Leon found more interest in looking back for a while, catching a glimpse of a few of the houses in the barren landscape.

Finally the edge of the forest could be seen, the bright blue of the sky bringing the rusty tree line into sharp focus. There were still a few fringes of yellow and gold mingled in Autumn's patchwork quilt of color and the sun seemed particularly pleased with these little patches of brightness. In spite of the sunshine there was a briskness to the air that bit and teared the eyes if you bothered to stick your head outside a train car to look at the scenery. Leon watched the scenery and the others sat on boxes and watched Leon.

A mile and a half of scenery had passed when they rumbled over a wooden bridge spanning 20 Mile creek. It was one of those spring fed streams that started in the hills, being fed by little freshets as it tumbled down toward Lake Superior some 30 miles distant. At the bridge it was wide enough and deep enough to support the Brook Trout that darted back and forth from pool to pool. Most were dark tinged from living in the shady realms of the undercut bank, with bright red and white spots for contrast. In the warm spring days of June, hundreds could be caught and eaten and shared with neighbors and friends.

But Leon wasn't pondering on that so much. He was still restlessly scanning the tree lines ahead of them, on either side of the car, when he noticed the first signs of the Johnson farm coming along the right hand side. Just a half-mile from the bridge was an open field, a fenced pasture with a pretty two-story frame house in a clump of trees at the far southern end. White sheets tied to a clothesline waved stiffly in the breeze from along side the house, while a woman continued to pin more in place. Emil was just coming out of the barn when Alfred blew the train's steam whistle. He waved and smiled. Now that the trains would be running more regular, it would be easier to catch a ride to town, with plenty of room for groceries and such on the return trip, as the cars were empty going out.

At the sound of the whistle, Martha Johnson nearly dropped a pair of Pa's clean pants, but waved and smiled just-the-same. With the trains running more regular, she thought, it would be easier for visitors to stop by for coffee and cake and little get-togethers with music and games.

"Is that Andrea?" asked Leon as he continued to wave vigorously.

"You can stop waving now, boy, we've been out of sight for a few minutes," teased Cooper.

"That was Andrea, wasn't it? You said we'd pass the Johnson farm. Well was that it? Was that Andrea?"

"Nope," answered Buck spitting out the door of the car, downwind. "Martha". He rubbed at a little bit of spittle that had refused to leave his face.

"Are you sure it wasn't Andrea?" Leon asked while the others smiled.

"Buck probably learned to tell his sisters apart some time ago and seldom makes a mistake now. Wouldn't you say so, Buck?" injected Jake sarcastically.

"Vell, certally," nodded Buck. "Martha," he said again and spit once more, having to remove spittle from his chin as before.

Leon suddenly wasn't as interested in the country-side and sat somberly on a box just out of reach of the wind. Of the others, only Cooper seemed absorbed with the passing scenery, a fondness he tried hard to keep to himself. He didn't want Jake or anybody for that matter, to know how delighted he was to be in this country, to watch the scenes of nature unfold before him, to be a witness to the change of the seasons. Something about this wild lonesome country instilled him with energy and livened his senses.

Feeling the wind a bit too deep within his clothes, Cooper soon moved from the doorway and sat down alongside Leon.

"Well, a few more miles should bring us to the first switching point at Camp #8," said Cooper.

"Camp #8?" questioned Jake. "We don't have a camp #8."

"Well, we will next year," said Cooper gruffly. "You can't have all the camps put in, in the same year. But next year I was thinking that switch point would be a good place for a car camp. There is a nice stand of timber to the east of there that I'd like to get at, and maybe some to the south."

"What's a car camp," asked Leon only half interested.

"Oh, it's just a camp that we set up with a few of these box cars instead of building shacks. There's bunkhouse cars and a cook car and a supply car...all kinda together on side tracks."

"Oh... well, what kinda camp are we going to?"

"This year we set up camps 7, 9, & 11. You'll see at least two of them before the days through, but you'll be living and working at camp 9 for the winter.

"Living in what?"

"Fine warm houses, my boy. Ain't that the truth, Buck?"

"Ya," agreed Buck, smiling.

"Camps 7, 9 & 11," mused Jake. "Mr. Cooper, if you needed help with counting, why didn't you just say so. I would have helped you, or least found a second grade student at the school to give you a hand."

"Don't pay any attention to what Mr. Jacobs has to say. He seldom says anything worth troubling your ears over. Truth is, I've had plans for camps laid out on a map shortly after I first cruised the timber here a few years ago. Numbers don't mean much, unless it's money numbers, of course. And we put in the camps when the time is right whether the numbers go in sequence or jump around. Still, for record purposes, it's easier to keep the names the same as I laid them out on the map."

Cooper focused on the signs of nature rumbling by while he fumbled in his pocket for a cigar. Finding one, he struggled to light it in the strong breeze, finally resorting to crouching on all fours behind the biggest stack of boxes. His head suddenly popped up again with wisps of smoke surrounding him like a halo before it was whipped out the door by the passing wind. Sitting again beside Leon, he continued.

"In fact, in thinking about it, Camp 1 was the only camp we ever put in, in sequence. That's the Johnson place now. Our first camp," he sighed. "Remember that, Buck?"

"Ya," grunted Buck. "Lousy cook."

"Old man Meyers. What he did to perfectly good food should have been a capital offense. Oh well, in spite of the perfectly lousy food, I watched Buck grow from a gangly kid into this fine specimen, over one winter. He's a survivor, that boy."

Buck's face flushed crimson and sober. "Ya, maybe," he mumbled, "but I survive better vith a gude camp cook."

Just then the train whistle blew again, long and sorrowful, and the heavy machine began to slow gradually.

"Must be the Camp 8 switch point," speculated Cooper out loud. "Won't take but a few minutes, but I better get out there and make sure we switch in the right direction." He was up from his seat rather quickly and jumping out the right hand door was gone in a flash.

Alfred was already down from the engine walking slowly forward when Cooper joined him. The switch was a good 20 yards ahead.

"Nice day for a walk, Al," opined Cooper. "Nice day for anything, actually."

"Unless you have the remutismus," mumbled Al. "It's a day for that alright. This leg's been botherin' me since..."

Just then a partridge exploded from the brush along side the track. And then before the men could still there fluttering hearts, there was another and another. Five in all were startled from their cover while Alfred and Cooper looked on.

"Say, I shudda brought my gun, them was fine partridges," said Alfred.

"Yes, indeed. Sure got the ol' heart in working order," agreed Cooper rubbing his hand over his chest. "We're heading south, Al. Switch'er to the south, ok?"

Al looked up the tracks at the switch and then back at Cooper. "It's already switched south. Ya want me to switcher east then switcher south again?"

"Why did you bother stopping the train then?"

"Well, I didn't know which ways you were going. You never told me. You never tell me much, jus run the train, is all you say."

"Well, get back to the engine and run the train, then." He patted Al on the back. "And Al, when we get to the next switch up ahead, we want to go west. West, to the camps," he repeated.

The terrain began to change as they headed down the south track. The ground began a gradual rise with rocky crags and butts thrust up here and there in random patches of gray. The engine, with such a light load, barely gave evidence of it's climbing work at hand.

Only Cooper seemed to notice or care about the change. He stood at the doorway, as long as the speed was slow and the wind didn't bite too deep, and watched the unfolding changes in terrain with a tight clinch on his cigar. He usually put the cigar in a tight clinch whenever he was trying to stifle a grin or smile or any other emotion he found unseemly to his character.

The next switch was already in place for a west transfer when the engine drew near. Alfred eased back on the throttle enough to slow the train to a walk through this section, gradually increasing speed after the engine had passed.

"We're on the west leg now, boys," Cooper said. "Another couple of miles will bring us to Camp 7 and we can get rid of some of these supplies."

"Where do those other legs go," asked Leon, "the ones we turned off from. On to Ashland or someplace?"

"Son, this isn't a passenger coach you're riding in. This is a logging train. It's gonna haul my timber to Pratt so I can get it switched over to the Omaha line to New Richmond and St. Paul. Just a work horse, nothing more," answered Cooper stepping back from the door.

"Then those other legs go..."

"Nowhere, absolutely nowhere," interrupted Jake with a smirk.

"Unless you'd call fine timber lands 'somewhere'," added Cooper. "That south leg now, goes over past the Atkin's Lake area, fine country, beautiful country. It just kind of ends out there for now, waiting for us to cut timber and move it on. Same as with the east leg pretty much, and this one. Why, by the time we get done we'll have tracks all through this country from Pratt to the Namakagon and east to Ashland County, and perhaps beyond. Yes sir, good little workhorse this 2-Spot."

They were going cross country now, west along the base ridge of the Great Divide area, the far west end of the Penokee range running through Upper Michigan and Northern Wisconsin. Great mining efforts were made along this range of rock in the Town of Pratt, in the latter part of the 19th century. But the dreams of great riches, hitting the motherlode in copper and silver and gold, disappeared in just a few years. Now, timber was the focus, the everyday work and worry of a hardy class of people. No dreams of riches here, no motherlode, just hard work. John Cooper pondered some of this while he shivered at the door of the boxcar.

Within two miles of making the switch west, the engine slowed again.

"Should be camp #7," said Cooper. "Might as well get up and get ready, Mr. Jacobs. You can see to the unloading. I assume you got this mess organized by camp loads?"

"Wouldn't surprise me a bit," sneered Jake.

"Elmer Rose and a few of the boys should be around this time of day to give you a hand, but Jake, I want to see you carrying something this time. No slacking!"

"Someone ought to supervise, don't you think?"

"Cook'll tell you where he wants something, or don't want something. You carry something, Jake."

"I'll help," added Leon, "I don't mind."

"Ya," said Buck.

The engine was switched onto another short spur of track heading a little north to where Camp#7 lay nestled in among the large pines and hardwoods. When the engine finally stopped, Alfred blew a long shrill blast on the whistle, that echoed off the distant hills of the great divide and returned to settle in the trees.

Camp #7 was a medium-sized camp by Straddle Creek Co. standards. There were two long bunkhouses, side by side, built with rough logs and covered with black tar paper held in place with vertical slats. And a cook shanty, with rows of plain wood tables and bench seats, enough to seat sixty men. Nearby and down wind, was a horse barn and blacksmith shop and supply shed, all similarly built.

Leon paused in the doorway of the car a moment, for the view of the camp was good there, and scanned the area. A few of the fellows were coming down worn paths to the spur, knowing quite well what the train would bring. The men were muscled and stocky, with woolen shirts and trousers held together with suspenders.

"Might as well move out son," said Cooper intruding in Leon's thoughts. "You'll see plenty of camp life before this winter's over." He put his hand on Leon's shoulder and gave him a warm smile.

The other men didn't pay much attention to Leon, but greeted Buck and Jake warmly enough. Cooper disappeared right away, heading up the path to the camp kitchen in long hurried strides while fumbling in his inside coat pocket for a fresh cigar. He always used long hurried strides when there was business to attend to. He found Elmer Rose talking to the cook who was slowly stirring a huge kettle simmering on the wood range. Elmer had a cup of coffee in his hand and was peering into the pot, dodging the cook's stirring arm each time it came around.

Cooper stopped in the open doorway, unlit cigar clenched tightly in his jaws. While silently observing the two at the stove he took the chrome plated watch out of his vest pocket and noted the time; 10:15, or thereabouts if the watch was running right.

"Elmer!" Cooper grunted loudly. Both men jumped, Elmer spilling his coffee down the front of his shirt. "Is it coffee time all day around here?"

"Mr. Cooper... didn't know you was coming out with the engine."

"Obviously so," said Cooper. "Cook, put down the spoon and go watch over your goods, they gotta last you awhile."

"Yes, sir," replied the cook, and hurried out the door, wiping his hands on his food stained apron.

"Now, Elmer, let's have a little walk through this burg. You know I gave you the candy camp, and by God, there should be no trouble and plenty of wood cut before long."

"Yes sir, Mr. Cooper," nodded Elmer. "As soon as I get the rest of my crew we should be getting along just fine."

"Hrmmph," ejaculated Cooper. "Well, let's go have a look-see. That barn looked a little small to me and the rest of the teams could be along as early as next week."

By the time Elmer and Cooper had wandered around the camp once or twice, looking at this and peering at that, the supplies were nearly unloaded. They were coming down the path as the last bundles came down the planks from the car, with Jake bringing up the rear carrying a small brown bag. He held it up high for Cooper to see, wagging it back and forth and boldly walked up to the two men.

"Your peppermints, Mr. Rose, as you requested," he announced holding forth the bag. Elmer looked sheepishly at Cooper.

"Settles ma stomick," explained Elmer. "Thanks, Jake." He took the bag, examined the contents briefly, then closed it up and moved it behind his back.

"Well, Jake," said Cooper testily, "thank you ever so much for unloading that car. Now that you kinda got the hang of it, the next two stops should be a piece of cake. Let's get aboard this thing and get going."

"Aren't you staying for lunch?" asked Elmer.

"Not this time. I had a chance to take a good look at that stew in there, Elmer. Guess we'll head on over to the other camps and get this job done."

"Ok Mr. Cooper. I'm ready for the men and horses anytime now, so you just send them on out when you've a mind to. No need for you, yourself, to come though."

"Nooo...sir," said a voice from behind the men. "No need at all." It was the cook. "And that's fine stew... ain't poisoned nobody yet... least none that complained."

"Cooper stared at the man in the dirty apron for a few seconds, then smiled. "Fire her up, Alfred," he yelled over his shoulder.

Alfred was already in the engine cab checking gauges when he heard Cooper's yell. He let a shrill blast of the steam whistle go which turned every head in the area.

"Well, Elmer, give'r the snoose," said Cooper heartily. And with that he walked off to join the others in the car.

"Snow coming soon, Mr. Cooper," Elmer yelled after his retreating form. "Pretty thick skins on the onions I've seen... means a hard winter for sure!"

The day held bright but cool to high noon. Where one could stay out of the slight breeze and soak up the sun, it was actually quite a pleasant day. Unfortunately, the on-going track lay mostly in the shadows of tall timber.

The engine was still puffing noisily along to the west, with Cooper in the doorway of the car, coat pulled up around his neck, and hat pulled down. In a moment though, even Cooper gave up and went to the corner of the car farthest from the wind.

"Remind me to put a caboose on this thing next time, will ya Jake?"

"How much farther, Mr. Cooper?" asked Leon, "To the camp where Buck and I are gonna... uh, work."

"Couple of miles, I'd say," answered Cooper. "I'll have to see what Muggsley's cooking before we decide to stay for lunch though."

"Muggsley?" questioned Jake. "Has he ever cooked before?"

"Must have," replied Cooper, "at least a little bit, anyway." He watched bemused as Buck suddenly showed an interest in the conversation.

"Everybody knows how to make flapjacks," said Buck suddenly. "And boil pataters. Who's the helper?"

"Joe Kinder," answered Cooper. "And of course Leon, here, is Choreboy, I told you that, Buck."

Buck turned to Leon and looked him over for a few seconds, as if newly assessing him for the task at hand. "Yew cook much?" he asked.

"Not at all." replied Leon. Buck rolled his eyes and groaned softly.

It wasn't long before the engine slowed again. Cooper announced that it was probably just the next switch line, one spur to Camp #9 and the other to Camp #11. As the engine switched onto the Camp #9 track, they watched the other spur disappear to the northwest in a gradual swing. Still they rode on through great groves of pine and hardwood, the land rising gradually into rocky crags to the south, and falling gently to the north toward the White River valley. They crossed the north/south wagon road, a crude path that bumped over the tracks and wandered down the hill toward town, a shortcut to whiskey if the need be.

"Well, boys, I suspect you're home," announced Cooper as the train began to slow and the whistle echoed off the hills. "I expect you to make yourselves useful to Pete in any way he deems appropriate." Leon and Buck nodded silently. "Pete'll have his hands full with the crew I'm bringing in," continued Cooper. "Good lumbermen, no doubt, but some can make trouble just for fun. And some I picked up in St. Paul that won't know one end of the axe from the other, but they are big boys and they'll work hard just the same if you give them a chance and teach'em how."

"Buck, things will be slow for a bit. Not real slow, but nearly tolerable, so I sent along a few bottles for medicinal purposes. Care you don't get sick too often though."

"Yaa," grinned Buck.

Camp #9 was a small camp. Only one bunkhouse building and a smaller cook shanty, but the other buildings were about the same. The foreman made his own little addition by adding a small attachment to the cookhouse, however, containing a small office and two bunks. It didn't fit well and looked slightly askew from the larger building. Smoke was coming from the kitchen area, and Buck sniffed the air tentatively, hoping to smell good baking smells, or a little stew. He seemed a little disappointed when it brought no memories.

"Jake, you take care now to unload the car," said Cooper as he got ready to exit. Then as an after thought he turned back to add, "and if there's any peppermints in this load, let some other guy struggle with 'em." Jake made no reply as Cooper jumped down and disappeared in hurried steps.

Jake, Leon and Buck all stood in the door of the car surveying the scene before them. The size of the camp not withstanding, the location was nicely picked. There was a little creek running from the west that cornered north at the edge of the camp. The bunkhouse was perpendicular to the track spur on the north side, as was the horse barn and blacksmith shop. The cookhouse and supply shed were just opposite on the south side, a neatly laid out arrangement.

"There's Ox-Pete," said Jake pointing at a burly looking man near the horse barn. He wore a large mustache that curled at the ends and a black felt hat that had seen better years. His green wool trousers were patched here and there, and drooped some in spite of the red suspenders attached. The sleeves of his plaid wool shirt were rolled up revealing white winter underwear on thick strong arms.

"Why do they call him Ox-Pete?" queried Leon.

"Hell, can't you see?" answered Jake. "Strong as an Ox, he is."

"Oh," murmured Leon.

"And nearly as smart," he added patting Leon on the back. Buck laughed out loud suddenly, startling the other two.

"Yaa," said Buck, "almost as smart, hah." He jumped down then and wandered in the direction of Ox-Pete, who was talking with Cooper with forceful hand gestures.

"Say, you don't think Buck would repeat what I said, do you?" wondered Jake.

Leon gave him a toothy grin. "You shouldn't say things you don't want people to hear," he said. "Well, I suppose we should get going on this stuff."

"Yeah," sighed Jake, "I suppose."

The few camp men about were gathering at the car for the unloading by the time Jake and Leon got the planks down and started moving stuff toward the door. Cooper and Ox-Pete watched from the other side of the tracks by the blacksmith shop.

"See that fellow there?" said Cooper pointing toward Leon. Leon would appear and disappear from their view while hauling loads of supplies from the rear of the car.

"Dat skinny one?"

"Yes, dat... that slender one. He don't look like much, but he's wiry strong and will do his job. His name is Leon Mancheski."

"Pole? Vell, dats gude. Poles, dey vork hard, like hard vork."

"Now, Ox, he....."

"Vhat yew say?"

"Don't they call you Ox-Pete?"

"Yah, some peoples do, but only vhen I don't hear."

"Can I call you Ox?"

"If I call yew mule," replied Pete.

Cooper studied the woodsmen for a few seconds, decided he was dead serious, then backed up. "Well, pardon me, Mr. Swenson," he said, contritely. "This Leon has never been in a camp before so he may need some proper guidance. I've asked Buck to kinda keep an eye on him, but just so you know."

"You giff me de haywire camp, for sure," complained Pete suddenly.

"Well, Pete, I did at that," admitted Cooper. He drew a draft on his cigar and blew the smoke lazily into the sunlight where it swirled and curled as he watched. "But only because you are the best bull of the woods in these parts," he added.

"Yah?"

"None better."

"Py golly, vee cut some good vood dis venter, Mr. Cooper," said Pete, suddenly enthused. "Py golly, vee sure do!"

Cooper was back down by the car as the last load came off. It surprised and pleased him to no end to see Jake actually working up a sweat.

"Well, well, Mr. Jacobs, I'm impressed. I take back almost half of the nasty things I've said about you." The crew chuckled good-naturedly at that, leaving Jake with no suitable reply. That, too, pleased Cooper.

"I think we'll take a chance and join these fellows for lunch today. Give us a chance to see how ol' Muggs is doing."

"Must be doing somewhat fair, as they haven't hanged him yet," speculated Jake. As they spoke, a clanging arose from the cookshanty.

Cooper took out his fine chrome plated watch and noted the time. It was still 10:15. He bumped it against the side of his shoe a few times and listened to it, finally hearing a ticking.

"Why, I believe, Muggs is a few minutes off," he said.

The crew filed into the cookshanty in orderly fashion as Muggsley supervised by the door. Each man removed his hat and went quietly to a table already set with tin plate, cup, and utensils. There were large coffee pots full of strong smelling brew and serving pots full of stew; a mixture of potatoes, beef and vegetables in heavy gravy. Joe Kinder was busily filling cups with the coffee as the men filled their plates from the serving pots, all done in complete silence.

There were only 10 or 12 men at the camp just then but their appetites were sharpened daily through their winter wood cutting and building efforts. It was an easy life actually, compared to what was ahead. Leon, Cooper and Jake sat at the far end of the table while Buck had joined the rest of the crew. Leon, not understanding lumberjack cookshanty etiquette, was amazed that a group of men this size could sit so quiet. He had sampled the coffee, and decided it was a bit strong for him, but the stew was actually quite tasty and heartily filling.

"Not bad!" he declared to no one in particular. And he was surprised when no one in particular had anything to say in return. "Coffee's a little strong, though," he continued. "Kinda stiffens me up." Still no one said a word, but went about the business of eating quietly, with little wasted movement. He barely noticed that Muggsley had wandered over to stand behind him.

"Say, Mr. Cooper, I was wondering when..." That was as far as got when Muggsley whacked him on the head with a wooden spoon. There were a few stifled chuckles from the crew, but still no one said a word.

"Hey! Don't..." And whack, the spoon came down again on his head. Leon's face flushed and he started to get up in anger when Cooper grabbed his arm and pulled him back down.

"It's a rule, son," said Cooper calmly. Then turning quickly to the cook he added, "And don't you even think of hitting me with that spoon, Muggs, or you'll be walking back to town to look for a job."

"Hrmmph," grunted Muggsley and wandered off back toward the kitchen.

"It's a rule," he said again to Leon. "The rule is that no one talks in the dining hall. There's generally too many mouths to feed so seldom time for both talking and eating. You ask a jack later, which he is apt to give up, talking or eating."

Leon said nothing more, nor the rest of the crew. There was plenty of eating and the coffee was consumed until coarse grounds were about all that would come out of the pot. Still some swished these around in their mouths, even chewing a bit trying to savor the strong flavor. When the meal was done, which took less than half an hour, the men arose and went back to the work at hand, without instruction or complaint. All save Leon, Cooper and Jake. Even Buck was off, already to work with the crew.

When Cooper came out of the cookshanty, he didn't go far. Just outside he pulled up a good sized wood chunk and sat down carefully on it, while Leon and Jake stood nearby. He reached in his inside coat pocket for a cigar but came out empty.

"Well, drat!" he uttered. But before he could expound further, he saw a cigar hanging in front of his nose. He followed the hand back to it's owner and found the sleepy smile of Jake looking back at him.

"Mr. Jacobs, you are worse than a wife. Half the time I want to boot you in the ass, and the other half of the time... well..." He took the cigar and bit the end off, then from his vest pocket he retrieved a wooden match and striking it along his shoe, he set fire to the cigar, puffing heavily. "You're not a smoking man, Jake, now what made you think of bringing along some extras?"

"I know how cranky you can get if you don't have something to chew on," answered Jake. "Well, better the cigar, than one of us."

"As bad as all that, eh?" Cooper chuckled. Then taking a more serious tone he added, "Say, Jake, go on down and have Alfred fire up the engine. It's time we moved on over to Camp #11 and got rid of the rest of those supplies."

"I think Alfred's all ready to go."

"Then go on down and wait for me in the car."

Jake got the message, finally, that there was some private business yet between Cooper and Leon. He turned to Leon unusually serious and offered his hand. "Good luck," was all he said. But to Leon, it felt warmly spoken. And then he was ambling down the trail to the spur.

Even when they were alone, Cooper stayed silent for a few moments, enjoying the sunshine and watching the smoke curls dancing in its light. Then suddenly, he spoke.

"I know there are a few things in your past that you would just as soon forget. Well, son, this is just the place for forgetting. Most days you'll be too tired to remember your name. And when you do, there will be plenty of folks to tell you how unimportant it is."

"Well, I..."

"Let me finish. I don't know what kind of people you are used to dealing with, but I would guess they were not Wisconsin woodsmen. These men are tough, hard men, most of them. They are generally honest, except for an occasional tall tale or two. They will expect you to work just as hard as they do, dawn to dusk mostly, and kid you and ride you and perhaps torture you, in ways. And then they will turn around and give you the shirt off their backs or defend your honor, or loan you money."

Cooper looked up at Leon very seriously. "Just treat them honest and fair. Watch what you say, and how you say it. Listen more than you talk. That's good advice to anyone. Just give it your best shot."

Leon nodded silently.

Cooper stood up and stretched. "I have to be moving on, now." He held up his arm toward the North. "Pratt is about 4 or 5 miles through the woods there, if you follow the track back to the wagon road. Only a couple of miles to Camp #11 in the same direction. Well, like I said... just give it your best shot. I'll look out for things in town... you'll hear from me if there's anything you should know."

They shook hands warmly and then Cooper was gone. Leon barely remembered the train pulling away, or the lonesome eerie sound of the whistle as it bounced around the rocky crags to the south. He just suddenly found himself standing alone outside the cookshanty wondering what to do now. Just then Muggsley stuck his head out the door.

"Well!?!" said Muggsley.

The Tenth Chapter

Muff Brown meets the Wolf King

The friendly blue skies of the morning began to fade into dull gray by late afternoon. The air was wet and cold with a slight western breeze snatching at any remaining leaves within reach. Dusk brought a stiffer wind, full of leaves, and moisture and just a little bit unpleasant. A view from above would show clouds covering a wide area. It was snowing in Duluth. It was snowing in St. Paul. It would be snowing in Pratt before long.

John Cooper had been peering out the window of his office from time to time, restless as the breeze. He watched the leaves scramble by, listening to the clack clack of the branches on the roof like knitting needles in his mother's parlor. Finally, he could stand it no longer and went and threw open the door. The wind, in a sudden gust, removed his hat and tossed it across the room. But he smiled in spite when he felt his face being anointed with a hard driven sleet.

The beginning of the timber season, he thought. Hard ground, frozen swamps, snow on which to slide vast loads of timber. He may have been the only one in Pratt with a smile that night.

Or perhaps not. Joe Johnson was at a window too, watching the storm move in. His smile was borne of sliding memories, of sleigh rides and snowball fights. There wasn't a day in the life of the world that Joe couldn't find use for, and each one a new adventure.

Well adventure begins with the first step. Joe knew from the sound exactly what it was; the barn door being abused by the wind. Had he forgot to latch it? No distinct memories of that, but probably so. Might as well take care of that before Pa wakes up and raises a fuss.

Down the stairs he went, creeping on barefoot tiptoe, and out the door. He was careful to shut the door behind him, so as not to start that to swinging too. And then a dart, still with bare feet and flannel nightshirt, to the barn. It was easy enough to shut and latch the door, but oh, the night... what a wonder of blowing snow across the fields, swirling around the well pump, dancing through the broken corn stalks and leftover garden plants. It was cold. Joe danced from foot to foot, to keep them from going numb, finally giving up and running briskly back to the porch.

He paused with the door cracked open and turned to look again at this restless night, and suddenly a hand reached out and pulled him in through the door.

"Geez, Andy, you about scared me half to death," he sputtered.

"Well, serves you right. Are you trying to catch pneumonia?" She removed the blanket she was wrapped in and put it over his shoulders. "What were you doing out there in the middle of the night?"

"Well, what're you doing up?" he shot back.

"Never you mind that. Just look at you, nightshirt all wet, and your feet must be frozen." Joe could see that there was no anger to her words, and through the darkness of the room he could sense just the hint of a smile at her lips.

"Nice night, huh, Andy?" he whispered close to her. She tweaked his nose in return.

"Glorious," she whispered back.

Early the next morning the wind abated and allowed the snow flakes to bunch up and waft lazily through the crisp air. About four inches of flakes had wafted by noon. Those that watched the accumulation from the warm side of a window, thought it pretty. Those that were outside working in the midst of it only slightly disagreed.

It was the first real storm of the season, the harbinger of winter, here to stay. Oh, the days may flirt now and again with the warmth that once was summer, tease with thoughts of sun and spring, but winter, alas, is truly a harsh mistress, especially in Northern Wisconsin.

Only John Cooper could accidentally stumble, slide all the way down the hill on his posterior, and arrive at the bottom with his dignity intact. Even those that happened to observe, swore he did it on purpose. He arose and dusted himself off, clearing his throat a few times. Walking stiffly, he crossed the tracks and headed for the restaurant.

As he was opening the door, someone was opening it from the other side to come out.

"Oh," said Charlie Mathers, one of the Pratt & Southeastern roundhouse crew, "I was sent to look for you, Mr. Cooper."

"Well, did you find me, Charlie?"

"Not in there."

"Did you check in my office up there on the hill?"

"No."

"Why not?"

"Cause you're not there," observed Charlie nervously. "I figured you'd be having a late breakfast down here."

"Oh?"

"I'm a little hungry myself, you ate yet, Mr. Cooper?"

"No, I was just gonna... say, what do you want, anyway?" asked Cooper.

"Well, Sam sent me to tell you there's sorta trouble with the track crew," answered Charlie.

"What kind of sorta trouble?"

"I dunno, but they say they ain't going back out there today."

"On account of a little snow?"

"I dunno."

"Oh fer... I'll go see for myself," grumbled Cooper.

He walked east down the tracks, with Charlie trailing behind far enough to avoid further conversation. The roundhouse wasn't far, just a block or two, and they could take the main Pratt & Southeastern spur right to it. But even before they got there, Cooper could see the section line crew and a few of the roundhouse boys standing around by the tracks, pointing southeast down the line.

"Hey! What's going on here?" shouted Cooper when he was still some distance away. Five heads turned as one from the east in startled fashion. Three were part of a section line crew, two were roundhouse crew, Sam Fieldstone, foreman. All started talking at once. Cooper could make out a few words out of the babble, words such as 'wolf' and 'big' and 'teeth'.

"Ok," he said when he got up to the group, and they all fell silent, "Sam, you and your boys get back to work now, this is between me and the section crew." When the three men of the section crew were all that remained, Cooper continued.

"Now what the hell is this all about? You, Carl, you tell me, and when I hear something I don't like, I'll let you know."

"Wolves, Mr. Cooper," said Carl. "Six, maybe seven of 'em circling round us."

"Wolves?"

"Big ones! We yelled at 'em but they just kinda eyed us from a ways. Gaunt lookin' and mean," said Carl.

"Yeah, mean," agreed one of the others.

"Thought we should come in, Mr. Cooper. We didn't have a gun or anything. You can't tell about wolves when you can't scare 'em off like that. No telling what they might do."

"Yeah, couldn't scare 'em at all," mumbled the third man.

"Oh, so," nodded Cooper. "That could be a problem, I suppose. Wolves, eh?"

"Big wolves," corrected Carl.

"Yeah, big... big wolves," added one of the others."

"Where abouts did you run into trouble?"

"Well, we were fixing up that line near the 20 Mile Creek bridge. You know, afore the Johnson place? Couple of rails were loose. Don't know what makes 'em loose this time of year. In the spring, when the ground is heavin'... well then, I can understand it. But this time of year, loose rails, I dunno."

"Yes, yes... by the Johnson place." Cooper peered east down the spur, as if to see the wolves standing about the distant rails. Instead he saw a small form trudging along, kicking up snow, walking the rails, flinging snowballs. It was young Joe Johnson. They all watched as Joe continued along merrily until he joined the men.

"Hello, Joe," greeted Mr. Cooper, "what are you doing out and about?"

"Nothing."

"Well, I mean, shouldn't you be in school?"

"Don't have to, teacher's sick," smiled Joe.

"Well, I hope it's nothing serious," said Cooper.

"Ma says it's a delicate condition. Don't know much about conditions, though," said Joe packing a snowball. "Think she'll have it tomorrow too?" The men all smiled at one another.

"Well, it's hard to tell about those, uh...conditions," admitted Cooper. "Say, Joe...did you just come in from your place?"

"Sure... you know, I saw a couple of wolfs too."

"You did?" smiled Cooper, "Well, what did you do?" Joe threw the snowball against the side of the roundhouse building and then bent down and started building another.

"Well, I got nervous at first, cause Pa says you never can tell what a wolf'll do. Specially, when there's a bunch of 'em. But I had my lucky quarter... the one the Omaha flattened that day, and boy it sure works swell, Mr. Cooper. You ought to make one for yourself."

"So what did you do?"

"Well, I rubbed my lucky quarter... for luck... and then I threw a few snowballs at 'em."

"And they ran?" prodded Cooper.

"Nah, they just dodged them old slow things. So I scraped away the snow next to the tracks and dug me up some rocks. I can wing a rock just about better'n anybody. Hit that big one right on the nose. Never saw it coming, I think."

"No kidding?"

"No, I'm not kidding. They all ran away, honest!" Cooper put his arm around the lad in genuine admiration. It was a while before he spoke, and the other men found an excuse to look at their feet and around, anywhere but in Cooper's direction.

"I know, son. They all ran away. I wish half the men in this village had your courage."

"Really?" beamed Joe.

"Really, son. Now you run along. I've got some business with these men here, and then maybe I could buy you a soda or something."

"Geez, Mr. Cooper, that would be glorious!" exclaimed Joe, and suddenly became animated again, skipping gaily down the rails. Cooper smiled wide until he turned once more to face his section line crew.

"Well, are there any questions, Carl? You wouldn't want me to send Joe along for protection, would you? Or get you a lucky quarter?"

"No sir, Mr. Cooper. I guess we got work to do. We'll just get going on that, Mr. Cooper."

"Good idea."

The men started walking off toward the handcar glumly and muttering to themselves. Cooper just started to walk back toward the restaurant when he heard Carl call out once more to him.

"I don't suppose anyone would have to know about this, would they Mr. Cooper?" Cooper offered no response, just waving them on, somewhat in disgust.

Later found him in the Mercantile re-addressing camp supply items with Bill Farley. There were a few people about, Mrs. Gillis for one, but weather was mostly the topic of conversation today. Until Muff Brown walked in. No one knew what his real name was. Some speculated that it was Matthew, or Mickey or Ruffus. Nicknames came easy to a northland full of odd characters and foreign names. But he had been Muff since his arrival in town nearly a year ago.

Muff wore clothes that were tattered and dirty and sported an unkempt beard, stained with tobacco juice down to his chin turning it a sandy color. He limped, too, which just added to his already miserable image. Some of the families in town had tried to include Mrs. Brown in their activities, and the children, too, but most offers were met with silence and evasive eyes darting nervously about until finally communication stopped all together. Muff's presence now just inspired speculative conversation.

And Mrs. Gillis, of course, was up to the challenge. The back of the store was all a buzz. Cooper looked up briefly to register his immediate disgust, and then it was back to the books.

"You don't have to worry about any of this, Mr. Cooper," said Bill. "Jake has all the facts and figures... everything has been taken care of... really."

"I suppose you're right, Bill. I know Jake keeps on top of these things pretty well. It just seems like I should know something about this, somehow be involved, or I might as well be in New Richmond."

Muff was walking along the aisle, conscious of the whispering in the back but acknowledging it only with an occasional sneer. He would peer at this pot or bottle, or pair of overalls, or mackinaw, and mumble to himself about overpriced junk, then move on, handling everything.

"You know," said Cooper, "just between me and you, I'm kind of afraid I might not make it to work one morning, for one reason or another, and no one will notice. No one will care. Things will probably go on just as smooth as before. And Jake will probably be smoking my cigars and drinking my brandy on top of it, hang it all."

There was a clanging and a banging in the second aisle as a washtub rolled over. It was Muff.

"Pretty careless the way things are laid about here. A man could get hurt if he wasn't careful. Darn careful, this worthless junk laying around and stuff," he started loud but trailed off into a mutter, kicking the washtub and moving on.

"You know, Bill, I try to like everybody I meet. The rich, the poor, the stupid, even smart-alec geniuses like Jake. But mean people... mean for no reason people... they kinda scare me, Bill, and I don't like it."

"Want me to toss him out, Mr. Cooper?" offered Farley.

"Nahhh. This guy isn't worth the effort. Let him curse and crow all he wants. And if he don't buy nothing, give him a few peppermint sticks for the kids anyway."

"Whatever you say, Mr. Cooper."

"Thanks, Bill," he sighed. "Well, I might as well throw myself out of here. Guess I'll wander over to the Hotel and see what Jake has taken care of over there for our woodsmen coming into town. I expect to have full camps by next week."

"That's what Jake said," added Farley. Cooper smiled a weak contented smile.

"I want one of these," growled Muff, throwing a pair of leather boots on the counter. "How much?"

"Hmmm," pondered Bill. "A pair of River Boots are about $3.00, but you can pay on account if you'd like."

"I didn't say 'pair', I said one. One boot. The other ain't near wore enough for replacin'."

"One? No one wants just one boot."

"I do," insisted Muff. "Just one. That's all I need, that's all I want."

"I can't sell you one boot," said Bill.

"I can," jumped in Cooper. In fact, I'll sell you this one on my foot right now."

"Awwwww...."

"No, seriously. And I'm going to deliver it to your back door in about 30 seconds." Cooper eyed the man sternly, fire smoldering in his blue eyes. In a second, Muff knew that if there was a bluff involved, it was his and not Cooper's. He cleared his throat quietly.

"Well, I guess I don't need it so badly," he muttered. He shuffled off, looking carefully over his shoulder several times before he reached the door and then hurried out.

Bill clapped Cooper warmly on the shoulder. "Now that's something that Jake couldn't do," he said sincerely.

"Oh, I don't know," replied Cooper. "Jake might have sold him both boots and convinced him the other one was a spare." Bill smiled heartily at the joke, but Cooper wasn't so sure it wasn't true.

When Muff came out of the store, he was just a little bitter about them rich folk who would threaten him, just on account of him being careful with his money. And the first thing he saw was Joe Johnson talking with his daughter, Emily and her younger brother Billy. His kids had climbed down from the wagon seat and were sitting on the steps of the Mercantile with Joe, talking mainly about the teacher's 'condition' and the glorious weather, certainly innocent behavior. But Muff was naturally mean, and recently tainted with bitterness.

"Hey, you kids," he yelled angrily. "I thought I tol' you to stay in the wagon?" He didn't wait for a reply, grabbing both kids by the collars of their shabby coats and dragging them through the snow.

"Rotten kids," continued Muff. "You, Em... don't you be talking to that Johnson boy."

"But Pa, I jus..." Muff didn't let her finish. He threw the kids toward the wagon and cuffed Emily aside her head.

"I tol' you never talk back to your Pa! You hear me?"

Joe winced when Muff had struck at the kids. But it never occurred to him to do anything, until he heard Emily cry. Not a loud cry... as if she was used to a silent crying to avoid further abuse, but a sob that struck Joe squarely in his backbone.

"Hey!" cried out Joe. "You can't do that!"

"Shut yer face, ya little piss ant. These are my kids," shouted back Muff.

It was enough to bring Bill and Cooper to the door just ahead of the gossip squad, in time to witness the flying attack of one ferocious piss ant. Joe, his fists a blur of fury, lit into Muff's back. It was all Muff could do to contain this attacking dynamo. Finally, he got hold of both arms and tossed him back.

"Why, you little... I got a good mind to take the strap to you right here and now. C'mere, piss ant!" Muff started toward Joe, who backed up just as fast.

"No pa!" yelled Emily.

"You shut yer face, Em! I'm gonna teach this little bastard a lesson." Cooper was just out the door when Muff got a hold of Joe.

"You got a problem there, Muff?" yelled Cooper, a bit of strength showing in his voice. "Or you looking for one."

"None of yer business, Cooper. Someone oughta teach this... this... kid to respect his elders."

"Let'em go, Muff," Cooper insisted. It was said strongly enough that Muff heard the unvoiced threat that went along with it and he let him go.

Muff spit copiously in the snow and stared at Cooper for a few moments, rubbing his chin. Then without a further word climbed up on the seat of his dilapidated wagon along side his kids and slapped the reins. He turned the wagon in the street, making Joe jump out of the way, and headed slowly up the street.

"That man shouldn't even own horses, let alone be taking care of kids," said Bill. "Did you see those animals? They'll be lucky to make the winter." He shook his head sadly.

Cooper watched Joe curiously as he reached down and packed a snowball, small, but solid and hard. He was about to throw it, when he paused suddenly. Cooper thought he had had a change of heart. But Joe reached inside his pocket for a second, then hauled back and threw, lurching forward as he did. Through the air it arched, catching Muff squarely in the back of the head, knocking his hat off and scaring the heck out of him. He urged the horses on in a frenzy of anger and madness, without looking back or retrieving his hat.

The people on the porch, including Cooper, were just a little bit impressed. It was quite a throw and Joe was all smiles. He turned to Cooper to see if he was in trouble, but Cooper too, was smiling. Joe retrieved something out of his pocket and held it up for Cooper to see.

"Lucky quarter," he grinned.

K. Wallin

The Eleventh Chapter

Leon adjusts to camp life

As the lumberjacks poured into town in the following days, the Straddle Creek Lumber Co. would lodge them in the Pratt Hotel until such times as they could be delivered by train to the appropriate camps. Farmers they were by summer, lumberjacks by winter, many of them. Some brought in teams of horses, heavy, healthy animals that would be used and fed by the Lumber Co. for the next several months. It was a way for the farmers to save on feed expenses, as well as to add a few dollars to their daily wage. The horses too, were often brought to the camps via train unless the farms lay closer to the camps than to Pratt.

There were others, of the old school of logging that held the ox to be stronger and therefore superior to the horse for the hard work of lumbering. Peter Swenson was just such a fellow, leading people to associate the man distinctly with the animal, hence the sobriquet; Ox-Pete. It was a name he never grew accustomed to and many was the man who learned of his disdain the painful way.

The town grew used to seeing these men come, gather and then disappear. The saloons remained quiet in spite, for this was the beginning of the season, when the money was still scarce and the men were fresh from the influence of their families and friends.

They were a mixed lot, these hardy woodsmen. Swedes, Norwegians, Finns, Poles, Germans... some new from their homelands, while others were nearly Americanized. Most were used to hard work; dawn to dusk labor at a variety of physical tasks. But Leon wasn't.

It wasn't bad at first. Well, not real bad, he thought. There were 8 or 10 fellows of a moderately tame nature to put up with, to wake in the morning and clean up after through three meals. They worked through the day chopping firewood, adding finishing touches to the buildings and occasionally fixing track if required near the camp. Evenings were quiet affairs, of chatter and minor mending of garments and card games. But by the end of that first week of snow, the bunks were nearly all filled and Leon's tasks took him longer than he thought possible.

He sat just inside the back kitchen door, a pile of potatoes at his feet, his wool shirt open at the throat down to his mid chest. Sweat dressed his hatless head, for though the weather outside was cool, the kitchen was nearly always hot. If Muggsley wasn't cooking one of the three meals of the day, he may have been baking pies or cookies, for quite to everyone's surprise, he was good at both.

It was a relatively quiet evening. At 6pm it was about as dark as it was going to get for the night, so kerosene lanterns provided a yellowish orange glow in the bunk house and the kitchen, and the little shanty of an office that Ox-Pete called home. Right now Leon liked the small draft of cool air that found its way around the kitchen door to fall in upon him. In a month or so, however, he would be complaining about the airy conditions.

Joe Kinder was at a washtub behind Leon, up to his elbows in soapsuds, the surrounding areas piled high with plates and cups and saucers.

"I'm gonna need some more hot water here pretty soon," he said wearily.

"I've got some warming on the stove, Joe," replied Leon, "I hope it's enough."

"Should be, I guess."

Leon tossed peelings into a bucket as he pared them off. Muggsley had measured out exactly how many potatoes, counted them actually, that he needed for tomorrow's meal.

"I still don't understand why he needed these done tonight, not that it would be any easier tomorrow. But I would have had time after breakfast to get at them," complained Leon.

"That is breakfast," said Joe. "Ox is going the men full bore come tomorrow. Muggs figures they'll need a particularly good breakfast, so he's gonna shoot the works; potatoes and ham and flapjacks and beans and a million gallons of coffee."

"Beans? For breakfast?" exclaimed Leon.

"Yaa up," grunted Joe. "Supposed to be cold tomorrow too. Sumpthin about a gut full of grub that keeps a body warm in all that weather. Muggsley knows."

"Yeah, Muggs knows. I wish he knew how much I hate peeling potatoes." Both men paused and looked at each other affording a weak smile through the sweat.

"Well, that about does it. The last potato," muttered Leon. He held it up admiringly for a few seconds before tossing it onto the pile.

"I suppose I could retire now, eh Joe? Unless you need help with those dishes. You don't, do you?"

"No," said Joe. "I'm not far from done. You go ahead and get some sleep... but don't forget to load up the stoves or there will be hell to pay."

"Yeah, the stoves... I better do that, I guess. You'd think they'd do this business in summer, when it's warm," he complained again. "Lousy stoves," he mumbled as he went out the back door.

The air was cool, but not biting, kind of refreshing actually. A few flakes of snow fell lazily, noiselessly, coming from a black starless sky. Leon took a deep breath. It revived him a bit and allowed for another weary smile. It didn't ease his tiredness any, but it cleared his head. Then it was back to the woodpile.

At 4:29 am the next morning, a great roar of snoring could be heard throughout the bunkroom. From the musky darkness a variety of grunts and wheezes and undulating cracks and groans permeated the room. In time, Leon would learn to identify each man by his snore, but for now he was not even sure of their names.

At 4:32 am the alarm clock hooked up under Leon's bed sounded it's frightening ring. It was a large affair, with two round bells on top, and quite an earth shaker in it's right. It's ringing was loud and clearly distinct. The first morning he had been slow in reacting to it's clamor and suffered quite an abuse from the rest of the men who could continue sleeping for a little while. Boots and hats and a variety of other missiles were tossed his way to painful result. It was several days later that Buck gave him some sound advice: Wrap a sock around the bells to muffle its ring and then silence it as quickly as possible.

Now Leon's arm shot out automatically, in search of the offending sound, fingers fumbling for the little switch along the side that would silence this intrusion on sleep. This done he was inclined to snuggle up in his wool blankets and drift back into fond dreams. But that too, he had learned, would bring on abuse.

He was given instruction on his duties, one time and one time only. If he failed to live up to the every unspoken intent of the instruction, he was roughly and rudely handled by both Ox-Pete and Muggsley. He often thought of walking off from this menial work, taking the cut across into Pratt to catch the train, or taking the tracks wherever they may lead. But his pride was still intact. He would not let it be said that he couldn't handle the job at hand... mere physical labor. He would not let it be said to Mr. Cooper. And he certainly wouldn't want it to be said in front of Andrea.

And so he arose quickly and felt for his pants. It was cold in the bunkhouse. He tried to dress in a hurry, but his shaking stifled his movements somewhat. Once in boots and pants, he made his way to the stove, near the center of the room. Nearby was just enough kindling and wood to fire it up. He cracked the door to the inner chamber and the sudden draft produced an orange glow from within. He added some kindling waiting for the telltale sounds of cracking and snapping, and then added the chunks of hardwood. He opened the drafts a little to facilitate the ignition, then clomped off to finish dressing.

Next were the cook stove and the office stove across the tracks. The bunkhouse stove was loaded for courtesy and convenience, but the cookstove was critical to the well being of all the crew, especially Leon. Thirty hungry men could definitely be considered a threat to a man's well being.

Leon found the early morning air quite colder than yesterday. It was crisp under a clear sky, with stars brightly twinkling, seemingly close enough to reach out and touch. But he paused only briefly once outside, to cough a little and admire the wisps of warmth coming from inside him. Then it was quick steps across the tracks, the moon on the snow enough to clearly light his way, though the path that was worn there would have been easy enough to follow.

He stopped at the cookhouse first and got a good roaring blaze going in the main stove. Then he crept as quietly as possible (in boots) into the office and added a couple of chunks to the smaller stove there. Between Ox-Pete and Muggsley, the snoring was almost as bad as the total bunkhouse crew. Pausing at the door, Leon mused to himself that Cooper probably picked his Camp Boss by who ever snored the loudest. Joe Kinder also slept in the little shack, though hardly a peep could be heard from him. Ox-Pete allowed that he was entitled to the better accommodations because he helped out with the books, as well as helping Muggs in the kitchen.

Leon shook Joe lightly, and he sat up in bed. Joe looked at him and blinked. His graying hair was tousled and his teeth were missing, his mouth moving open and shut as if he was tasting something. Finally he focused on Leon's form in the dim light and silently nodded. Joe, in turn, would wake Muggsley when the time came.

With all the stoves aglow with warmth, Leon moved back across the tracks to the bunkhouse to wake the teamsters. Each teamster had animals to take care of before breakfast, to feed and prepare for the day's work. By the time their particular chores were done, the rest of the crew would be reluctantly roused.

Breakfast was at 5:15 at Camp #9. Not a moment before. Muggsley would wipe the sweat from his brow, set the white cooks cap squarely on his head and go to the large iron triangle hanging outside the cookshanty door. The clamor that arose from the dinner bell would scare the birds and animals nearby, and certainly startle any human that was not expecting it. But the crew was expecting it. They expected it three times a day and never late. And as the winter grew long, it would be one of the few things they would look forward to. Another being sleep.

By the time Muggs had finished the breakfast ringing, the men were converging on the cookshanty as bees to the hive. Freshly washed, fully dressed and ready for the day they came, and hungry. Muggsley was a stickler for silence and good behavior in the cookhouse. He marched solemnly around the tables, a tight grip on his large wooden spoon, ready to enforce the rules on any blasted miscreants who felt frisky and talkative. Muggs was a big man, and strong, but the crew would have taken just so much abuse if he hadn't turned out to be a darned good cook too. His flair for providing meals and pastries made them downright docile and appreciative. Heaven help the man who tried to tamper with the cook!

During the meals, Leon helped Joe keep the coffee coming and the food piled upon the tables. It was enough to do. Muggsley sweated in the kitchen flipping flapjacks and boiling potatoes and frying thick slices of ham in a skillet, and in a free moment, patrolled the tables for speech violators. It was a morning routine that was to remain pretty much unchanged through the winter.

When the men had finished and wandered off to have a smoke or gather their tools, Muggs and his kitchen crew sat down to finish off their own breakfast. Muggs wasn't so obsessed with silence during these moments and would often regale Joe and Leon with his thoughts on most any subject. It was there they learned the secret of Muggs success. He had been a cook in the army and had learned the hard way that a good cook is appreciated, as much as a bad cook is abused. He learned fast, his new trade, and under good tutelage.

"So Mr. Roosevelt says to me... he says, 'Muggs, for a man that likes to eat as much as you... you should learn the culinary arts'. So the next thing

I knows, I was peeling potatoes. You think this is a lot of potatoes? You should see what the army eats in a day! Specially if they're fightin'.... and their always fightin'. And coffee? You think this is strong coffee? This ain't strong coffee... I know what strong coffee is! Mr. Roosevelt says to me one day when I was putterin' round with the coffee... he says, 'when you kin float a cannon ball in there, Muggs, the coffee's just about right'. Well, cannon balls were a little scarce, even where we was... fightin' and all, but I heard tell a horseshoe works just as good... so I kinda worked that out... and you know what he says the next time? Mr. Roosevelt says... 'Private Muggsley, the coffee sure is powerful today... but ain't it supposed to have a little water in it?' And I says... I says ... if it's anythin' that's gonna get us up that hill, Mr. Roosevelt, it's the coffee. And the rest is history, sure as I'm sittin' here. He got the credit alright... but sure as hell it was the coffee."

Joe and Leon listened with rapt attention to these stories... more to please Muggsley than through any particular interest. And maybe just to hear the sound of chatter in the usually silent hall.

By first working light, the crew would be in place to begin their labor. In the beginning, the work was done near the camp, the trees cut and limbed, the logs dragged to the landing by teams of oxen. For lunch they would be called by the dinner bell to the cookhouse for a well-prepared hot meal and at the end of the day, much the same.

These things they would come to appreciate as the area around the camp was cleared and the distance to the standing timber work increased until it was more timely for lunch to be brought to them instead of a return to the cookhouse. The oxen labored then, in steamy breaths, to bring the long sleds to the landing on icy roads, often piled with a thousand feet of logs.

It was dawn to dusk, this labor. Seldom were the men trudging back from the day's work with any light from the day still about them. Six days a week they did this. But even hearty men such as these, need a bit of rest now and again. Sunday was their day.

As the first week of labor came to a close that Saturday night, Leon reflected on Cooper's prophetic words; you would be so tired you would hardly remember your name. Leon thought he just might be right about that. He knew his name was Leon, but he thought it just might be 'mud', at least for the rest of the winter. He started to smile at his own joke, but as soon as his face relaxed in the effort, he drifted off into sleep.

The Twelfth Chapter

ᎨᎠking the Bull by the Horns

With a full complement of woodcutters in the camp and living in close quarters, it was inevitable that there would come a rattling of the horns; a test of territorial rights and privileges. Ox-Pete had the haywire camp for sure!

Nestled into this rough wood shelter of sweat and darkness were a disagreeable lot. There were the Sweet brothers, John and Henry, wily and mean and quick with a knife. Jack Larson, burly and tough. Ed Simms with the character and composure of a grouchy old bear in early Spring. And there were several others whose reputations for fighting fell on the wrong side of fair, and some whose conscience was not overly burdened by what was legal and right.

But the new "cock of the walk" in the woods around Pratt this season, is Mr. Patrick J. Finnigan, commonly referred to as "Bull". Bull is a lumberman of vast experience in the piney woods of the east before coming to Wisconsin, though some say his departure from that area was insisted upon by the local authorities. It was thought that Bull Finnigan got his nickname from his appearance; strong and stocky, with an abbreviated thick neck and a wide face with two small dull eyes that betrayed little emotion at any given time. It could have been his looks... but it could just as well have been his attitude. Mr. Finnigan was not overly blessed with cleverness or tact.

Buck Johnson suffered no little reputation himself, though it centered more on manly feats of strength and shooting ability and less on transgressions. His years of work in the woods and on the farm, his genetic heritage, and his propensity for a good meal all combined to develop a magnificent specimen of Swedish-American manhood; a working machine capable of almost half the things that were said about him in story and jest. Buck was pretty much of an even temperament, however, and seldom called upon to defend for pride and honor. But neither would he be trodden upon.

And so it was, that two such men in a small bunkhouse at the beginning of a long winter of work, must sooner or later bump together with calamitous results.

It was on this first Sunday after the first full week of work that trouble found its way to Camp #9. The men were a bit ugly and unsettled getting into the rhythm of the arduous labor and there was much growling and snapping all around. Bull managed to bang a few heads and bruise a few ribs of his bunkmates that mistakenly fell on the wrong side of his attitude this morning, but narrowly missed feeling the sharp knife of the French Canadian, Johnny Sweet, before charting a new course. As it was, the new path chosen led him directly to Buck.

Mr. Cooper's parting gift of two bottles of medicinal whiskey were three fourths gone by the time Bull knew they were in camp. Buck had never considered it any more than his right to "manage" both bottles carefully, determining his own "medicinal" need as much for the mind as for the body. Now he felt Bull carefully maneuvering to a position that would allow him to claim the rest through right of conquest. The battle line was about to be drawn.

"I didn't even know there was whiskey in camp," announced Bull to no one in particular but giving Buck a flash of his dull black eyes, "but now there it is, practically being wasted."

"Hey, there's whiskey?" cried someone from the corner.

"Yep... good Irish whiskey if I'm not mistakin'. Fit for an Irish King... or an Irish gentlemen at least...but certainly wasted on a dumb Swede. Why, it's only natural... the whiskey belongs to me."

"You never had no whiskey," said Jack Larson.

"Well... I'm Irish ain't I?" explained Bull. "An' I cut more trees than there are houses in Boston, cut more timber than Paul Bunyan hisself. That ought to count for somethin'. It's mine, I tell ya. By rights!"

It was starting to bother the Bull a little bit, that Buck seemed totally unconcerned about this significant claim to his medicine. He lay back on his bunk, propped up with a pillow, and gently nursed the half empty bottle, his eyes unblinking, following Bull. No anger was on his face, no reply upon his lips.

"Well, swede?"

As anger, frustration and a little bit of fear started to color the short stretch of neck of Mr. Finnigan, Leon slipped quietly out the door and ran as quickly as he could to find Ox-Pete, sure that whatever trouble was about to erupt, Buck was apt to suffer at the hands of the stocky Irishman.

But Pete wasn't to be found. In hurried steps Leon discovered that he was not in the office, not in the stable, not even in the latrine. So he came running breathlessly to the cook shanty where Muggsley and Joe Kinder were playing cribbage at one of tables.

"Where's Pete," gushed Leon.

"Went home, I figger," said Joe Kinder without looking up.

"Home?"

"Well.... he said so didn't he," exclaimed Muggsely. "Now git, you're distractin' me." Then turning to Joe, "It's my crib ain't it?"

"There's trouble... "

"Nope," returned Joe. "My crib.... you got 3 last time in your crib." As an afterthought he reached out and moved the four cards of the crib a little bit closer to his side of the table. Then turning back to Leon he asked, "What kind of trouble?"

"It's Finnigan... and Buck... and I think there's gonna be a fight," gushed Leon urgently.

"Oh, is that all," spat Muggsley. He didn't like the count of the cribbage board much. His half-matchstick pegs had a ways to go, but Kinder was within reach, especially with his current run of luck. "Men fight... that happens," continued Muggs. "Was bound to happen... I tol' Pete. Just stay out of their way." Then turning back to Joe, "you have the darndest luck, Mr. Kinder. Or is you cheatin'?"

"But...!" stammered Leon.

"Oh...for Christ sakes!" exclaimed Muggsley throwing down his cards. "Ok Joe... let's go watch the dang fight or we'll never get this game done." He stood up and turned to go, then as an afterthought turned back and removed the pegs from the board. "Might as well start over," he added, "even though I probably woulda won." He picked his cards up again, fingered through them carefully, and then set them back on the table face down. "Yep..." he said. "Well...lets git on with it."

"Dang it, Mr. Muggsley!" cursed Joe.

Back in the bunkhouse Bull was finally able to get a rise out of Buck by insulting his parentage, a pretty risky business no matter who one chose to badger. As soon as the words were in the air, everyone in the room knew... it would come to blows. Even then, Buck's movements were slow and deliberate. In spite of his youth and good nature, he affixed a gaze so steely and mean that it made the big Bull nervously step back a pace. Then the big Swede began to move, ducking under the edge of the top bunk to rise formidably in front of his antagonist. Bull stepped back a little more then, thinking to himself that he didn't remember Buck being so high, or so broad, or so... so... hard. Buck stood a good four inches over his head and now it seemed that whatever energy his confidence had once given him, had begun to ebb away. But even Bull knew; there was no turning back now.

"Vhat yew say?" Buck said purposefully.

"I said the whiskey is mine by rights," replied Bull less forcefully than he intended.

"About my Mama and Papa. Vhat yew say?"

Bull stroked his chin wondering just what he was going to do or say now, unsure if he should just haul off and hit the big Swede or talk it down to a lower level of intensity. His own bullish ways now seemed a burden to him.

"Vell, vhat yew say, yew say again. Say nice and loud for all to hear. Den vee know for sure who is bastard!" Buck's own words brought a fire to his blood. His hands curled into hammer like fists at his side, while his body shifted slightly to improve his balance.

But before much more could be said or done, Muggsley and company strolled in. The intrusion turned all heads and simmered the encounter briefly.

"What's this?" gruffed Muggsley. "A fightin' mood is it? And maybe break all this furniture that Mr. Cooper so generously provides? I think not!"

"Stay out of it Muggs," said Jack Larson. "You ain't the boss an' you got no right to..."

"Well, I'm the cook ain't I? I don't need no rights. Ox-Pete told me to take care of things while he's gone... and I'm gonna take care of things."

"He *is* the cook," agreed Ole olson. "And if the cook says somethin', why I don't know if'n we all shouldn't go along with it. You gonna make some more of them cinnamon buns, Muggs?"

"Shut up Ole," answered Muggsely not impressed with the patronization. Then turning back to Bull and Buck, "Now its only natural you boys want to kinda lock horns for one reason or another...over whiskey or women or maybe just because... and that's reason enough, don't get me wrong. But a free-for-all just might grow too big to handle an' Pete don't want to lose no bodies or answer to Cooper if'n there's a hole in the wall next time he visits."

"Especially if there's a head stickin' through it," added Jack Larson sarcastically.

"And it might be yours, Jack Larson," replied Muggsley.

"Well, I figure I got a right to that whiskey," argued Bull. The swede's been hogging it... and there's only bout half a bottle left. And it's Irish whiskey!" said Bull.

"Oh, it's whiskey is it? Well...." says Muggs rubbing his hands together and pondering where to go next. "Half a bottle, you say? Not much to share I guess. Well..." pondered Muggsley with some difficulty, "I guess the best thing you boys can do now, is wrestle. Bring that table over here, Ed."

And Ed Simms moved a small table into the center of the room while Ole Olson found two small stools for the men to sit on. Muggsely himself roughly maneuvered each man to a chair, while the rest of the lumberman stood back, not sure arm wrestling was going to solve anything but ready to watch and expecting the worse.

In a few moments, both men were sitting across from one another glaring menacingly. Buck took a gentle swig of the whiskey while keeping his eyes on the Bull, then set the bottle under the table near his feet. Watching the Swede savor the taste and burn of good Irish whiskey set a fire under the Bull making his dull eyes seem to smolder with courage and determination. Leon had never before seen such intensity.

"Well... that's the way it is then," said Muggs. "Arms on the table and fists in the air. Lock hands but don't budge an inch 'till I say so. Bull's solid stock of arm fell a little short in tightly grasping Buck's big hand, lifting his elbow off the table just a little. With a little effort he anchored it again, adjusting his grip. Buck let a little grin slip past his ugly mood at the thought... the leverage was his!

"This is the end of it then," continued Muggsley, "this finishes all, I won't have it any other way. And if it don't finish it, I'll go git my frying pan and then by God, we'll see!" He looked at both men to see if those words left any impression, but both woodsmen were staring at each other again, afraid to look away lest the fight begin too soon. The others crowded around mumbling encouragement to one or the other, placing bets, thinking about the whiskey.

"Get back you dumb bastards," exclaimed Muggsley to the crowd as they nudged a little too close. "Can't you see what's gonna happen here? Then turning back to Buck and Bull he asked, "Now you two ready?" not really needing an answer. "First one to get the other man's hand to the table, gets the bottle. All the rest of it. You hear? All the rest. Be sure of that, for every man-jack in this room will see to it." Muggsley paused a moment then, thinking maybe there was some way the bottle could come into his own possession, but another look at the two solemn faced lumbermen before him indicated otherwise. So he let out a little sigh and signaled the start of the contest, quickly withdrawing to a safe distance.

Through the years tales of this little foray, in the middle of the woods during a winter's log cutting, would take on such heroic proportions that it was eventually unrecognizable by the participants, filled with death and disorder. The truth of such matters often lie buried deep in the unmarked graves of mediocrity, a fitting place, perhaps. For any tale that cannot be enriched by events should surely be enriched by the teller before passing on to posterity.

Well... there was no death, but there was certainly disorder. At the sound of the start, the contestants locked their arms, muscles bulging out the fabric of their flannel and seeming to grow before the on-lookers, the blue veins in their wrists choked with power and blood. In the first few minutes it appeared that the two men were pretty equally matched. What Bull lacked in leverage he made up for in brute strength and determination. He huffed and puffed until his short neck was swollen and pink, his eyes remaining lifeless and dull in concentration. Buck too, began to show the strain. His face tight and drawn, his body solid and erect, teeth gritted against the work before him. They stayed that way for some time, neither giving way so much as an inch while the crowd howled and cheered and whipped them on with profane oaths and curses.

Then slowly, very slowly, Buck's arm began to give ground. It was almost imperceptible at first, at least to the on-lookers. But Bull sensed it and it drove him on. Little by little, Buck's arm gave way, withdrawing toward the table, though you could not see a change in the expression on his face. Still, with each minute gain, Bull felt the power, felt the win within his reach and it fed the fire inside him.

With Buck's arm nearly at a 45-degree angle to the table, he suddenly did a strange thing. He affixed the Bull with a steely stare and then broke out in a grin... growing into a broad smile. It nearly silenced the crowd and it certainly perplexed the Bull. It threw his concentration off for a moment, and then he re-doubled his efforts, squinting his eyes and grunting softly in strain.

Buck, still with the smile on his face, reached down with his free hand and picked up the bottle of whiskey from the floor by his feet. Calmly he bit the cork, pulling it out with his teeth and spitting it at Bull, hitting him in the forehead. Bull pretended not to notice, but it was distracting him severely.

Buck tipped the bottle up then and began to drink, all the while his arm was outstretched, six inches from the table, struggling against hope to re-gain the ground he had lost and him seeming not to care. As each swallow passed, his throat made a gurgling sound. At each swallow, Bull gave a little way, distracted, unsure, baffled at this turn of events. Then... mad! Mad with anger, mad with frustration, mad with power. He didn't care anymore. He didn't even notice as Buck finished off the last of the bottle right before him. He brought his other arm to bear and using them both put all his weight into pinning Buck's arm to the table, wrenching it painfully with the bluster and force.

"I win!" he shouted, "the bottle's mine!" unaware it was now empty.

"And here it is!" cried Buck and swung it up and over, then down upon Bull's head with such force that when Bull went down in the hail of broken glass, the table went down too and the two of them fell in a tumble to the floor midst the blood and debris. It was then, as was customary to say at the time, that all "hell" broke loose. Bull never lost consciousness from the blow and came up swinging, blood in his eyes limiting his vision so that he didn't even know it wasn't Buck he had by the throat. In only minutes there was not one soul in the room who had not been drawn into the melee from an accidental or deliberate blow.

And so it was, that Muggsley's worst fears were realized. Furniture was broken, heads were bruised and really... there ended up being a hole in the wall to explain to Ox Pete that evening. That there was no ones head still in it was merely chance.

It was quiet in the bunkhouse that night. Most of the lumberman slept soundly, weary and bruised from the day's events. Ox Pete tried to be serious and angry with Muggsley about this situation getting out of hand, but he had to chuckle just a little at the rosy welt around his eye. Then shaking his head, he wandered off to his own bunk, satisfied that this inevitable right of passage had been all for the good, and almost sorry that he had missed it.

K. Wallin

The Thirteenth Chapter

A Jail for Pratt

Joe Johnson always took the Pratt & Southeastern tracks home from school. It was an easy trail to follow, right up to the north pasture, and it also afforded him a chance to watch the train go by from time to time. The train was running more frequent now that the camps were in the woods and logs were being brought in. Whenever the engine would draw near he would wave at Alfred or one of the other engineers and when they waved back, he would raise his arm up and tug it down a few times, a signal that asked them to blow the whistle. This they were more than happy to do for Joe, especially after news of the wolf incident circulated around town. They would toot the whistle and Joe would jump and wave and watch the cars go by, loaded with timber, bound for the Omaha line and on to the mills and lumber markets of St. Paul.

Joe found school just a little bit boring, what with all the excitement of trains and lumbering and snow sledding and such. Which is why he was carrying such a particularly heavy load home today. A report card tends to get heavier, the lower the grade. And Joe's was heavy indeed.

Normally this, a Friday, would be a glorious day, the weekend coming on and Thanksgiving just ahead. But the shadow of the card loomed gray and melancholy in his mind. Robert Walden, much like Joe in spirit, had had the same burden, and sharing that made Joe's load seem lighter for a time. But when Robert waved goodbye and headed south up the hill, Joe was reminded that he would face his Pa alone.

Joe was unusually good that night. He put his books away, and did his chores, bringing in plenty of wood, feeding the chickens, cleaning the barn, sweeping the porch. No one seemed to notice, save Andrea, who always seemed attuned to what Joe was up to. She already suspected the reason.

At 6:00 pm they gathered around the supper table; Martha and Andrea chatting about social affairs as well as those of the heart, little Emma talking to the doll in her arms in soothing tones. Alma was at the stove, fussing with this and tasting that, humming to herself an old Swedish tune that Pa often played on his violin. Pa stood behind her, watching her for a moment and smiling. Finally he hugged her from behind with long strong arms.

"Oh, Papa, go sit down," she scolded half-heartedly. "Supper vill be ready in a few moments."

"Maybe I should sample someting," offered Papa.

"Oh, yew are vorse dan Yoseph, for goodness sakes. Now go sit down," she waved her spoon at him menacingly.

"Yaa, yaa, I sit down," he smiled. "Vhat ever it is, it smells goot."

Joe was the last one in from the cold, making less of a fuss than usual, even washing his hands before settling at the table. But when he offered to say the grace, Andrea could contain herself no longer. As the family added their own 'amens' and picked up their forks, Andrea jumped in with the first topic of conversation.

"Martha, didn't you tell me that the Cable school handed out report cards today?"

"Why, yes," responded Martha innocently. "I talked to Amy Stewart just this afternoon at the Mercantile. Her sister, Katharine, is teaching the intermediate at Cable this year. Kate says she had such a lovely class of students, all so bright and interesting."

"Did you get a port card too, Joe?" jumped in Emma.

"I don't go to Cable school, dummy." evaded Joe.

"Yoseph, don't yew talk to your sister dat vay. Yew be nice, now," scolded Mama, "and eat your supper."

The table was quiet for a few minutes then and Joe was somewhat relieved that the situation had died in rudeness. He was eating fast... the faster to escape the table and lose himself in the barn or someplace else outside. Tomorrow, he knew, would bring another day, yet another chance to postpone the inevitable.

"Sooo, Yoseph," said Emil between bites. "This report card. Do yew have a card from the Pratt school, or do they not do such tings anymore."

"Well, Pa," jumped in Andrea, "of course the Pratt school gives report cards. How else would you know if a student was doing his work?"

"I see," said Pa. "And vhen do they give these cards, soon yah?"

"Well, I would think so," continued Andrea playfully. "But the teacher has been ill, and perhaps needs time to catch up on all the things there are to do."

"Yaa, yaa I suppose dat's true," nodded Emil. Turning to Joe he added, "Yew haf no card den, Yoseph?"

Joe swallowed hard a few times, then sat up straight before he answered. "I have one, Pa. I was gonna give it to you after supper." Emil didn't answer right away, merely kept spooning mashed potatoes into his mouth. Then finally he spoke again.

"Yaa, dat's gude. After supper yew bring me this card and vee see how vell yew do in school." With that matter settled, at least as far as it could be for now, the talk turned to other matters.

"I heard Mr. Farley say today, that the town is going to get a jail," started Martha. "Imagine needing a jail in Pratt."

"A yail?" asked Alma. "A yail, Papa, a yail in Pratt. Vee don't need a yail vhen vee first come here."

"Vee don't need one now," said Emil. "I tink somevun yust vants to spend money and say, 'Pratt is big city, it even haf yail now'.

"Mr. Cooper said that it's for the lumberjacks, mostly," added Andrea. "In the springtime when they are uhhhh... feeling frisky with all that money in their pockets."

"Like Buck," jumped in Emma. Joe sat silently. He figured there would be plenty of time for trouble later, so no sense adding to it. Emil eyed Emma carefully and she smiled sweetly in return.

"Yaa," murmured Emil, "dat Buck."

"Buck is good boy," spoke up Alma. The others at the table, including Emil, all shared a secret smile of knowing. Buck was indeed a "good boy", good at heart leastwise. But he could be as frisky as the rest of them.

"Vell, maybe a yail vouldn't be so bad in Pratt," added Emil after a bit. "For the bad boys, I mean. Better dan the yail in Vashburn. I vonder though, vhere they put it?"

"Put vhat?" asked Alma only half listening.

"The yail, this Pratt yail," said Emil. "It must be someplace. Ve don't haf yail house." They all looked at him in sudden surprise.

"You know you're right, Papa," added Martha. "I wonder where they will put it?"

"They could put it in the school house," jumped in Emma. "Lots of room in the schoolhouse."

"Why, Emma, the very idea. That would be silly. A jail in the schoolhouse, wouldn't that be a laugh?" suggested Andrea. Her and Martha giggled softly at the thought.

"A good place to learn a lesson," added Martha, and they all laughed out loud.

"That's enough, this talk of yails. Vee vill hear no more about yails at this table," chastised Alma. But she too, was reluctantly smiling.

Conversation dwindled for a time then. Food was passed back and forth and consumed with great voraciousness, as Alma was indeed, a good cook. Joe was still fidgeting quietly in his chair.

"Are we having a turkey next week, Mama?" asked Martha, breaking the silence once again.

"Vell, yaa. It is Thanksgiving. Vee have a lot to be thankful for. The Lord is gude to Yohnson family."

"A big turkey?" wondered Joe aloud.

"Vhy yes, Yoseph, a big turkey," smiled Alma. "Mr. Farley has ordered special for us, a really big bird."

"Mama," said Andrea, "I was thinking. Mr. Cooper said he would be in Pratt all next week. He's so far from his family and has no one to be thankful with... and we will have such a big turkey."

"Vhy Andrea, such a nice thought. If Papa says ok, Mr. Cooper should come and eat vith us."

"Yaa," said Papa. "Mr. Cooper should be here if he cannot go home."

Andrea waited a bit, and when the matter seemed to drop she kept looking at Martha. But Martha was not paying attention, so she kicked her foot under the table.

"Ohhh!," she exclaimed suddenly.

"Vhat's a matter, Martha?" asked Alma.

"Oh... oh, I was just thinking. I was thinking that with Mr. Cooper coming here to eat, that nice nephew of his will have no place to go. He doesn't know anybody at all, in Pratt."

"Is dat so?" mused Alma.

"I heard," said Joe between bites, "Mr. Muggsley is cooking a turkey at the camp, and ...oww!" He looked at Andrea from whence a kick had come. "Well, maybe it wasn't a turkey after all. It was a partridge, I think. A small one."

"Vell," said Emil, "I think vee have one more chair. If Mr. Cooper comes to be vith us, the nephew should come too. Don't yew think so, Andrea?"

Andrea sprouted a rosy color starting at her neck and working it's way up. "If you say so, Papa," she said.

While dishes were being done, Joe wandered back outside to see to a few additional chores, hoping that somehow time and labor could erase the memory of his report card. The night was clear, with stars twinkling brightly in the dark November sky. With the ground covered with snow, the countryside was easily illuminated by moonlight, casting shadows in blue-black tones dancing here and there about the edge of the field and around the buildings.

It was a silent world, this winter night. Not nearly like the chatter of Spring, the bird and animal sounds calling to you most of the time. The winter calling was only the wind, wild and cold, rattling the window shutters and making the branches of the trees talk to each other in groaning and clacking sounds.

Joe found the barn warm enough, the heat from the animals making it seem almost comfortable. He wandered over solemnly to the Molly cow and stroked her muzzle affectionately.

"Well, I might have done better," he said to the cow who looked at him with big brown unblinking eyes. "It's not that I don't understand it at all, but it's just so boring. Why don't they ever talk about pirates and injuns and stuff like that, Molly? I could learn that kind of stuff." Molly nosed his hand at the sound of her name, as if she understood.

With a heavy sigh Joe threw himself down in a pile of straw, putting his feet up and snatching a strand to stick in his mouth like some long cigar. He stayed like that for a while, daydreaming of the adventures of the Pirates of Pratt, with fleeting thoughts of a dilapidated hay wagon careening down the street. He sure would have enjoyed that ride a lot more if he had known that everyone would live through it. Suddenly he heard the barn door creak open slowly and Andrea's head popped in. Seeing Joe, she came in and shut the door again. She was wearing a warm shawl about her shoulders, but hugged her arms about her in the chill night air.

"Pa is ready to see your card," she said softly. "Oh is it that bad, Joe?"

"No, not that bad, I guess," he allowed, shifting the piece of straw in his mouth. Andrea sat down in the straw with him, folding her legs under her. "I did as good as I ever done."

"What's wrong then," she pressed. "I've never seen you this quiet before. It scares me, Joe. Like you're sick or something."

"Heck, Andrea, I'm not sick. I never get sick."

"What then?"

"Well, I might've missed a few days of school. Nice days... where a body ought not to be in school anyway. And I been tardy, three times," he said holding up three fingers. "What's Pa gonna say about being tardy? It's bad enough I don't do as good in school like he wants, but when he sees I skipped school and been tardy, it's the strap for sure."

Andrea studied him for a moment in admiration. This boy alive with energy, so full of curiosity for the ways of the world, his imagination so ripe with thoughts and plans. And here he sat, three days tardy and his world spinning down.

"I've always found that it lessens the blow if you'll tell him you promise to do better next time," she offered. "But then you have to do better. Not just on going to school and on time, either, your grades will have to improve at least a little to find Pa's full forgiveness."

"Aww Andy, I try. I try real hard. But my head keeps filling with other things and I forget what she's sayin'. I don't do it on purpose, Andy... it's just that... the lessons are so boring. I just can't help it. An... an... and when I'm walking to school... and I see a fox running across the trail... well I gotta see where he's goin' don't I? To make sure he's not heading this way to steal chickens or nab one of the cats. And there's other things, too, important things. Why there's dozens of important things that kinda get in the way of school."

"Yes, I suppose there is. But you're just going to have to wait and do them some other time. School's important Joe, you know how Pa feels about that. He wants you to be educated and be a good American. Pa never had the chance to go to school himself, you know."

"Well maybe if he had, he'd know it wasn't no fun."

"He knows, Joe, he knows. He knows a lot more than you think he does. Not much gets by our Papa. He just doesn't always tell what he knows.

"He sure knew who wanted Mr. Mancheski to come to Thanksgiving dinner, didn't he?" smiled Joe.

"You're not so dumb yourself," she replied, then nearly laughed out loud at seeing the missing tooth in his grin once again.

"Ok," she said, "now go and see Pa. You tell him you're sorry and that you'll try to do better next time."

"Ok," nodded Joe. Then he suddenly added thoughtfully, "Thanks, Andy. I really will try harder. I'll suffer horribly, but I'll try.

"I know you will, Joe." It was worth a kiss on his forehead.

"Yew could do much better Yoseph," said Pa sitting back in his chair next to the woodstove and adjusting his glasses. "Much better, I tink, eh Mama?" He passed her the card.

"Vhat's this Yoseph? Absent? Tardy?" she exclaimed.

"Yes, Mama," he replied soberly, "four times absent, three times tardy."

"Four times gone? Where you go?" asked Emil. But Joe just shrugged his shoulders. "Three times tardy, Yoseph? It is only 2 miles to school. Did Mama not get yew off to school in time each day?"

"Yes, Papa."

"Then Vhat?"

Joe looked about the room for support but Andrea and Martha had withdrawn and taken Emma with them. He was alone to face the music.

"Vhat is it, then?" insisted Papa.

"Well, I... that is ... well one time, I was on my way, but the Gustavel's cows had broken down the fence, and I... I chased them back. I was afraid they might get on the tracks and get hit by the train."

"Yaa, this is gude. I see yew have reason for vun tardy. Vhat else is reason?" continued Papa.

"I don't remember," shrugged Joe.

"Ah, yas, vell vee know vhat vill make yew remember gude, eh?"

"Yes, Papa." There was a throat clearing in the other room suddenly, coming from just the other side of the door to the kitchen. "Oh, Papa?" added Joe.

"Yas?"

"I promise to do better next time."

"Yas, I vould hope so. But still I think vee take a little valk out to the vood shed." He stood up and looked at Alma, who remained silent. "It is for his own gude, Mama," he added. Alma nodded solemnly. "Yew come now, Yoseph."

It was behind the woodshed they went, near the garden, in the cool night air. But Emil Johnson was not a mean man. While Joe bent over expecting the strap, Emil paused and put his foot up on a fence rail and reached for his pipe. When Joe sensed the aroma of pipe tobacco, he stood straight and turned around.

"It is nice night, yah Yoseph?" He said while exhaling smoky wisps.

"Yes, Papa."

"Vee come to this country many years ago, to Vashburn first," he continued wistfully. "And I tink... I tink this is fine country, this Vashburn. And your uncle Swan tells me, yew come down to Pratt and see vhat fine country this is tu. So I come and see, and Pratt is fine country tu. Like in old country, like in Udavella. It makes me vant to farm and raise nice family."

While he talked he stared out across the field, now snow covered, with half beaten down corn stalks and garden debris littered about.

"But it is hard, Yoseph. It is hard to make money out of the ground sometimes. And vee vork hard. Your muther, vorks very hard. It is our land, now, this is land of Emil Johnson, who never had land before. And it is gude, this land. But vee vill pay for it vith our sweat and our blood the rest of our days. And maybe it still von't be enough. Vee be so smart. Vee clear more land, to plant more food and grain, to sell in Pratt, to sell in Ashland even. But is hard vork clearing land... so I think... vee should be smart... blow up stumps and move rocks... blow them all up. Boom!" He paused then, shaking his head sadly.

"Now... my leg... it don't vork so gude... and now no vork in camp for me. No vork. Vee be so smart. Now vee tell Martha she cannot go to school to be teacher, because vee cannot pay. Vee tell Andrea she cannot go to visit my sister, Esther, in Chicago and see big city. Vee cannot do all these tings, because vee are so smart and vant big farm." He rubbed his leg, now suddenly seeming to pain him, though the pain was deep within his mind as well, and a shadow on his conscience.

He turned around and pointed his pipe stem at Joe.

"But yew, Yoseph. If yew do vell in school, yew can do better dan Emil Yohnson. Maybe some day yew be like Mr. Cooper and run things, and tell people vhat they do. Ahhh, that vould be proud day for Mama. Yoe Yohnson, important person, vearing nice clothes for no reason and telling trains vhen to run. A good day for Emil Yohnson, tu.

"But, Pa," said Joe, "I don't want to be important... I just want to be like you." Emil turned his face away then. Back to the fields of his never-ending toil, and then to the starry sky. The cold night air brought a bit of a mist to his eyes.

"Yew do gude in school, Yoseph," he said finally, when it was easier. "Yew do gude in school."

"I will, Pa."

The town meetings in Pratt are held on Thursdays. Not every Thursday, of course, although it was once meant to be. But there was so little discussion from week to week that it was soon set for only the

2nd Thursday of the month. This allowed the townspeople to gather their grievances and concerns over a month's time and made for some lively discussions then, which was entertainment for some.

A small town, like Pratt, has small affairs and therefore has a small town board to deal with these concerns. In this case, Pratt is run by a Town Chairman, two board members, a secretary and a treasurer. Altogether they would address most town matters rather efficiently, generally following the will of the people. Sometimes, however, the people didn't know it was their will until the Town Board explained it to them. Such was the case of the jail.

The jail was the inspiration of Samuel Hackett, present Town Chairman and owner of a confectionery located down by the tracks, as well as the town's only hotel. It was rumored that he had suffered at the hands of a few drunken lumberjacks the preceding Spring, a bit of rough handling during a rather ordinary bar room tussle. Sam seemed to take offense at this, though few involved remembered much about it. Now there would be a jail to confine and punish such roustabouts.

The jail had been ruling the gossip mill for most of the week, ensuring a good turnout at the meeting this night. All the discussion had provided a few pros and cons about the issue, and an urgent anticipation for the entertainment of the meeting.

Cooper was still in his office on Superior Street as darkness settled about the town on that Thursday. It wasn't that he was that busy, as Jake had been caring well for the camps and keeping the books as the train loads of logs were switched unto the Omaha line bound for St. Paul.

Truth was, Cooper liked his little office on the bluff, liked watching the sun set at the western edge of White River valley. And when night rushed in and extinguished the last glow of daylight hovering about the edge of the world, he would put his feet up on his desk, light a sweet cigar and wallow in the serenity of it all.

This night was much the same, until Jake poked his head into the back office and said, "It's near six."

"Is that important?" mused Cooper.

Jake and Mr. Cooper had been getting along pretty well lately. Once Cooper let go of the reins somewhat, the horse found an easy trot. At least those were Cooper's thoughts on the subject. Now casually they strolled down the street toward the lights in the Modern Woodmen hall where the town meeting was convening. Due to the keen interest of the jail issue there was a good turnout.

Hoping to avoid some of the fanfare, Sam had moved the meeting up to 5:30, alerting only the town board members to the change. So by the time the hall was filled and every chair taken, the meeting was nearly over. The jail issue hadn't even been discussed. The last few people that came in stood back against the far wall, looking here and about for available chairs that were not to be found.

Despite the cool of the evening, the hall was already beginning to get a little warm with the body of people that were mustered. The wood stove along the north wall, while at first barely able to raise a glow, now had people moving their chairs at odd angles to deflect the errant heat. Some wondered if Sam hadn't "loaded it up" a little more than was necessary.

The board members sat at a table toward the west end of the hall away from the door. Sam, as chairman, was in the middle, a gavel atop a pile of papers in front of him. The board members, Amos Bandy and Carl Larkin, were on either side of him. Lance Jackson, the secretary was on the other side of Carl and Bill Feeny, treasurer, was on the other side of Amos. All were unusually reticent this evening.

Amos Bandy sat smoking his pipe, tamping it at times when the conversation was awkward. It nearly caught him by surprise when Sam suddenly announced that he would entertain a motion to adjourn.

The people started to whisper to each other, and Carl and Amos looked at Sam nervously.

"Well, I guess I... " started Amos.

"What about the jail?" someone yelled from the crowd. Cooper and Jake were just entering the building at the time, immediately sensing the tension in the room.

"Go ahead, Amos... you had a motion to make?" prodded Sam.

"Before you adjourn," jumped in Cooper loudly from the back, "I have a question for the board."

"We were about to adjourn," answered Sam.

"But you haven't yet," insisted Cooper. "Surely the board wouldn't mind answering one little question."

The crowd turned their heads almost in body from Cooper to the board and back again as the discourse continued.

"Very well, Mr. Cooper," capitulated Sam nervously, "the board is all ears to hear your question. I'm sure it must be very, very important to tie up these good people's time." He made a vague gesture to the crowd before him, most of who missed his sarcasm.

"Yes, well, seeing as how I missed most of the meeting," he paused and took out his watch, "hrmmph, watch must be slow. Anyway, seeing as how I missed most of the meeting, I was wondering if the board had any 'specific' recommendations on how to deal with this traffic problem. The few automobiles in town are scaring hell out of the horses!"

A look of relief swept over Sam's face. "Yes, well... ah... we're aware of the problem... yes, yes... and ahh... well, we've given the matter alot of thought. We think some signs limiting the speed will just have to be posted here and there. Don't you think so Carl?"

"Yep," said Carl, "speed limiting signs."

"We don't want to have to do it, mind you... but for the safety of everyone... we feel we have to," added Sam for effect. The crowd of people nodded their heads, some whispering tales of car/horse near mishaps, or speeding machines careening from ditch to ditch. Suddenly there was laughter in the back.

"What's that?" asked Sam.

"It's Greg Fuller, Sam," answered Hank Martin. "Greg says the speed limit for his automobile is set on how fast he can push the dang thing." More laughter rippled through the crowd as the lines were repeated to those who hadn't heard. Sam almost relaxed. Amos stopped tinkering with his pipe and chuckled along.

"Well, what limit do you propose," asked Cooper as the crowd quieted down. The board members put their heads together for a moment, and then separated and Sam snapped the gavel down on the table. " T h e board hereby sets a speed limit of 10 miles per hour for automobiles operated within the town limits," said Sam. "Clerk is hereby directed to make and post said signs on all streets within the town proper." Lance Jackson busily recorded all directions and comments into the large ledger book before him.

"Anything else?" asked Sam. Immediately, he knew he had made a mistake. Cooper's talk about the automobiles had relaxed him, taken him off his guard... now with the opening he had just created, he was sure the jail issue would be coming straight at him. He was right.

"Mr. Hackett?" said a weak voice in the front row. Sam had to scan the faces quickly to figure out where the voice was coming from. "Mr. Hackett?" the voice said again. Sam pinpointed the face. It was Marvin Munson, a small, thin bit of a man, wearing overalls and big boots. He was the only one in the crowd who had not removed his hat upon entering the hall and his gray hair stuck out from under it like unkempt straw. His bony hand was part ways raised, a weak attempt to garner attention.

"Yes, Marvin?" replied Sam. He figured he was saved. Marvin couldn't possibly have any interest in the jail issue... and he wouldn't let himself get trapped like that again. "Go ahead, Marvin," he said, "and speak up nice and loud so the people in the back can hear ya."

Marvin cleared his voice a few times, his adam apple bouncing up and down midst the loose skin of his neck. "Well, sir," the weak voice started, "I was wondering kinda... where they was gonna put that jail?" A whispering chatter swept over the crowd at once, while Sam sat red faced, eyes and mind a blank.

"What's this about a jail, Sam?" jumped in Cooper. "Did the people vote to buy a jail?"

"Yeah, Sam, what about this jail?" asked Hank Martin.

"We don't need no jail in Pratt," added someone else.

"What we want a jail for?" asked another. And then, with the floodgates open, a dozen voices were talking at once, but the only word you could distinguish from time to time was 'jail'. It appeared that some were for it and some were against it. Some had no opinion but enjoyed listening to the others voice theirs. And Sam sat back in his chair in the front and let the chatter continue. From time to time he would look to Carl or Amos, or Cooper in the back of the hall with the unlit cigar in his mouth and the smile on his face.

"Let's have some quiet here, now," said Sam finally tapping the gavel on the table. It wasn't loud enough.

"Hey! Let's have some quiet!" he shouted, slamming the gavel down mightily. That brought a gradual lessening of noise in the room. He tapped the gavel again a little lighter this time and the noise ceased altogether except for an occasional low rumble of laughter.

"Well," said Sam, "I think we're about done here. I'll entertain a motion to adjourn now."

"Done?" exclaimed Hank Martin. "Aren't we going to vote on it?"

Sam cleared his throat uneasily, then said, "Vote on what?"

"The jail," said someone in the back. "We got to vote on the jail."

"We don't need a jail," said another. And then the chatter started up again. And the gavel came down again, a little harder.

"Well, are we going to vote, or not?" shouted Jake from near the back door, getting into the spirit of things.

"We don't need a vote. The board will take the issue under advisement and make an appropriate decision," answered Sam.

"We ought to vote," insisted Hank. "It's an important town issue and the people should have their say."

"We have all the information we need," defended Sam.

"Wait a minute," said Charley Halverson. "I'm a town people and I didn't have my say."

"Yeah, me neither," said Fred Smith, "I'm a people, too!"

Everyone chuckled at Fred's revelation. Then the chatter started again. There were many for the jail, many against, but all were in favor of a vote on the matter.

"We better have a vote, Sam," whispered Carl. Amos nodded. Sam gaveled for silence again.

"Well, you all think you should vote on this, huh?" he said loudly. "Well, go ahead and vote on the dang thing then, but we're buying it anyway." The hall grew silent again.

"Can they do that?" asked a husky voice from the crowd.

"We already did," admitted Carl. He fidgeted with some papers in front of him, glancing up at the crowd only briefly. "Sent for it already. We got a two cell cage coming all the way from Kenton, Ohio."

Amos cleared his throat. "Sam said it was in the best interest of the town... and it did seem like a good idea at the time."

"Well, ya can't undo what ya already did, I guess," said Hank Martin calmly. "But I still think we should have voted on it."

"It's just as well," added Greg Fuller. "When it gets here, we can put Sam in it." That bit of wisdom made the crowd relax into smiles and laughter, easing the tension again. Sam was grateful in spite of the nature of the comment.

"Now if there is nothing else, I'll still entertain that motion to adjourn," sighed Sam.

"Well, I guess I can... " started Amos once more.

"Mr. Hackett?" cried a weak voice again. It was Marvin Munson, his hand raised slightly.

"Yes, Marvin, what is it?"

"I was kinda wondering... where ya gonna put that jail?"

It was then that Sam and Amos and Carl finally realized they hadn't put quite enough thought into the matter.

K. Wallin

The Fourteenth Chapter

Leon goes to Town

Leon was not happy with himself. He used to wake up grudgingly when the alarm went off. Sometimes, at first, the alarm would ring long before he would even hear it, until someone would bring it to his attention by throwing a boot at him. Now, however, he awoke usually minutes before the alarm went off. Awoke from a deep sleep and fond dreams to stare at the face of the clock, wondering what it was that made it so. Getting up at 4:30 in the morning is a bad habit to get into, he thought. If it weren't for the chores of a lumber camp, what would one do at 4:30 in the morning anyway?

Then he remembered something that made his heart sink a little. It was Sunday. He could sleep in. And here he was wide-awake at 4:30 in the blessed morning.

It was a good time for thinking though, something he didn't ordinarily have time for. He lay there looking at the dark and wondering about things. He wondered how far away Spring was, and freedom from the camp. He wondered if the snoring would ever stop. He wondered if he would ever not have the smell of sweat and old socks in his nostrils. It occurred to him then, that he was repugnant even to himself. And he thought of Andrea. Did she even remember him? Did she think him a twit, or did she think of him at all. How many times did she comb her hair at night to give it that lustrous sheen? And the smell of violets, he could almost smell it now, her hair, shiny chestnut brown and smelling of violets. He let a heavy sigh escape his lips and looked at the clock again. Only 4:37. My how time crawled by sometimes.

149

He decided to get up in spite of himself. He should load the stoves up anyway, he thought, as the cool air started to penetrate his long underwear.

After getting dressed and loading up the stoves, he found himself in the kitchen area looking for something to eat. Muggsley was up, putting coffee on and poking at the coals in the cookstove with a long rod.

"It's ok to sleep in a little later on Sunday, boy," he said generously. "I can get things going, go on back to bed."

Leon shrugged.

"Can't sleep, eh? Well, that happens. I knowed a man once that had the same problem, one winter in a camp and he never slept again." Muggsley smiled. "You done pretty good," he added, "for a new man, I mean. I've seen worst chore boys." He put the lid back on the stove and centered the coffee pot on it. Leon could feel the warmth starting to glow.

"So whatcha gonna do, anyway?" asked Muggs.

"Oh, I don't know. I was thinking it might be a good time for a trip to town, maybe pick up a few things," replied Leon.

"No train today," warned Muggs.

"Aw, that's ok, I feel like a walk anyway. It can't be more than a couple of miles."

"Well, yaa, if you traipse through the woods. If you walk the tracks, maybe 8 or 10."

"The snow doesn't seem that deep, guess I'll cut through the woods," said Leon. He was kinda surprised at himself. He had never been in the woods before this camp, now here he was talking about a 4 or 5 mile walk by himself.

"Say, would ya do me a favor?" Asked Muggs.

"Well, I..."

"You know my daughter, Mary, don'tcha? Well, I need to tell her about coming out here for Thanksgiving. Her Ma is down Hudson way with some sick relatives or sech, so I figure she might as well come out here. Cooper's running a train that day and Alfred'll be here too, and Albert. Cooper's getting us a coupla a nice birds, he says."

"I've never met your daughter, Muggs," said Leon, figuring that let him off the hook.

"Mary? Everyone knows Mary. You ask around, someone'll tell you how to find her. You'd do that wouldn't cha?"

"Sure Muggs, I'll tell her. Or leave a her a message at least, if I can't find her."

"You do that, boy, you do that. That's good," muttered Muggs as he started stirring up some batter. "You know, I've eaten so many flapjacks, I don't think I could do without 'em one morning. Know what I mean?"

But all Muggsley got for an answer was the door swinging shut behind Leon.

"Heh? Hope that boy knows to wait for daylight afore traipsing off. Could be we'll be looking for him later." Muggsley chuckled lightly to himself, shaking his head.

Once outside, Leon paused at the corner of the building and stuck his hands in his pockets. His breath came out in hoary wisps as he looked around the sleeping camp. Moist warm air was rising from the barn area where the horses and oxen were tethered, and he momentarily considered riding a horse to town. But these were not riding horses. They were huge muscled beasts bred for labor, not jaunty riding.

Even from across the tracks he could hear the snoring of the crew. It was a ragged coughing melody, but it gave him some comfort to hear it, knowing he was not alone in the wilderness. He figured it was about time for Ed Simms to make a visit to the little shack out back, as was his usual.

As that thought crossed Leon's mind, he could hear the back door to the bunkhouse squeak open and in the light of the moon, he watched a dark figure lumber on. It was a contrary stomach, Ed claimed, that made him visit the outhouse sometimes 3 times a night. And it was his lack of sleep from these trips, thought Leon, that made Ed, himself, so contrary. A contrary man, indeed, one of the few that Leon had not learned to like a little, though Buck said he was a competent woodsman.

Soon the smell of Muggsley's flapjacks would permeate the odor of sweaty socks and unwashed bodies in the bunkhouse and raise the men reluctantly from their warm bunks. They would stir and grumble and cough and snort as they did every morning. And they would probably want to wonder what Leon was doing up and about so early on Sunday, what he was doing and where he was going.

Suddenly Leon felt the urge to move, to get away from this place at least for a day. To talk to faces that were not weather worn. To talk to gentle souls who would not have to pause for an unsightly spit every now and again.

He walked up to the tracks and stared east. The moon glinted off the metal rails showing imperfect parallel lines through the woods, dark and foreboding. Eight miles by rail? Well, it would be daylight by then. He could always return by way of the woods to shorten the journey. Return? What an ugly thought. Leon spit into the snow.

When he heard the door on the outhouse slam shut he started walking down the tracks east keeping between the rails, his hands in his pockets. He walked for some time, his mind wandering over events, real and imaginary. The uneven lay of the ties made him stumble and to his surprise, an involuntary vulgar curse erupted from his lips. It was then he stopped and for the first time noticed that he was alone in the deep woods of Wisconsin. The dim lights of the camp had long since faded, the moon being his only light. Even in the dark he would be able to follow the tracks, if he switched off in the right direction. But the imposing gloom of the woods was starting to close in on him. It was the first time in his life he had heard such silence, no streetcars or automobiles as in Chicago. No train whistles. No fighting neighbors or yelling kids in thin walled apartments. Not even the comforting snore of the hearty woodsmen.

Leon shivered in the morning air. The cold seemed particularly biting today or was it the woods? Unfriendly and dark it appeared, as yet untouched by the woodsmen's axe, and from it strange sounds; cracks & creaks, whines & moans; the sounds of nature. Sounds he had heard many times since being in the woods... sounds that now unnerved him somewhat, though he tried to think of other things.

He had walked quite a ways, though he didn't know how far. It seemed like there was a dim glow in the eastern sky, which encouraged him. But he was a little bit cold, a little bit lonely, and just a little bit nervous. And as the morning glow tried to brighten, it was shaded out by heavy grey clouds hanging low with the promise of snow. It was light enough, however, to see the ties on the track or to pick out individual trees in the woods, but surprisingly it did not lighten his mood. Gusts of wind and snow swirled around him and tugged at his clothes and soon he wondered if it was farther to go ahead or go back.

Suddenly the wind got behind a tall, dead tree and heartily pushed. The tree fought back momentarily, creaking and clacking it's branches, reaching out for a hold. But the wind was too much and the tree too far old and rotten. It had to give. And it did so in a loud crack and crash that carried it swiftly to the ground in an explosion of broken branches and billowing snow. Less than 50 yards away from nature's pruning effort, it pushed rationality far from Leon's mind. He bolted like a frightened deer, but not nearly as graceful, and ran like a madman down the tracks, his heart beating loudly in his throat.

In minutes he began to tire and his feet were less apt to find firm footing along the ties, but wildly he continued until his foot caught an upraised timber and tumbled him cruelly upon the tie and rail. He grunted painfully and rolled off the rail to find himself continuing to roll down an embankment coming to rest against a stump. He was up in a flash, ignoring the pain of banged up legs and tender ribs, and looked quickly about expecting the worst from whatever it was that could topple trees, and tumble him down. But the wind merely laughed at his ragged form, this novice in the woods.

When Leon's calm nearly returned, he was able to look about and see where he was. He had fallen where the south road to Pratt crossed the western track in a winding trail. He didn't know that at first... but it was a path heading in the general direction of Pratt and should have to lead somewhere warm and lighted, he reasoned. He climbed back up to the grade and looked at where he had tripped. The ground had shifted and the ties and rail on the north side were in need of repair, possibly due to the occasional wagon traffic. He must remember to tell Cooper when he got to town, for it could prove dangerous to the engine.

Now, though the morning was still gray, his mood brightened. He set off down the hill on the south road to Pratt and within minutes crossed the other western branch of the Pratt & Southeastern, the one that led to Camp #11. He was delighted. He now was pretty sure of where he thought he was, but even more, of where he was going.

As Leon neared the town of Pratt, he paused on the hill just south of town to take in the view. It was the hill where the pirate ship first lay that Halloween night, the beginning point of the famous ride of the Pirates of Pratt. Leon, however, was unaware of this historical significance.

Before him lay the small village, houses sleeping peacefully in the early morn, wisps of wood smoke tied to their chimneys. There was nary a tree to block the view, having been cut in the early logging period, even before the town had taken root. He even had a glimpse of the White River valley to the north, though it was just so much hazy white at this time of year. The roads through town, east/west and north/south, were ugly with mud, marking a crosshatch pattern on the white background.

He could hear a dog barking somewhere, and the sound of a cowbell. Never in his wildest dreams could he have imagined that these things would have meant the signs of civilization to him. Yet now they were a comfort. When he continued down the hill some of the weariness in him was lifted, at least temporarily.

There was no one in the Straddle Creek Co. office, of course, this being Sunday and early at that. But Leon stopped there first anyway. Then he walked down Superior Ave. a ways, past the Pratt Hotel. Lights were lit in several of the rooms, he noted. The day had begun for some of the residents of Pratt.

A black dog came trotting down the street, stopping at a bush here, a tree there, or a wagon wheel... to sniff and snort and perhaps leave his mark. He gave Leon a cursory glance and a little snort while lifting his leg on the corner of the hotel building, and then continued on his route.

Leon moved to the edge of the plateau looking north and admired the view once more. He could make out a few of the distant fields over toward village of Mason, standing out from the woods pattern in smooth white tones. He couldn't see White River of course, or it's nearer Long Lake branch running cool and clear just a mile north of town, but he had been told that they were there, clean to drink from and full of trout.

Squeaky hinges drew his vision in from the vast scene of the valley to the row of buildings along the tracks just below him. Mrs. Williams was edging her way out the door with a pan full of dishwater, for to throw it in the alleyway. Without pause she re-entered the restaurant. The town was alive below the tracks. There were lights in the depot, the restaurant, the bunkhouse. There was someone stirring outside the blacksmith shop. Only the saloons remained silent as the sun peaked around the edge of the mass of gray clouds.

John Cooper was a bit surprised when Leon walked into William's restaurant. He was just getting ready to dig into two eggs over easy, with bacon and toast, when he waved the young man over.

"Well, now... surprised to see you here," he said, motioning to the chair opposite him. He watched Leon's face carefully for a trace of fear or a sign that this was goodbye. He found only weariness there.

"Well, it's Sunday. We don't work much on Sundays," answered Leon.

"I suppose not, gotta rest sometime. So you came in to chat did you?"

"Well, no, not really. I just came in to... uh... actually, I just wanted to get out of camp for a while. It's alright, isn't it?"

"Certainly."

"And I'm supposed to give Mary Muggsley a message from her father," added Leon.

"Say, how is old Muggs getting along anyway? Many complaints? Are the men treating him O.K.?"

"Treating him ok?" said Leon incredulously. "Muggs is a fantastic cook. The men wouldn't even think of getting him even the least bit upset. If he says, 'jump', they say ok Muggs, we'll jump."

"No kidding," said Cooper. "Imagine that. I figured I would have to be out there putting down a rebellion by now. Muggs, a good cook... what next!"

"Well, are you gonna eat, or just watch?" queried Mrs. Williams.

Leon looked at Mr. Cooper's plate and hesitated. He was used to eating a good-sized meal by now... but he hadn't given much thought to his finances. He was, in fact, broke.

"Go ahead son," urged Cooper. "I'll add it to your tab and we'll settle up later."

"Well, I suppose I'll have a little something. Some eggs, maybe... scrambled, and some bacon, and a few flapjacks. And... do you have any beans?"

"Beans?" asked Mrs. Williams.

"I see your appetite has adjusted to your new surroundings, son. Good for you. Mrs. Williams, bring this lad whatever you got... I'm sure he will do you proud." Mrs. Williams smiled and shook her head as she walked back to the kitchen.

"Say, Mr. Cooper," said Leon suddenly remembering something. "On my way in this morning, I noticed some bumped up ties on one of your western branches."

"Loose ties?"

"Yes sir. Where the Namakagon road cuts across the track heading into Pratt. They were bumped up a bit, making the rail somewhat uneven."

"Drat!" Uttered Cooper disgustedly. "Are you sure?"

"Well, yes, quite sure. I tripped over it."

"Which line... there's two you know. They split not far east of the south road, one going to Camp #11 and the other..."

"The other leading to our camp. I know. It was the south most line... the one going to our camp."

"Drat! I knew this would happen. I hoped it wouldn't, but it did. A spade is a spade and that's that," he muttered almost to himself.

"What are you talking about?"

"Muff Brown," he said. "I hired him last week to inspect the lines. He should have been out on that line yesterday but he had nothing to report. Or so he said," Cooper explained. "He was a fine fellow once, you know" he added wistfully. "I just thought if he had a chance... well, a spade is a spade, I guess."

155

"Say, what's the story on him anyway. Have you seen how he treats his kids? I've seen dogs treated better."

"I know, I know. He's no better to the Mrs."

"He was a fine fellow once? That's hard to believe," allowed Leon.

Just then Mrs. Williams brought two plates full of food; eggs, bacon, flapjacks. She set the plates in front of Leon and returned shortly with a mug of coffee. Then she stood expectantly by the table.

"No beans?" asked Leon.

"Hrmmph," she said and stalked off.

"Kinda forgotten our manners out there in the woods, my boy."

"Oh, sorry, you're right. I'm not even used to talking when in the cookhouse, as you well know... just a grunt and gesture here and there to get the food passed down. Appalling, isn't it."

"Appalling."

"So what about this fine fellow business?" asked Leon, as he started to attack his plates of food. Cooper sat back and reached for a cigar in the inside of his coat pocket. A fatherly smile found it's way to his lips as he watched Leon wolfing down a man-sized breakfast, remembering the first time they were in William's restaurant.

"Yes, well... it's pretty much true. Muff was foreman on a crew down in the Chippewa Valley country some years back." His eyes took on a pensive look as he attempted to bring these dusty memories to the forefront of his mind. "Well, now... I guess it's been a few years at that," he added briefly pondering how time had passed. "Anyway... he was a pretty good man at the time, I guess. I didn't really know him then... but he was recommended to me once, by the head boss of the outfit. Turns out I didn't need a foreman just then, but I kept the name filed away in the back of my mind for future reference. Then there was an accident, not so uncommon in this line of work. Muff got his legs broke. Both of them. One healed fair enough... but the other was kinda crooked. It turned him. Turned him mean on the world.

"It sure seems like it," said Leon with a mouthful of eggs.

"The current Mrs. Brown came complete with kids, a boy and girl, meek as lambs for the most part.

"I suppose."

"And though Muff's the source of their trouble, he's also the only chance they got to try to get back on their feet. Well, there I go again... thinking I know what's good for people. But seems like they could do alright if they had a chance." He turned pensive again, smoking the cigar and staring out the window.

"I gave Muff a chance, a good chance. All he had to do, was do the job. But damn his ornery hide, he couldn't do it. He just couldn't do it. I can just see him climbing up the south road to that first crossing, seeing it was in pretty good shape... then figuring no sense in climbing up further. If one was ok, probably the other was too. And how was that old fart to know the difference. Drat!"

"Old fart?"

"Oh shut up and eat your eggs!"

They talked of many things through Leon's breakfast, most of them pleasant. And when Leon was finished and the bill had been taken care of by Mr. Cooper, they walked outside continuing their discourse.

"By golly, Muggs a good cook," mused Cooper. "As good as Mrs. Williams?"

Leon hesitated a few seconds wondering if he was being baited. "Well, I guess so," he offered.

"No kidding! Well, I've got to get out to the camps more often and have a look-see. But this damn business stuff... even with Jake's help, it smothers a man. Papers! George always wants things down on paper. Why, we could turn all this lumber into paper and still not have enough to do the paperwork on the lumber we just processed." Cooper kicked at a rock along the path in frustration... and missed.

"Good thing I missed," he laughed, "I've got a corn on that foot that wouldn't have taken lightly to that kind of outburst. Say," he continued a few minutes later, "now that I'm downwind of you, I realize that the bacon at the restaurant hadn't soured after all."

"I smell?" asked Leon.

"Smell? Son, you stink." They both smiled.

"I guess you're right," agreed Leon. "The facilities are somewhat lacking at Camp #9. I must take that up with the superintendent at once and register a complaint."

"So noted by the superintendent," said Cooper. "And though you stink no worse than any other woodsman I've ever met, I suggest you bathe before addressing Miss Mary Muggsley. They have a tub at the hotel you can use. And if you hurry, you have time to wash the smell off and still meet Mary coming out of church at 10:00."

"Thanks, Mr. Cooper."

"Well, don't thank me, son, it was self-defense. Whew!"

"I know, I know," said Leon softly... "but thanks all the same. For everything."

Cooper nodded soberly for a second then slapped the young man on the shoulder. "You enjoy your day off in town," he said, "but come see me before you head back to camp. I've got to run out to the Johnson farm with some mail and other things that Jake forgot to put on the 2-Spot for them, but I should be back by early afternoon. Some things have come up that we need to discuss." Leon was unsettled by the serious look that clouded his face.

"What is it?"

Cooper forced a smile. "It can wait, son," he said. "Just stop and see me before heading back to camp. We'll talk then." He turned to walk away, but Leon caught his arm gently.

"The Johnson place?"

"Well... don't tell me you've taken an interest in farming now," said Cooper turning back to see a smiling face. "Very well... meet me at the livery around 10:30 and I'll take you for a little ride. Might do you some good at that." And then the older man was off in great strides toward the path up the bluff leaving Leon with plenty to think about.

The Pratt House, the only hotel in town, was managed by the Hackett family, Sam Hackett, proprietor. Young Tim was tasked with hauling the hot water for the bathtub situated in a little room off from the first floor office, among his various other chores. Leon waited until the tub was nearly half full before shucking his clothes and settling in. It was mildly cool in the little room this early in the morning and the water was steaming in vapors above the tub. Pure luxury, plain and simple, thought Leon, his tired muscles and aching bones beginning to relax at once as the weeks of weariness settled about him, numbing his senses and lulling him to a peaceful consciousness just short of sleep. Tim continued to bring the pails of steaming water, carefully dumping them into the foot end of the tub.

Now, a regular lumberjack, one used to years of arduous toil, would not feel the effects of a couple of weeks work in the woods no more than a mosquito bite on an elephant. But Leon had never worked so hard in his life, nor so long. His weariness was real, hard earned and with depth. He vaguely remembered Tim taking his clothes so that "ma could have a go at 'em," and then his whole body gave up at once and he passed into a restful slumber.

It was an hour later perhaps, or two, that he suddenly sat up in cold water with panic in his eyes. It was moments before he could place where he was. His dream had been of cold creek water and he shivered. When he finally regained his senses, he noticed his clothes, clean and folded on a chair. The door creaked slowly open and Tim stuck his head in.

"Ma says, if she'd a knowed you was gonna sleep, she would've rented you a room." Leon nodded to the boy and the door closed again.

When he had dressed, he suddenly noticed the water in the tub was a dirty gray color with not a bubble of soap to grace its surface. He had to get into town more often, he thought.

From the hotel, Leon wandered down Cudworth Street, south toward the church. Before he was halfway up the block he noticed the people leaving, getting into carriages and wagons and waving goodbye to one another, so he ran. When he got up to the church more than half of the people had already started on their way. Noticing the preacher standing on the porch, he approached him.

"Excuse me, Father," said Leon.

"Well, hello," replied the preacher smiling pleasantly. "It's Pastor, actually. This is a Methodist church. I'm Pastor Nicholson."

"How do you do, Pastor... could you possibly tell me where Mary Muggsley is?"

"Yes, yes... I believe she was just here. She's on her way home, now... there, up the street." He pointed to the west where several people were walking. Leon thanked him and then ran to catch up to the people.

There was Frank Thomas and his family. Then two lone females, one rather heavy-set, and the other he could not see very well at the distance. If one of these ladies were Mary Muggsley, it must be the bigger one, he thought, picturing a mental image of Muggs as a female.

"Excuse me," he said tipping his hat politely. "Miss Mary Muggsley?" The woman turned around and he was pleased to see a friendly-faced woman clutching a bible in her hands. She giggled at once.

"No, no," she smiled pleasantly. "Sally Beardsly, Mr. Mancheski. Is there something I can do for you?"

"Oh, I'm sorry. I have to find Mary Muggsley. I have a message for her... from her father."

"That's her up ahead," offered Sally. Leon tipped his hat once more to a giggle response and ran ahead to Mary.

"Mary Muggsley?" he asked as he approached. The woman paused and turned slowly, not recognizing the voice. Leon nearly gasped when he saw a delightfully pretty face of delicate features, a light dusting of freckles on fair skin framed by golden curls escaping from the edges of her bonnet.

"Yes?"

"Why, uh...uh... you're Mary?"

"Yes?"

"Well, I uh...well..."

"You're Mr. Mancheski aren't you? Mr. Cooper's Nephew?"

"Yes, I am," he answered clumsily.

"Well, how nice it is to finally meet you, I've heard so much about you."

"Oh?"

"I hope you'll be staying with us for awhile and not be running off to Ohio or where ever it is you're from. Say you will be staying, Mr. Mancheski." Her hand reached out and rested gently on his arm.

"Well, yes...I...I..." he stammered. "I'm working in the woods, now... but I get into town once in awhile. We have Sundays off."

"How nice. Perhaps you will be around for our Christmas party then... we have such fun. You'll come in for Christmas won't you?" Her hand remained on his arm, though he was starting to feel it on his heart.

"Yes, I'd like to," he said sincerely. They stood looking at each other for a few moments then, pleased by what they saw and smiling.

"Did you want to see me for something?" she asked finally, breaking the spell.

"Oh, I almost forgot. I have a message from your father. He says to take the train out to Camp #9 on Thanksgiving Day and join us for a turkey dinner. He thought with your mother being gone and all... that you'd want to spend the day with us... uh, him, to spend the day with him at the camp. Cooper is running a special train out with the turkeys that day and the engineer and fireman will be staying for supper and you can go back with them."

"How delightful," she clasped her gloved hands together and smiled a bright smile. "And you'll be there, won't you Mr. Mancheski?" He nodded. "Well, I should be getting home now, I suppose. I will see you on Thursday then, Mr. Mancheski?"

"Yes, yes of course," he answered, while Mary turned away from him and continued on her way. He was so captured by her charm and beauty he had neglected to tip his hat again as he had planned. He did it anyway, to her back.

It was nearly 1100 when he strolled out of the Mercantile, a small wrapped package in brown paper under one arm. He was so preoccupied with his thoughts that he nearly walked into the horse and carriage that was shifting restlessly out front just beyond the stoop. It was Cooper.

"Oohh... Mr. Cooper," he stuttered, "I... I guess I forgot."

"I guess you did! Well, are you getting in the carriage or do you plan to wander around through the Bibon swamp with that silly look on your face?"

Leon smiled sheepishly as he climbed into the vehicle. He was nearly seated when Cooper jerked the reins and sent them speeding up the road, nearly losing his passenger in the process.

K. Wallin

The Fifteenth Chapter

An Impromptu Visit

Though the day was cloudy and gray the temperature was quite mild, alleviating some of the gloom that comes with a lack of sunshine. The men trotted up the muddy ruts of the south road full of conversation and good humor, anticipating a pleasant visit with the Johnson family and perhaps a biscuit or two. Cooper admitted quite freely that there was no real urgency in the packages he was bringing... but then an occasional personal indulgence by an old fart should be allowed from time to time without begging explanation. He "hrumphh" a few times, clearing his throat to make his point on the matter, then changed the subject.

They turned off the south road on a less traveled muddy path that led past barren fields to the Tuttles farm and the Gustavels, Olsens and the Johnsons. It was a spirited horse pulling the carriage and so took no little urging to find a brisk pace though the trail was often in sad repair, jostling the men and making conversation difficult.

So they sat quietly, each with their own thoughts on this and that, while the carriage bumped them along closer to anticipated warmth and conversation just a mile or so ahead.

Country life can get kind of lonely sometimes, especially in the north woods, so visitors arriving are a celebrated event. The carriage had hardly ceased rocking, midst the excited squawking of the chickens in the yard, when members of the Johnson family appeared from every corner, interrupting their chores to welcome their unexpected guests and usher them into the parlor.

Leon felt a little awkward with all that attention, being newly introduced and bombarded with questions. And Andrea was strangely absent, though the presence of Martha surely lightened his heart. She had disappeared briefly when they first arrived and now she fluttered around them smelling of perfume and looking like a freshly cut flower. Still, he wondered where Andrea might be and if she knew he was here, her dancing partner and friend. He sat quietly looking about, twisting his neck at each little sound like a nervous partridge.

Martha finally took pity on him, offering to show him about the farm and he gratefully accepted, following her out the door while the remaining Johnson's converged on the remaining guest, who seemed to prosper well under their cookies and questions.

Martha strolled with him about the yard, talking to him cheerfully about dances and dresses and styles of fine clothes. Though he was numbed to speechlessness by the girlish chatter, it would be safe to say he enjoyed it and preferred it to the snortles and chorts of the men at camp.

"It isn't often we get such distinguished visitors, Mr. Mancheski, so if all the attention is a little overwhelming... well it's well meant."

"You have a very nice family," he said sincerely. "I can see why Mr. Cooper makes up excuses to come out to visit."

"Why, Mr. Mancheski, you don't need an excuse to visit... just come out and see us some time. It's nice to be able to talk to someone who's been someplace... or done other things. Really, some of the local boys think that when they see Ashland, they've seen the world. Appalling, isn't it. What's it like in Ohio?"

"Oh... it's alot like this, I guess," he stammered. "Don't you have another sister? I mean... it seems like I danced with a young lady who said her name was Johnson. Perhaps she was a relation to you."

"Tired of me already, Mr. Mancheski?"

"No... no... I... I..."

"It's alright," she said laughingly. "I was wondering when you would get around to asking. You know, I do seem to remember another sister." Martha was leading him toward the barn, bumping him, crowding him until he seemed to find the barn door on his own accord.

"An ugly little thing that we keep hidden... talks in horrible whispers... walks like an ape... why, I don't even know if she could be related."

"Oh, no!" he said taking her seriously, "she's nothing at all like that. I was meaning someone more pleasant looking, like you, and gentle and fine... I...

"Pleasant looking? Oh, Mr. Mancheski you are the one!" She jostled him into the barn and by the time his eyes adjusted to the light, she had disappeared. He wondered about that only briefly as he heard snuffling sounds coming from the far corner.

"That's it little Nell... you don't need your mama anymore... see? Good milk... gooood milk for babies." She was squatting near the calf with a bucket, reaching in and bringing milk to it's lips with her hand, letting the calf suckle and lick her fingers greedily as the milk dripped back into the pail.

She was unaware of his presence, so he watched her for a while making her cooing noises, being mother to the calf. She was dressed in a worn and shabby coat over a plain dress, her hair chestnut brown and shiny was pinned back out of the way. There was rose color in her cheeks... painted there by the brisk fresh air of Autumn, and in spite of the drab appearance of her work clothes, it accented quite well the simple beauty of her face.

"That's it, little Nell," she encouraged, "that's it." As the beast slurped noisily she would lower her hand toward the milk in the bucket, hoping it could discover that her fingers were not needed. But when her hand was devoid of milk, the moonfaced calf would merely stare at her, blinking stupidly, wondering in its thick brain why it was so.

"Cows are kinda dumb, aren't they?" he said finally. It didn't startle her nearly so much as he thought it would.

"She's just a baby... aren't you little Nell?" She kissed the calf on the nose. "Babies need a little time to adjust to these kinds of changes. I don't think she's dumb at all."

"Is she having trouble learning how to drink from the pail?"

Andrea nodded. "Want to give it a try?"

"I don't know much about cows, I'm afraid."

"Here... try it. Maybe you have a real flair for it and don't know it. C'mon." she persuaded, making room for him in the pen. He squatted down beside her, a bit dubious but game to try, though the calf shifted uneasily at his presence.

"Scoop the milk up in your hand and let her start to taste it. Then gradually move your hand down toward the milk in the pail so she can find it. I've tried everything with this one... but she's a bit stubborn and still wants her mama."

He did as she instructed, wincing as the calf began to suckle at his outstretched hand. Suddenly he withdrew his arm in a jerk. "I think she bit me," he said looking for marks.

"Why, don't be silly," she admonished. "Little Nell wouldn't hurt anyone... try it again."

"Ok... but I think she really did bite me... there isn't a mark, but I felt it." He shifted a little, putting the pail between him and the calf and cupped some more milk, bringing it up slowly. Just then one of the cows in the stalls let out a loud bellow and the calf jumped forward knocking the pail and spilling it into his lap. In reaction, he flung himself backward into Andrea knocking them both down in the straw.

In mere seconds, calm returned and both of them started to laugh.

"Look!" cried Andrea. The calf was licking the milk off his pants leg, nosing around, finally finding the pail laying on its side and drinking milk from a small pool that still remained.

"You did it!"

"Well, I..." he turned to look at her and found her alarmingly close in the heap where they'd fallen, bodies bumped up next to each other. Her eyes were moist yet from the laughter, and the color of a bright blue October sky. It tied his tongue in knots. "It was just... just an accident really. I... I...

"Andy?" came an excited shout. "Andy? Andy, you in there?" Leon shifted out of contact with Andrea then, looking in dismay at his pants that were milk-wet in spots from his thighs down to his boots.

"Andy?"

"In here Joe, in the calf pen. We were trying to teach little Nell..."

"Andy," exclaimed Joe nearly breathless as he ran up to them. "Oh... I didn't know he was here," he said noting Leon.

"We were trying to teach little Nell to drink from the pail... and look... she's a smart little calf isn't she."

"Andy... I need some help. Bob's stuck and I can't get him out... can you come Andy... right away?"

"Where's he stuck? Where is he?"

"Down at the creek. We were crossing the beaver dam to get a look at that fox hole in the far bank and his foot got stuck... we gotta go get him outa there, Andy. Should I get some dynamite from the shed?"

"Dynamite? For heaven's sakes, no! You want to kill him?"

"Well, I gotta get him outa there. He's supposed to be home soon and better not be wet, his Ma said."

"Oh Joe!"

"I'll help," offered Leon.

"Where is that boy," mumbled Cooper outside near the carriage while checking his watch. The low hanging gray clouds made the day seem later than it was... and made Cooper antsy... wanting to get on back to business now that his "visiting" was through. There was a pleasant and filling lunch of course and an offer to stay for supper, politely refused, for it was a wise man who knew not to overstay his welcome on an impromptu call such as this. Still, the inner man had been fulfilled in ways that even Cooper didn't understand.

"They're not in the barn," said Martha coming across the yard. "I even checked the loft." She turned away from Cooper when she realized what she had implied and stared across the pasture field. There, trudging along were three figures, dark and faceless at the distance. Martha squinted her eyes and was sure at once of one of them being Joe, skipping along as if he were in a parade. The other two... she couldn't be sure... but it seemed briefly like they were holding hands, then separated again.

Cooper was dropped off at the office, leaving Leon to return the carriage and walk back up the hill by himself. He figured it was penance for making him wait at the Johnson farm. A little later found him off the path, in back of the Straddle Creek Co., coming in via the back door through his old lodgings. It startled Cooper when the door to the back room slowly creaked open. Leon found the older man sitting pensively at his desk, feet up, smoking a cigar.

"I'm not used to people sneaking up behind me. You get lost?" he said curtly.

"Just admiring the view," returned Leon sheepishly.

"Splendid, isn't it?" said Cooper immediately softening. So... you've done all that you've needed to do, I take it. Had a refreshing visit, no doubt, judging by the smile on your face."

"Splendid," agreed Leon.

"Were you able to meet up with Mary Muggsley?"

"Splendid," repeated Leon to Cooper's amusement.

"Sit down..." Cooper motioned for Leon to take the chair in front of the desk and he did so, feeling once again like he was being called to task in front of the teacher. There was something about that chair... or the desk.

"What's eating you?" Leon asked, sensing the mood had changed.

"From what I can gather," started Cooper, sitting upright and leaning on his elbows, "there were people in Chicago that were not real happy with you, and that's why you left. Does that briefly sum it up?"

"I'd say so."

"Well, it's been over a month... at least a month, and apparently they're still not happy with you. What the hell did you do down there?"

"What do you mean?"

"I got a call from Ed Harding yesterday. A telephone call! We couldn't talk as much as we'd like to because the depot was full of people at the time... but from what he could tell me, there's been a little trouble in St. Paul. It seems there are a few rough folks that have taken to asking questions with a blackjack and fisticuffs."

"Anyone hurt?"

"Not seriously... some close calls... but the point is, these are not forgiving people. Perhaps we should discuss exactly what it is you're involved with here. If there is a chance some of my people may be in danger, I'd like to know how and why."

"Well, I don't want 'your' people involved at all, so if they just stay out of it, they won't be in any danger. It's as simple as that."

"Oh, cut the crap, mister," said Cooper, sincerely aggravated by Leon's attitude. "A person doesn't choose who he cares for or who he looks out for... it just happens. You're here, and whether you planned it or not, whether you like it or not, the people have a vested interest in you. And I would hate to see any of them get hurt because of it."

Leon shrugged. "Maybe I should leave," he said defiantly.

"Maybe you should," said Cooper just as defiantly. Then he backed off a little. "Look, son, all's I'm saying is that you've handed me some kind of ugly animal in a sack... I just want to open the sack and see what kind of beast it is I'm playing with. What's this trouble down there that these folks won't forget after so long a time. Did you kill someone... maybe by accident?"

"No...no, I didn't kill anybody," replied Leon. "But I saw... " He paused for a second as the memory came back and his face became crimson with the thought. "I saw someone else get killed."

"I see."

"No, you don't see. You don't see at all. He was a very good friend... and my partner. We were going to be hotshot private detectives... kinda like the Pinkertons...like my father... but I guess we got in over our heads."

Cooper said nothing, sitting there pensively smoking his cigar, his eyes digging deep into Leon's soul. He was afraid to move or say anything... afraid Leon would stop now... now that he was so close to speaking the truth.

"Tom stumbled onto something down along the waterfront, some scheme involving undocumented ship cargos and altered manifests. It seemed simple enough at first. I was working on another case, some missing jewelry that it turns out wasn't so missing after all, and I didn't really get a chance to see exactly what was going on." Leon's calm had returned as suddenly as it had vanished.

"Then one night he stopped by around midnight. He banged on my door in a frenzy and when I opened it, I could tell he was scared. His eyes were wild and there was panic in his voice. He had been running, because he could hardly talk without gasping for breath. He shoves a leather case at me, tells me to hide it somewhere until he can come back and not to tell anyone about it, not to even think about it. I tried to get him to come inside, but he was nervous as a cat... kept looking over his shoulder... and when he heard a door creak open, he took off down the back stairs and I went back inside and locked the door." He spoke smoothly now, unruffled, as if he was talking about politics or the weather. He didn't look Cooper directly in the eyes, however... merely glancing up every now and again. Cooper thought it was of shame or embarrassment.

"I lived on the third floor of this apartment building, see. After Tom left... well... the next thing, I hear voices outside in the back, so I go to the window... a few thugs got Tom and are beating the crap out of him. Then another man comes up and... and... he sticks a knife in him. Just like that. In the chest, a couple of times. Just like that. And when a few lights come on, they suddenly disappear."

"Where's the leather case now?"

"Tom's dead, Mr. Cooper. He never had a chance."

"I know that son, that's why we have to start talking about you, now. Where's the leather case?"

"I hid it. And the next day I lit out. I stayed with some friends of mine for a while, until I contacted Mr. Harding. The rest you know."

"What was in the case?"

"Uhhhh... I don't know. I never even opened it."

"Well, why didn't you just bring it to the police."

"The other man? The one with the knife? He was a policeman... or was wearing some type of uniform, at least. It didn't look like the uniform the cops on the block usually wore... but he was definitely a policeman."

"Probably one from the lakefront area... maybe even a private guard, hard to tell, I would suppose, under the circumstances," allowed Cooper. "But it sure seems like they want whatever was in that case pretty badly. Could be it would be mighty important to the Police, too. I know you don't want to hear this, son, but you should consider going back and getting that thing to the Police and letting them have a go at figuring this thing out."

"I don't think that's a good idea," said Leon right away. I think maybe they'll forget about this after awhile... if I'm up in the middle of the woods all winter. I never have to go back to Chicago, you know. And I never will. Never!"

"I see. Well, I suppose that's possible. Unless they know you were witness to the murder." Cooper watched as Leon's face darkened. "They did see you in the window, didn't they."

"Not very well."

"Well, son... if you won't go back to Chicago and confront this thing, there's nothing left to do but get back to camp and forget about it. I'll keep my eyes and ears open for anything strange going on here... if someone from Chicago ends up in this neck of the woods, they shouldn't be too hard to spot. They'll stick out just like you did when you first got here. And with all your new woodsmen friends out there, I suspect you'd be as safe as any place. Could be that you're right, that they will forget all about this in time, when they see that you've no intention of exposing their activities."

Leon thought perhaps that last comment was a bit condescending, but said nothing.

"Well, you'd better be off to camp before it starts getting dark. I have some things for Ox Pete you can bring back with you, if you don't mind, but better give them to Joe Kinder, or they'll get lost or thrown away." Cooper reached into a drawer and pulled out a leather case, handing it to Leon.

"I don't mind. I bought a few things at the store, too, on credit. Do you mind if I stick them inside."

"Go right ahead." Cooper moved from around the desk and held out the case. "You take care of yourself, son. And I'll do what I can for you."

"Thanks, Mr. Cooper."

"And say hi to Buck and the boys for me, will you? Say, that reminds me... we are invited to the Johnson's for Thanksgiving ... you may as well come in with Buck on Thursday."

"Sure," said Leon opening the door. He looked at Cooper again, the older man returning the gaze for several seconds, but no further words were spoken. And then he was outside with the cool wind on his cheeks and a heavy burden on his mind.

The Sixteenth Chapter

Ꝓunkhouse ꝏales

Leon trudged out along the south road with mixed emotions about his visit. He tried to put the Chicago problem behind him by thinking of his Thanksgiving dilemma; to stay in camp to be with Mary Muggsley, or to spend the day chatting with Andrea Johnson. The thought of both lovely girls filled his mind and did not leave much room for any other thoughts, good or bad. My but the twists and turns of life were interesting.

The day was still cloudy and Leon was glad he had left town when he did so as not to face the woods at dusk or thereafter. And though the gradual climb up the south hills along the Namakagon road would normally tax him, his gait suffered little borne on the strength of his Thanksgiving thoughts.

He stopped once, where a trail led off and pondered for a moment on a side trip to Camp #11, but good sense prevailed. And soon he came to the first set of westward tracks, up and over the grade and on up to the second set some farther distance, where he rested. The woods were a lonely business on a gray day in November. If not for the thought of warmth and company at the end of these tracks, Leon would have had trouble going on. But home, such that it was, was onward down the line. And so his journey continued.

At the camp, his first stop was to the cookhouse to let Muggsley know he had made contact with Mary. Entering silently, he watched Muggs poking at the stove ashes, pausing to scratch behind his ear and snuffle and snort to himself. The image of golden curls and delicate features flashed into Leon's mind and he shook his head in wonderment.

"Hi Muggs," he greeted. Muggs turned around sharply.

"Oh, it's you. Made it back did ya? Figgered we'd be looking fer ya by now."

"I can take care of myself," Leon replied indignantly. "And I spoke to Mary... she is delighted to come out and have dinner here on Thanksgiving."

"That's good, that's real good," said Muggs wiping his hands on his apron. "That'll be real nice. What else did ya do in town?"

"Oh, I bought a few things and talked with Mr. Cooper a little."

"Oh?"

"And took a bath."

"A bath?!? On purpose?" exclaimed Muggs.

"Mr. Cooper says I was starting to bring tears to his eyes. I was just being polite."

"My God, a bath this time of the month! You'll just need another by tomorrow, ya know. That's the way of it."

"I got some stuff for Ox Pete," said Leon tiring of the conversation. "Is he around someplace?"

"Everyone's someplace," sighed Muggs. "Pete's place is over in the bunkhouse just now."

Just about the whole crew was in the bunkhouse. Outside, dusk was approaching at a fast pace, bringing with it cooling air and a bit of snow. The kerosene light and anticipated warmth of the cabin were beckoning.

Ox Pete was standing in the center of the room, one foot up on a box and a pipe in his mouth. The "boys" were sitting around on the bunks near the center of the room, telling tales and laughing at their own lies.

"Hah," said Ed Simms when the latest bout of laughter subsided. "You ain't seen real birling, lessen you seen Tom Oliver and Jim Stewart birling for the Lake States championship up in Ashland a few years back. Now that was birling!"

"Vell, seems I remember dat one," says Ox Pete pulling the pipe out of his mouth midst a swirl of smoke. "Vas Labor Day, I tink. Dat Stewart quite a birler."

"But Tom was no johnny-come-lately," added Simms. "No sir. Why only Tom and Jim and about 10 others made it past the preliminaries. Must of been hundreds there... but they dunked 'em all."

"Ya don't say," says Olson from behind the stove.

"Ya, and before ya knew it, it was Jim and Tom left on a log, and there they go. The log was spinning and spinning, this way, then that. But both them boys... they was good."

"So who won?" asked Ed Albertson, adding a slug of snoose under his lip.

"Well, it weren't that easy, win or lose," continued Simms. "Them boys went at it all day, neither could shake the other, though Tom got the edge now and again. Jim was a big boy, like Buck there," he paused and pointed a fat bandaged finger at Buck resting back on his bunk.

"And Tom, he was a little less so, but game to the core. Why them boys birled til nigh onto 7 that night and both still standing astride that log."

"So what hoppened," prompted Frank Mueller.

"The judges decided it was enough for the day. They called the boys from the log in a temporary draw and decided to finish the contest in the morning. There was hell to pay in Ashland that night. Whoooeeee! Thousands of lumberjacks were in town for the birling and fair, and they hit the town like the 4-Spot a rolling down the grade. Let me tell you!"

"Ya," mused Ox Pete, "like da 4-Spot vith no brakes."

"Come morning, the boys were on the log again...

"Same log?" asked Olson.

"Same log, Ole," continued Simms. "They started about 10 in the morning, on the same log... a twisting and a turning and a rolling. Best birlers in the world."

"Bowlers?" asked Leon as he stepped through the door, hearing only the last part of the tale. "They have bowling up here?" The lumberjacks all faced him in unison, with the same incredulous look. The looks were enough and silence reigned for the next several moments.

"As I was sayin'. Them boys were the best birlers in the world," started Simms again. "They went at it all day long, without a break, until Tom Oliver collapsed in exhaustion. The big fella won cause he had a little more oomph than Tom, but as birlers, they was equal. Ol' Tom lasted til about 4:30, but no longer. Jim, he was declared best birler in three states, and got a hunert dollars too, and a watch."

"Yaa," added Ox Pete. "But Bill Delyea over in Minnesota beat Jim da next year. Alvays somevun better, or bigger. Alvays vill be, I guess. Ain't dat so, Ole?"

"Hard tellin', not knowin'" says Ole as he leaned over to spit in the snoose bucket.

"Yaa," agreed Buck.

With the end of the story, Ox Pete stuck both hands in his suspenders and waded through the men toward the door. As he got close, Leon held out the leather case. He was so flustered that he forgot his own purchases were still inside.

"Mr. Cooper sent this along for you," said Leon.

"Gude," grunted Pete, and was through the door.

Common chatter returned to the room as soon as Pete had left.

"Hah!, for my money, ain't no birlers like the Thompson brothers," says Tom Gulliver.

"Jack Flemming," said another.

Leon edged closer to Buck who was still leaning back calmly on his bunk.

"Took a bath, dint ya?" says Buck.

Leon nodded. "How'd ya know?"

"New fellas alvays seem to need a bath every couple a veeks," said Buck wagging his head. "You'll get over it." He smiled and it eased Leon a bit.

"Cooper says to say hi, Buck. Guess him and I are going to your place for Thanksgiving."

"Ya... dats gude. Mama is the best cook, you'll see."

"Buck? What's a burler, anyway?"

Buck was just getting into his explanation of log rolling, why it was important and how it was used, when Ox Pete came bursting into the bunkhouse in a rage. To Leon's chagrin, he marched right over to where they were sitting.

"Vhat's dis?" he shouted. He held up the thermometer he had found in the leather case.

"A thermometer," replied Leon.

"I know it's damn thremometer. Vhat's it doing here? Don't I alvays tell vhen it's too cold to vork? Don't I alvays let yew know so's yew von't freeze yer asses? Who tinks he needs to know better dan Pete?" Pete's face was flushed by the time he finished and Leon was perplexed, but not into stupidity.

"Must of been Cooper," said Leon shrugging.

"Cooper! Cooper!?! Bah!" he spit out. "Cooper don't know shit about veather, dat I know." Pete turned on his heel and slammed the door as he left the bunkhouse. Leon turned back to Buck with relief on his face.

"Hope Cooper forgives me that one," he said.

"Dat Pete. He alvays tells us vhen it's too cold to vork," said Buck. "Dat's why no thermometer. But it's never been too cold to vork."

"Never? Not even 20 below zero?" asked Leon.

"How yew know? Vith Pete, it's never too cold, alvays yust right."

"Why it was so cold once," started Tom Gulliver, on another tall tale. And so on and so on.

The following morning it was business as usual; early morning breakfast and then to the woods to cut and haul the logs. Leon could hear the trees fall and the calls and shouts of the men whenever he passed outside on some chore. He did notice, however, that the men were getting farther and farther from camp with their work.

Ox Pete let it be known that Thanksgiving would still be a workday, though work would stop at noon. Some men grumbled about working the holiday, some were glad they were getting a half-day off.

And the weather held. Cloudy and gray it was, always the promise of snow and a brief flurry now and again, but the skies, for the most part, withheld their moisture and clung to the earth low and heavy. As long as the sky stayed overcast, the temperature would remain mild, men would say. Most speculated, at least, that a heavy storm was due. Ed Simms was sure his corns were telling him it would be Thursday. Bull Finnigan figured it was sooner, according to the way the squirrels were acting. But they all agreed it was only a matter of time... and it made them uneasy in the anticipation.

Thursday dawned gray and dark and unusually calm. Leon reasoned it was about 15 or 20 degrees out, not the least uncomfortable. He thought it a good break that there was no wind. The others knew better.

"It's about due," said Ox Pete looking at the sky after breakfast. "Vhat yew tink, Ole?"

Ole looked about him, concentrating on the western part of the sky. He spit snoose into the muddy remnants of snow outside the cookshack before speaking.

"Hard tellin', not knowin'" observed Ole.

"Vell, yaa," agreed Pete. "Not knowin', I guess vee should git to vork."

By 9:00 am the west wind started to blow, slowly in mild gusts, snatching at free leaves and dancing them across untrodden snow. It wasn't much to notice at first. Then the snow started in large floating flakes wafting through the air. It was kinda pretty, thought Leon, for he wasn't wielding an ax into sturdy pine, nor managing a team of oxen or horses pulling a sleigh laden with logs to the landing.

And slowly, sneaking up in swirling blasts, was a rip roaring western storm that engulfed the camp and the men in the woods in a howling fury of freezing wind and blinding snow. It was so sudden, from pretty lazy flakes to swirling storm, that the men in the woods were caught midst stroke of an ax, as the trees began to bend and twist in the onslaught.

Above the roar of the storm, Ox Pete howled too, in strong Swedish curses, and urged the men to seek shelter the best they could. Some wandered blindly in the direction of the camp, tripping over stumps and sprawling in the snow, then surging on.

Buck was making his way back with his crew when he heard a loud "crack" above the storm and wind. He turned in time to make out a huge white pine nearly cut through and caught in the fury of the storm beginning to topple. And in its impending path were 2 or 3 of the men struggling up the side of a depression, unknowing of the danger they were in. Buck struggled back shouting and reached the men just as the tree came crashing down.

At the Johnson farm, Alma was busy cleaning the house for the company to come. Andrea and Martha were helping likewise, in different rooms, while Emil and young Joe were in the barn finishing chores.

At 9:27 am, Alma suddenly sat down in a daze. For moments she stared at the doorknob on the closet door, her face careworn and somber. She was unmoved from that position until Andrea came into the room.

"Mama," she cried out, and rushed to her side. "Oh, Mama, what is it?" She knelt at Alma's side and took her hand in her own trying to make contact with blank eyes.

"Mama!" she cried again, and Alma began to blink. She looked at Andrea sadly, and tried to smile. "What is it? Are you alright?"

Alma nodded. "Yaas," she said. "I am fine. Vee don't tell Papa... vee don't tell Papa... vee don't tell Papa that I see..." She struggled with the words, thinking, trying to decide what to say, what would make sense.

"Who was it Mama? Was it bad? Was it really bad?"

"It vas Buck, I think. A little bit hurt maybe, maybe storm, I don't know." She looked up at Andrea feeling just a little bit foolish, and a little bit troubled. "Vee don't tell Papa that I see.... Vee don't tell Papa nothing.

Andrea nodded. "I wonder about Buck, though. Is he alright Mama?" Alma looked weary. She turned away and gave no response, wanting Andrea to go away now.

Andrea left her then to stand at the window, looking out at the pasture and down the trail, trying to see all the way to Camp #9. The wind was pushing hard at the house and swirling snow was sweeping across the woods and fields. It made her shiver involuntarily.

"I guess we'll know in a little while," she shrugged uneasily.

K. Wallin

The Seventeenth Chapter

Thanksgiving Day

Even from inside the house they heard the train whistle blow that afternoon. It sounded rather hollow and eerie, trying to make itself heard above the dwindling storm. The wind had subsided pretty much, leaving the snowflakes to find their own way to the earth at last.

From the window, Andrea could make out Cooper's stout form and wide brimmed hat stepping off from the engine platform into the gathering snow. Immediately the whistle sounded again... three short blasts and the engine began to chug slowly down the line on its way to the camps.

About 15 or 20 minutes later they could hear Cooper stomping the snow off his boots at the front door. He was all smiles and jocularity when the door was opened and the greetings were bandied about. There were snow marks still on his pants over halfway to his knees where he had waded through the field from the track line.

Emil soon had him in the living room with a tumbler full of homemade blackberry wine, inquiring into the news of the day. Andrea shared nervous glances with Alma and Martha as time ticked slowly by. They all knew, from Cooper, that the men would be working in the woods all morning and would not likely show up at the Johnson's farm until later in the afternoon. Many was the moment that Andrea convinced herself that it was all superstitious nonsense and that there was nothing out of the ordinary in this November storm. Yet, the uneasy feeling remained.

It was around 4:00 pm, near dusk in the gloom of gray skies, that Joe announced their arrival from his perch by the window. Even Cooper sighed with relief.

Leon and Buck, sober faced and silent, were nearly overwhelmed with the barrage of questions and attention from the worried group.

"Is everything all right?"

"What took you so long?"

"Did something happen?"

"Why are you so quiet?"

"Did you get caught in the storm?"

"Alright, alright," said Emil above the voices. "Let them sit down and rest. Andrea, yew bring some of dat gude vine. Martha, take their coats and hats. Here, boys, yew sit down near the stove." He moved them off by grasping each man by the elbow and ushering them into the living room.

Leon took a long swallow of wine before he spoke. "There was an accident, Mr. Cooper." Andrea's eye caught Alma for a second, then back to Leon's face, which she was finding particularly handsome just now, flushed with color and lined with character.

"How bad, son?" asked Cooper with a voice full of concern.

"Ed Simms is pretty banged up. Jack Larson, too. They would have bought it for sure, if it hadn't been for Buck."

"Dat right, Buck?" asked Emil. But before Buck could answer, Leon continued.

"They were caught in the storm. Came on real sudden like, right Buck? And before they knew it, no one could see anything or find their way back to camp." He paused and took another drink.

"A glorious storm," added Joe.

"Hey, this is good wine," started Leon once more. "Anyway, Ed's crew had this large pine nearly cut down when the wind picked up. They were trying to get away from it, but Ed and Jack got stalled somehow in going up a ridge and the tree come a crashing down." He made motions with his hands as a tree once standing and now crashing to the ground.

"Did it kill 'em?" asked Joe excitedly.

"Joe!" cried Andrea, Martha and Alma simultaneously.

"What happened, Buck?" asked Cooper.

"Buck saw the tree start to go," continued Leon, "and hollered at Ed and Jack, but they could hardly hear above the wind and so Buck rushed over there and tackled 'em both so that all three went flying, just as the tree came down on 'em. Buck managed to get 'em over so that the main trunk missed 'em, but they still got clobbered."

"Are you hurt, Buck?" asked Alma.

"Oh, he's not hurt much... just some banged up ribs and a gash on his leg. And Jack Larson got banged in the head some, so he's a little bit funny, and probably a broken arm or shoulder. But Ed... I don't know. He wasn't doing so well. A branch stuck right in 'em, pinning him to the ground, and all he could talk about was how he had been right... the storm did hit on Thursday. He was real happy about being right about that.

"Easy, son," said Cooper putting his hand on Leon's shoulder. We don't need to go into details just now. I'll check with Pete in the morning and find out all about this. I think you boys should just relax now. Why, Buck, you must be plumb wore out from all that talking."

"Yaa," nodded Buck, and they all laughed at the sarcasm, even Leon.

"I'm sorry... I didn't mean to go on so... I guess..." stammered Leon.

"That's alright son," said Cooper, "you have every right to be excited.

"Vell, I spose yew boys are probably not very hungry vith all this excitement," said Alma. "Vee could put this supper off for some hours or so. Vhat yew think, Papa?"

"Yaas, yas, I suppose. Everyvun too upset to eat now py golly."

"Well, if I don't at least get some pumpkin pie pretty soon, I'll just die," whined Joe, bringing more laughter.

The Johnson table was filled with an abundance of good food and surrounded by warmth and laughter. Emil sat at the head, with Alma to his right, Joe to his left. Cooper was at the opposite end. Somehow, Andrea ended up next to Leon, leaving Martha and Buck across from them. Little Emma was between Andrea and Joe, eyes wide and focused on a very large turkey stuffed with a variety of breading and spices.

With some difficulty, Emil was able to bring silence to the table to affect the "Grace", an honor traditionally held by Alma.

"Vee tenk yew Lord, for many things today," she started, after all heads were bowed and hands were reverently clasped, even Cooper's. "Vee tenk yew first for gude food vee are about to eat. Trough yer goodness we have fine harvest this year. Not like last year."

"Hrmmph," grunted Emil. He was thinking of the hard labor that went into that good harvest. The momentary glare from Alma silenced him immediately.

"And Lord, vee vant to tenk yew for our family and guests at this table tonight, and for our gude health. And vee tenk yew for helping our Buck to... for helping our Buck, Lord, Amen." Buck blushed awkwardly, while the rest mumbled their own amens.

Emil carved the turkey, lovingly laying the first juicy slice on Alma's plate. Everyone else was digging into the mashed potatoes and gravy, corn and pickled beets and sweet potatoes and breads and jams. And midst the intake of food, conversation found its way.

"Well, they got their jail," said Cooper. "Came in yesterday from Ohio. A two cell thing with nice strong bars."

"A yail, for goodness sakes," grunted Emil, not missing a stroke with the carving knife.

"Yep," continued Cooper, "a pretty little cage. But you'll never guess where they opted to put the da... dumb thing."

"Where?" they all asked at once.

"The schoolhouse. The schoolhouse of all places."

"I tol' ya. I tol' ya," chanted Emma.

"The schoolhouse, oh they couldn't, could they?" asked Andrea. "Not in the schoolhouse."

"Marge Hinkle says they hardly ever use the jail in Cable until spring," added Martha. "Her brother was in the jail once on account of fighting with that Blakewood boy."

"From what I hear, Lester Hinkle fights with just about everybody," said Andrea. "And I doubt if he's been in jail just once."

"Vell, dat's in Cable," said Emil. "They should send all our criminals to Cable den, to put them in yail. A yail in the schoolhouse?"

"That's Sam Hackett and the Town Board for you," added Cooper. "They never think things through. Not only did we not need a jail, but we have no good place to put it. Now they have to build a jailhouse to put it in, can't just leave it in the school. And that'll cost more money. They just don't think, that crew. Pass the lefsa, would you Andrea?" Leon watched as a plate of flat doughy pancake-like things passed in front of him.

"You know, Emil, you should give some thought to running for the town board next time," suggested Cooper. "I've always said that you have uncommon good sense." Alma smiled and patted Emil's arm in pride.

"What's this leftsop stuff," said Leon pointing at the plate.

"You have never had lefsa?" asked Martha.

"Lefsa?" repeated Leon.

"It's kind of a potato pancake," said Andrea reaching for one. "You can put butter on it, sprinkle a little sugar over it and roll it up like this." He watched as she prepared one for him. "Then you eat it from the end. It's very good." She handed it to him carefully. He looked a little skeptical, but was inclined to try it now that the entire family was watching him for a reaction.

He took a bite and registered surprise. "This is very good," he said. "Is it really made of potatoes?"

"Certally," said Buck wondering what all the fuss was about. Lefsa was as common a dish as bread in the Johnson household.

"I like it with jam in it," offered Emma.

"Aww, you like anything with jam in it," said Joe.

"Look who's talking, Joseph," said Martha. And Joe smiled.

Little by little the dinner disappeared. It was not unnoticed that Leon's appetite nearly matched Bucks and certainly surpassed most of the other diners. Slowly too, John Cooper and Leon Mancheski were comfortably wrapped in the warm friendly glow that was the Johnson family, a thought not lost on the two men.

When no more food could possibly be eaten, Leon had one more lefsa, while everyone watched.

"Yew like lefsa, maybe, Mr. Mancheski?" asked Alma, knowing full well the answer.

"Very much," he replied, taking another bite.

"It was a wonderful meal," offered Cooper, "I don't know when I have eaten better. It was kind of you to take pity on us poor bachelors and include us in your feast."

"Yew are alvays velcome at our table, Mr. Cooper," answered Alma sincerely. "And yew tu, Mr. Mancheski." Leon was overwhelmed at such feelings. He colored a little, mumbled a thank you, and silently ate his lefsa.

As the dishes started to be carted away by the women, Emil herded the men into the parlor for a little more blackberry wine. Cooper offered cigars all around and was surprised when they were accepted.

"These aren't the usual 5 cent cigars I usually smoke, I'll have you know," said Cooper as the men started to strike wooden matches. "These are 25 centers, my holiday smoke. I think you'll see the difference."

"It's gude!" exclaimed Emil. "A man should have a gude cigar like this at least 2 or 3 times a year, yah Buck?"

"I guess I'll stick to snoose," answered Buck waving smoke from in front of his face. "Yew don't have to breathe snoose."

"Say, Emil. I was somewhat serious about having you run for Town Board," said Cooper. "I think you would do a fine job."

"Oh so? Dat politics, Mr. Cooper," replied Emil shaking his head, "I don't know dat politics. Dat Sam Hackett... he knows."

"That's just the trouble. Too much politics and not enough getting up and getting things done. Why there are things to do around here, this is a growing town. There are roads to build, for goodness sakes. Take that Namakagon road, for instance. Why it's nothing more than a pack trail. Wagons bumping over my tracks causing the rails to shift... and who knows what that jostling does to the wagons themselves."

"Yaa, not much of a road, dat Namakagon trail," inserted Buck.

"Well, where does it go, anyway?" asked Leon.

"Where does it go? Where does it go? Why where ever you want it to go... out to Namakagon Lake and on over to Cable and south to the rest of the world if you like. Every road leads to another road and to the rest of world where ever it is," preached Cooper.

"We had a picnic once, over at the lake," jumped in Joe. "It was glorious fun... fishing and swimming... hardly any leeches even."

"Alls I'm saying, Emil, is give it some thought. I think you'd give Sam a real run for his money. Why all he does is sit around and tell you what he's done before, or what he thinks he might do, but he never gets around to actually doing anything. That's politics."

"Yaa, I give it some little thought."

"Excuse me, Papa," interrupted Andrea softly. Her nose wrinkled up at the smoke in the room.

"Yas, Andrea?"

"I'm going out to the barn to check on the Molly cow. She was a little off her feed today."

"Yas?" questioned Emil a bit puzzled.

"I just wanted to tell you so you didn't worry about where I was, if you were looking for me. I'll be in the barn for awhile." Emil looked at Buck, who shrugged.

"Dat's a gude girl, Andrea." Andrea smiled shyly and wrapped a shawl around her shoulders. Then moments later the door was heard to open and close and a wee draft of cool air felt it's way along the floor.

"A fine young woman, Emil," said Cooper beaming. This scene was not lost on him. He knew she was basically telling Leon she would be alone in the barn if he wanted to come out and talk. Or whatever it was that young people of the opposite sex got around to in this day and age.

The hint may have been lost to Leon, but the opportunity certainly wasn't. He waited for a while, joining the men in more talk of politics and weather and people. Then he stood up and announced he was going to seek a little fresh air and find out what was left of the storm. Nobody paid much attention to him, so he put his hat and coat on and went out the door.

Andrea wasn't in the barn, but just outside the front door of it, looking toward the heavens. The storm clouds had cleared finally and stars twinkled brightly in the dark November sky. Her arms were wrapped around her for warmth, for with the clearing of the clouds, the temperature had begun to drop.

Leon was struck by her simple beauty. Surely not like the beautiful and delicate Miss Mary Muggsley, but with plain and attractive features that were nice and comfortable to look at. Leon felt the blackberry wine take hold of his senses. He wanted to go to her now and take her in his arms...

"Oh, it's you, Mr. Mancheski. I didn't see you at first."

"I'm sorry, I didn't mean to sneak up on you."

"It's alright," she exclaimed quickly. "I was just looking at the sky. It seems so deep sometimes, and yet... if you stare long enough, it feels as if you could reach out and touch a star."

"I heard some men talking the other day... just talk, I guess... but they were saying that some scientists think there will be men on the moon someday."

"Why that's silly. They must have been just joking with you. How could anyone get to the moon?"

"Oh, I don't know," he replied fidgeting a little, dragging his foot in the snowy dirt. "If it was Cooper... he'd probably push a railroad on up there and charge everyone two bits just to see the man-in-the-moon." In the pale light he saw her smile briefly.

"If it was up to me, I'd never let anyone travel to the moon," she said softly and seriously. "It was meant to be seen from down here, the way it turns colors and shapes through the seasons. It's everyone's moon from down here. It's everyone's, but still it can be your's alone, if you know what I mean. It can be whatever you want it to be; a friend to talk to, a dream keeper, a light to shine the way."

"It's just a moon," he said, then realized at once that it was the wrong thing to say, at least to her, at least tonight. "I'm sorry..."

"That's alright," she smiled again. "Just a moon... and that's all I want it to be... ever!"

"Is the cow alright?" he asked to change the subject.

"Cow? Oh...yes, Molly's fine," she replied, looking directly at him, wondering about him. Her feelings about him changed like the fickle winter wind, confusing her, exciting her. "Would you like to see Molly?"

"Sure."

In the barn it was warmer, and Andrea had already lit a lamp. The air was thick, however, with cow smells and hay, and Leon found his nostrils adjusting to these new odors with some disdain. He patted Molly on the nose with little affection and no reaction from the cow. But the nearness of Andrea warmed his heart and he could make out the faint smell of violets through the barn smells.

Andrea wandered over to a couple of bales of straw and sat down, wrapping her long skirt around her legs to keep the cool air out. Leon followed and stood nearby, pretending to look at some tack hanging on a post near the stall.

"I think your job must be pretty exciting," said Andrea.

"No, it's mostly tiring. Why, I barely have a moment to myself what with hauling water and wood and washing dishes and peeling potatoes and stuff."

"What? No, no I mean your real job. Writing for the magazine, traveling and meeting people. I'd love to travel to a city... a big city, like Chicago."

She saw him wince a little at the mention of his job, thinking he was disappointed and surprised that someone knew about his writing career. Actually, it was the mention of Chicago that made him react.

"Oh, you know about that?"

"Well, yes, I guess a few people do. I hope you don't mind talking about it. I won't tell anyone else."

"No, it's ok... it's just that, well... everything is not exactly what it seems." She gave him a quizzical look, which he could only return with a warm smile. "I'd rather hear more about you," he said softly. His fingers started to play with the harness straps he found hanging on the post, something to pay attention to, if her eyes probed too deeply.

"There's nothing to tell," she said. "I'm just me, Andrea Marie Johnson."

"How old are you?"

"Seventeen," she said hesitantly. "Almost eighteen. I graduated last spring. I was supposed to go to work for my aunt Ester this fall, taking care of her children... my cousins, I guess."

"But you didn't."

"No... Pa hurt himself this summer and couldn't work in the camps, so we don't have much money. I was trying to save enough on my own but... Pa needed my help around here anyway. Martha was going to go to school, but she has to wait, too."

"I'm sorry it didn't work out for you."

"Oh, I'd probably miss this stodgy old town, anyway. It's ok."

"I've noticed that you speak very well... with no accent I mean, but your mother and father... and Buck... well it's pretty noticeable. Swedish, isn't it?"

"Yes. Swedish. It's the way we were brought up. Mama and Papa learned English after they got to America. And Buck...he was taught too, by the family and some in school, but he didn't go for very long. The rest of us learned most of our English in school. Papa said he wanted us to speak English like good Americans."

"But you know some Swedish, too."

"Mama taught me, but not so very much. You don't speak Polish?"

"Nno..," he stammered. "But I'd like to learn Swedish sometime. Perhaps you could teach me?"

"Perhaps."

They looked at each other warmly then, with the promise of another meeting, barely understood. But after a few moments Leon felt the need to look away, as if she was seeing too much of him, as if she knew that he wanted desperately to kiss her.

"I'm glad you didn't go off to your Aunt Ester's," he said bravely, "or I never would have met you."

"I'm glad you came to supper tonight," she said, coloring a little. She pulled the shawl closer around her shoulders.

"Me too," he answered, "it's nice to see you again and talk to you. And it's nice to get out of camp for awhile, even if Muggs is a good cook."

"Mr. Muggsley is a good cook?"

"Sure. I don't know how good he is with turkey, though. Maybe that's why he invited Mary out there for dinner... to help cook."

"Mary Muggsley?"

"Yes, do you know her?"

"Why of course, we went to school together. She's very beautiful, don't you think?"

"She sure is!" exclaimed Leon a little too heartily. To his dismay, Andrea suddenly got up and strolled to the door of the barn. Leon watched her warm breath turn to vapor from the cool air coming in the crack in the door. He walked up behind her, wondering why she had bolted like a skittish colt, hoping that it wasn't him.

He wanted to tell her that she was as beautiful as Mary Muggsley. That the lingering smell of violets in her hair stirred him so deeply that he could smell it long afterwards; that the sound of her voice was music personified. But all that came out of his mouth was, "it's getting colder out, isn't it?"

187

"Yes," she nodded. He put his hand on her shoulder tentatively and turned her gently to him. She looked up at him with rosy cheeks and lively blue eyes, her lips full and trembling.

"Andrea, I'm not very good with words, but..."

"So don't say anything," she said, putting her fingers on his lips to silence him. He hugged her close to him, then, her head on his shoulder and the smell of violets settling deep within his soul. They stayed that way, wrapped in the warmth of their embrace, rocking back and forth ever so lightly.

"I hear music," she said softly.

"Oh, Andrea..."

"From the house," she said pulling away. "Papa is playing his violin." She began fussing with her hair, adjusting hairpins and tightening her bob.

Leon could hear it now, a soft and sweet melody familiar to him from the dance at the Modern Woodmen hall. Before he could say another word, Andrea was dashing from the barn toward the house, fresh snow flying from her heels.

Leon sighed. He was confused by a rush of feelings he was just not prepared for. Even when the barn was once again closed up and he was standing out in the night, he hesitated to go in and join the merriment. He wanted to think about things. But the music was calling to him, like a pied piper tune, it drew him unavoidably to the house. He would have plenty of time for thinking at the camp in the next couple of months, he reasoned. And the thought of that evicted a more wearisome sigh.

Inside the house was a merry little group. Emil was picking up the pace on the violin, Buck was giving it a go on the mouth harp and the rest were clapping and stomping along, including a less than dignified Cooper. As Emil finished the sprightly number, he paused to sip some more blackberry wine. Alma, seeing Leon standing at the entrance to the parlor, pulled him in and handed him another glass of wine.

"Papa," said Alma, "play something to dance to. It isn't often we have gentlemen to dance with in our own home." Leon smiled. The next tune started and Alma held out her hands to him. When they began to dance, Leon clumsily so, everyone clapped and laughed. Martha could hardly keep from dancing by herself, finally dragging Buck up out of his chair. From the way he got up, it was evident that he was a little stiff and yet with pain. So Martha sat him back down and held out her hands to Mr. Cooper.

"You'd dance with an old man?" he asked.

"I'd dance with Muff Brown himself, tonight," she replied gaily, pulling Cooper onto the more open floor.

Young Joe danced with Emma, her little feet dancing twice as fast to keep up with his lanky form. And the night wore on. No one was inclined to call it an evening, even when Emil had to pause frequently and wipe the sweat from his brow. They changed partners often, Leon even mockingly dancing a few steps with Cooper to everyone's amusement.

Finally, when Emil was just about wore out, he sat down and rested. They all sat down then and it was in this momentary silence that they heard the train whistle. Cooper took out his pocket watch to check the time. He shook it a few times, then shrugged and put it away.

Emil took his watch out then, opening it carefully and letting a musical tune emanate from its golden form. He held it out for Cooper to see the time.

"Now that's a beautiful watch, Emil. I'd give a pretty penny for a watch like that. Makes this one of mine seem like a lump of coal."

"My Papa gave it to me, vhen I leave the old country. It is a fine vatch. He vas fine papa to me."

"Well, that must be Alfred coming back from the camps," said Cooper. "I told him to pick us up when he came back through."

"Us?" asked Leon, suddenly realizing that he would have to leave eventually.

"I figured you and Buck could catch a ride to town and walk up the Namakagon road to camp. Save you a few miles, anyway."

"Oh, uh...ya... that's right, thanks."

"Papa, play that tune, that one about the swallow," pleaded Joe. "I really like that one."

"Yoseph, Mr. Cooper has to be going. The train is vaiting."

"Please, Papa!"

"Yoseph," scolded Alma, "Yew listen to Papa."

"Well, let the darn train wait," said Cooper, "I like that song too." And the music played on.

As Leon walked with Buck up the Namakagon road, there was no sign anyone had been by since the snowfall. He wasn't sure if the warmness he felt against the cold was from the thought of Andrea, or from the wine and meal. It didn't matter. He couldn't remember ever feeling better.

They found their way by light of the stars and moon on the bright white of the snow. Easy to see well enough, thought Leon, but he was glad that Buck was along. The woods didn't seem so bad with a guy like Buck stomping along beside you. Leon didn't even notice Buck grunt a time or two as they stumbled up the hills along the path. Even Buck himself was unaware that he had bruised a rib in the foray with the pine, for he was not one for complaining. But it would be a week or two before he was at full speed again.

The Eighteenth Chapter

New Men in Camp

Jack Larson's logging days were over for the year. His shoulder would mend in time, however, and life would go on. But Ed Simms was a little more broke up inside than people at first thought. Doc Parker treated him the best he could, tended him through the night and stayed with him on the train all the way to Ashland the day after Thanksgiving. The doctors in the hospital checked him over and shook their heads sadly. It did not look good for Ed Simms. Mrs. Simms and the kids gathered around him and offered all the love and support a family could possibly muster... but silently he slipped away during the night. It was a sad occasion for the little town of Pratt. Ed Simms and his family had been permanent settlers there, running a small farm to the north of town near the Wheelers. Ed would be missed, to be sure, but the question remained, what would become of the Simms family?

"It's one of those things, Jake," said Cooper in the office Saturday morning. "Just one of those damn things." He shook his head sadly. "Ed was a tolerable logger... and he was good to his family. Why did it have to be Ed?"

"Who would you have preferred?" said Jake soberly. "I mean, it's not that you can choose. Ed's worked the woods a long time, he knew the risks."

"Suppose it had been Buck? I don't think I could've faced the Johnson's. You know, it almost was Buck, too. And the young fella, Leon. This is all new to him. It could just as well have been him," said Cooper.

"Well, it wasn't. It was Ed." said Jake, tiring of the conversation.

"Yeah," nodded Cooper, "guess I better go have a talk with his Missus, what's her name?"

"Dorothy."

Cooper walked into the back office, saying nothing more, his teeth clamped on an unlit cigar. For once Jake felt sorry for him. It was cool in the back office, but Cooper was not inclined to add wood to the stove. Instead, he went to the window to gaze out over the White River valley to the north. Usually it had a calming effect on him, settling his nerves, lightening the load of everyday work and worry. Today the view was stark and barren, dark shadows of trees in the distance on a white background, reflecting his mood. The color was gone. The warmth was gone. While Cooper watched, the sun suddenly appeared and brightened the white of the snow. It had a strange effect of making it seem colder. "It's funny," thought Cooper, "how the storms in our lives sweep through and then are gone. Now the day appears in such calm and innocence, like a regretful child apologizing for its brief fury and the trouble caused and promising to be good, until the next time. He shivered involuntarily, but it wasn't the cold.

"No work today, Mr. Jacobs," said Cooper reappearing from the back room. Jake was just about to add another chunk of oak to the stove.

"Oh?"

"You must have something to do. Get out of here, Jake. Enjoy your life a little," insisted Cooper.

"Well, I was pondering on the merits of a sleigh ride with ... with a companion."

"Go! Do it! It's a perfect day for a sleigh ride," enthused Cooper. Jake tossed the chunk back into the wood box and closed up the stove.

"And give my regards to your companion," shouted Cooper as Jake slammed the door on the way out.

Cooper stopped at the store on his way to the Simm's place and filled his pockets with treats for the kids. He had Bill Farley prepare a box of staple foods for Mrs. Simms as well. He then had the livery send over a horse and sleigh into which his parcels were loaded. As he settled into the sleigh, Bill came out with a scarf. He said nothing, but held it out to Cooper.

"You're a good man, Bill," said Cooper sincerely. As Cooper wrapped the scarf around his neck, another sleigh coursed by, its occupants all bundled in a blanket.

"Well, upon my soul," said Bill. "I'd almost say that looked like Mr. Jacobs and Sally Beardsly."

Cooper smiled. "I'd almost agree with you, Bill," he said, then snapped the reins gently, saying "heeeyup there girl".

The Simms farm was a small affair but well known for its vegetable garden supplying much of the town's needs. There were several small farms in the area, mostly cutover land with rich soil beneath the stumps and slash. The largest belonged to the Wheelers, located next to the Simms place and one of the first farms in the county.

Cooper could see the Wheeler's sleigh near the Simms house when he approached and was somewhat grateful. The children of both families were out playing in the yard, snowballs flying here and there and half-formed snowmen being worked on. Cooper was glad that he had brought enough candy for an army, gleefully distributing it to mittened hands midst a chorus of 'thank yous'. In spite of his generosity a snowball caught him in the back as he headed for the door, the kids scattering midst laughter at Cooper's mock fear and despair. It almost made him forget why he was there.

Mrs. Wheeler opened the door and tried to smile. "How nice of you to come," she said. Cooper nodded. He sensed that the aura of depression was wearing thin on the woman. The dining room table was already accumulating food from the efforts of friends and neighbors. Cooper set the box of staple goods in the kitchen, and followed Mrs. Wheeler into the living room. Mrs. Simms was dressed in a plain black dress and sitting in an old rocker, gently moving back and forth. She looked older than she was, older than Cooper remembered, a combination of the daily grind and recent misery. She held a handkerchief in her hands, wrapped around an object that Cooper surmised to be Ed's watch. Her eyes were closed, but the eyelids quivered from time to time.

"Dorothy," said Mrs. Wheeler gently, and the eyes blinked slowly open. "Dorothy, Mr. Cooper is here to see you."

"Mrs. Simms," started Cooper, "I just wanted to stop by and offer my condolences. I'm terribly sorry about Ed. He was a good man. A good logger, too."

Dorothy smiled weakly. She said, "He was very good to me and the kids." It was the way she judged his character, all other faults being forgiven.

"Mrs. Simms," continued Cooper, "I'm concerned about how... how you and the kids will get by. I know it's hard to think about that right now... but... Mrs. Simms, arrangements can be made, if... if you have no plans."

"I appreciate your concern, Mr. Cooper," replied Dorothy. "Ed always did think you a fine man, in spite of what others... well, I mean, he always liked you well enough, but we'll be fine. George Lundstrom stopped by this morning. Ed was a member of the Modern Woodmen society, you know. George told me there was a life insurance policy... he'll be back to help me with the papers in a week or two."

"That's wonderful!" said Cooper, a little too happily. "I mean, under the circumstances..."

"I know what you mean, Mr. Cooper. It was really nice of you to be concerned for me, but as you see, we'll be fine. We'll be missing Ed, but that can't be helped."

"Mrs. Simms, if there is anything I can do, anything at all, I wish you would let me know."

"Thank you, Mr. Cooper, you're very kind." Dorothy closed her eyes again, a subtle signal that the conversation was over and Mr. Cooper was free to go. He was grateful.

Mrs. Wheeler went to the door with him. "She'll be fine, Mr. Cooper, but only time will lessen the grief." She looked back toward the living room briefly, and then she said in a soft whisper, "even with a man like Ed Simms."

John Cooper started his sleigh ride back to town with a much lighter heart. The neighbors were seeing to the needs of the Simms family for right now and the insurance policy, while not providing great wealth, should see them through to better times. And he would tell Bill to see to it that the kids got some candy now and again. "Troubles and misery," thought Cooper, "like the storms of winter, are eventually replaced by sunshine and sleigh rides." But unlike the weather, real tragedies often leave holes that are hard to fill.

The boys at Lumber Camp #9 were affected only briefly by Ed's passing. Though everyone certainly regretted the incident, there was no particular affection for Ed Simms and camp life goes on. Ox Pete was the only one spared for the funeral on Monday. He attended a graveside service at the Pratt cemetery midst a curtain of lightly falling snow, a grave dug with pick and shovel in the frozen earth. He didn't admit it to anyone, but he felt a little responsible for Ed Simms; perhaps he shouldn't have worked the men on the morning of Thanksgiving Day. He stood graveside, hat in hand, snow gathering on his head and on his voluminous mustache, pondering on the whole affair. And when the pastor said 'amen' he stalked off to consult *Mr. Whiskey* at Charley's saloon.

So Ox Pete wasn't there that morning when the 4 spot came chugging in from the East with empty cars to be filled with logs and two new men to fill the bunks of Ed Simms and Jack Larson. No one expected Cooper to find extra men so quickly. After all, it was well into the logging season. Joe Kinder was wiping his hands on his apron when he heard the 4-Spot's whistle echoing through the hills, and sauntered down to the siding, rolling a cigarette as he walked. As he approached the engine, the two new men jumped off.

"Why, Helge Johnson, as I live and breathe," exclaimed Joe, fumbling with the cigarette.

"Hello Joe," offered Helge. He was nearly the size of Buck, but a little leaner with a handsome face. He was in fact, Buck's cousin, the second son of Swan Johnson, Emil's brother. The other man was about Leon's age, with sparkling blue eyes and tousled blond hair. Oddly, thought Joe, he wore no hat.

"Hello," said the other man smiling, extending his hand. Joe at once observed that the hand before him was rough and worked, leading him to believe that here before him was a man of woods experience.

"Didn't catch your name," observed Joe, but there was no answer tossed back as the men continued to look around.

"Nice place for a camp... some good pine from what I figure," said Helge. "The boys in the woods?" Ox Pete in the woods?" Helge had none of the accent that marked Buck's speech.

"Pete went into town for the funeral today," answered Joe.

"Oh, that's right, Ed Simms. Sorry to hear about that."

"The rest of the boys are in the woods of course, ceptin' Muggsley, myself and Leon."

"Leon? Chore boy?" asked Helge.

"Yeah, new guy... Cooper's cousin or sumpthin'. He's ok. Say, Helge, does Buck know you're coming out here?"

"Reckon not, Joe. I came over from Escanaba. Just got in last night and heard Cooper could use a man or two. Met this fella at Charley's last night," said Helge slapping the young man on the back a little too roughly. "Guess it was fate, wouldn't you say, Joe?"

"Fate," spat Joe Kinder, "has caused more than one man a bit of trouble." He lit the ragged end of the cigarette he had finally produced and drew at it thoughtfully. "Might as well move your things into the bunkhouse, the men will be in pretty soon for chow. I 'spect you'll be heading up Ed's crew, but that's up to Pete. Anyway, you'll find the bunks that Ed and Jack used to have. I imagine they're yours now."

"C'mon, smiley, let's go see to our luxury accommodations," said Helge heading across the tracks toward the bunkhouse.

Joe took one last drag on his cigarette, nearly burning his fingers, and then threw it in the snow. "Things are starting to get interesting," he said to himself.

Leon watched Joe greet the strangers from the door of the kitchen where he had aspired to gain some fresh air, noting how much the bigger man had made him think of Buck, though he hadn't considered why. When Joe returned with a few parcels brought by the train, Leon asked about the new men.

"Well," replied Joe, "that big fella's Helge Johnson. The others... well, I guess I didn't hear no name for him. They're gonna take Ed and Jack's place."

"Johnson?" repeated Leon.

"Joe nodded. "Buck's cousin. A likable fellow, but seems to lean toward trouble. Don't know if him and Buck always get along together neither. Gettin' interestin' around here, I'd say." Then he muttered more under his breath, "wouldn't doubt Escanaba sorta asked him to leave for awhile, that Helge." Joe spit into the snow debris from his cigarette that were still caught on his lips. He continued mumbling as he moved the parcels into the kitchen leaving Leon staring across the tracks at the bunkhouse.

The Nineteenth Chapter

Never teach an ox to sing

The two new men were already sitting at the table when the crew came in for lunch. True to form, and in deference to Muggsley, not a word was said as they gathered around and began the meal. Buck stared at Helge with a critical eye prior to digging into his plate of food, then ignored him and concentrated on the pleasure at hand.

Ox Pete had said he would be back by noon. He wasn't. In fact, he stumbled in just before dark, quite intoxicated and singing an old shanty song sometimes in English, sometimes in Swedish, but hardly ever in tune. The men were wise to steer clear and most knew this from long experience. He had left his coat and hat at Charley's so his exposed flesh; his hands and ears and face, were crimson with cold. It was the stable where he finally took refuge after abusing those few unlucky fellows he came into contact with. He stood in front of the oxen, talking to them in soft Swedish curses. He was staggering and nearly fell, grabbing onto the ear of an ox to right himself.

"Vell, thankee, Mr. Ox. I tink vee all sing a song now." He kissed the ox on the nose and began to sing:

"Not a ting on da river McClusky did fear
As he swung his goad-stick o'er the big boney steers;
They vas long, fat and thick, girt eight foot and tree--
Ha, ha! says McClusky, the laddies for me."

"Vee all sing now, eh laddies?" He pointed at one ox in particular and said, "yew sing da high part."

He was singing to the oxen when Leon went to throw out the dishwater. He could be heard bellowing across the tracks in the stable, where a lantern now lit, cast his staggering shadow about the room. Muggsley and Joe Kinder were pacing back and forth in the cook shanty, pausing from time to time to stare out the window at the stable.

"Damn, if it don't sound like them oxen are singing along," says Muggs.

"Well, if there's a man to teach 'em," nodded Joe, "it's Pete."

When the music stopped sometime later and still Pete did not emerge from the stable, Muggsley and Joe got concerned.

"Could be," said Muggs, "that one or tother of us should go have a look see, eh Joe?"

"Could be, I suppose," agreed Joe.

"It kinda feels like it's gonna get cold tonight," added Muggs. "There's a ring around the moon, bound to be cold."

"Bound to be," agreed Joe.

"Why don't cha go have a look see?" suggested Muggs.

"Me? Why me? You're the cook, ain't ya?"

"Certainly. But what's that got to... say, where's the young fella?" Just then Leon came in carrying a load of wood. When he straightened up after dropping his load in the wood box, he found both men looking at him curiously.

"What?" he asked.

"Would ya do me a favor, Leon?" asked Muggs. "I left one of my best pots in the stable. Wouldcha go get it for me?"

"I guess so."

"And whilst you're there, kinda check on ol' Pete, wouldcha?"

"Sure." Leon started out the door, but stopped half way through and stuck his head back in. "Where abouts did ya leave the pot?"

"Never mind the pot, jes go check on Pete," said Muggs pushing him out the door.

Ox Pete was sitting in the straw by the door, his eyes aglaze and Leon, for a dreaded moment, thought perhaps he was dead due to some unknown malady, until he spoke.

"Dat Ed, he done me bad," mumbled Pete. "He vent and died, Goddam him."

"C'mon, Pete, let's get you off to bed now," cajoled Leon.

"Izzat yew Ed? Py golly, yew done me bad."

"It's me, Leon."

"Didcha know Ed? He vas a tolerable fellow. Yust plain tolerable."

"C'mon Ox, I'll help you up." Leon grabbed him under his arms, and after several attempts, Pete was able to get to his feet. Arm in arm they stumbled in the snowy path, over the rails barely maintaining balance, and on to the back door of the small bunkhouse attached to the kitchen. Once there, in the light of the window, Pete straightened up tall and shrugged off Leon's help. He turned and looked the young man straight on, blinking, trying to comprehend the situation. Then he smiled.

"Vell, thankee little fella. Guess I'll get me to bed." Leon nodded knowingly. Pete was just opening the door when he stopped suddenly. He stood there for a few seconds as if struck by a thought. Then he turned and swung and hit Leon in the face, knocking him flat backwards into the snow.

"An don't call me Ox!" he said gruffly, then entered and slammed the door.

Leon was 'out' for a few minutes after the blow, which Ox Pete had rendered him. When he came to, he was cold and his head ached. "Well, that's what I get for my trouble," he said to no one. When he entered the bunkhouse, he found the men in their usual state of leisure. Ole Olson was cutting hair for those that were so inclined, several men were telling tall tales, others were mending garments. Socks and underwear hung from a wire near the stove.

"Where you been?" asked Charlie Louis as he pinned up a pair of socks.

"I was helping Ox... uh. I was helping Pete," answered Leon, feeling the edges of his eye where it was beginning to swell. He turned toward his bunk to flop down.

"Well, that explains the snow on your back and the welt on your eye," says Charlie laughing.

Leon was taken aback to find Helge resting comfortably on the bunk he had called home for these many hard weeks. "Excuse me," he said gently, "but you seem to have made a mistake. This is my bunk."

"No mistake," answered Helge, his arms folded under his head.

"I've had this bunk since the camp started. I've been here from the beginning," insisted Leon.

"Well, good for you. You seem to be good at picking out bunks, go pick out another one," said Helge. Leon looked around the room, at Buck, at Charlie and Ole and the others. Their faces were impassive, though most had heard. Not one said a thing.

"It's my bunk, ain't it, Buck?" said Leon, his eyes pleading for assistance. "Ain't it Charlie?"

"Well, if the bunk were yurn, you'd be in it by now, I spect," replied Charlie. "Maybe it ain't yurn after all."

Leon looked around and began to see the futility of the matter. He sized up Helge and decided at a glance that a fight would not be in his best interest. Red faced and full of humility Leon bent down and gathered his stuff from under the bunk. Later as he lay in his new bed, he reflected on the ups and downs of life. Tonight was definitely a down. His only solace was that he knew, that if he closed his eyes and let himself drift, tonight would go away and be replaced by tomorrow, a clean slate, a fresh start on survival.

And drift he did, after setting the clock. It was always the last thing he did before settling in, for he knew the harsh ramifications of not arising on time and getting the chores done. He set the clock within easy reach, remembering the first week of camp and the penalty of the slow reaction to its muffled bell. And each night he checked the sock wrapped carefully around the bell housings. Its rhythmic rat a tat tat was certainly preferable to the loud clang of a bare bell.

With all as it should be, Leon left the confines of the bunkhouse, within his sleep, and wandered over the land. He hovered over the Johnson house and watched Andrea sitting by the moonlit window staring out over the frozen landscape, her shawl draped about her shoulders. In his dream, she was thinking of him with tender thoughts and wishing she had kissed him in the barn that night, for he wished it too. But his dream led him on away from the Johnson farm, to a sleigh ride with a bubbly girl with golden curls and laughter filled with the music of life. And on and on his dream led him, forward and away from the past, away from the present, to a preferred and well-formed future, all wise and knowing. And there he dwell for the evening, in the safe haven of sleep.

He awoke with a start. It was still dark out and cold but he suspected it was near the time he would have to rise for long practice in this matter had trained him to know. He huddled in his blankets and thought of the day ahead, trying not to think of the day behind. But then his eye, slightly swollen and sore brought back the night. And as he lay there, in the pre-dawn darkness, he grew angry.

When it became obvious his thoughts and anger would not let him return to the nights dream, he sat up and wrapped the blanket around him.

He rubbed his eyes, wincing as he came into contact with the sore one. In caution, he picked up the alarm clock to stifle it before it could alarm. He squinted in the wan light to see that it was about 4:15 am. Yes, it wouldn't do, after all that he had been through the night before, to allow the alarm to trigger more abuse. He looked over at his old bunk and heard Helge snoring so peacefully where he had no right to be. And then he looked at the alarm clock again. A thought, like a burst of lightning, struck him wide-awake. He quickly worked his way into his clothes, but carried his boots. As silently as possible he loaded up the stove with wood, noting that not a body stirred. And he chuckled to himself, having to put his hand over his mouth for an instant.

When the chores were done in the bunkhouse, he tiptoed back to his bunk and retrieved the alarm clock. He unwrapped the bell housings and stuffed the sock under his pillow. Then he dug through his stuff, finding a spare shoelace to suffice for his intentions. Holding the clock, he wormed his way along the wooden floor of the bunkhouse until he was under his old bunk. And there he tied the alarm clock, beneath the center of the bunk, near it's head. He tied it firm, but made sure the bells had plenty of room to sound and would not be muffled by anything save for open air. And quietly as he could, he wound it full. Then he retreated, and gathering up his boots, he slipped into them near the door. It was 4:25 when he skulked across the snowy path to the kitchen, chuckling to himself. The old alarm clock was dependable. It alarmed as it was set, at 4:32 am, scaring the hell out of Helge, who awoke with a start. It alarmed and alarmed and alarmed. At first there were grumbles, growing into roars. Then the boots began to fly. As used to as they were, to Leon being in his old bunk, their aim was true and Helge began to be pummeled by heavy objects. He hollered back to no avail, and after being struck several times by missiles of considerable size and weight, scrambled to find the offending noise. He grabbed under the bed and felt all around, finding nothing within reach, for Leon had tied it up high. Finally, Helge crawled under the bunk, partly for protection, partly to find the clock. And when silence came finally, and the grumbling stopped, he had to smile to himself.

When Leon had finished his chores and the men were hard at work in the woods, he took a few minutes to return to the bunkhouse. He found his stuff back on his old bunk and atop the pile was the alarm clock, suffering no ill effects from its rousing duties. And Leon smiled. This then, was an "up" day.

After lunch, Ox Pete made a point of seeking out Leon who was in the kitchen peeling more potatoes. Leon looked up at him sullenly, then back down to his work.

"Py golly, vhat happened to yew?" he asked. Leon thought it was more abuse and didn't answer.

"I'm talking at yew, boy," insisted Pete. "Vhat happened to your face?"

"You hit me!" exclaimed Leon.

"Me?" says Pete incredulously.

"No one else," replied Leon.

"Now vhy vould I do sumptin' like dat?"

"You were drunk," answered Leon throwing a peeled potato down with force and picking up another one.

"Yass, maybe," says Pete stroking his chin and thinking about it. "Vell, vas I falling down drunk or standing up drunk?"

Leon looked at him curiously, trying to figure out his angle. Surely he must remember hitting him. He must remember singing with the oxen. Or did he?

"Falling down drunk, I'd say," he replied.

"Vell, now... dat explains it. A body can't account for everyting vhen he's falling down drunk. Vhy, I might've hit my own muther and I vouldn't have known it. It's an awful ting to be dat vay. Most folks know to leave me be, vhen I'm falling down drunk. Vhen I'm standing up drunk, I'm much sociable. But not falling down drunk."

"I'll remember," said Leon.

"Yew do dat, boy. Yew remember lots of vhat Pete says, and yew be better off."

Somehow it did make Leon feel better that Pete didn't remember hitting him. As if it was an accident, with no bad intent. But his eye blued up some after the swelling went down, and that, more than the pain, was the part unforgivable as a sign for everyone to read. He would do well to stay in camp until his normal color returned. By Wednesday of the week, it was decided that the men were working far enough away that lunch should be brought to them instead of vice versa. A wagon, on runners, was brought out for that purpose and a pair of sturdy horses supplied. It was Leon's job to see to this, aided by Joe Kinder, and in spite of the break from the usual camp chores, it was alot of work. Time was essential, as the food would cool off quickly enroute and they risked facing the wrath of hungry men.

Leon would bring the wagon around near the kitchen and the food, in large kettles, was moved directly from the stove to the wagon. The tin plates, cups and silverware were already pre-loaded so as to make haste with their precious cargo. This was the lunch meal only, the others still being provided at the cook shanty at the beginning and ending of each day. And as the weather grew gradually colder, the meals grew more substantial.

Joe Kinder carried a large triangle of iron with him to signal the lunchtime break. The lunch wagon would proceed out the same trail as was broke for the oxen hauling the loads of timber to the railway siding, and occasionally they would pass these loads. Leon was always impressed with the great heights of timber chained to these sleighs, loads seemingly impossible to move. As much as 1,000 feet to the load sometimes, Buck had said. Yet move them, the oxen did, slow and steady on roads kept slick with ice through the use of a water tank and sleigh. When the drivers would pass the lunch wagon on the way in, they would stop at the cookshanty and eat with Muggsley so as not to miss a hot meal.

Truth to tell, Leon had never really witnessed the harvesting of trees in such order of productivity before that first visit to the field. In the beginning when the men were working close to the camp, he was too busy with his own work, and getting used to camp life, to catch the feel of what they were doing. He had looked forward to that first chance to bring lunch to the men, to watch them, to see the lay of the land. And after the men had been called in, had consumed thick meat sandwiches and hearty broths of soup, and then returned to work, Leon made Joe Kinder wait.

He watched as the men went off together, and he followed them a ways until a view of the scene was his advantage. And there he sat on a stump, a mute witness to an aspect of life that too soon would fade into history.

It was Helge's crew that he watched in action, five men of similar stature and dress approaching a large towering pine. There seemed to be some discussion as to the lay of the tree, it's lean, and possible open areas toward which it should fall. Then Helge and Brent Williams stood on either sides of the towering wood, with axes of keen blades and shiny steel. Helge began the cut with a mighty swing, and Brent's followed as Helge's withdrew. In rhythm then, they continued their cuts, first one, and then the other with steady regularity until a sizable cut had been made. Then, with a large crosscut saw, they took a bite into the opposite side several inches above the low point of the first cut. The men worked the saw with the same rhythm of the axes, back and forth with strength and vigor, until the pine feels the bite and leans into it. One of the men produces a heavy steel wedge and drives it into the cut with a large sledge, making loud metal 'pings' with each stroke. As the blade is freed, it is daubed with oil and begins again, the seesaw motion. The wedge is worked along with the saw at necessary intervals, until a premonitory crack is heard. The sturdy sawyers take a final quick survey of their work, again noting the lean of the tree. Then continue with the saw until it begins to sway, and a much louder "crack" is heard, a note of finality in the life of the tree.

The men yell "timber!" together and as loud as they can muster, making the other loggers pause in their efforts to assess their safety from the falling wood. And suddenly, almost sadly, thought Leon, the huge monarch of the forest, once a hundred feet high or more, falls to the earth in a crescendo of swish, creak and crash and there it lies as the snow settles around it, a living thing no more. The men do not hesitate, bringing the saw and the axes, and a rough travois pulled by oxen. Two of the men begin to chop the limbs from the upper reaches of the fallen victim, while two others use the crosscut saw to cut it into the desired lengths. As a portion is freed, the end of it is loaded onto the travois sled with peaveys and there chained for its trip to the main sleigh trail. The oxen are encouraged in their labor, with a goad, a stick about three feet long with a sharp tack on the end. Leon noticed that some teamsters, those that he found to be mean with men as well, used the goads most freely.

At the main trail skidway, the logs are piled up, as they come in, tier upon tier by several men using a block and tackle, and oxen power to roll the logs, guiding them with peaveys and cant hooks to the top. Later, as the loading sleighs come along, the logs are piled high and chained in place for the trip to the railway siding, there to be loaded on the Pratt & Southeastern cars with the jammer.

The men did not tarry when one pine was done, but selected another and began the routine over again, pausing not, save to take a load of snuff under the lip or a pinch in the cheek and a spit or two as the work progressed. But these things were built into the rhythm and did not affect the work at hand or slow it down.

Leon tarried long watching these scenes of the American logger, until Joe Kinder called to him that he would be walking back if he did not present himself posthaste. As it was, they got a dressing down from Muggsley, who knew exactly how long it took to feed a crew and return.

And so that day, as every day, continued on with the harvesting of the Northern Wisconsin forest. One day was pretty much like another and so ran on into an endless week. Come Sunday, Leon examined his eye, which had regressed into a gentle rose color, but suffice to convince him that a stay in camp would do him no harm.

The Twentieth Chapter

Poker at Camp #7

"I think your hair would look pretty wrapped up like this," said Martha, holding it in swirls on the top of Andrea's head. "We could pin it up so you could see how it would look, sort of like the way Clara Williams wears hers when she goes to St. Paul. But you're much prettier than Clara."

Andrea moved away gently pulling her hair free, saying nothing. She went to the bedroom window and sat on the cedar chest that held her books looking out over the snow covered ground.

"I would've thought that... well," Andrea stammered, "that maybe he would have visited today." The sun was setting in the western sky, with a quickness that winter brings, and she shivered as the last tip of orange disappeared.

"Well, maybe he wanted to, but he couldn't. Maybe... maybe Mr. Peterson ...or Mr. Muggsley had him working today," offered Martha sitting down beside her.

"Maybe," said Andrea, "or maybe he visited with Mary Muggsley instead. She's much prettier than I... and ..."

"Oh, please, Andrea... Mary, Mary, quite contrary," Martha mocked in a high voice, "if I hear about our dear Miss Muggsley one more time I'll scream." It made Andrea smile to herself.

"Well, it's true. He could talk about Mary with some enthusiasm, but when he would talk to me, he 'wasn't very good with words'. Can you imagine... a writer telling you he's not very good with words. He must think I'm a perfect idiot."

"Don't be silly, Andrea, nobody's perfect," cooed Martha. Then they both giggled impulsively. When it was quiet again, Martha turned pensive and thoughtful... staring down at the floor. "Did you tell him that Mary's mother was a trollop from down at St. Paul?" she said without looking up.

"Martha!"

"Well, Amy Grant heard Mrs. Smith telling someone that she ran one of those places where the lumberjacks all go when they have some time on their hands and gold in their pockets. You know what that means. And Mary was already 4 or 5 years old when they got married... but no one knows who her father really is. Does Mr. Mancheski know all of that? Why, I heard from someone that Mrs. Muggsley still goes down there from time to time to..." She paused when she saw the look of disgust on Andrea's face. "Well, that's what I heard."

"Well, you shouldn't repeat it," said Andrea. "It's just plain mean." She turned away from Martha then, going to the dresser, picking up her hand mirror and looking at her reflection with a critical eye. Staring back at her was a lovely girl; lovely brown hair... too brown, lovely blue eyes... too blue, well formed rosy cheeks... too gaunt, full lips... too pouty, and strong nose and chin... too stark. She put the mirror back down solemnly, not at all pleased by what she had seen. Martha stood behind her and put her hands on Andrea's shoulders gently.

"If Mr. Mancheski cannot see the beauty in you, then he is as blind as the bats in his belfry," she said sincerely. "But I would not give up on him so soon. There's the Christmas party at the hall and a few Sundays before then. Who knows?"

Andrea turned into Martha's embrace and hugged her, saying, "Ya, Martha Johnson, who does know?"

"Besides," added Martha, "if he's not interested, there's always Seth Hackett. He's been in love with you since 1st grade."

"Ohhh Martha, paleaseeeee..."

Sunday at the camp, though restful, was often boring for these men of endurance. Ole Olson put out his shingle as barber for the boys and there was not just a few takers for this enterprise, some for the distraction it would bring, but then Ole was not a bad barber either. He hardly ever nipped an ear. Those waiting for haircuts were reading tattered copies of the Police Gazette, containing purported stories of real life crimes and the criminals who commit them. In spite of its dubious literary value, it was quite popular, and thus the few copies that found their way to the camp were well used.

"It says here," says Charlie, nodding toward the yellowed copy of the Police Gazette in his hands, "that most criminals return to the scene of the crime. Now why would they do that?" He looked around to see if anyone was inclined to answer.

"Why, cause they're dumb," replied Butch Akers from the designated barber chair. "That's why they're criminals, cause they're dumb." The others nodded agreement, or grunted approval at that observation.

"Never did meet an old criminal, by gad," added Louie Stuminski, from over near the stove. "Guess they either get to jail, or get kilt."

"You know, I think Louie's got sumpthin there," added Bull Finnigan. "I mean that figgers."

"Well, now, I don't know as how that figures anything," said Helge. His voice instantly got Buck's attention. "Criminals are just like any other people, I'd say. Some criminalize for awhile, then they go and do something else for awhile. Just like lumbermen."

"You saying lumbermen are criminals?" asked Louie.

"Well, some are and some ain't, I suppose," continued Helge. "Depends on the circumstances."

"Circumstances?" questioned Leon, reposing on his bunk.

"Everybody's got to do something. Some cut lumber, some deliver mail, some drive trains. Some criminalize. Like as not, they don't know what else to do at the time. Them that are good criminals don't get caught and you don't know much about 'em. They ain't in jail and they ain't dead. Just like some men are good lumbermen and some aren't."

Everyone in the room figured that they were being grouped with the 'good' lumbermen, so they smiled and nodded to one another. Helge put one foot up on a crate and started to pare an apple, the attention of the others not lost on him as the wheels turned in his brain. When he first joined in the conversation he wasn't sure where he was heading with it, but now he began to suffer from inspiration.

"Fact is," he added calmly, "that not many men are really taken to it. Lumbering, I mean. Only Swedes are born to it."

"Swedes?" questioned Bull Finnigan, standing up.

"Well, sure. Now you take Ole there," says Helge pointing at the barber in residence.

The barber looked up suddenly as if awaking from a dream. "Me?" says Ole, "I'm Norwegian."

"And not much of a logger neither," answered Helge, "that's my point. And you, Frank and Bull... not a lumberman among ya that could hold a candle to a swede. Why me and Buck could cut rings around ya any day."

"What?!?" spit out Bull. It was too much. He tackled Helge from a jump, suffering a wound from the apple knife in the process. It stopped him momentarily as he spouted: "I been stabbed!" Then he lit into Helge with a vengeance. The melee had begun and a little blood was not of importance as yet, merely stoking the fire of anger.

The new guy that had come into camp with Helge now tried to go to his rescue. A few of the other men, Charlie and Butch, jumped in to break up the fight, but got so entangled in the affair that you could no longer tell who the peacemakers were. Buck gave Leon a push, saying, "go git Ox!" and then waded into the fight, pummeling this one and that one, tossing bodies off the pile.

Leon didn't question the order, speeding out the door so fast he forgot his boots weren't on. Across the tracks he went, stumbling and shivering from the exposure of his feet to the icy path, finding Ox Pete and Muggsley in the dining room playing cribbage and having coffee.

"Bull Finnigan's been stabbed!" shouted Leon in a flurry of excitement. "He's bleedin' real bad."

"Vell, shit," exclaimed Pete. "I tink maybe dat Helge gone too far."

"How'd you know it was Helge?" asked Leon.

"Vell, shit!" said Pete again, pounding the table with his huge fist, causing coffee to erupt from the cups on the table and douse the cards as well as Muggs and Joe Kinder. Pete, paying no attention to the mess on the table, jumped up and grabbed a hold of Leon and started out the door. Leon jumped and pranced across the snowy path once more, trying to keep his feet more in the air than on the cold ground, making him seem like an excited dog dancing around stolid Pete. But the big fellow paid no attention, already building up a head of steam to confront Helge.

When they entered the bunkhouse, all was calm. Ole was cutting Bull Finnigan's hair, a towel draped over his front to catch the locks. Helge and a few of the others were gathered around a little crate upon which they were playing cards. Buck was laid out on his bunk with the Police Gazette in front of him. The others were minding their own business, mending, chawing, reading.

"Vhat's dis?" expounded Pete, his hands on his hips. "Yew, Bull, yew been stabbed?"

"Jes a little cut, Pete," replied Bull. "It was an accident. Ole put some grease on it."

"Ya sure, Bull?" pressed Pete.

"Ya... ya," he replied.

"Ok den..." He looked around the room at the silent faces of the men, finally eyeing up Helge with his face turned toward the shadows, swaying ever so slightly. The new guy was crumpled up in the corner, unconscious.

Ox Pete spit and wiped his chin. "And yew," he said pointing at Leon, "put some boots on afore yew freeze yer feet." With that he stomped out and Leon closed the door behind him.

"What happened?" he asked Buck.

"Nothin'" said Buck, shrugging his shoulders. The truth was, Buck was mad enough to bring the wrath of Pete upon Helge... but in the moments after Leon had darted out the door, he had had second thoughts. Instead, he worked his way between Helge and Bull. The fight paused then... Bull unsure of what would happen next...Helge sporting a wicked grin. And then Buck slammed his huge fist into Helge's face sending him sprawling. It was the end of the affair.

Bull had discovered shortly thereafter that instead of a puncture, the knife had grazed his side, slicing him a bit, but nothing of a serious nature. And so, Buck having quelled his own anger, and the fighting spirit of the others, suggested that they keep the affair to themselves. Those involved instantly agreed, bringing upon the scene to which Leon and Pete had burst upon.

"Ya know what you need for that cut," says Ole, "is some of that Davis Pain Killer. Best stuff you can have for an accident like that."

"Naw," replied Louie. "Some of that Great Blood and Remutis cure. I heard Matt J. Johnson himself puts it in the bottle."

"I ain't got no remustisma," says Bull. "I been cut!"

"Well, it can't hurt ya none. I know'd old Matt when he was just a simple logger like me, and he was kinda partial to the juice and the snoose. Like as not, that's what's in the Great Blood and Remutis cure. That can't be too bad."

"Spose not," observed Bull.

"Say, ya know that's what we need some of," says Butch.

"What?" asked Ole.

"Some juice. I ain't hardly had no liquor since last year. My wife brung me right to Pratt to board the train for camp making sure I wasn't likely to dawdle none at Charley's saloon."

"Now that's a job for ya," mused Helge weakly, stroking his chin. "I just might get me a saloon some day... open'er at noon or so, and set back and ring up the till. A saloon's like a magnet to most fellas... especially lumbermen. Course some lumbermen can drink, and some can't. Seems like some are born to it... like Swedes," he added, looking around to see the effect.

"Say, now don't you go starting that again," says Bull. Helge just smiled a weak smile.

"Who's yer friend, Helge... ain't heard a name for him yet?" asked Charlie. "I might not have hit him so hard had I know'd his name."

"He ain't got one," replied Helge still rubbing the bruise on his chin.

"Everyone got a name," observed Bull from the barber chair. "Even if it ain't a pretty one... still gotta call'em something."

"Well... guess he's got a name somewhere... only he don't remember it, leastwise that what he says. Seems like he just kinda woke up on the train and don't remember a thing; where he's from, where he was go'in or who he is. So he got off in Pratt and sat at Charlie's Saloon hoping it would come to him."

"But it dint?"

"Nope it didn't. He just sat there smiling. I asked him what was so funny... and he dint even know what he was smiling at. That's when Charley told me about Ed Simms and Jack Larson so I figured I'd ask him along."

"Does smile a lot, don't he?" said Bull eyeing the prostrate form of the stranger in the corner, mouth open and breathing with a slight nasal wheeze.

"Yeah... for no real purpose I can see. But he kinda took a like to me... like a stray dog and ya feed him once and next thing you know he's camping on your porch. Nice enough fella, I guess."

"Well, he gotta have a name," insisted Bull. "What if he got in the way of the 4-Spot and I wanted to warn 'em... what would I say? Hey, you there... look out? How'd he know I was talking to him?"

"Gotta have a name," agreed Ole. "It ain't natural... not having a name."

"Smith," said Louie Stuminski. "He could be a Smith I guess."

"Naw..." joined in Emil Larson, "he don't look like no smith... maybe... well, he looks like an Olafson a little."

"Olafson? Olasfson," said Ole. "Nope, it's not Olafson."

"Why don't we just let him decide for himself," opined Leon. "It is his name we're talking about."

"Cause he don't know nothing... can't remember nothing. I think he'd probably appreciate it if we helped him out a bit.... give him a name, don't you Buck?"

"Yaa... gotta have a name. Pete's gotta write it in the book. Gotta have a name."

"Well, it's settled then... we gotta find him a name," said Bull.

"How about Jack?" said Emil. "Jack Pine." The others all burst out laughing.

"Hey... that's good though... he's a lumberman now... might as well name him after timber, what'd ya think?" said Bull.

"Oak," said Ole.

"Elm," said Emil

"Maple," said Peter Sweet suddenly taking an interest. They all paused and looked at the sleeping countenance of this blonde blue-eyed stranger. His complexion seemed pasty white against the dark shadows of the corner.

"Birch," said Leon. And everyone smiled, nodding, thinking about that moniker for this fair complexioned boy.

"Birch it is," said Helge. "Smiley Birch". The others all mumbled that to themselves over and over.

"Smiley Birch," said Buck. "Maybe somebody ought to go vake ol' Smiley up and tell him somevun remembered his name for him."

Just then the train whistle could be heard coming up from the east. To all the men it was a welcome sound, even if it meant spending some time unloading stores.

"Why don't you come with these things on a work day, when the men are working anyway," said Muggsley to Alfred over coffee in the cook shanty. The men were unloading the staples and grumbling to Pete good-naturedly about all this business on a 'day off'.

"Well, I would... but Cooper, he thinks Sunday is a work day. Got me delivering to all three camps today. Says I can pretend tomorrow is Sunday and sleep in 'til 6. Not that I normally would, mind ya, but my rumetismas been bothering me terrible lately."

"Take anything for it?" inquired Muggs.

"I tried some of that Johnson Great Blood & Remutismus cure, but I think there's somethin' unnatural in it. It went through me faster than..."

"We're all done, Alfred," interrupted Helge. "You heading back to Pratt?"

"Not afore I stop at Camp 11. You didn't take them peaches now did ya? Them peaches are for Walter Benson from his folks."

"Were there peaches?" probed Helge.

"Never you mind," replied Alfred.

"Say, you been to Camp 7 today, anything going on?"

"Just the usual poker game. Elmer sets 'em up in the cook shanty on Sunday as nice as ya please. Says it keeps 'em out of mischief. Some of them camp 11 boys are there too."

"Well, that's just the ticket, Alfred. Mind if some of the boys and me tag along with ya back to the switch... we'll walk from there."

"Suit yourself. I gotta get going though. If you ain't ready when I get the engine turned around and headed east, I'm going anyway."

There were seven men, including Leon, that decided to head for the poker table at camp 11. Buck wasn't inclined to go, not being much of a gambling man, but they wanted an even seven, for luck, and persuaded him by saying where there was poker, there was liable to be whiskey as well. It made sense to Buck, so he joined in. Also with Helge and Leon, there were Bull Finnigan, Louie Stuminski, Emil Larson and Smiley Birch now awake and feeling his aches. A hand to draw to, for sure.

And so the men gathered in the supply car, the caboose not being attached for the supply run, and huddled in the leeward corner while the engine pulled them on. And though the cold wind found them, it could not damper their enthusiasm. It did seem to quiet them some, however, at least for the duration of the trip. At the switch point, they were still about a mile from camp 7, so as the engine slowed almost to a stop, Helge jumped out of the supply car and joined Alfred at the engine. In a few minutes he was back.

"This is as far as he's gonna go," he said climbing back aboard.

"Then what you getting on for?" asked Louie.

"I think I forgot something," answered Helge, rummaging through some parcels. "You boys go ahead and wave 'em on. I'll be right along."

Alfred was already backing down the trackway to camp 11 when Helge jumped off the supply car and climbed back up the bank to the tracks. He had a bag with him, a bag they all knew he hadn't brought aboard with him.

"So what's in the bag, Helge?" questioned Leon.

"A little insurance," he replied, and offered nothing more.

Camp 7 had changed quite readily from the camp Leon and Buck had seen on their first trip out to the camps. No more was it in the shadow of pines, the land around having been stripped back by the logging harvest. The camp was on a spur jutting north of the main track on a gentle slope. The men could see the welcome signs of smoke from the chimneys as they walked up the spur, jingling of money and expectations. They bothered not with the other buildings, picking out the cookshanty and converging on it almost in a bunch. They were so eager there was a tussle on who would get through the door first, but Bull Finnigan, having a slight lead, was squeezed through by default. The room was smoke filled and ringing with rowdiness and laughter. There were about fifteen men there and even when they spied the newcomers, the play was not interrupted.

"Hi Buck," greeted Elmer Rose upon seeing the men. "Come to try your luck, eh... well the boys could use some new money around here, that's for sure. But you'll be lucky to wrangle in."

"Hah! Two Pair!" said a rough looking man that Buck didn't recognize. And while the others groaned aloud, he hauled the pot in across the table.

"What's that, Elmer?" said George Gottley through teeth clenched around a cigar. "Got a few neophytes waiting to deposit some money in the bank of George?" A few of the men chuckled but a few just grumbled 'deal the cards, George'.

"Say, who you calling neofighters," complained Bull. "We don't want no trouble... jes lookin' for some poker, that's all."

"Well, boys, you come to the right place... but we haven't the room for ya, now," said George. "Could be in a couple of hours or so, I'll be sending these puppys home with only lint left in their pockets. But 'til then, why I dunno."

"We have enough for two games here," offered Helge. "What say we split up, so we have a few of us at each table." The men playing poker all looked at one another and then one by one into the money before them. All save George were fighting a losing battle at the game.

"What'll ya say, Elmer?" asked one of the players.

"Fine by me. But keep it honest... and no trouble!" admonished Elmer. It seemed to Leon that the last remark was addressed mainly in Helge's direction.

In a brief time there were two games going, with all of the boys from Camp 9 involved except for Buck who was sulking in the corner with Elmer, who had explained to him there was not a drop of whiskey to be had, not even of the 'medicinal' variety.

Then too, there were almost as many on-lookers as there were players. At Leon's table, there was Smiley Birch and Emil Larson from Camp 9, three men from Camp 7 and one from Camp 11. He was introduced to the rest but almost immediately forgot their names, being so enthused about the game. It was his thought that poker was one of the few things that he was good at, having learned the expensive way among his friends in Chicago. But then, each man that plays, figures that he is good at it some time or another. The proof most often is in the pocket at the end of the night.

Helge and Bull joined three fellows from Elmer's camp, including the one named George, and two others from Camp 11. When all was said and done, Louie managed to convince 4 other fellows that there was room for a third game and they waited only until another deck of cards was found, noting it was missing the jack of clubs but electing to proceed anyway. And then the serious business began.

Poker in a lumber camp, though certainly a social endeavor, is indeed a serious business. Cheaters are most unwelcome and roughly handled in the best of situations. Talking is tolerated to a certain extent, unless it leans toward distraction. Spittoons are gathered around the fringes of the participants, as snoose is conducive to heavy thought and clever playing... but often it is only chance that the spittle actually hits this target. Several participants seeking the joys of tobacco but disdaining the use of snoose, expertly rolled cigarettes from fine papers and coarse tobacco, accounting for the layered levels of smoke hanging in the stagnant air and settling on their clothes. Leon thought it a welcome change from the usual bunkhouse smells. Alcohol was scarce, and down right discouraged by camp boss's, accounting for little actual bloodshed during these games. Still, with money at stake, there was a propensity for seriousness at the table.

Helge Johnson was running short of money in no little time, due primarily to a shortage of funds to begin with as well as basic flaws in his betting philosophy. This, however, he did not immediately let on to, preferring instead to feign thirst and set aside his cards in search of good cold water. As he temporarily retired from the table, he carried his sack with him and after his cool drink, sat amongst the observers chatting amiably. Reaching into the bag casually, he withdrew a round fruit and bit voraciously into it, emitting spurts of juice from around his lips.

"Peaches!" somebody yelled. And those not holding cards, gathered around.

"You got more peaches in that bag?" someone asked.

"Oh, a few," answered Helge slyly. "They're kinda hard to come by out here, ya know, especially these fresh juicy ones."

He took another bite and dribbled more juice for effect.

"I love peaches more than anything," said a young man from camp 11. "Do you think you could spare one or two? I can pay."

"Well, I don't know," teased Helge, "these are special peaches sent to me from my dear family in St. Paul. It wouldn't seem right to sell them too cheap."

"I understand," nodded the youngster.

"On the other hand, if I eat all these peaches, I'll be proper sick. And if I don't eat them, they'll go bad. Sooo, I guess I could part with a couple for... oh, say, a dollar a piece." Most men groaned or chuckled then walked away. For most of them, that was a day's wage for one peach. Helge took another bite, then chewed seductively around the pit.

"Mister, I'll take two of them peaches," said the youngster.

"Guess I'll have me one, anyway," said another. And a few more coughed up the required funds until Helge had enough money to re-enter the game. He sat back down in his chair as if he had just stepped out for fresh air.

"I knew Walter would have to have one," said a man at the table. "That boy is just crazy about peaches. Keeps trying to get his family to send him some from St. Paul. Imagine, a dollar for a peach."

"Imagine that," replied Helge.

"Got any left?"

"Nope."

"Well, not that I would have paid a dollar for a peach anyway."

And the day wore on. Money exchanged hands quite readily for a while, making piles dwindle and grow from time to time. At Helge's table however, George was losing... and was not happy about it. Bull was winning, and was delighted. Bull was also more than happy to announce his mounting success quite frequently.

At another table, Leon was holding his own, staying a little ahead of his original investment, money he had borrowed from Joe Kinder. It was partly his planning, holding back until the time was ripe and the pot was full, and partly because his cards were not quite worthy of more success. But luck sometimes comes to he who waits.

"I'll bet five dollars," said Smiley Birch with less than a poker face smile. Three men called, two dropped out up to Leon.

"Hmmm, I'd more than swear that's a bluff," Leon said soberly. "I ain't losing this hand to hot air."

"So call or bet," pushed Smiley.

"Well... I'll see your five and bet five more," he said pushing the money out to the center. Smiley's smile never faltered. Reaching into his pocket, he set out a ten dollar gold piece.

"Your five, and five more," he said. The others re-examined their hands, searching for more cards than they had. Two more men dropped out, leaving Smiley, Leon and someone from Camp 11 named Paul. Paul only called and it was back to Leon.

"Well, if you've a better hand, it's time to prove it," he said. "I'll bet..." he paused and looked down at his dwindling pile of money. "I'll call your bet and raise... three more dollars." There was just three dollars and change in front of the Smiley as well.

"I'll just call," he said. "What'd ya have?"

"Wait a minute there boys... there's still three players in this game," said Paul. "I'll call that little bet and raise twenty dollars on the nose. Either call or shut up." The other two were stunned. In sizing up each other they had forgotten about the third man.

"Twenty dollars? I don't have twenty dollars," said Leon.

"Not my problem," said Paul. "Call or fold."

Leon looked around the room for friendly rich faces and settled on Bull. He was the only one likely to have twenty dollars on him at this point. Leon looked at his hand again and was relieved to see the three aces and two fives were still there.

"Hey Bull, can you loan me twenty dollars on account?" he yelled.

"On account've he ain't got no money," said one of the other players to rings of laughter. It was likely that Leon wasn't going to get it, until George added his own little jab of 'stop chattin' like women and play cards'. Bull looked at him squarely, and then counted out the money from his stash at the table.

"On account," said Bull. Leon passed the money from Bull's hand to the pot. It was now up to Smiley. He too, re-examined his hand, the grin still emplaced on his face. It was a flush. A pretty red flush with a king high. He seemed to falter only a second, then reached deep into his pockets and came up with a shiny twenty dollar gold piece, dropping it heavily on the table with a clunk.

"Well, I'll be damned," muttered Paul. He turned over his hand and Leon nearly let out a gasp. Three queens there were, and two tens. But it seemed to Leon for a second, as if there was four queens. The grin faded from Smiley's face briefly, but Paul was chagrined to see Leon all aglow.

"Full house, aces up," he cried. But before he could even gather in his winnings, trouble erupted at Bull and Helge's table. It had been building for some time as Bull was not a gracious winner. He gloated, he flaunted the money by playing with it and counting it and he laughed much too loud. Helge was about broke and disenchanted with his attempts to reap the profits he had imagined, so once again he leaned towards trouble, courting it with some amusement. He fired up George every chance he got.

Leon had no idea what was coming. He was so involved in playing out his own hand he hadn't heard the raised voices and the angry taunts. The word 'cheater' hadn't taken hold of his ears like the warning it should have. So as Leon leaned forward with the glint of gold in his eyes, the table in back of him erupted in a frenzy of money and fighting bodies. The fray was growing by the moment, as the punches landed carelessly on the uninvolved, and swept the entire room into turmoil. Leon's own table collapsed as two bodies landed upon it wrapped in struggle. It was all Leon could do to scramble on the floor searching for his hard won pot and in the end his hand clutched only the twenty dollar gold piece before he, too, was caught up in the bedlam.

After several futile minutes of dodging swinging fists, he suddenly felt himself lifted to his feet, and found Buck pushing him toward the door. By the time Leon found himself outside, the others were already running down the spur, Bull clutching a fistful of dollars and shouting insults at the men back at the shanty. Leon turned around to thank Buck for getting him out of there, to discover a hoard of people scrambling to their feet and heading toward them with ill intent. When he turned back, Buck himself was making tracks up the spur and Leon, too, followed that discretion as quickly as he could.

Feeling the weight of the twenty dollar gold piece in his pocket as they were walking along, already far from Camp 7, Leon suddenly wondered to himself how Smiley Birch had come to have so much gold in his pockets.

"Where'd you get these gold pieces," he asked, fingering the one in his pocket and looking at Smiley.

"Gold pieces?" asked Helge.

"Yeah... Smiley kept throwing 'em in the pot. Must have had a few..."

"And me buying you drinks at Charley's," sighed Helge. "Where'd you get the gold, Smiley boy?"

"Found it," he replied softly.

"Found it? Where?" questioned Leon.

"In my pockets," he said soberly. "It was just in my pockets when I woke up on the train."

"Wish I had pockets like that," mused Helge. "Mine just got holes in 'em."

It was a merry band that stumbled and laughed their way along the miles of track back to Camp 9. Bull had high praise for Helge, who apparently had diverted a near lethal blow with a cast iron pot meant for him. The others chuckled like schoolboys about this punch or that. Oddly, the only one who suffered any noticeable bruise, was Leon. His face hit a chair when the table collapsed and brought them all down. It was the other eye, for a time giving him the look of a raccoon, and keeping him in camp yet another weekend. To add insult to injury, Bull claimed the shiny twenty-dollar gold piece he had scrambled for, as payment for his loan on account. And in Camp 9 the fracas grew in ponderous proportions until the seven men suffered near death, and Leon's black eye became a badge of honor. Just the boost the camp needed at that time of the year. It would do well to stay away from Camp 7 for a while, however.

The Twenty First Chapter

Ꝺays of winter fun

There were many places along the rise of land where the Town of Pratt was situated that were well suited for winter sliding, but none more so than the north road. After all, the trail was graded and already cleared and packed by wagon and horse traffic. However, due to the occasional vehicle and the remote chance of an express train coming through it was often discouraged by the town constable and other elders.

Though the children of Pratt most often started their sliding fun on the North road, when they were forced to evacuate they moved west along the bluff to a spot where rain water runoff had cut a gouge in the bank, offering a rather fast and steep course but with a long landing area at the bottom. At times, when the trail was packed and on a good run, the sled would make it all the way to the tracks. The children of Pratt would often gather in groups in the winter months, as if by some in-borne instinct, all seeming to come together as if called. Sliding equipment ranged from store bought sleds, to crude homemade affairs, or merely smooth boards from packing crates. Any vehicle, any size or description, as long as it would slide on packed snow.

Joe Johnson stood on the north road hill where Superior Avenue joined it from the west, near the Straddle Creek Lumber Co. office, and gazed over the terrain below. Images of the last horrific ride by the Pirates of Pratt on Halloween night flashed through his mind and he grinned. Now that was a glorious ride if ever there was one, especially so since no one got killed.

Joe had with him a pair of homemade skis that Emil had fashioned from good yellow birch, soaking them in boiling water and patiently working a bend in them. The bottoms were waxed and smooth. But Joe and the skis made an odd pair, the skis being almost twice as tall at 10 feet in length. Robert and Henry Walden appeared on the scene just as Joe was considering launching a slide down the hill. They "hulloed" from nearly a block away, and broke into a run when they recognized Joe, so he waited until the boys drew up panting. It was a good day for a slide, the sky clear and brilliantly blue. The temperature had an edge to it that turned cheeks rosy before too long, but stiffened the snow and made it squeak. All the boys had woolen mittens on, and caps with earflaps, woolen trousers and boots. Henry's pants were being held up with a rope in lieu of a belt, but effectively all the same.

"'member that ride on Halloween, Joe?" gushed Robert.

"Yeah," sighed Joe. "There was hell to pay that night."

"Mamma says we're not supposed to say 'hell'," joined in Henry.

"Shut up, Henry," said Robert shaking his head. "Yeah, Joe... some hell to pay, alright. Pa nearly whipped my hide. Nobody told about the wagon, but plenty guessed about it, I'd say. Like Ma said, it did sound like sumpthin' that we'd do."

"Cause we're the wild Pirates of Pratt," beamed Joe. "Why, if this was a hunert years ago, I betcha we'd a been real pirates, and fair successful too."

"Yeah," said Robert.

"Yeah," repeated Henry.

"You?" challenged Robert. "A real pirate?"

"Hell, I even bled all over, remember?" smiled Henry.

"Yeah," agreed Joe. "Henry'd make a great pirate, alright. He was bleedin' like a stuck pig." And Henry smiled until his face hurt where the cold wind had tightened his skin.

"Well, matey's, time for a ride," said Joe. He put the skis close together and sat on them, his feet to either side dug in to prevent a premature start. He looked behind him, and saw no one, and in front, the same, so he pushed off. The skis were made well and slick, and Joe had a swift start. Down the hill he went with only a slight element of control over his destination and speed, that through the use of his feet. After a quick, slick ride through wagon wheel ruts and bumps, he skillfully abandoned the trail when the Wheeler's wagon turned onto the north road from the west. In a flurry of exploding snow he violated the smooth untouched surface of the right hand ditch leaving the skis behind and breaking trail with his tumbling body. It was a relatively tame landing for a wild pirate and Joe soon dug the snow out of his hat and mittens and boots and retrieved his skis. Never one to miss an opportunity, he quickly put the skis back on the road facing up the hill and grasping a hold of the back of the wagon, was pulled ever so slowly back up the path.

Mr. Wheeler was aware of this practice, of hitching a ride, and didn't discourage it. He thought it showed ingenuity. "But that Johnson kid," he said to himself, "one of these days will take a chance too many and end up with broken bones. Like as not, however, it won't slow him down terribly much."

Robert and Henry were waiting for the Wheeler wagon to pass before attempting a slide and were delighted to see Joe wobbling, weaving and waving from the rear end of the vehicle when it approached. By that time there were several other pirates and Pratt children about, most of which were heading for the cut in the bank to the west. Joe greeted the other kids with a grin of rosy cheeks.

It was Robert's turn now. Robert and Henry had one sled between them, an older brother's hand-me-down. It was sturdy with metal runners, but had a proclivity for steering to the right of it's own accord. Robert sat on the sled and put his feet in the steering holes, holding the rope in his mittened hands, while Henry knelt behind him, putting his hands on Robert's shoulders for balance.

"Move up, Robert, I ain't hardly on, yet," whined Henry.

"Awww, let me go alone the first time, Henry."

"Ma says we gotta share!" Henry reminded him.

"Awww gee."

"I'll push ya," offered Joe. And quite before the Walden boys were ready, he did. And off they went, a scramble and scream of rocketing youth weaving down the trail. Joe laughed out loud.

"Gee, I wish I had a sled," said a weak voice from behind Joe. It was Muff Brown's youngest, a slight built boy named Billy. He was wrapped in a coat just a little too small, and no hat was upon his head, nor gloves upon his hands shoved deep within his pockets.

"Hiya Billy," greeted Joe warmly. "How come you're out and about? I thought your Pa made you work all the time."

"Pa's gone to Ashland this mornin'. Ma says we should go out and play some, but be back afore Pa."

"You don't have no sled, Billy?"

"Naw... Pa says we ain't got no money for tomfoolery. You think sleds are tomfoolery Joe?"

"Tomfoolery? Why, they're a down right necessity in winter. You can do all sorts of things with sleds and sliding things. Ya can haul wood better on a sled, and water, and go places faster. There's a hunert reasons to have a sled."

"How come you don't have one, then?"

"Why, I coulda had one. But these skis are faster for sliding down the hill. I expect maybe I'll get a sled pretty soon, though, maybe for Christmas this year."

"Really?"

"Why sure. Maybe Santa Claus will bring you one too, now that ya know ya need one."

"I dunno. Pa says Santa Claus ain't likely to stop by our place this year. Says he don't like miscreants like us," Billy said sadly. "Joe? What's a miscreant anyway?"

"Awww... I think it's someone who don't believe in Santa Claus, maybe."

"I believe in 'em, Joe, honest!"

"Then ya ain't a miscreant no more," smiled Joe. "Say, ya wanta slide with me, Bill?"

"Gees, can I?"

"Sure! These skis are near 10 feet long. I could slide a passel of kids, if I was a mind to. C'mon!"

Joe lined up the skis and got Billy situated with the briefest of instructions: "Don't fall off". As Joe settled in, he noticed Robert and Henry tugging the sled back up the hill, pushing and arguing along the way.

"Hey Robert!" shouted Joe. "It's me and Billy Brown." With that, he shoved off with a grunt, settling in behind Billy.

Joe soon discovered that in view of Billy's lack of sledding experience, he should have provided a few more instructions. From the start, they were in trouble. Billy couldn't keep the balance required and weaved from side to side as they took the bumps and occasionally his feet would stray to the side and catch the snow, making the skis careen a bit out of control by the time they hit the tracks. The bump of the track crossing was too much and the skis started to separate. Joe, trying to save the day, jerked his foot on the right ski trying to bring it back in line. Instead, it caused them to careen wildly off to the left, completely out of control. The move left was so sudden, however, that the Walden boys didn't anticipate it and with a sudden shock, they saw that the rolling ball of arms and legs and skis was about to crash into them. No one was hurt, though snow found it's way into every possible crevice in the boy's winter wear. They all stood up laughing and screaming and shaking snow from their clothes.

"Geez, Joe, ya nearly kilt us," laughed Robert.

"Yeah... I think this thing needs work," replied Joe shaking snow out of his mittens.

"Work?" exclaimed Henry, "It needs a steering wheel!"

The blacksmith shop was the nearest refuge for the youngsters after a decision was made to warm the frosted parts of their bodies. It was the first building west of the north road crossing on the north side of the tracks and was also substituting now as a "garage" for the few automobiles that were to be found in Pratt. Jack Bender was the owner/blacksmith/mechanic in residence and he had a warm fire aglow in the stove in the back of the shop. The kids greeted him by name, one by one saying, "hi Jack" as they came in through the door. He barely acknowledged the boys as they sauntered over to the stove and started to remove their outer clothing. He was busy with some engine parts, immersing them in kerosene and scrubbing them lightly with a brush, stopping to peer closely at them from time to time. He was a big man and bewhiskered to such an extent that his most memorable feature was his dark brown eyes staring out from his hairy face. He was a single man, by preference, and not one to lean toward conversation unless absolutely necessary. Mostly he replied with grunts and nods when people requested service.

The boys scattered out articles of clothing around the stove, hoping for a quick dry, but willing to settle for a damp warm if the need be.

"We need some ways to keep the skis together," remarked Joe offhandedly. "They gotta be goin' the same way."

"I wish there was a seat," added Billy, "so's all of me would stay on."

"It needs a steering wheel," reminded Henry

"Maybe it should have brakes," suggested Robert and all the boys laughed.

"We always stop sooner or later," added Joe, bringing more laughter.

Jack Bender gave the impression of ignoring their chatter, going about his business as if they weren't even there, but he did take notice. He took notice of Billy Brown. He knew who he was, who his Pa was, and he was a little surprised that he was able to join this bunch, these pirates, as he heard them refer to themselves. His big heart found pity for youth so restrained.

"Can we borrow a hammer?" asked Joe after the boys had decided on a course of action. Jack stood and wiped his hands on a rag.

"A hammer? For what?"

"We need to make some adjustments," explained Joe. "To my skis. We're gonna nail 'em together."

"Eh? I dunno. Them skis are yer Pa's ain't they? Does he know about them adjustments?"

"Well, I..."

"You better talk to yer Pa about that. Then you can use all the tools I got, if ya need to."

"Thanks, Mr. Bender. I will. I'll talk to Pa tonight maybe."

"Hrmmph," grunted Jack, then turned back to his work.

The boys continued their sliding routine most of the day, trading off rides on the skis and the sleds, frolicking in the snow and delighting in the speed attained going down the hill, in spite of some not-so-glorious endings. When the afternoon train whistled its approach, Billy Brown lit out of there like a house on fire.

It was another Sunday in camp and Leon was getting restless. Helge and a few others had chanced another poker visit to camp 7, but Buck and Leon and even Bull declined the adventure, and the walk.

Leon lay on his bunk drifting in and out of sleep as the day wore on. It was the dreamy sleep of a person seeking relief from the drudgery of life he had found himself thrust into. Now and again he would slip into consciousness, hearing the talk and tales of the other woodsmen confined to the bunkhouse realm on this brisk day of early December.

"Vell, I spose Vhiskey is ok on days like this, to kinda kindle the heart and sooth the nerves," says one lumberman philosophically. "But on a day, hot in July, dusty and miserable, vith no vind atall, kinda still like and yust hanging on ya so's ya kin hardly breathe. Vell, den, dere's beer. Cold, cold beer. Nothing like it... nothing better... not vhiskey or rum or dem fancy brandies and sissy sweet stuffs. Yust beer... cold, cold beer. Man, I kin drink me a barrel of it in July."

It was kind of a long soliloquy, for a lumberman, and the rest of the men pondered long and hard on the words.

"What kind of beer?" pondered Bull.

"Vhy, any kind vould do," returned the lumberman. "But real, real cold, like a January day on the Namakagon and the fish ain't bitin'. Dat cold.

"Oh, I like beer well enough," says Emil Larson. "But I like it made nearby. I like it made with good branch water. That's where the cold comes from."

"That so?" says Bull. "There's a Pratt beer?"

"Well, none to speak of," admitted Emil, "but Ashland's got some fine stuff that must be made with branch water. I remember last Spring when we came outa the woods, ol' Charley couldn't keep a keg tapped on accounta we was draining 'em so fast. Good local Ashland beer!"

"Pratt's got whiskey, though," says Bull. "Mr. Poppy's own brew. Bibon brandy some call it. Not bad either, but kinda sneaks up and knocks your legs out from under ya, if yer not careful. Ask ol' Muggs about Poppy's brew!"

"Vish I had me some of Poppy's stuff," says Buck wistfully. "Yust a little... vell, maybe not so little." The others laughed.

Leon made a mental note to bring Buck a bottle of whiskey when next he visited Pratt. Next Sunday, perhaps. Maybe he would saunter in and have another bath at the Hotel... buy some cigars, smell some other smells... have another talk with Cooper about the ways of the world. Maybe run into Miss Muggsley. Miss Muggsley of the golden curls and winning smile. Why, the Christmas party... must find out about the Christmas party that Mary spoke of. She invited him, she certainly had. Hope it's on a Saturday night.

That settled it. He had to get to town to find out about that Christmas party. Wonder if Andrea is going to go. Why sure, she'd be there. Her father would play the fiddle, her mother probably baking pies and cakes. And mistletoe. Somebody would bring mistletoe for sure. Kisses, sweet kisses, from rosy lips. But he was near a stranger... no one kisses strangers even under mistletoe. But not to Andrea... he wasn't a stranger to Andrea... he ate dinner at her home, he works with her brother. No stranger at all.

"Hey! Chore boy!" intruded the voice of Bull Finnigan. "What you smiling at?"

K. Wallin

The Twenty Second Chapter

Another visit to town

Leon looked forward to those trips to the men in the woods, bringing them a moderately hot lunch. He learned to keep a few items on hand to further ingratiate himself to these hardy men; tobacco, peppermints, an extra pair of gloves. It was not his intent to "buy in" to the kinship of the woodsmen... but he sincerely felt in awe of their long hours and arduous labor.

He noticed at times that some of the men suffered hurts of various origins; a sprained ankle, bruised legs and hands, frozen fingers. But he never heard one complain... in the woods. In the bunkhouse it was different. Men would go on about their ills and woes for hours, both imagined and real. Leon determined it was more for conversation sake than actual complaint. And wisely enough, no grumbling ever intentionally reached the ears of Ox Pete.

But with all the admiration he had found for the durability and general character of the lumberjacks, he was slowly becoming aware of the devastation wrought by their great work. The forest fell before them, day by day, leaving cleared acres of slashing's; those remaining unusable limbs of logs and debris. It was what he imagined war to be like, after the battle, after the cannons had worked the ground leaving no salvageable remains of the opposing force, their weapons, their horses, their men. He had heard stories of such things, what battle wrought during the War Between the States. But perhaps that was the necessary way of those conflicts. Destroy one thing to preserve another. It was beyond his grasp to understand or contradict the philosophy of war. But the devastation of the forest was another matter. What nature had created and preserved, what strength had long endured, now fell to the woodsmen's ax and saw in total capitulation. Perhaps it was because he was not born a woodsmen and had not led the woodsmen's life, but little by little, as the axes bit into the sturdy pine and hardwoods, the thought of it bit into his soul.

Through the next week, Mr. Mancheski was somewhat content. He had plans for Sunday... and not staying in camp no matter what the weather would bring. He would ask Buck if he wanted to tag along; Buck was always good company on a traipse through the woods. He would offer to try to bring back the most recent copies of the Police Gazette, the Svenka Post, the Bayfield County Press and the Ashland Press, and any other magazines, books and papers he could find. With the cold settling in, the men in the bunkhouse at night were a restless lot and needed what entertainment they could get. It was no wonder, thought Leon, why the breakup of the camps in the Spring could cause such an uproar in the saloons and bordellos up and down the Chicago & Northwestern line.

And so it was, that on that Sunday in December, not three weeks from Christmas and in the presence of a delightfully warm winter day, Leon and Buck headed down the track line to the Namakagon road and north to Pratt.

Leon did his best to try to convince Buck of the merits of a warm soothing tub bath at the hotel. Buck at first smiled patronizingly at him and nodded politely where an answer had been expected, but was not convinced just the same. He did allow as how he would be content to converse with Leon while he was in the tub... and wait for him to cleanse himself of the odoriferous tapestry of camp smell. After all, it was early in the day... even Charley's saloon was not yet open for business.

After breakfast at the restaurant, which was magnanimously charged to Leon's account with Cooper, the men headed for the hotel. While Leon languished in the steaming tub, and an oily scum began to replace the soapy surface of the water, Buck leaned back in a chair and loaded up with snoose. He even had the good sense to pull a spittoon close so he didn't have to expend too much energy in spitting.

"Ya know, Buck, I can see where this camp life could wear thin on a man. Too many hours, too many men in close quarters for too many months."

"Yaa, I spose. Sometimes I think it's not so bad, den sometimes I think, maybe I vill do udder things. Like on railroad, maybe."

"Well, that's not what I had in mind, really. I've seen them boys work a fair piece too, unless you mean driving the train. Now that can't be too hard... it's not like you can steer it anyplace or anything."

"Hah! Dat ain't vork at all."

"Anything you get paid for, is work," allowed Leon. "If you get paid for thinking, then that's work. Some men do better at thinking than at working. I know, now, having spent just a couple of months in the woods, that I could never be a lumberjack. I just don't have the spirit for it."

"Yaa. No spirit, nor no gumption neither. You're right vhen yew say it's hard vork. And I think, tu, vhile I am vorking, I think about alot of things. But I am not paid for thinking them things." He leaned a little to the left and let some spittle fall from his mouth into the spittoon.

"Well, I didn't mean..." started Leon a little disturbed by that gumption comment.

"I think about my fadder and how he vorks so hard on farm, for so little. About my mudder who vorks hard too... about Yoseph, who vill be vorking too, someday. I think this America is fine country... but sometimes I think like you say; dat some men get money for thinking... and is usually thinking how they can take money away from those that are vorking. I think about this lots of time.

"Well, Buck, I suppose you're right," said Leon pensively. "I never really thought about it like that. But Cooper's a thinking man and he seems square enough."

"Square, yaa," agreed Buck. "But is all his money. God make the trees, Buck Yohnson cuts them down, Alfred hauls them to the mill and Cooper puts money in his pocket and buys good cigars."

"Yeah," mused Leon.

"But Cooper, is a square man. He's ban very gude to the Yohnsons."

"He's been very good to me, too," observed Leon.

"Yaa."

Leon sunk lower in the tub and fell into thought, surprised that Buck could provide such food for his thinking. Later when he was dressed in clothes lacking the familiar smells, he decided to put off the heavy thinking until later, concentrating instead on Mary Muggsley and plans for a Christmas party that he was not apt to miss. He separated from Buck, then, to seek out on his own this vision of loveliness that should be leaving church any minute.

"Excuse me, Miss Muggsley, could you spare a moment to talk?"

"Mr. Mancheski! What a pleasant surprise. It's so nice to see you in town again."

"Thank you," he gushed, suddenly remembering to remove his hat. "I was wondering if you could elaborate on that Christmas party you spoke of. I would certainly be interested in attending such an affair."

"Why certainly," she smiled. "It's at the Modern Woodmen hall of course, and everyone will be there. There will be plenty to eat and drink and music and dancing. It will be absolutely splendid." Leon followed her bright blue eyes as she spoke, his ears lost somewhere in the melody of her voice. So there was a pause after she stopped speaking, when Leon just plumb forgot to respond.

"Mr. Mancheski?"

"Oh...oh, yes... it does sound splendid. I was wondering... when the party would be. What day, to be exact, and what time a person should be there."

"Oh, of course. This Saturday night at 6:00 pm it is, though doubtless I will have to be there at 5:00 to help with the preparations. These town affairs depend so much on our help, my mother and I, and for guidance as to what is right and socially acceptable. Mother spends alot of time in Minneapolis, with the right people, if you know what I mean. And I go there quite often myself."

"Saturday is perfect," he replied. "I'll be there for sure. We don't work on Sundays you know, the whole day off."

"Yes, I know."

"Well..."

"I hope you won't let me down, Mr. Mancheski... I hope you will indeed attend our Christmas party."

"Well...of course..."

"A couple of weeks ago you invited me to the camp for Thanksgiving, but then you went off someplace else and left me with the rest of those dreadfully mannered men. I was very disappointed not to see you there. Very disappointed." Her sunny smile retreated behind a cloudy frown.

"Well I... I... Mr. Cooper and I... we were invited to the Johnson's for dinner. I didn't really want to go... but I felt I owed it to Mr. Cooper. He's been very good to me."

"I see... you'd rather spend an evening with those Johnson girls than with me... why Mr. Mancheski... I just..."

"No... no it's not that. Gee, Mary, I'd rather be with you than anybody else, really!"

"Really?" She tested.

"Really," he said. And then she knew that he was in the right frame of mind for anything she might think of, anything that might help her with her own personal plans. Both of them stammered about unimportant things for awhile, noting the condition of the weather on at least two occasions. Finally, growing cold, Mary suggested that they walk along and so they did, continuing their idle chatter.

Andrea had hoped yet again that Mr. Mancheski would have found a reason to visit the Johnson farm on a Sunday. But Sunday was here and Leon was not. Though Martha often tried to convince her of her natural attractions and an interest showed by the boy, Andrea was convinced that she had made no impression at all. As a diversion, Martha suggested they take a sleigh ride into town and look over the Modern Woodman hall for Christmas decorating ideas. Joe insisted on coming along... to protect them if necessary from awful men and thieves, and so the three slid merrily along the road to Pratt, it being a slightly longer and more wandering journey than the railroad line.

It was a wonderful day for a sleigh ride. And listening to the jangle of the bells on ol' Jess and being so close to Christmas, brought a cheery euphoria to the riders. Soon they began to sing... first Martha with a strong clear soprano voice, singing a sprightly Christmas tune. Then Joe, whose voice cracked on occasion, but whose enthusiasm for life never wavered... and finally Andrea, caught up in the mood of the moment and storing her moody thoughts for reflection at a later time.

They passed the Gustavel farm and waved vigorously to the children in the yard. And more houses as they got closer to town. And finally, along the village streets of Pratt, where the greetings were more numerous and gay... waves and jubilant shouts of 'Merry Christmas', warm and sincere.

They were standing outside the hall when they first saw Mary Muggsley and Leon strolling down 2nd Avenue. Truth to tell, Mary was growing weary of his company, but upon seeing the Johnson girls, picked up her smile once more as well as her step, not wanting to miss them.

"Oh, my goodness... it's... it's... him," said Andrea putting Martha between her and the oncoming couple. "Ohhh! And walking with Mary Muggsley... don't that just beat all?"

"Pay no attention to them, Andrea," replied Martha. "We'll just ignore them when they pass by."

"No, no... let's get in the hall before they get here."

"Who?" asked Joe, kinda lost from the conversation.

Andrea tried to get around Martha to move toward the hall door, but Joe was in the way and they fumbled and danced for a moment, with Joe still confused as to what was happening.

"It's, too late, it's too late, their waving," cried Martha. Andrea rolled her eyes, then tried to form a smile as sweet as could be mustered under the circumstances. And so they waved back weakly, and waited for their fate.

"Well, Martha and Andrea Johnson, don't you two look just delightful with the rose in your cheeks," gushed Mary.

"Hello, Mary, Mr. Mancheski," nodded Martha. "It's nice to see you again."

"What brings you to town this time of day? It's not often we get to see you both, and so prettily dressed," she added with sinister charm. Andrea was suddenly aware of the state of her clothes, imagining wrinkles and stains, though they were free from both. And suddenly, her dress was rather drab, she thought.

"Kind of you to say," replied Andrea politely, her eyes avoiding Leon's. "About our pretty dresses, I mean."

"We're here to look at the hall, to get some ideas for decorating for the Christmas party," jumped in Martha.

"Yes, I was just telling Mr. Mancheski about the party, the food and the music. Why, he's made me promise to save him a million dances. I told him there were so many others that it may be difficult... but I shall try." Leon started to color, finding his collar a little tight at the throat. He started to say something, opened his mouth and made stuttering sounds... but nothing substantial came out.

"Well, how wonderful for you, Mary... all that dancing... such a wonderful way to exercise and wear off those extra Christmas pounds," chided Andrea in a tone reminiscent of Mary herself.

"Well... uh... I mean, I like to dance, but I don't need to dance. Oh, you know what I mean," she stammered. "You don't think I need to dance, do you Mr. Mancheski?"

"Sure," he said missing the point.

"You do? Well!"

"No... no I mean...well, I'm not sure I know what I mean... but I think... don't you want to dance?"

"Of course you do, dear," said Martha to Mary, ignoring Leon's stammering. "We all like to dance, don't we Andrea?"

"When we can find young men to dance with that aren't prone to stepping on our feet." Andrea finally let her eyes reach out to Leon...

searching a little for his thoughts among the whimsical looks crossing his face.

"I think we should probably let you dears get back to your work," said Mary, having quite enough of the conversation. "Decorating is such hard work... not at all like the making of pies and cakes. Why you poor dears will simply be exhausted by tonight. Come, Mr. Mancheski... let us continue our stroll." At that, her nose went into the air and she clutched Leon tightly. With his free hand Leon tipped his hat awkwardly and they stumbled off.

"That went well," laughed Martha.

"What?" asked Joe, still pretty much in the dark.

"Oooooh," mumbled Andrea.

"What?" asked Joe again.

"Oooooh," shuddered Andrea. Suddenly she bent down and scooped up a large handful of snow. She carefully packed it hard while looking off in the direction of the strolling couple. Martha caught the look in her eyes.

"No, Andrea, don't do it," she half whispered. But Andrea whipped her arm back and let fly a snowball catching Leon in the back from a hundred feet and knocking his hat off, as well as scaring a years growth from his life. The shock of it sent him sprawling. He turned and stared at the three Johnsons who all looked about as surprised as he was.

"Shame on you, Joe Johnson!" scolded Martha suddenly, shaking her finger at a surprised Joe. His mouth fell open, but no words of denial came forth. Andrea joined in.

"You wait till Pa finds out about this, young man," she said, also shaking a scolding finger at him. Leon stood up and replaced the hat on his head.

"It's ok" he yelled, "I'm not hurt. It's ok" and he waved. Mary just grabbed his arm and pulled him along.

The Johnson girls each grabbed one of Joe's arms and dragged him along into the hall, breaking into fits of giggles as they entered the protection of the building.

"I'm sorry, Joe," said Andrea when finally gaining composure.

"It's ok," he replied. "That was good shot, Andy, but I coulda threw it harder if ya woulda tol' me."

"That *was* a good shot!" laughed Martha. "I didn't know you had it in you."

"Not so good as you think," replied Andrea. "I was really aiming at Mary. But I'm glad it turned out that way."

"Did you see the look on her face?" laughed Martha.

"No," replied Andrea in suddenly sober tones. "But I saw the look on his."

"Well, I think it's time you give him some of his own medicine," suggested Martha. "Him and his silly stupid grin."

"What do you mean?"

"Seth Hackett!"

The Twenty Third Chapter

Christmas time is coming!

Except for that snowball incident, Leon had a wonderful trip into town. The ever charming Miss Muggsley completely captured his heart and sent him into a tailspin of feelings that left him sighing at the thought of her. The other men just thought he was tired of camp life and was thinking of Ohio or home or some other such place. Home was, in fact, the farthest thing from his mind.

No, Pratt was a new beginning for him. He relished the thought of it, this new life, unimpeded by past mistakes. He wallowed in the good feelings these simple farmers and loggers could generate so easily. And his misconceptions of what life in a remote lumber town was like were gradually going the way of the forests, falling before the ax of time.

It was a quiet cold evening in the Northern Wisconsin woods. Ole had put away his scissors, for every man jack in camp had a Christmas haircut for which to greet his family. The stove in the center of the room glowed hot and occasionally made snapping noises form the air pockets in the hard chunks of wood. The men were busy sewing up rents in their wool garments or writing letters or reading tattered magazines for a 3rd or 4th time. Several were practicing dance steps with each other in anticipation of Christmas party. A few men were gathered more or less in a group near the stove, as much for the warmth of sociability as from the fire. Tales were told around that circle that Leon, years later, tried hard to remember, but most had faded into vague smiles and warm thoughts. The actual events had blurred, with lies and truth a soluble mixture. Still, Leon was worldly enough to appreciate the character and flavor of it.

"Met this gal down St. Paul way," said Bull. Then while the men were digesting that tidbit, he fitted some snoose into his lip. When he was ready to continue, he noted with satisfaction that the boys in the stove circle were waiting for him expectantly. "Nice ol' gal with the name of Sal."

"Sounds like a song," threw out Leon. Months ago he may have suffered abuse for jumping in, but now that he was practically a lumberman, the others chuckled, even Bull.

"I reckon it does. Nice ol' gal with the name of Sal," he said again and smiled. "Sal was a friendly type gal."

"Friendly?" inquired Helge.

"Yep," replied Bull leaning over to spit. "Friendly like them gals down at Swede Annies." That brought more laughter. Swede Annie was a well-known madam of the red light district in St. Paul. Most lumbermen in Northern Wisconsin and Minnesota had at least heard of Swede Annie, if they were not indeed personally knowledgeable of her charms.

"Ol' Sal had an ass on her like a $40 dollar mule," continued Bull. "That ain't no lie. A fine figure of a woman. Why, I almost give up life in the woods on account of her. It's no secret she was partial to me."

"She was partial to most of St. Paul, I exspect," added Helge while starting to peel an apple. He paused and looked up to see if perhaps he had triggered an angry look from Bull... but the Bull was placid and content with the response to his tale.

"Maybe," he said, "but she was especially partial to me. Wanted to get married and settle down, she said. Thought I would be the perfect husband for her, so big and strong."

"And smart too," said someone in the group, but Bull wasn't sure who, so he let it pass.

"So, why didn't you settle down with this gal named Sal?" asked Leon.

"Waall, I was gonna. She was purty and lots of fun, ol' Sal was. So I went home with her, to her house up on Maple Street. A big ol' house. And when I walked in, there was kids coming at me from all directions. Why she musta had fifteen kids, if there was one. And none looked the same, all different, like they all had a different Pa. There was one looked just like you, Charley." Charlie Helgestrom colored, though he tried hard not to.

"Naw, Bull, I ain't never been to Maple Street," defended Charley to peels of laughter.

"Why, I lit outa there," he continued, pausing for a moment to spit again, "before one of them brats could call me Pa."

"You going to the Christmas dance, Buck," Leon asked when there was a break in the tall tale telling.

"Vell, certally. I don't dance so much, but lots of gude stuffs to eat... and drink. And my family. Ya, I think I vill go to the dance."

"Dance?" asked Smiley Birch. "There's a dance?"

"A Christmas dance in Pratt," acknowledged Leon, "at the Modern Woodmen hall."

"No kidding! Do you mind if I go with you. I've only been to Pratt once, on the way out here, but it seemed like a nice little town." Leon looked at Buck's placid face but found no objection there.

"Sure," he said. "It's this Saturday night. We can walk in after work."

"Or take the train," suggested Ole. Ox Pete tol' me there was a special running that night after work." All the fellas that had dancing on their minds beamed at the news. Without having to walk, all the more energy left for dancing.

"Alfred should be happy about that," observed Helge.

"You going?" asked Smiley. Helge took a bite of apple slice and acted as though he was pondering the weight of this heavy question.

"With bells on," he replied.

With that settled, some joyous dancing and story telling went on. You'd never have guessed that these men had worked in the woods from sunup to sundown in vigorous labor. Leon and Charley Helgestrom, the youngest of the lot, were the only ones that yawned and sighed on occasion, suggesting their newness to camp life. As the night wore on, the men seemed to gather closer to the stove though they were not necessarily conscious of it. They may have been unaware that the temperature outside was dropping down to a squeaky cold. Ox Pete knew. He walked from the cook shanty to the barn on hard packed squeaky trails with his breath trailing in wisps and ice forming on his whiskers from the moisture. The oxen seemed warm in spite of the night.

A cat had shown up at the camp, a female that no one would claim responsibility for. Some men even suggested that she might have been the half-breed offspring of a panther and a bobcat, but Ox Pete figured more on the common variety barn cat that had found its way out with the train and was looking for a meal. It was a tiger cat, with white breast and paws, and friendly to everyone who would bother to stroke it's fur or sneak it food. It was more of a concern to Pete, on this cold night, than the sturdy oxen. To his satisfaction, he found the furry animal asleep on the broad back of an ox, warm and content. It was enough to make Pete smile, though he checked to see if anyone else was around before allowing himself this pleasure.

"Kitty knows, eh?" he said softly. "Oxes gude for more dan hauling logs. Gude oxen." He patted the ox on the nose and then likewise the cat, which stretched up to his touch and purred almost instantly. Ox Pete backed off then, not wanting to disturb the beasts further and content that all was well. On his way back to the office, he took note of the clear windless sky and brisk cold. Never too cold to work, he thought, but maybe keep an eye on the men, to spot where frost bite may be settling in, and to ward off such possibilities. He would tell Muggs... much hot soup tomorrow, on the sleigh to the woods, much hearty food for breakfast.

There were others who noted the dropping of temperature. In the Johnson girl's bedroom, Andrea noted the frost creeping up the window in pretty snowflake patterns illuminated by moonlight. She was grateful, now that the cold had settled into winter, that Martha was still here to add warmth to the bed they shared. Good ol' Martha, now soundly asleep next to her. Martha didn't seem to share her penchants for deep pondering of events, past, present and future. Andrea thought about it all the time, her dreams to travel, to see the cities of New York, Chicago or even St. Paul, perhaps to visit foreign and exotic lands. Yet, here she lay, with only the money she had saved from working odd jobs and late hours at the shops and saloon in town, hardly enough for fare to Ashland, let alone to the far reaches of the world. With no job as yet, though Mrs. Williams often mentioned she may need help in the Restaurant. With no money for school. With no money for a new dress, even. A Christmas dress. A Christmas dance dress.

She pondered too, on whether Martha may marry Nightowl Bill, or some other young gentry that would take her away from the Johnson household to parts unknown. Or whether Martha would be taking that job as Nanny to the Benlick family, as they had mentioned only once, taking her away as early as Spring. While she lay there in the silence of a winter night, warm and snuggled in the bed with Martha, she heard a light clanking sound in the downstairs, then a light cough. The thought of a burglar never crossed her mind, but her curiosity was enough to make her remove herself from warm comfort, slip into her slippers, now cold, and tiptoe down the steep stairs with her worn robe wrapped around her nightgown. Before reaching the bottom step she could make out a small form near the door. Without a doubt it was Joe. He was standing in his bare feet in a nightgown just a little too large, and opening his mouth wide, amused to see the warm vapors escaping. He figured they would be even more pronounced near the draft of the doorway.

"Joe," whispered Andrea. "What are you doing?"

"Nothing," he replied guiltily. Andrea glided down the stairs the rest of the way but went to the wood stove and held out her hands to feel the heat. Joe joined her there.

"Kinda coolin' down, ain't it Andy," he said.

"I'll say. What are you doing up at this hour, and in your bare feet for heaven's sakes?" She opened the door to the stove and found the cherry blush of hot coals were all that remained. Crouching low, she stared into the glow, taking pleasure in the color and the warmth.

"I was thinkin' Andy. Sometimes thinking wakes me up. And when I'm awake, I think even more and then I gotta go have a look-see. I was thinkin' it was cold."

"Well, you were right about that," she replied. Andrea reached into the woodbox and slid a considerable sized chunk of oak onto the coals. In a short time, small flames began to lick at the new source of fuel.

"Andy?"

"Yes, Joe."

"That's not all I was thinkin'."

"Oh?"

"I was thinkin' that it was almost Christmas. Almost, anyway."

"So it is."

"And I was thinkin'... that is, I was wondering... why Santa Claus only brings kids presents... and not grownups. And when does a kid stop getting presents cause he's getting to be too much grown up?"

"Some pretty serious thinking, Joe."

"Yeah, I know. I had to get up, Andy."

"I see," she said patronizingly. The one piece of oak was simmering over the coals, the ends hissing and bubbling with the water in the wood beginning to boil. But the feathers of flames were having trouble sticking to the wood. So she retrieved another chunk from the wood box and laid it diagonally across the first one. Within minutes, the flames took hold of the first piece of wood and began to lick and burn in bright yellow.

"Well, what do you think, Andy?"

"I think, for some reason, it always takes at least two pieces of wood to get a good blaze."

"I mean about Santa Claus," insisted Joe.

"Oh, yes, Santa. Well... Santa is pretty smart... he brings kids presents because they are too young to appreciate other Christmas things."

"Other Christmas things?"

"Well, like singing Christmas carols and dancing and kissing someone under the mistletoe. And the birth of baby Jesus."

"I know about Jesus," said Joe. "Mamma reads me about him once and awhile on Sundays. He had it kinda tough, didn't he?"

"Kinda tough, yes," she mused.

"And his birthday is on Christmas day."

"Yes, it is." The stove was beginning to cook now, emitting snaps and crackles as the fire bit into the wood. Andrea added a few more pieces, until the stove was fairly filled up, and then closed the door, the drafts already set to their customary nighttime positions.

"If Jesus was around today, I'd take him sliding down the North road hill. He'd like that," said Joe sincerely. Andrea tried on that vision and it brought wetness to her eyes. She stood up and wrapped her arms around herself for further warmth.

"Andy, I miss Buck," said Joe.

"You do?"

"Yeah," admitted Joe, "he snored somethin' terrible, but he sure was warm." Andrea tousled his hair in sympathy. Upstairs her bed would still be warmed by Martha, while Joe would return to a cold room and cold bed. Even Emma, on these cold nights, could climb in with Emil and Alma, though not if she approached Emil's side of the bed.

"Whatcha gettin' me for Christmas, Andy? Something glorious?"

"I guess you'll just have to wait and see, Joe. Now you just get upstairs and into that bed and let Christmas come when it's ready."

The Twenty Fourth Chapter

ᘯhe Christmas ᗪance

Saturday morning dawned bright and cold in the North Country but by mid morning the cold was softening, breaking a three day cold spell that had bit into Pratt woodboxes with enthusiasm. There was no mistaking the cheery disposition of the men in the woods. There were fewer complaints and a certain vigor to their work. It was the Christmas spirit working it's magic, getting stronger as the day drew near. Not a man was thinking of the months of hard work and cold weather that lay ahead... their vision had narrowed to a single event that was close at hand.

Joe Kinder and Leon were busy loading up the dinner meal into the sleigh, but had paused long enough to note the weather had taken a turn for the better.

"Could be near 20 degrees," offered Joe. "Maybe 22 or 3."

Muggsley came to the door of the kitchen as the last bit of food was loaded upon the wagon. Both men looked back at him expecting comment or new orders. But Muggsley just looked about the sunny blue sky. He spit copiously into snow already so marked, then wiped the excess spittle from his mouth and wiped his hand on the dirty apron he wore around his thick middle. Saying nothing, he retreated to the confines of the kitchen to begin the makings of yet another meal.

"Doesn't it seem strange that he can cook so well," mused Leon out loud. "I mean, if I was to have a gander at him for the first time, before sitting down to eat... well I wouldn't expect much. Do you know what I mean, Joe?"

"Yep," replied Joe. "Sorta fools ya don't he. I know'd Muggs for three or four years now, never knew he could boil water but he'd burn it somehow. Yep, yep. Turns out he used to cook in the army. Cooked for Roosevelt himself, or so he claims." Joe climbed up on the sleigh with Leon and they started off down the well-packed trail.

"I always figgered that the Lord made everyone good at sumptin," continued Joe. "I always figgered Muggs was mostly good at begattin' though."

"Begatting?"

"Begattin'... like in the bible. Muggsley got married and begat Mary. You know, Mary... Muggsley's daughter?"

"Yess," replied Leon cautiously.

"Begat by Muggs I guess. And as fine a job of begattin' as I seen done. Hard to figger, maybe, exceptin' if it's the one thing Muggs is good at; begattin'. Ceptin' he's a tolerable cook, too. Maybe he's good at two things."

"Mary," mumbled Leon to himself, and for no more reason than to hear her name again.

"What zat?" asked Joe.

"I was wondering what you were good at?"

"Most everything, I exspect. Well, almost everything," smiled Joe.

"Vee vill haf to bungle up gude, now," instructed Emil to the rest of the Johnsons. This direction was of course, lost in the flurry of excitement and the concentration on not forgetting anything. Andrea and Martha were fussing with their dresses, straightening bows and checking lace trim. Emil watched his family hurrying about for a few seconds then went back out the door.

"Oh darn... this lace is coming undone from the sleeve," cried Martha. She looked at Alma with pleading eyes and stamped her dainty foot.

"I can do it, Mart," said Andrea. Grabbing Martha by the hand, they hurried up the stairs.

"Well, I'm gonna wait with Pa," said Joe.

"Yoseph, yew stay clean now... and dry... yew don't do nothing outside. Tell Papa vee be ready soon." And Joe was out the door.

Andrea and Martha came bouncing back down the stairs shortly, faces aglow. "I'm going to dance every dance tonight," said Martha gaily twirling. "Every one."

"And you Andrea?" smiled Alma.

"Oh, I thought I would sit out a dance or two, maybe. Some of those gentlemen have big feet and aren't too careful where they set them down."

She gathered up her shawl and wrapped it around her before sliding on her coat.

Emil had the sleigh parked just outside the door, with ol' Jess and another horse, Blackie, hitched and waiting patiently. When Emil had Andrea, Martha and Joe settled in the back, and Alma and Emma in the front, he produced several hot bricks from a metal bucket and with mittened hands slid them in at their feet.

"Oh, papa... we are too excited to have cold feet," laughed Andrea.

"Yaaas...maybe is not tu cold now, but on ride home it vill be late, it vill be dark and yew vill be cold."

"And so will the bricks," mumbled Joe under his breath. It brought giggles from his sisters.

"Let us go, Papa. All this talk is making us late," scolded Alma.

"Bah! I wait for.... heyup there Jess, hiii Blackie..." He snapped the reins and horses jolted the sleigh into motion. "I vait for yew... yew girls and yewr fussing. All dat fuss to look so pretty. For yew... looking pretty should be so easy... heyup Jess, yew go now, heyh." The girls smiled at the offhand compliment.

At the Modern Woodmen hall there were sleighs and wagons and a few buggys gathered around. Greg Fuller's automobile was stuck in a ditch nearby with men gathered around scratching their heads and wondering at the contraption. Two other autos were parked on the street.

It was near darkness by the time the Johnson's arrived and those that had doubted the need for warm bricks at their feet now crowded their warmth. Joe wrestled his way to the edge of the sleigh and dropped to the snow covered ground before it came to a stop, disappearing into the crowd of boys and girls running about outside the hall. Inside, the hall was gaily decorated, in part by the Johnson sisters, with green and red ribbons and snowflakes made of white paper. There was evergreen boughs over the doorways and along the tables, and candles here and there, flames bouncing this way and that as the door was opened and the cool night air found its way inside.

Once the girls were inside, they paused to look about the room, seeking to know who was there and with whom, and who was yet to arrive... for certainly everyone would come who was able. Alma noticed that Mrs. Simms had come and was sitting with the Wheelers. She had a smile on her face, but Alma could still see traces of sadness about her... as if she was thinking; 'now wouldn't Mr. Simms have enjoyed this'.

It was apparent nearly at once that the Pratt & Southeastern had not yet returned from it's roundup of the camp men. Several members of the orchestra were missing as well as the rowdy group who always seemed to find the whiskey on these occasions. Sam Hackett came rushing up to Emil, who was just now taking his coat off after having to take care of the sleigh and horses, and grabbed him by the elbow.

"Emil, Emil... there's no one here to play music. What are we going to do? The people are ready to dance."

"Vell, hello du, Sam, py golly," returned Emil clutching his hand. "Merry Christmas! But dere's no orchestra... vhere's the orchestra?"

"That's what I'm trying to tell you... they're not here! What are we going to do? A solo maybe? You could play a solo on the fiddle to get them started?"

"No, no... no solo, Sam. Find Mrs. Humphries for the piano, she's got to be here. And James Finley and his guitar, he's not a camp man this year. And Amos Bandy, py golly... vee give'm some music den."

"Ben Walden's here too, Emil. Did you know that he plays the Mandolin?"

"Vell don't yust stand dere Sam, go get 'em, go get 'em. Emil opened his case and gently removed the violin. It was from the "old country" and he treasured it dearly, for its music and for its memories. He held it up to his ear and picked at the strings, tightening one, then another until a smile spread across his face at the sound. Then he picked up the bow and peered down its length for loose hairs. He chalked it softly and with care... then drew it lightly across the violin and smiled once more.

"Emil, are you coming?" yelled Sam from halfway across the room. Emil waved the bow at him and when Alma turned around to look for him, he was gone.

"Give us a good one, Emil!" shouted someone from the milling crowd as he made his way toward the traditional playing area for the orchestra.

"A fast one to dance to," said another, "my feet are still cold."

"What song do you have in mind, Mr. Johnson," said Ben Walden. "I know many of the regulars."

"Vell, den... vee start to play and yew yump in vhere yew vill," Emil replied. He played a short burst of music over the violin, then paused. "And hang on the best yew can!" he added. Then jumped into a lively tune that the rest of the present orchestra followed to perfection. To Ben Walden's credit, he found the rhythm and "hung on". The crowd was waiting for the music in avid anticipation. The first chords were hardly struck before the floor was filled with a dancing throng; men with women, girls with girls, kids. A happy bunch filled with the joy of the season.

Several songs later there was a brief pause while the orchestra conferred about the next couple of numbers. In the waning silence as the door opened to admit snow-dusted children, the long low whistle of the Pratt & Southeastern was heard. All knew it would bring the men of the camps... slightly smelly, but full of vigor for dancing and fun. Fathers, brothers, husbands, they were... and some of no relation at all, but welcomed as warmly and well. Within a half hour the Modern Woodmen hall was inundated with this hoard of smiling woodsmen, wild in spirit, yet strangely tamed now in the presence of women and children.

Leon was so bubbling with excitement he could hardly contain himself. He removed his hat and greeted Alma Johnson politely at the food table... but took notice that Andrea was not near by. Smiley Birch hung at his elbow, not knowing many of the people and feeling a bit shy. Even the woodsmen he had come in with he had not known long. Helge had disappeared into a crowd of men who were smoking pipes and discussing politics. Buck, too, paused only long enough to kiss Alma softly on the cheek before finding the corner where a bottle was being passed. Cooper had arrived at about the same time as the woodsmen and immediately sought out Buck in the corner.

Buck eyed him suspiciously as he approached, his hands in the greatcoat pockets.

"Well, Buck... I... well... I just thought you should get a chance to see what real whiskey tastes like... before you kill yourself with that rotgut." He pulled a fine bottle out of his pocket and pushed it toward him.

"Vell, tanks, Mr. Cooper."

"Merry Christmas, boys," returned Cooper gaily and then he withdrew to the men of politics. The bottle lasted not all that long in the midst these men of hearty thirst.

The music had begun once again, this time with added members of the orchestra, men from the camps with instruments brought in by their families. Though Leon was actually seeking out Andrea, he bumped into Mary Muggsley first. Mary of the golden curls and sweet smile, with just a dusting of freckles across her nose and cheeks, all dressed in finery with a red bow in her hair. It ignited the passion in Leon all over again, and his search for Andrea was immediately set aside.

"Why, Mr. Mancheski, I was hoping you would be here soon. I've been saving a dance especially for you."

"Hello, Mary. You sure look beautiful tonight," gushed Leon. Smiley cleared his throat a few times when it seemed the conversation stalled with the opening shots.

"Well, who do we have here?" she inquired.

"Mary Muggsley, I would like you meet Smiley Birch, a new woodsman at our camp."

"Mr. Burch is it? I don't suppose you are related to any of the Burches of St. Paul are you? Mary's eyes were alive with interest.

"Uh, no. I don't know no other Burches 'cept me."

"Oh," she replied somewhat deflated. And so Leon once again was the target of her intentions. Looking at him she said, "shall we dance?" He nodded and offered his arm.

Together they joined in the dancing throng that was more or less centered in the hall. On the fringes were the ladies talking and setting up food on the tables, sampling each other's favorite recipes and passing the latest gossip along with the plates of food. And too, were the children talking and playing, the men in one corner imbibing in the Christmas "spirits" and those smoking near the door and wallowing through political opinion and the state of the country. And then too, there were those women, or girls rather, who were of the dancing, kissing and marrying age, who grouped together and whispered secrets and hopes and dreams to one another as they followed the happenings in the room.

Andrea and Martha, from the midst of gathered females, followed the movement of the dancers while they themselves were resting from the same activity. And Mary Muggsley, not one to keep a low profile anyway, made sure that they could see her dance by with Leon in tow, in a bubble of sunshine and laughter.

"Well, they probably deserve each other anyway," observed Andrea, half whispered to Martha.

"Her feet are certainly doing well dodging his clompers. Upon my word, I think she's added a few new steps to that dance," laughed Martha.

"Serves her right," replied Andrea. "Oh Mart...what I wouldn't give for a snowball right this very minute."

"I'll getcha one, Andy," said Joe suddenly appearing from behind them. "It's not that great a packin' just now, cause it's too cold... but I could do it."

"I know you could, Joe, but I was just joking. I wouldn't really throw a snowball at those two," said Andrea, "at least not in here."

"Awww shucks," said Joe, "it would have been glorious, Andy."

"Well, you run along now and play, young man. You find enough trouble as it is. Scoot," said Martha giving him a gentle push. Then turning to Andrea she said, "I'd venture to say we were pretty safe while he's about. Oh... Oh... look at that Mrs. Hatch!" Andrea turned to see a very pregnant Mrs. Hatch hovering over the food table, a large plate in her hand.

"Would you look at that! She's eating Mrs. Porterfield's baked beans, of all things."

"Well... what of it? I've had some and they were delicious," said Andrea.

"And ham... she's eating ham!"

"Martha... what has gotten into you? It's all delicious."

"For normal people maybe... but not somebody that pregnant. It's obvious she hasn't read the book for mothers by Dr. Aldrich. Ohhhh... and layer cake... not the layer cake. My goodness what will become of that baby?"

"She'll be fine, Martha... "

"And I wouldn't put it past her to even dance... though could you imagine the sight that would be? That poor baby!"

"Oh, Martha, really!"

"Well, it's right in the book... right in the book! I've seen it."

"Look how she parades him around," said Andrea changing the subject and returning her attention to the dance floor. "If she only knew how silly they look." It was enough to divert Martha's attention back to serious discussion.

"And with a corset that tight, it's a wonder she can breathe," observed Martha, "why, she's liable to fall over in a faint at any time... wouldn't that be a sight... the swooning Miss Muggsley attended by all these gallant boys."

"Yes," murmured Andrea, "all the gallant boys... that's just what they are... boys."

Leon was unaware of the observation. And though his feet stumbled through the steps of the waltz now playing, his mind danced lightly through visions of fond embrace. Had he not been so blinded by these visions, he would have noticed the look of pain and boredom on the face of his partner. With every misstep she endured she reminded herself that this was all for good reason. Was this man not of literary success? Was he not well known in the social circles of New York, a renowned journalist for Harper's magazine? Was he not surely well-to-do, perhaps even wealthy from his literary endeavors, or perhaps a family inheritance? For that's what the inner circle of gossip was saying.

She had decided on him as a ticket out of this drab little town almost from the beginning, when the gossip mill had churned out his "secret" story. If bruised ankles and boredom were the price to pay for such a ticket... then let the music of fate play on.

She forced a smile once again to her ruby lips and lit the glow of womanhood about the face that could charm its way into the coldest heart. Not a teacher, she, nor a store clerk, or a maid and nanny. Not a housewife with snotty brats tied to her apron strings. She deserved more... and more she would have. She would have a life of parties and pretty dresses, away from these boors, away from the drudgery of everyday life. Yes, she determined once more, this was the ticket, the only such ticket just now available. And the music of life played on while fate laughed a merry laugh.

Mary Muggsley's dreams and schemes were not completely unknown to all inhabitants of Pratt. Her wily female ways had worked their magic on more than one poor soul who became entranced with golden curls and a voice like silk. Those that adored her and admired her, and there were many, saw the other women who occasionally spoke against her as jealous and spiteful... for someone with visage so fair must certainly have a heart and soul to match.

But Andrea knew. And as she watched her now, with her smile and humor feigned, she struggled with her own feelings of inadequacy and grew angry with herself for feeling that way. And angry with Mary for bringing it on.

"Just one snowball," Andrea said again, quietly but with feeling. "Just a small one. Well, maybe not so small."

"Oh, Andrea, you are so physical some times," chided Martha. "That's not what a proper lady would be thinking. A proper lady would be thinking; now how could I outshine that girl, how could I make the men prefer my company over hers." Andrea smiled at the thought.

"A little shoulder perhaps, or an ankle shown in an accidental move, then covered in sudden modesty. You'll see, it will do wonders."

"Oh, Mart, you are as bad as she is. For goodness sakes it's winter, my shoulders are too cold to peek out of a dress... besides, this dress has no room for showing bare shoulders. And mother would feint. And Papa would... well who knows what Papa would do. I'd probably be locked in my room."

"Oh, fiddlesticks. If you want to attract bees, you got to show a little honey," replied Martha.

"Mart, bees make honey, not... you mean bears, don't you...oh for goodness sakes, I think he's waving at us."

"Wet your lips, he's coming over," said Martha excitedly. She wet her own, then checked that Andrea had done the same. Satisfied, she straightened her dress and stood suddenly nonchalantly watching the dancers. He was followed closely by Mary, who was not sure she was happy with this meeting. She didn't need any competition, Leon was her ticket.

Leon was full of smiles and good feelings approaching the Johnson girls. And full of good will for the world. And just generally full of it.

"Hello, Andrea, Martha," he nodded, "it's good to see you again."

"Mr. Mancheski," greeted Martha, "are you enjoying the dance?"

"Oh, yes, Mary and I have been dancing so much... that she needed a rest. I guess, having worked in the woods now for these months that I have more stamina than I thought. I'm ready to dance the night away and hope it never ends. I thought perhaps you would favor me with a dance, Andrea, while Mary rests. You don't mind, do you Mary?"

"Why, no," smiled Mary. Then looking at Andrea added, "You go right ahead dear. You should dance at least one dance tonight." Mary took Andrea's hand and put it on Leon's extended arm. Andrea's face remained impassive, but Martha's was tightening. As the couple moved back onto the dance floor, Martha could stand it no longer.

"Mary Muggsley," she said sternly, "if you know what's good for you, you will stop these childish remarks and let the man choose what partner he would."

"Upon my word, Martha Johnson, how rude... but it's something I would expect from you and your sister. Just because you are jealous is no reason to start threatening me. It's not my fault that Mr. Mancheski and most of the other young men, including Bill Gusteval, are constantly buzzing about me. Why, I don't do a thing to encourage it. Heaven knows I have no use for these crude lumbermen." She threw up her nose in a huffy manner and daintily stalked off.

Martha steamed. And as many thoughts streamed through her head most unkind, there was one that involved a snowball.

Andrea was stiff and formal on the dance floor with an expressionless face. Leon was puzzled by it, thinking surely his charm, having worked its magic on Mary, should again see him in good stead. He felt clumsier with Andrea, noticing this time that his feet were not always bumping against the floor, but instead, bumping the dainty feet of his partner. Andrea did nothing to mask this intrusion, wincing at times when his boots made contact.

"Sorry," was all he said. And she nodded politely.

But the magic that was love, or chemistry, or any other name one would choose to apply to that feeling that draws two souls together, was playing with their hearts. Andrea's stiff mechanical movements began to soften and warm. And Leon now, too, was more conscious of his movements. Closer they fell, in dancing embrace as the music in their hearts played on and the others about the room fell far from their thoughts. Andrea braved a look at the man, so boyishly handsome and gay, his gray eyes flickering so bright, the strong chin on a tender face. Then suddenly she was conscious of his touch, his hand warm in hers, his movements, though clumsy and mistimed, so vigorous and lively. Her heart reached out to him, but was restrained by her mind... still caught in the vision of Mary Muggsley in his arms. She had the sudden urge to rub the back of his neck... would he notice, would he care? But her hand would not move from the middle of his back.

He caught her looking at him that instant. He held her eyes for only a moment before she turned away but it made him wonder, it made him suddenly care even more on whose feet he was occasionally tramping on. She was lovely, he noted. Not in the way that Mary was... but strangely, he thought, in a warmer, more subtle beauty. A beauty that grew as it was studied. He drank in her looks for a moment, trying not to betray his feelings. The chestnut hair falling softly about her shoulders, the graceful line of her face, blue eyes of such depth and feeling. Suddenly an audible sigh escaped his lips. She saw it as boredom, he as a betrayal of feelings. It made them both uncomfortable and she stiffened once more in their dancing embrace. When the dance was over, it was Andrea who broke away and returned to Martha's side without a word. He followed.

"Thank you, Andrea. It was a pleasure to dance with you, and I'm sorry... I'm not too light on my feet. I haven't really had much practice, you see. But perhaps we could do it again later?"

Andrea just nodded and pretended to seek out other friends in the crowd. When she spied Sally Beardsly talking with Seth Hackett, but looking her way, she waved.

"If you will excuse me, I must have a dance with Seth, he's such a sweet dear." And with that she escaped his company to join the others.

"And Seth is quite fond of her," whispered Martha. "It's a wonder they aren't engaged... everyone thinks they would be the perfect match... just perfect."

Leon nodded absentmindedly. It was true that Andrea's sudden interest in Seth Hackett caused some disturbing feelings to shadow his thoughts for a time... but the bright light that was Mary Muggsley could easily dissolve the shadows into bits and pieces best pondered at a later time.

So where was Miss Muggsley? Leon stood there awhile looking about the room, his eyes searching the various groups of ladies for yellow hair. Strangely, she was not easily found.

"If you are looking for Miss Muggsley," said Martha happily, you will find her 'resting' in the company of that group of men over there." She pointed toward a crowd gathered around Mary as moths to a flame. And never did a flame burn so bright as when the moths were in so great a number. Smiley Birch was there, up close and friendly, and several others from the camp on the outer circle. Mary directed her attention to the better dressed of the bunch, those with some semblance of wealth and position, such that it was in Northern Wisconsin. But even those, whose cause was long lost, hung on her every word, as if addressed specifically and singularly to them.

Leon was at first mortified, then attacked by the well-known green-eyed monster. He left Martha's side in great strides to cross the room and reclaim Mary's attention.

Martha smiled. But it was a smile borne of some relief of not finding Bill Gustavel caught in the same web as the others, at least not yet. He was pulling at the bottle with the men in the corner just now... building up courage to make proper advances in her direction. At least it had better be in her direction, or she just might have Joe build a snowball for her, a big snowball.

And the night wore on. Emil Johnson would pause on the orchestra breaks to wolf down lefsa and great pastries, and, unbeknown to Alma, sample the homemade wine that was in plentiful supply. In due time his cheeks were rosy and his eyes quite lively, the image of St. Nicholas in his cheery disposition. And he played and played the violin, his fiddle, his friend. All was well with the world. Ben Walden's appreciation for this man at the violin grew as the night wore on, fueled too, on the same homemade wine. Comrades in musical arms, they were. It was a mutual appreciation, safe to say.

At some point in time, Cooper noticed Leon fawning over Miss Muggsley as some ill stricken puppy. It amused him some, but he also felt the fatherly feeling toward the young man. He made up his mind to throw in his two cents worth... whether it was listened to or not, and after that, to mind his own business.

"Say, Mr. Mancheski, I see you've been dancing up a storm here tonight."

"Mr. Cooper, what a wonderful dance. I've never danced so much in my life."

"I see," said the older man, "and nearly learned how by now."

"Well, I'm getting better, I think."

"I'm sure you are. Plenty of girls that are willing to give you a dance lesson too. They're all very pretty."

"Yes, well, I've got to... I mean there's Mary and I should... um."

"Well, ok son... but do me a favor and stop by and see me tomorrow before you head back to camp. Business stuff, you know." Leon nodded impatiently. He was a little worried Mary was giving Smiley Birch a little too much attention. "You might want to see about a room at the Hotel tonight. It's kinda cold in the office... haven't had a fire in there all day, what with Jake on a holiday. And I've been at the store with Bill, you know... so...anyway... you might want to try the hotel."

Leon nodded again, only half listening, but he understood that he would have to stay in the hotel tonight. And then before Mr. Cooper could make further use of the conversation, he was off. He didn't get very far before he felt the cold bony hand of Mrs. Gillis on his arm. She was dressed in festive attire; a red dress with white lace, a stylish little hat on her head. She smiled politely as she turned him around to her, then hooked her arm in his, locking him in place. He was caught. And within the circle of his captivity were several other women of the town, aged but gay, with expectant expressions on cheerful faces.

"Mr. Mancheski... it's so nice to see you again. I trust your work has gone well so far." She winked at him them, at their shared secret, and it made him weak.

"Yyyes... fine," he stammered.

"The lumberman's life is quite exciting isn't it?" said Mrs. Porterfield.

"Yes, and so... interesting," added Mrs. Smith.

"But..." said Mrs. Gillis, "the women have an interesting story to tell, too! Your education in the woods would not be complete without hearing the woman's point of view."

And so they told him. For nearly twenty minutes while Mrs. Gillis clung tightly to his arm, they told him of the trials and tribulations of living in a lumber town in the wilderness. They told of their work with the anti-saloon league and the terrible problems that whiskey had caused; of the deprivations of living in the woods; of the low wages for their men; of the disease and pestilence that often followed the transient lumberjack population. And they told of woman camp cooks, who slaved for 20 hours a day over a hot stove and still managed to raise and educate a family. Had he been listening, it would have been a real education for Mr. Mancheski. But once again he had lost sight of Miss Muggsley and it had been all that he could do to resist tearing himself apart from these vultures to go in search of her.

As it was, he finally tore from their grasp by suggesting that he had to use the "necessary room". And so he fled... scanning the room as he went, looking for golden curls to fill that void in his life that had become so apparent as of late. It was not easy. There were hundreds of people crowded in and around the hall, milling about, laughing, singing, sharing their lives with one another, a complex tapestry of diverse cultural backgrounds and religions woven tightly into the panoramic quilt that was the American experience.

Finally, he wandered outside... to get some fresh air and some semblance of peace from the festivities inside to help clear his head. As he leaned against the building, breathing the crisp night air and feeling through the wall the rhythm of life that played on inside, he came to the conclusion that this truly was a wondrous place, this northwoods frontier, this lumber town, this Pratt.

A wolf howling in the distance made him shiver and look to the east from whence it had come. No wolf could he see in the bright moonlight... no wild and woolly rogue... or did he? There beneath the shadow of a tree a half block distant... two forms standing near. There was conversation... unheard, a hand reaching out, a hand meeting the other halfway. And then the two forms came together... a warm embrace until the two shadows seemed as one, clinging to each other for a time. They stayed like this then, until finally one form broke away and running down the street entered the circle of light where golden hair caught the glow and took on a light of its own, until quickly being swallowed up by the hall.

Mr. Mancheski felt his heartbeat waver and dim for a moment, his mind clouded by the image of two forms joined in the moonlight. An uneasy feeling settled over him like a cloak, sheathing his mood into the shadows of the night.

But there were others about with yellow hair, he reasoned... many others. Mary was truly interested in him and no one else... she had as much as said so. It was not possible that she would let another man... that she would... no, it was not possible. And with only that bit of rationale staying his heart, he went again in search of Miss Mary Muggsley, while still the cloak of uneasiness hung about his shoulders. And after he found Mary innocently chatting with some of the other girls, instantly fawning over him, bumping into him, touching his arm tenderly, he found it was not enough to lift the heavy feeling in his heart. There was something about this girl, something hidden, something strange. But still he was drawn, the clumsy moth to the bright flame, to suffer whatever fate she would graciously bestow.

The more Andrea watched the confused Mr. Mancheski flutter about the light of Miss Muggsley, the more attention she paid to Seth Hackett. They danced close and intimate, and briefly she had rubbed the back of his neck, thinking of Leon as she did so, embarrassed when she realized it was a smiling Seth who responded to her touch unaware of the surrogate role he was playing. Such was the emotional tangle of life this festive evening.

Toward the end of the night, when the orchestra was getting too tired or too drunk to continue with the same enthusiasm, people began to load up the sleighs and wagons with leftover food, tired and sleepy children, and spouses overwhelmed with spirits. Andrea discovered by accident, Martha in the cloakroom kissing Bill Gustavel. A sprig of mistletoe hung limply above them, and though it was dark, Andrea could see that the passion was not lacking in either one of them. So without a sound, she withdrew and then making clumsy walking sounds, she approached again.

"Oh... uh... I think this is your coat, Martha. Isn't it?" he asked.

"Why, yes, I believe it is," returned Martha, cheeks flushed with color and hair just a little bit mussed. "Thank you, Mr. Gustavel."

"No, that's Emma's," laughed Andrea. "Your's is the red one, Mart. You two!" she wagged her head, smiling. "Of course if someone hadn't put out the lamp in here you could have found the coat much easier."

"It must have been the wind," suggested Bill. "I've got to go now Martha... I thought maybe you'd... well maybe we could take a sleigh ride tomorrow. If your folks wouldn't mind, that is."

"That would be lovely, Bill. I would be very pleased."

"Well, I'll see you tomorrow then. For the sleigh ride I mean."

"Yes, that will be nice."

Bill started to vacate the room, but stopped suddenly. Turning around he shrugged his shoulders, "I don't have a sleigh."

"We have one, Bill," said Andrea. "You go on now." Bill smiled and left.

"Thanks, Andrea," said Martha. She rolled her eyes and laughed. "I bet we fooled you."

"You go help Mama load Papa into the sleigh, would you, Mart. It seems the homemade wine was especially good this year." Martha nodded and donning her coat, paused to give Andrea a hug before leaving.

Andrea sighed. Martha would be marrying soon, she suspected. The thought of it saddened her suddenly, and a tear found it's way down her cheek. She rubbed it from her face and sniffed. She felt for some matches along the windowsill to re-light the lamp and finding several wooden stick matches, she struck one, her face alight in the dim glow as she fumbled with the mechanics of the kerosene lamp. Another tear formed unexplainably. "Well just look at you Andrea Johnson," she said out loud. "Even good news makes you cry. You must be a sight."

"Yes, you are," said Leon from the doorway. "A lovely sight." It startled her and made her pause and turn. As the match burned on, it suddenly warmed her fingers and she dropped it. "Oh!" she said.

"I'll get it," Leon said softly. And fumbling along the windowsill, he found another match and lit it. Closer now, he could see the shiny wetness of a wiped tear on her cheek and it puzzled him. She backed away slightly as he drew near, until she was up against the coats, but said nothing. Gently he rubbed the wetness from her cheek with his thumb, and in the glow of the match found new beauty in her looks. He felt he was about to do something important, or say something meaningful... but no words came out, their bodies remaining motionless.

And then the match burned him. "Ow!" he exclaimed and dropped it. It made her smile weakly. But in the darkness, she could feel him leaning closer, feel his breath upon her face.

Then there were voices and footsteps coming in the direction of the cloakroom, and Andrea adroitly slid by him and caught up another match. This time her actions were swift and deliberate and in seconds, the lamp was lit and filled the room with light.

It was Hank Martin and his wife, Dorothy, arguing about the wine and the dancing and the food and every other little thing. They were so caught up in their own little affairs that they made no notice of the other two... picking coats off the rack and continuing the discussion. Andrea found it a good time to gather up the Johnson coats as well.

As the squabbling Martins again withdrew she started to follow. Something made her pause at the doorway, however, and she turned back to eye him. He had a sheepish look on his face, a confused little boy look, a hurt look, perhaps, for the way he had fumbled in front of her. It warmed her, this look, this image. She was going to turn and go... perhaps say something in the nature of; 'good night, Mr. Mancheski and Merry Christmas.' But she suddenly noticed he was standing almost directly beneath the mistletoe. She was aware that he did not even know this... and it amused her.

So instead of saying something clever, instead of gathering her wits and retreating with the Johnson coats to the safety of the main hall, she did something that surprised them both. She suddenly walked briskly up to him dropping the coats, and with her arms wrapped around him, kissed him full on the mouth, as warm and passionate as it was brief. And then realizing what she had done, gathered the coats in a bundle and ran out.

In the hall, she found the Johnson clan gathered together near the door. It seems Alma was having trouble parting Emil from Ben Walden... they were singing old songs and playing imaginary instruments (the real ones having been put away), while the ladies tried to get them heading in the right direction. By the time they had Emil and the kids settled in the sleigh, with the help of Buck, they couldn't find Joe. The girls grumbled and Andrea was nearly out of the sleigh to go look when Joe appeared carrying a piece of tin with hot bricks on it.

"I've been planning this," he explained, "ever since Pa put'em on the sleigh. I didn't know they got so hot, though." His hands were slightly blistered.

"Oh Joe!" exclaimed Andrea and Martha in unison. They helped him into the sleigh and promised soothing grease and salve the minute they got home. When the girls were settled in the back with Emma and Joe between them, Buck covered them with a blanket, then took the reins. As they rode along, tears once more found Andrea's cheek, tears she herself couldn't really begin to explain. But Joe saved her the explanations.

"Don't cry, Andy," he said. "They ain't burned so bad." Andrea smiled. Reaching around she grabbed a handful of snow off the back of the sleigh and packed it into a snowball. Handing it to Joe she said, "see, snowballs are good for lots of things. Keep this in your hands for awhile."

"And your hands 'aren't' burned badly, not 'ain't', added Martha. "Never say ain't."

"I'm not cold," said Emma. "I like sitting in the middle."

"Did you have a good time, Emmy?"

"umhmm," she nodded. "I even got to dance."

"Oh, my," exclaimed Andrea, "which handsome gentlemen did you dance with?"

"Joe," she said beaming. "And once with Bob Walden cause Joe made 'em. Joe takes care of me, don't ya Joe."

"Awwww," was his only comment.

"Joe takes care of all of us," added Martha and leaned over to kiss him on the forehead. He tried to dodge, but it was no use.

"Well, don't tell any of the pirates about this kissing stuff," he said to their amusement.

Over the icy paths they rode, the horses sure of the way to the Johnson farm and happy to be headed toward home. The moon lit the way for the most part, over road and snowy field, but when the path cut through a dark patch of woods, Buck got out and led the horses. It would not do to go astray on a cold snowy night.

The Johnson's were a contented lot, each for their own reasons. Andrea decided not to tell Martha about her mistletoe experience for a while, so she could mull it over herself and come up with some rational reasons for her odd behavior. There were other things said between Martha and Bill and that would be related in time and be of no small importance, but tonight, Martha would savor their meaning privately. Joe had had a glorious time. Emma was asleep under the warmth of the blanket and bricks, with visions of sugarplums dancing in her head. Alma was filled with the latest gossip and had been lauded for her pastries. And Emil, also sleeping, was done singing and playing for the night.

Buck, full of Cooper's good whiskey, thought of a few good songs of his own to sing, but not the type that would fall gently on delicate ears. Perhaps he would sing in the barn to the cows. Such was the joy of the evening.

K. Wallin

The Twenty Fifth Chapter

A Christmas Tussle

It took Leon a few minutes to realize that Mary Muggsley was probably waiting for him. Somehow that fact seemed less important now than it did a few minutes ago. But with a heavy sigh, he picked out her coat from the rack, and his, and returned to the main hall.

Though there were still milling crowds of people wishing each other Merry Christmas and saying goodnight, the hall was thinning out and it was getting easier to see from one end to the other. When Leon burst out of the cloakroom, still half in a daze and with a smile on his face, he was momentarily accosted by a scene at the other end of the hall, real or imagined, of Mary in an embrace. He blinked and Mary stood back. Perhaps it was his imagination, perhaps it was the angle, or perhaps it was someone altogether different. When he got close, he found Mary was standing with her father, and Smiley Birch. He naturally assumed, if there had been an embrace, it was with her father, who was quite drunk and tipsy.

"Some a them fellas need to learn a thing or two about Mr. Roosevelt," said Muggs. "Why, I could teach'em all by myself. And these are my teachers!" He slapped a big fist into his open other hand.

"Roosevelt?" asked Leon.

"Teddy Roosevelt," answered Smiley. "Seems a few of those gentlemen think President Roosevelt should mind his own business when it comes to railroads." He nodded toward a bunch of loud staggering men near the hall side door.

"Bah," spit Muggs. "Them yahoos don't know snivel about Mr. Roosevelt. I spose they're Democrats, too."

"Help me get him home, will you Leon? Mr. Birch?" pleaded Mary. "He'll make a scene and I'll just die of embarrassment. Wouldn't the Johnson girls just love to hear about that. Oh, why did mother pick this time to go to Minneapolis... she knows how he gets!"

"C'mon Muggs," offered Leon grabbing the bigger man by the elbow. But Muggs just grumbled and groaned and jerked away. He was still mumbling about Democrats and Railroad men in general as he lurched off in the direction of the men. Leon and Smiley stood there next to Mary nervously shuffling their feet, not sure what to do.

"Hey, you Democrats!" yelled Muggs. "I'm gonna kick your asses like Roosevelt did to Parker in '04." And with that he threw himself into the group starting a fracus that luckily fell to the outside quickly.

"Well, don't just stand there like a couple of idiots, go help him," cried Mary, giving the boys a push. And so, these sober and quite innocent boys reluctantly threw themselves into the drunken spectacle that was beginning outside. Like a snowball rolling down a Pratt hillside, it was getting bigger all the time. But for the most part, Muggs was outnumbered and reeling badly by the time the boys came to his aid.

At first they tried to break it up with shouts and threats, but when the punches finally began to be directed their way, they too were caught up in the snowball. It was going bad for Muggs and his helpers. These Railroad men were a hardy lot and looking for just such an excuse to brawl. It seemed to Leon there were twice as many of them as what started, but where they were coming from he didn't know. He was on the ground with a particularly large fellow on top of him, abusing his face with a large fist when in a daze he thought he spotted Cooper. He tried to call out, but it took too much concentration away from his already weak defenses. It was Cooper. He was standing near Jake and a few of the bachelor woodsmen who were nearly around the corner of the building.

"Well, would you look at that, would you?" said Cooper when the fight caught his attention. A few of the men peered around the corner and smiled at the melee in progress. "It's always someone who has to break up these merry festivities. I think I'd be all in favor of leaving the bottle at home on these affairs." He got dubious looks from the men around him with that revelation.

"Hey, I think that one fella is Leon Mancheski," said Jake.

"Is that right?" replied Cooper, "Well, I certainly would've thought that he would know better than to get involved in something like that."

"Yes, you think you know some people," observed Jake, "and they surprise you every time." He looked back at the fighting again. "Seems he ain't doing too well at it either."

"And who's that other guy?" mused Cooper. "Is he one of ours? That yellow haired fellow?"

"Looks like Smiley," said Bull.

"Smiley?"

"Smiley Birch... come in with Helge that day," offered Bull. "And he ain't doing too well over there neither."

"Yeah, ya know, that reminds me of a fracas I was in, in Escanaba one time," joined in Helge. "It was just me and four or five other guys that had taken offense to something innocent I said."

"Something innocent?" questioned Jake.

"Well, it was an observation, really. I observed that the whores of Hurley were lots better educated then them in Escanaba." The men gathered around chuckled at that. "Well, I saw one of 'em reading a book once," he added to more chuckles. Meanwhile the grunts and oofs and smacks and hits continued along the side of the building.

"Took exception to that, did they?" asked Cooper.

"Yaa... and I even allowed as how the whores in Escanaba were better lookin' too. I thought that would calm them some. But it seems they have this thing for ugly whores. They like 'em!"

"A fracas was it?" inquired Bull Finnigan.

"Well, not a fair one, I'd say. And not a man to come to my defense, no sireee. Not one to help me out with such odds."

"Pitiful," agreed Frank Wiesal. "Ya just can't count on some peoples."

"Well, so I backed myself into a corner... kinda take 'em on one at a time... and then I..."

"Hey!" yelled Frank Wiesal, "That's our cook! They can't do that to our cook!" And all the men suddenly took an interest, and upon identifying Muggsley in the tangle of flying fists and heaving bodies, rushed to participate.

The ensuing fight tipped the other way, with the influx of Cooper's woodsmen. Even Cooper himself managed to throw a punch before he ended up in the snow with his lip beginning to swell. He could have sworn it was Muggsley that threw that punch. But before long the railroad men were routed and peace nearly restored. There was blood upon the snow where the struggle had been... no telling whose or from how many people. It was too late for the sober boys. Both were unconscious on the ground.

"What'd I tell ya, mangy Democrats," mumbled Muggs, just before he fell to his knees, paused then fell face first in the snow.

The next day was bright and blue and warm, for a winter day. The snow was still crisp but the temperature was crowding the 25-degree mark. At the Johnson house, activity began at an early hour, as usual on a farm. There were cows to milk, chickens to feed and wood and water to be hauled. Breakfast was served early, and almost as hearty as a woodsmen's.

Andrea sat in her upstairs bedroom, on her cedar chest at the frosted window, long after breakfast had been called. When Martha returned once to check on her, she allowed as how she wasn't hungry and declined to get involved in a more lengthy conversation. And so on this Sunday morning, after Alma ensured she was not coming down with something, she was left alone. A victim of womanhood, Martha said of her. In Andrea's mind, the night before played on in visions that changed the events to suit the mood. She had kissed him, but he had kissed her back, didn't he? Perhaps he had wanted to kiss her, but was afraid. Perhaps he was going to kiss her, but the Martins interrupted.

Or perhaps he was thinking about Mary Muggsley the whole time, even while they embraced. And she would draw her legs up and hug her knees, bowing her head down to rest on her arms. It was hard to sort through these emotions. But one fact was clear, at least in her mind; the kiss had awakened in her, a desire she felt uncomfortable about. She had been kissed before, a few times, but never did it generate such warmth within her.

"Mamma, what is it about men?" she asked when Alma came up to feel her forehead.

"Vhat is vhat?"

"Why do they make us make fools of ourselves, for no good reason. Why do they act so... so... contrary."

"Aah... it is a man is it?" She smiled a knowing smile. "You try to figure out men, yaa? As girls vee think sometimes there is answer to man's foolishness. Some deep secret vee must learn. But vhen vee become voman, vee know."

"We know?"

"Vee know there is no secret. Men act that way because they are really boys, not man at all. Girls, they grow into vomen and mothers, but boys, they stay boys all the time, only in big strong bodies. But up here," she pointed at her head, "they think they are men."

"Perhaps it's true," smiled Andrea.

"Tis true enough," sighed Alma, "perhaps is God's plan. To make muther to watch over husband and children."

"Does Papa know this?"

"Papa? Papa only knows there is supper on the table and a varm bed to come to on cold nights. Is enough for him. It is enough for me, also. I kiss him on forehead, goodnight, like all my good children. Papa is good boy."

Andrea hugged her then, her eyes misting at the simple thoughts offered to comfort her. She would remember the kitchen smells about her mother, the gentle, sincere embrace.

"Now, yew come eat something. Yew missed breakfast, but I make yew someting; eggs, bacon, vhatever yew like."

"It is a day for cookies, mama, can we bake some when we get back from church?"

"Vell, certally. Vee must have Christmas cookies," beamed Alma, happy with the change in her daughter.

The valise wasn't as heavy as he thought. But it wasn't empty... he checked it again and again and then slowly he crept down the back stairs as quietly as could, and peering out the back door, he saw his friend and the three men not twenty feet away. He would have to make it fast. He had no gun, so it would have to be rough and tumble. They could surely handle three men, even if one was a policeman. A Policeman! So he cautiously opened the door, prepared to throw himself into the rescue. But wait! The door creaked. They heard it. They are watching the door. The policeman turns and looks, stares, a defiant sneer spreading across his shadowy face. A body on the street! Blood all over. And now the door won't open. Now there is a box, in a church... with flowers. And someone's mother is crying. The pallbearers... the three on the left... the ones who... where's the valise? Where's the valise?

It was the church bells that woke Leon. He woke violently, sitting up and barely stifling a yell, barely catching his breath, and sweating in spite of the cool temperature in the room. When the Chicago scenery had finally faded from his vision, all that remained was four bare walls and the gentle snoring of a body next to him. A warm body.

It took him several minutes to shake this fear even after he realized that Chicago was 500 miles away. He sat there, shaking and softly crying, involuntarily reliving the horrible moments that had eventually sent him to the Northern wilderness seeking refuge. Slowly his breathing began to calm, and the images faded farther and farther away until he could put them away altogether for awhile. He could suddenly feel the ache in his head and his ribs, then. And his face. And the night came back to him, at least somewhat.

Muggsley, the fight, Mary, he struggled through the scenes in his mind. Mary? It couldn't be... he wasn't drunk... he would have remembered. Horror struck his heart as he studied the body next to him, completely covered by blankets. It couldn't be. He tried to think. The last thing he remembered was the fight... of losing the fight. Of Mary urging him to go to the aid of her father. Perhaps she had found him afterwards, nursed him of his wounds... was thankful that he had been so brave. No! It couldn't be!"

And it wasn't. When Leon whipped back the covers, Smiley's curly head showed. He snorted, shifted, and reached for the covers to regain the warmth.

"Get up you idiot," nudged Leon.

"Is it breakfast?" murmured the lazy form beside him.

They were in the Pratt Hotel, in room 4, where Cooper and a few of the boys had placed them after the struggle had concluded that evening. There were still bloodstain's on their clothing and dried on their faces. In fact, they were still dressed save for shoes, Jake suggesting that it had been the least that they could do; remove their footwear. It was cold in the room and Leon was quick to gather his boots and go to the downstairs where the stove puffed away in contented warmth. There was another gentleman in a chair near the stove, reading the Bayfield County Press, who gave no notice to him but a grunt and a nod. When Sam Hackett came out of the back room to the desk, he stopped and stared at Leon for a moment.

"You're a mess, ya know that?"

"Yeah, I guess I am. I don't suppose there'd be any hot water... I mean, enough for a bath?" asked Leon hopefully.

"Well, the stoves hot...Tim!" he yelled. "Tim!" he yelled again, and a young lad appeared from the kitchen with jelly around his mouth.

"Yes, Pa?"

"Mr. Mancheski would like a bath... put on some water."

"Yes, Pa." The kid retreated quickly.

Turning to Leon, Sam said, "won't be but awhile. I think Phoebe should have a go at them clothes as well. Seems you got them full of paint or something."

By the time Leon had soothed his aches in the tub and cleansed himself well, his clothes too, were ready. His jaw was still sore, but he remembered with a smile landing a few good punches of his own. While he had pondered the previous days events in the comfort of the tub, he remembered Cooper's words; he wanted to see him before heading back to camp. Hard telling what that was all about. Probably more papers for Ox Pete or something.

Freshly scrubbed, he walked out the front door of the Hotel and looked down the street toward the Straddle Creek office. No smoke from the chimney. But there... some kids nearby with sleds and skis. He decided to walk down that way and take a look. He first stopped at the office door and peered in... still dark and cold. The kids caught his attention once more, laughing and playing in the snow. A little melt of the day before had frozen again, making the northern road hill slick as could be. He drew closer and watched them, Joe Johnson and the others. Some he recognized but knew not their names. But Joe, and Robert Walden as well... he would not forget, for it was their fighting spirit at the October dance that led him to meet Andrea for the first time.

"I beat ya again," said Joe, beaming. "Fastest skis in the whole world, I'll bet."

"You didn't beat me. It was a tie at least," said Ryan.

"Did too!"

"Did not!"

"Did too, didn't I, Robert?"

"Looked like it. I think he beat ya Ryan," replied Robert.

"Let's try'er again then... I'll beat ya this time, Joe. This time for sure!"

"Joseph!" came the cry from up the road some ways, a female voice that Leon recognized right off. "Joseph Johnson, you wait right there." Andrea came up on the boys slightly out of breath.

"What's a matter, Andy?" asked Joe.

"Did you forget that we're going to the Olson's this afternoon?"

"Nahh, I know that. But it's early yet. We got some slidin' to do." And he started to turn around to position his skis.

"Joe! Papa says you're not supposed to be sliding on the road. You might get run over by a wagon or Greg Fuller's automobile or something. If you're going to slide, you go over on the sliding hill."

"Geez, Andy, this is the best slidin' ever, the roads as slick as can be. We'll watch out."

"No... I don't think you'd better, Joe," said Andrea.

"Oh, let the boys have some fun, their not hurting anything," jumped in Leon.

"I will kindly ask you to stay out of this, Mr. Mancheski. After all, they are just boys." Her words were cool, but saying them brought to mind her mother's words, that all men were boys, and she smiled condescendingly at him.

"Well, I didn't mean anything by it. It just looked like such fun. I guess I don't see why they shouldn't be allowed to do it."

"You want to slide, Mr. Mancheski?" asked Joe suddenly. "You can use my skis, they're the fastest."

"No, no... I don't think so... I just meant..."

"What's the matter Mr. Mancheski, afraid?" The words were from Andrea, much to her own surprise. "It's ok for the boys to risk life and limb... but it's too dangerous for a man like you, I must say!"

"Well, I didn't mean that... I'm not afraid, but..."

"But?"

"Well, ok then... I'll go... but only if you go with me."

"Ohhhh no," said Andrea. "This is a boys game... hardly the thing that ladies would be caught doing."

"So who's afraid now?" he taunted.

"I'm not afraid..." she stammered. "Ohhhhh..." She grabbed Joe's skis out of his hands and set them down on the road. Leon, too, took Ryan's skis and sat beside her. They both looked behind them to see if anyone was coming, or watching, and then from side to side and in front. Andrea wrapped her dress close around her legs and buttoned her coat up high. Robert handed Leon a pair of hand knit mittens, noticing he had none, and Leon nodded thanks.

"I'll say go," offered Joe. "The winner is the champion of the world!" Then stepping back he ordered the other kids back as well. He wanted it to be a fair match... he had confidence in his skis... and in Andrea.

"Ready... set... go!" And they were off. Neither realized at first just how slick the road was, nor how fast the skis could travel and so just after they bumped over the railroad tracks they were nearly out of control. They were going neck and neck, but jostling into one another, whether on purpose or not, neither would tell. And so they rushed headlong down the road, mouths open in joy and surprise, peals of childish laughter escaping from these two 'adults.'

The boys at the top broke out into excited shouts and laughter as the two sliders lost complete control near the bottom of the hill, bounded into each other and then in a combined blustery tumble, slid into the snow bank, a tangle of arms, legs and skis. When all came to a stop, Leon was somewhat embarrassed to find himself atop Andrea, looking down at her rosy cheeks and full lips, half pursed in a rather womanly smile. Their eyes locked for a moment, and then he was suddenly moved, without clear thinking, to bend his head low and kiss her on the mouth. It was a warm wonderful kiss, although brief, and she seemed to return the effort. Rising up again, he expected the smile to widen, her eyes to soften. Instead, a look of shock was upon her features and suddenly she slapped him hard across the face. He fell off her, confused.

Andrea huffed out of the ditch, slipped at the top and fell back again on her posterior, which made her even more furious. Then almost in a panic, she managed to crawl out of the ditch and storm up the steep hill in a steam of anger. By the time Leon could return to the top of the hill, the Johnson's were gone and he could only turn the skis over to Robert and Ryan before stalking off his own self.

K. Wallin

The Twenty Sixth Chapter

A Perplexing Situation

It was breakfast at William's Restaurant then, to fill his stomach and mull things over. Inside, there were the usual clientele; the bachelors, the transients, the railroad men. He spotted Charley Halverson across the room, saloon owner, sitting by himself sipping coffee and puffing contentedly on a pipe. Few other chairs were available during this busy time of the morning, so Leon asked Charley politely if he would mind the company.

"Sit down, Mr. Mancheski. Take a load off," he said.

"Thanks Charley," said Leon sullenly. He sat there quietly, playing with a spoon and looking around the room. Even when Mrs. Williams came over to take his order, he was barely responsive.

"Ahhhh," said Charley. "This speaks of woman problems or a dead ox, one or the tother."

"I don't have an ox," replied Leon with a weak smile. "You know anything about women, Charley?"

"Well, I guess I would know just about as much as any man could know. Not so much sometimes, too much other times. The truth is," he paused and puffed deeply on his pipe for a second, blowing hazy blue smoke into the air, "the truth is, that women are quite perplexin'. Mighty perplexin'."

"Perplexing?" repeated Leon.

"Said so, didn't I?"

"How do you mean?" asked Leon.

"Waaalll," said Charlie thoughtfully. "Women are kinda like... like... the weather. Some days they are all sunshine and sweetness, gentle on the eye with voices like a soft breeze. Good weather. Damn good weather, sometimes."

"Yeah," said Leon dreamily.

"But weather is perplexin' ain't it? I mean, you start to cutting hay, and wham! it starts to rain. You have a picnic and it storms and storms. Ya just never know about weather. Even when you want a little rain... sometimes it won't. And the Almanac never knows for sure, it just guesses. Ed Simms was about the best weather guesser we had around here. He was more right than the Almanac, most times, bless his soul. And that's about all ya can do with women. Take a guess at what they're thinkin' or what they'll do next. Rain or sunshine, it's hard to tell one day from the next. And do you know why?" Leon pondered that a moment, then shook his head, no.

"Why, it's because they're so perplexin' that's why. Ain't you been listening? They don't know themselves some days, whether they're happy or sad about somethin'. If you see a woman crying, you don't never know if it's sad crying or glad crying. It looks about the same."

"So what do you do? When it's storming and raining, I mean. What do you do then?" asked Leon.

"What'll ya usually do? Go fishin", I'd say." Charley sat back in his chair and drew on his pipe. "That's about all ya can do when the weathers like that. Can't cut hay, might as well go fishin'.

"Yeah...." murmured Leon caught up yet again in the days events. Just then Mrs. Halverson arrived looking for Charley, for he was dawdling as usual. She would be sure to point that out to him. He always said he couldn't get no better unless someone pointed out to him where he was going astray.

"Charley?" she called in a high-pitched whiny voice.

"Oh, oh!" said Charley, "storm a brewin'!"

Leon left the restaurant and tried the office again, but this time from the back of the building, fumbling around in the stack of firewood briefly, piling it up nice and neat, before sauntering in through the back door. Cooper was there, poking at the stove and adding chunks of hard maple, startled at the young man's sudden appearance.

"Well, where've you been, anyway?" Cooper asked.

"Fishin'" Leon replied with a smirk.

"Huh?"

"Nothing. I was just out and about. Me and Smiley kinda slept in late this morning, then I took a bath... and had breakfast."

"I see. Truth is," said the older man straightening up with a groan, "I kinda slept in myself. Must have been the dancing."

"Yeah," agreed Leon. "Say, what did you want, anyway. I was thinking I would mosey on back to camp pretty soon."

"Yes, well... this won't take long. Have a seat." Cooper settled back in Jake's usual chair near the stove and motioned for Leon to take the chair on the other side.

"You see... well... I guess I'm going to throw my two cents worth in where it don't belong. I was hoping you'd feel obliged to listen to me anyway." Leon said nothing, but started to study Cooper's face. Careworn and friendly it seemed this morning, he thought.

"It's about Mary Muggsley."

"Mary?"

"Yes, Mary. Now she's a beautiful girl, mind you. None prettier in my book. But she's got plans. She's..."

"Plans?"

"Well, schemes, really. I mean she's a nice girl and all. But she's very wise for her age... too wise... in the ways of womanhood."

"What on earth are you talking about?"

"Womanhood, the ways of womanhood. Mary... well... Mary knows how to use the ways of womanhood to make a man feel important and good about himself. She makes a man see things... that aren't really true. To think things, that..."

"I still don't see what this has to do with me. What's your point, Mr. Cooper?"

"I knew we should have had this talk in the other room. I knew it."

"The other room?"

"Forget it. We are talking about Mary Muggsley."

"No, you are talking about Mary. And I don't really appreciate the things I think you're saying."

"I was afraid of that. I never would of pointed you in her direction, but I thought you needed a little attention about then, the way you were mooning about. Look, son... I'm just trying to save you some grief. Mary is not exactly who you think she is. There are other women around here, girls really, that are much more suited for romance."

"Like Andrea Johnson?"

"Oh, I wouldn't go fooling around with her either if I was you. No sir. She's a beautiful girl too, but too nice, much too nice, and from a nice family too. No, you'd better put that thought out of your head."

"It's just as well, Andrea's not who we think she is, either."

"Then who is she?"

"Not who, but what."

"Well, what is she then, mister?"

"Perplexing... that's what she is, downright perplexing." Cooper shook his head in bewilderment for a second.

"Now what the hell are we talking about? Either this hangover is worse than I thought, or... Have you been monkeying around here? I kinda suspected something with this 'barn' business on Thanksgiving, but after seeing you with Mary last night... well, I thought I was being a little too anxious for nothing."

Leon was quiet, just sitting there scratching his head, as if he didn't quite know where the conversation was going, not sure if he wanted to go with it, and not sure where it had been.

"Truth is, you haven't made up your mind, have you? You don't know if the beguiling Miss Mary will fix what ails you or not, do you? Well let me tell you... Miss Muggsley is like a bright light to a June bug. You light a candle and the bug's gather 'round, dancing and preening, not sure what they're doing. But I'll tell you this. If they get too close, they get burnt. You think you're the only fella that's been attracted by the light of Miss Muggsley? Not by a long shot, mister. Why, Buck himself, and Helge, were closer than thieves before Miss Muggsley wedged between them. Next thing you know, there's a fight and Helge's off to Michigan and Buck's off from women altogether. Two that got burnt, right there. And why? Just a whim of Miss Muggsley, a break in the boredom. I always figured it was Helge she was in love with, but just couldn't resist setting him off against Buck. Women will do that, you know."

"I'm not so sure you know as much about women as you think you do," observed Leon cynically.

"Maybe not. But I do know that Mary has been asking an awful lot about your so-called career, this journalist thing. She's practically charmed the bejesus out of Jake and even has taken to befriending Mrs. Gillis, for heaven's sake."

"So?"

"So do what you want."

"I will."

"But stay away from Andrea Johnson."

"Will you make up your mind?"

"Well, I don't want to see her get hurt. Mary can take care of herself, emotionally. She's had to take care of herself for a long time, what with the stories of her mother's past and all... well, she's a very strong young lady that will end up with just what she wants someday."

"And Andrea?"

"If you hurt Andrea, Buck will kick your ass from here to St. Paul and back. And I guess I'd be of a mind to finish whatever he left."

"Now why would I want to hurt her, for God's sakes. You make me sound like quite a rogue, or something."

"No... no that's not what I mean. Have you forgotten that there's a little unfinished business you left in Chicago?"

"Oh, that."

"Yes, that. You may think that it's all gone away now that you are out here in the bush, but I know these people. At least I think I know the kind you got mixed up with. Ask Ed Harding what St. Paul was like a few years ago, before people like your father became involved in cleaning it up. It's the same people, different location. These people play for keeps. It's a never-ending story, until one side makes it end. Think of what might happen someday, if they find you. Think of what might happen to the people that are close to you."

"I know, I know," said Leon wearily, not wanting to deal with it.

"I still say you should consider going back and talking to the police. The more I think about it, the more I think that the man in the uniform was some sort of waterfront security guard and not an actual policeman."

"Maybe. But why go looking for trouble. I'm pretty safe here. Who would look for me in the woods, a Chicago boy like me?"

"All the same, I think it would help if you'd let me tell a few people about your trouble, sorta garner some help in case you need it later on."

"Why would they want to help me? And what could they do, anyway, a bunch of farmers or clerks or storekeepers. No... no, telling them would just get them mad at me for possibly bringing trouble and disrupting their lives. Just leave it alone."

"You're wrong, son."

"Just leave it alone!" And with that, Leon retreated... left Cooper sitting there, frustrated at not having reached the young man's soul and conscious. Left the Straddle Creek company office and off down the street in a huff of troubling thoughts.

The Johnson's shared a dinner of Lutefisk at the Olson's farm in a festive pre-Christmas celebration. This Scandinavian treat, a North Sea fish soaked in brine, was hard to come by in Northern Wisconsin, so this occasional delight, served with a white gravy, was greatly appreciated when it chanced to be available.

Later back on the Johnson's own farm, it seemed to Andrea that Joe appeared strangely distant. He put the horses away in the barn, rubbing them down and feeding them oats, but then didn't return. So Andrea, herself a bit restless, searched for him in the barn and found him in the haymow, curled up with a few of the barn cats and staring out at the starry sky through the upper doors.

"What's the matter, Joe? I would think you would be quite excited, it being this close to Christmas. Yet here you sit, talking to the cats."

"That's just it, Andy. I've been thinking again. I don't have much money for presents... and I can't knit things like Mama and Aunt Serena."

"Oh, Joe..." she said, sitting down beside him and taking one of the cats on her lap. "You don't have to buy us anything. Why, none of us have very much money. I thought that I could save enough money to visit St. Paul or Chicago this year... but that's not going to happen either. I could give you some of that money... to buy presents with."

"Really, Andy?!? I'd pay you back, I really would. I'll find a way to make some money somehow."

"It's ok Joe, I know you will. But you know... the best present you could give Mama and Papa is to be good... to be awfully good. That would be the best present of all."

"Well, maybe I could give'm that present next year," he speculated. "How much can ya spare me, Andy?"

"Oh, I think I could spare $2.00. Do you think that would be enough?"

"Are you kidding? Two dollars would be glorious, Andy. Just glorious." He sat up, sending the felines flying and embraced his sister warmly. "I didn't want you to go away anyhow, Andrea, even for awhile."

"Well, I don't think you have to worry about that. I think you'll be stuck with me for a very long time, Joe. A very long time," she sighed.

"Andy?"

"Yes?"

"Do you want me to hit that Mancheski fellow with a snowball?"

"Nooo," she said smiling, "I think I can take care of that all by myself."

"Kinda crabby, aren't ya?" asked Smiley as they trudged up the south trail toward camp.

"You could say that this whole weekend hasn't exactly lived up to my expectations," allowed Leon. "If you know what I mean." Smiley just nodded and smiled. They paused to rest when they reached the railroad tracks leading to the camps, sitting down on the rails.

"Say... did you ever remember who you were... you know... who you really are," asked Leon?

Smiley looked around carefully before answering. "I know who I am," he said softly. "And I know who I was. Now that I am Smiley Birch... well that suits me just fine. I don't want to be anyone else."

"Smiley Birch has a past, then eh? I know what you mean," sighed Leon.

"Everyone has a past," he continued... except Smily Birch. Smiley Birch just has a future. And that's the way I'm walking."

Leon saw the sad wisdom in the simple statement, not sure if it didn't apply to himself as well. "Amnesia, huh? I wish I would have thought of that." And thinking about it now made him wonder a little about Cooper and what he was up to in the beginning. "I guess I'm walking toward the future too," he said after a moment of silent thinking. "I'm just not sure what direction that is."

Smiley decided to change the subject to something a little lighter on his mind. "Some dance though, huh?" he said. "All that dancing... and the food... and I think I fell in love, too."

"Fell in love? With who?"

"I'd not like to say... I guess. You never know how these things turn out." And Leon couldn't agree more.

The Twenty Seventh Chapter

Christmas Eve

Christmas comes, as Christmas will, too fast for some, too slow for others. The Christmas spirit had settled in about the streets and houses of Pratt some weeks before, painting smiles on the younger set, investing them with dreams and giving the older folks a good excuse to be kind and gentle to one another.

Except, perhaps, for Muff Brown. He was in the company store on Christmas Eve day, looking at ax handles and Malone trousers and other such merchandise while his kids checked out the few toys available. The kids talked in excited whispers, trying hard to suppress the growing magic of Christmas.

"But I need a sled, Em... and I ain't no miscreant... I believe in Santa... I really do!" Billy whispered a little too loudly.

"Shhhh," breathed Emily... "don't let Pa...."

"You, kids!" shouted Muff from across the room. "Shuddup, now. You don't need none of that stuff. Ya can look, but that's all."

Bill Farley winced. He could stand alot of things... but not the abuse of children. And snuffing out childish hopes and dreams was certainly abuse. As Muff continued banging around the tools, Bill gripped the counter so hard his knuckles turned white.

"Pa?" tried Billy, weakly. "If we could write to Santa Claus, maybe he..."

"I tol' ya to shuddup. There ain't no Santy Claus... cept for rich folk. Just forget about Santy Claus." Muff wandered past the counter where Bill was still trying hard to contain himself.

"Bill, I got to go down below the hill for a bit," he said wiping his hand across his mouth, "to...uh... to see a man about somethin'. The brats'll stay here."

"Fine, Muff. They'll be no problem, I'm sure," agreed Bill.

Muff grunted and nodded and walked out the door without looking back. Bill thought the kids looked a little relieved.

"Hey, you kids," he called to them. "Come over here for a moment."

"We didn't do nuthin, Mr. Farley, honest!"

"I know that, kids... come over here anyway. I want to talk to you." The kids walked over to Bill like scolded puppies.

"Your father is a smart man," said Bill. "Only he made one mistake. Of course it's a mistake that many people make."

"A mistake?" wondered Emily.

"About Santa Claus. Why, Santa Claus loves all the children all over the world. He doesn't always get a chance to visit their houses every year... but sooner or later he does. Especially if he gets a nice letter from good children, telling him what they'd like for Christmas." The kids looked at one another, secretly wanting to believe beyond hope that there was a chance that Santa would find them, somehow.

"I suppose you two are too busy for writing letters, but if you had a mind to, why I got plenty of paper and some envelopes."

"We're not too busy," said Billy. "I expect Pa will be gone awhile."

"I expect so too," replied Bill. "Why don't you two sit at that table over there and I'll bring you the stuff. The rest is up to you." In moments he had them situated at the table, chewing on the pencil end and considering very carefully what to say. Bill tried to stay out of their way, giving them some time to mull things over and put things in their own words.

People came and went for over a half hour, and still they sat... staring off into a world that was suddenly laid at their feet. They thought long and hard on what to ask for, and how to ask, so that it didn't just sound like a greedy request from ungrateful children. Mrs. Gillis came in later, while the kids were still working on their letters. She studied them for a moment, concluded who they were, then strode by shaking her head and making clucking noises with her tongue. When she saw Bill stacking shoe boxes in one of the aisles, she sauntered up to him.

"Those are the Brown children, you know," she said. Bill nodded quietly.

"How can a mother let her children dress like that. Practically rags. Why if I was their mother..."

"But you are not," said Bill.

"Well, if I was... you can be sure they would not be dressed like that. Practically rags. Where's their mother now, I wonder?"

"I don't know," sighed Bill, already tired of the conversation.

"Then where's their father? He can't be far. Charley's Saloon, I expect. Hmmmph! The way he just leaves those kids around really makes you wonder about that man."

"Can I get you something Mrs. Gillis?" asked Bill finally.

"Well, I need a few things... but I'll just take one wooden spoon today, Mr. Farley. Broke my old one over the mister's head."

"Certainly, Mrs. Gillis," smiled Bill, "I'll get it right away. One wooden spoon."

"Yes, and..." she paused and looked around the room, then sidled a little closer to Bill. "Give them little ones a candy cane, too," she whispered. "One for each, but not until I leave. I wouldn't want them to think I was giving 'em charity. Not that they don't need it, now and again."

"We all do, now and again Mrs. Gillis, thanks," said Bill. And after she had paid for her purchases, he bid her a sincere Merry Christmas. The candy canes he broke slightly, telling the children he couldn't sell them that way, so they might as well have them. Their smiles lit up the room.

The store was empty and near closing when the children hesitantly approached Bill at the desk.

"Thank you, Mr. Farley," said Emily. She put the extra paper and the pencils on the counter and looked up at him with big brown sad eyes.

"I could mail them for you, you know. You could just leave them here," he offered.

"Gee, Mr. Farley," smiled Billy.

"No," said Emily. "That wouldn't be right. We'll find some way to mail them, Billy."

"I really don't mind," said Bill.

"No," she said firmly. "Its Christmas Eve... we may be too late already, but we'll mail them somehow and maybe next year..." Her voice trailed off as a thought crowded into her mind. She looked toward the door where the winter light was quickly fading to darkness. "How long will you be staying open," she asked.

"Oh," said Bill looking at his watch. "I usually stay until 6 or 7 o'clock, sometimes later. You are certainly welcome to stay."

"Thank you, Mr. Farley," she replied somberly. It was only moments later, as the kids settled themselves back at the table to stare at their letters, that Muff came back. Bill knew at once that he had been drinking. He stood in the doorway and said, "c'mon" motioning with his arm. The kids waved at Bill and filed out after their father.

Bill thought of many things that were unfair with the world. But in the isolated reaches of a Northern Wisconsin lumber town, this seemed to manifest itself in his heart as most tragic. Who was he to judge, however, he argued with himself. Perhaps there was an underlying love that outsiders could not see. Perhaps they were cared for and loved, more than anyone could know. There were people who felt it necessary to put on a front when in the company of other people. Mr. Jacobs was a good example. Those thoughts seemed to make him feel better.

He damped down the stove and began closing up the store, putting things away, locking the money up in Cooper's old safe beneath the counter. It was already near black outside as he closed the door, so he fumbled with the keys. When the door was locked, he straightened up and took a deep breath of fresh night air. It was a starry night, this Christmas Eve, a wonderful night for Santa to be making his rounds. As he took a step he noticed something in the snow that he nearly stepped on. He picked up two envelopes with child-like writing on them.

"To Santa," he read to himself by starlight, a lump forming in his throat. He shook his head sadly, then slipped them inside his coat pocket and walked off into the night.

Emil and Alma lay awake in their bed, close enough so that the sides of their bodies touched and produced a combined warmth. Emil was absentmindedly brushing his mustache, his eyes alive and quickly darting to and fro as his mind wandered.

"Vhat is it, Papa?" she nudged gently, "Yew are so far avay."

"Nooo," he replied, "I am right by your side, like alvays, Mama. Varm and content, like two old bears in a cave."

"Vhat is it then? There is someting. Yew only brush your mustache vhen your thoughts are troubled."

"Can't a man brush his mustache vithout there being wrong things on his mind? I think maybe I cut it some. Is too much hair in my mustache."

"And too much thoughts on the mind," she said. Emil smiled in the darkness. Alma always knew. But he lay there a while longer before saying anything.

"Vee can give them so little this year, Mama. But they deserve so much."

"The children understand this, Papa."

"Vhat they understand? That Papa cannot give them things they should have? That Papa cannot send Martha to school to be teacher? That Papa cannot send Andrea to Chicago so she can see the vide vorld? Emma should have a new dolly, vhy, the head is only hung on vith a pin on dat ting. And Yoe, a sled or a knife, I think. And dresses for my grown up girls, and perfumes. Yew, Mama... vhat yew should have, I cannot give."

"Vhat I should have, yew have already given, Papa. Vee are in America on our own land. Our own land," she emphasized. "Vee have fine children. Vee have food to eat and vood to burn. Vhat vee should vant for? And vee have something that many people do not have."

"Vhat is this thing?" he asked wondering.

"Vee have the music of the fiddle," she cooed softly, "to lighten our hearts." Emil smiled again at these comforting words. But in the darkness he brushed at his mustache still. They lay there quietly for awhile, each with their own thoughts. Then suddenly, Alma leaned over and kissed him on the forehead.

Later when most others were sound asleep, Andrea still thrashed around in restless contemplation, causing Martha to mumble grumpily from time to time.

"Andrea, for heaven's sakes... can you lay still for awhile."

"Sorry, Mart... I... I guess I was just... listen! Do you hear singing?"

"What?"

"Singing... and laughing... and... from outside." She jumped up out of bed grabbing her robe from the chair as she flew to the window. In moments she was joined by Martha asking, "what is it," while still rubbing sleep from her eyes.

"Down there... see them? Looks like half a dozen fellows... there's Jim Porterfield... the fat one on the left... and Seth Hackett and Stanley Perkiss, Bob Hugdale and... and... isn't that Bill Gustavel?"

"Bill? My Bill? Oh, for heavens sakes what are they doing?"

"Caroling, I guess... but not too well... listen!"

There was a great attempt at singing 'Hark the Herald, Angels Sing' but most were out of tune or ill timed, resulting in as much laughter as there was singing.

"Why they're drunk... every one of them," exclaimed Martha. Andrea disappeared from the window then, slipping on her slippers and heading out the door. "Andrea! Where are you going?"

"To shut them up before they wake Ma and Pa!"

Down she went to the front door, flinging it open and calling to the men in whispered shouts. Finally getting their attention, they stopped singing and all stared at her.

"Shhhhh" she said, putting her finger to her lips.

"Shhhhh," they all replied at once, breaking into laughter once more.

"Hey!" said one, "Silent Night!" And so they gave that song a try.

"No, no..." she pleaded in a hoarse whisper. In desperation, she motioned them over to the door and they all came scrambling just as Martha came up behind her, all primped and combed with rose color in her cheeks.

"Hiya, Andy," Seth Hackett said rather loudly.

"Shhhh," motioned Andrea. "You're drunk!"

"So am I," replied Seth.

"Bill Gustavel... is that you out at this hour?" whispered Martha.

"Oh... Oh... Martha... I wanted to sing to you... it's Christmas and... and... my but you look lovely."

"What? I'm in my sleeping clothes... and you boys shouldn't even be here. Are you really drunk, Bill?"

"Not so much, I don't guess... am I Jim?"

"Naaaw," replied Jim. "Say... it'd be pretty courteous of you girls to invite us in for a sip of somethin'"

"Yeah..." added Bob, "it's getting mighty cold out here." They all tried to crowd in at once then with the girls teaming up to hold them back.

"No... no... you can't come in... you'll wake, Pa."

"Whose Pa?" asked Seth.

"If we could keep them in the kitchen, Andrea... maybe..." started Martha giving in to her heart.

"We'll stay in the kitchen... won't we boys?" promised Bill. There was a chorus of affirmation from the fellows who once again crowded in, this time succeeding in squeezing by Andrea and stumbling through to the kitchen following Martha who led with nearly a constant stream of shhhs. In the kitchen Martha lit a lamp, trying to dodge the boys stumbling around. As light filled the room all movement stopped and the fellows looking around simultaneously put their fingers up to their lips and chorused another shhhh with barely suppressed laughter.

"There's some blackberry wine in the pantry, Mart... might as well warm 'em up some."

"Yeah... warm us up," repeated Seth trying to snuggle closer to Andrea.

"Seth Hackett! Unless you want a cracked head for Christmas you'd better back up." Seth backed up a little, still aglow with the smiles of whiskey.

"Well, grab a glass everyone," said Martha as she finished filling them with wine. There was a minor struggle as the glasses were grabbed and the men jockeyed for position, Bill maneuvering to Martha's side.

"To the Johnson girls!" he saluted, his glass held high in the air. "With beauty and hospitality unequaled."

"Here, here." cried the men holding their glasses high. Then they all brought them down at once and threw back their heads to consume the wine.

"Say! That was great wine," exclaimed Stanley Perkiss smacking his lips. "Is there more?"

"Sweet as a kiss," added Jim.

"Now there's an idea," said Seth. "Where's the damn mistletoe, anyway." Then with a mischievous grin he started to advance toward Andrea.

"Say there, Seth," said Jim stepping between them, "I think you'd better back up some."

"Get outa the way, Jim... or I'll..." and before the others knew what was happening a struggle ensued with the immediate casualty of a large glass pitcher shattering on the floor. It brought an instant silence to the group, Seth and Jim stopping mid struggle. They all looked at one another soberly.

"Hello?" said Papa's voice from upstairs. "Hello? Andrea? Marta? Py golly I'll see about dis?"

Before there were even steps on the stairway, the boys had disappeared in a mad scramble, miraculously quiet and adroit leaving Papa to find only two rosy cheeked angels at the bottom of the stairs. They whispered vague apologies for waking him up, kissing him on the cheek as they passed before he could muster up the wakefulness to ask the right questions.

"G'night, Papa" they whispered sweetly from the hall, then disappeared in a swirl of barely stifled giggling, leaving Papa to only shake his head and wonder.

Things were pretty quiet at Camp #9. On this Christmas Eve, most of the local men had gone home to be with their families. The remaining men were somber and thoughtful, thinking of other Christmas' in their lives, happier ones, warmer ones.

Leon was kinda hoping to be invited to the Johnson's this night, but the more he thought of it, the more he realized that it really wasn't appropriate. He had thought of spending the evening with Cooper, but their last conversation had not exactly been invested with the Christmas spirit. And then he heard from Alfred that he had left on Monday for New Richmond to be with his own family.

Yes, Christmas was a time for families, and feeling this made Mr. Mancheski a lonely man. He lay now on his bunk, arms crossed beneath his head, staring at the rough boards of the ceiling. Buck was home. Helge, Muggs, Charley, even Ox Pete were home. Home. Chicago. The thought of it weighed heavily on his mind. He had just begun reliving that night when he was interrupted by Smiley. He was grateful. A knot was growing in his throat as the old images started to color and enliven.

"Is Mary kinda your gal? he asked sitting on the bunk next to him.

"My girl?" It sounded nice when Smiley said it. "Yeah, you could sorta say that."

"She sure is pretty," said the other, his smile lighting up the darkness. "You're a pretty lucky guy."

"Yeah," sighed Leon at the thought of her. Somehow Mary and sound reason seldom shared the same moment.

"She's almost as pretty as Andrea Johnson," added Smiley.

"Andrea Johnson?" exclaimed Leon sitting upright.

"Yeah, Buck's sister. Now there's the gal for me. Sweet as a jar of honey, that girl. And what a dancer! Did you get a chance to dance with her?"

"Yeah, we danced. Say, just what have you got in mind anyway?" asked Leon surprised at his mounting anxiety.

"In mind? Well, nothing special, I guess. I don't think she knows I'm around even," said Smiley. "But I figure some Sunday after Christmas I just might go callin'. Maybe take her for a sleigh ride or something. Or maybe write her a note... I think maybe I can write better than I can talk."

"Oh, oh.... oh I wouldn't do that if I were you. Noooo not at all. I'd stay away from her... far away."

"Really? Why?" asked Smiley.

"It's Buck. No telling what he might do if he found out someone was... was bothering his sister like that."

"Bothering her? I wasn't gonna bother her. I was just gonna go callin'. There's nothing wrong with that," said Smiley.

"Buck hit me once," allowed Leon truthfully. "Right in the face. Wham!!" He banged his fist into his other hand with a smack. "And brother, I was out for a day and a half."

"Why?"

"Why?"

"Why did he hit you. He must have had a reason," exclaimed Smiley.

"Reason? I'll say he had a reason. I was drinking to someone's health. That was the reason. And he objected to it. Happened right in Charley's Saloon on a night before the camp even started up and before Buck even knew me. Just hit me, whack, like that." He smacked his fist into his hand again.

"I'd hate to see what he'd do to someone that was bothering his sister. No sir. I wouldn't like to see that at all," pressed Leon.

"Yeah," was all that Smiley could say. He had a mental image of that big fist coming at his face and it wasn't a comforting sight. "Yeah," he said again.

And when Leon lay back down again and closed his eyes, he was painfully aware that Cooper had been right about one thing. He had not really made up his mind about anything.

K. Wallin

The Twenty Eighth Chapter

Christmas Day

Christmas morning in the Northland dawned bright and beautiful. The long awaited day, so distant for all these weeks, now suddenly burst upon the residents of Pratt. For the adults, it was a matter somewhat of relief. To the children it was the culmination of hopes and dreams that had been invested with good behavior for such an awfully long time.

There were a few new sleds on the North road and the western sledding hill long before midday. Children of many ages, many in newly knitted mittens and mufflers were calling to one another gleefully espousing the generosity of Santa Claus. And the lingering feeling that all was right with the world would continue in the days to come until it gradually faded into the dreary days of winter.

There was no particular joy in the Brown house. The Mrs. fixed a sparse breakfast as usual and the children ate in required silence. Muff, nervous and surly, smoked a crudely rolled cigarette and stared at the sullen faces of his children. For a moment he felt pangs of compassion welling within him... that this merry season could bring no joy and laughter to his house. Their stark life had fueled his dislike for anyone who could afford the things he couldn't, simple things that a man ought to have.

Yet memories flitted through his mind like butterflies, bright with thoughts of the happy moments of his childhood, the magic and promise of Christmas morning. Memories made long before his life had turned sour, long before his dreams had faded into misery and contempt.

287

But the happy butterflies of thought passed quickly, being replaced by feelings of guilt and frustration. When you know how it had been, how it could be... it was much easier to be disappointed by how it was. And it was not particularly good in the Brown household.

"I tol' ya," said Muff suddenly, "Santa Claus don't visit us poor folk." Expressionless faces looked up in unison. "We'll get along better someday, and Santa will come around. Maybe when it ain't even Christmas."

"We know, Pa," said Emily softly.

"But Mr. Farley says..." started Billy, but Muff's fist was brought down on the table hard enough to make the dishes rattle. Both children and their mother, jumped in fear.

"I don't give a hoot what that man says. He never been poor, so how's he know what a man... what Santa can do or... well damn him anyway for putting thoughts into yer head!" Mrs. Brown stayed quiet. She saw the fire in his eyes and knew when it was important not to interfere, not to contradict or complain, even when her own heart was breaking. She nervously wrung her apron in her hands and waited until Muff's rage subsided and his quiet brooding returned.

"Run out and play, children," she called softly. Immediately they obeyed. Muff too, put on his coat and stomped out the door leaving her alone.

It was easy to see the disappointment in Joe's eyes, and Emma's, when they tumbled down the stairs early that morning. Joe figured there had been some mistake. He had distinctly told Santa he wanted a nice new sled instead of the cumbersome homemade skis that he was obliged to use. He had explained that the sled would come in handy for hauling any number of things in winter... and how he would be sure to give Emma a ride once and awhile.

But there were few packages beneath the tree, and certainly nothing as big as a sled. Emma clutched her doll tightly and looked wide-eyed at the scene before her. No fancy doll was anywhere to be found. Certainly Santa would not have forgotten her.

"A lovely morning, isn't it?" greeted Alma as she came from the kitchen. "I believe vee got some snow last night."

"Did Santa come last night, too, Mama? Was he here?" asked Emma.

"Vell, I tink so. Yew two... yew go put on some slippers now, and wrap in your robes. It is still some cold in here."

"Yes, Mama," they said in unison, and slowly they trudged back up the stairway, just as Andrea and Martha were coming down fully dressed.

The older girls were more gay and lively in their mood and greeted Alma warmly, with a hug and a Christmas kiss on the cheek.

"Merry Christmas, Mama!" they cried.

"Merry Christmas, my two beautiful girls. Vhat a pleasure it is to have yew here vith me."

"Oh, Mama. We are not so beautiful," said Andrea.

"Speak for yourself, Andrea Johnson," said Martha, "beauty is as beauty does. Why just the other day I was told by a fine gentleman just what a lovely lady I am. I certainly have no reason to doubt him."

"Bill Gustavel," laughed Andrea, "now there is a boy in love. And they say love is blind!"

"Well, Bill is a man, not a boy," said Martha suddenly, but that only made Andrea laugh harder. "I heard someone say that you were beautiful too, Andrea." The statement made Andrea stop short.

"Who?"

"I'll not tell unless you promise to stop making fun of Bill," she sniffed.

"Martha Johnson, you tell me right now or I'll box your ears," threatened Andrea.

"Andrea! I vill not have that talk in my house, especially on Christmas morning. Now yew girls go into the kitchen and eat your breakfast. Yew go now!" said Alma sternly but with a trace of a smile on her face. And off they went, Martha leading the way and Andrea at her heels. As the kitchen door closed, there was a squeal and more giggles until finally the girls fell into hushed whispers and stifled titters of laughter.

Emil came in from the outside and stomped the snow off his boots. He looked at the Christmas tree sadly and shook his head as Alma took his coat.

"Vee could get by vith not so much money in the sugar bowl, I tink," he said.

"Maybe," replied Alma. "But vinter is long... vee don't know vhat vee vill need. And vee do not add to sugar bowl in long time. It is not so bad Papa, the children understand." Emil nodded solemnly.

"Vee make it a happy day vithout fancy presents," she added. "Vee eat good meal and give thanks to the Lord for all of us together. And vee sing, and vee dance."

Emil nodded again, saying, "Ya ya, all this vee do." Just then they heard footsteps on the stairs and turned to find Joe and Emma coming back down fully dressed.

"Good morning, Papa," greeted Joe with little enthusiasm.

"Merry Christmas, Papa," greeted Emma.

"Yes, Merry Christmas my children, it is beautiful Christmas Day."

"Vhere is Buck?" asked Alma, "still in barn?"

"Yaa."

When Buck did not come in from the barn for some time, some began to wonder. But it was Andrea who finally put on her boots and threw her shawl around her shoulders to go out and check on him. She found him in the back, in one of the empty stalls, sitting and staring at something on the floor, a contraption of sorts with skis and boards. At the sound of footsteps he looked up to see Andrea standing over him, blushing a bit as a school boy caught in some wrong doing.

"Andy..." he gulped. "Vell, vhat yew think?" She surveyed the work before him. He had sawed the skis down to sled size and fastened a box atop them to hold them together and provide a seat. It was an old dynamite crate that still warned of 'explosives' in large letters. At the front of the box he had bent some tin over the bottom to allow for smooth travel over snow. To the top of the box he had attached a length of rope for pulling, and had just now finished his work.

"It's wonderful, Buck, just wonderful," she said as tears welled in her eyes. "Joe will think it's glorious for sure."

Buck beamed brightly. He was not fool enough to think it would replace a brand new sled, but optimistic enough to think that it would help.

And soon they all gathered around the tree and opened packages of mittens, hats, scarves and other knitted things made over the last several months. With money he had borrowed from Andrea, Joe produced crudely wrapped packages for Alma and Emil. They were overwhelmed. For Emil it was a package of his favorite pipe tobacco, for he had taken to smoking a much cheaper brand and not as often in these lean times. He tousled Joe's hair unable to speak, for it made the absence of 'Santa's' gifts seem that much more empty and tragic, though the children had not mentioned it again.

For Alma it was a new sugar bowl, with a slight chip in one of the handles... marked down in price accordingly. It was money well spent, for a gratitude in cookies would be meted out in the following days.

Martha produced a new doll for Emma, or rather, an old doll with a new face and newly sewn clothes. It brightened the young girl into smiles, and though the doll with the pinned on head would remain close to her, it would have a cheery companion to talk to and take naps with.

Martha and Andrea were each given handkerchiefs with their initials sewn in the corner. And Joe a new pair of winter boots, sorely needed. Finally, Buck brought in the sled, thinking how badly it looked, how inadequate, until he looked at Joe's face. And then he knew it was right. The word "glorious" was bantered about a dozen times and then it was announced that the sled would have a name, and that name was "dynamite".

But still Emil's heart was heavy and he smoked his pipe, with his fine tobacco, in silence, watching his family gushing over meager presents. Alma noticed him and allowed him a kiss on the forehead, which was returned with a weak smile.

"It is fine Christmas," she whispered to him. Joe overheard the comment.

"It is not fine, Mama," he said. His parents looked at a pained and troubled expression on his face. Then it suddenly brightened into a big grin. "It is the best Christmas, ever!" he suddenly beamed. "It just needs music. Will you play, Papa?"

"Ya... Ya..." he said, waving his pipe in the air. And so they sang and danced in joyous celebration of Christmas... in joyous celebration of life and family.

And later in the evening, as they were all gathered around the table with clean and smiling faces, dressed in their "Sunday" clothes and the mood of the season still bracing their spirits, Emil paused to savor the moment. "Levande ljus," he said under his breath; a warm glow over a festive table. And when Alma finished saying grace, Emil said "Yaa" and really meant it.

Bill Farley was a troubled man. He said nothing to his wife, Francis, that night, about the letters in his inside coat pocket. But he could not get them off his mind, the childish scrawling, all of their Christmas dreams sealed in yellowed paper envelopes. He could open them, he thought, but what then? Muff Brown was not apt to allow his children to receive charity, even in the guise of Santa.

But, by God... they deserved something. Any child and every child deserved the chance to dream, to challenge their stark reality by daring to believe in something better in their life. So when his wife went singing into the other room, Bill dared to open the letters. He had just finished reading them when there was knock on the door. He swallowed hard when it turned out to be Muff Brown.

"Merry Christmas, Mr. Farley," said Muff gruffly. As an afterthought, he removed his hat.

"Merry Christmas, Mr. Brown, won't you come in?" He held the door open for him and led him into the kitchen.

"Why, Mr. Brown," greeted Francis, "Merry Christmas to you." Muff merely nodded. "And how is Adeline?" she asked as she poured them both a cup of coffee.

"Good," he mumbled. Then noticing the men's uncomfortableness, she left them alone.

"You have a nice house," observed Muff a few minutes later, while munching on a Christmas cookie.

"Thank you," replied Bill. When Muff offered nothing more in the way of conversation, Bill decided that perhaps he should lead the way.

"Muff, I think there is something you should see," he began, and with a little bit of guilt, he offered up the opened letters for Muff's review. When he saw what they were, Muff swallowed hard.

"I threw 'em away," he said.

"I know. I found them in the snow. It's none of my business, Muff, this I also know. You can throw them in the stove now, if you wish. But I think you should read them first."

"I don't need to read 'em," he said defensively, "I know what the kids want. I know what they need. It's not that I don't want to give 'em something. I've been on hard times. It's hard enough to eat sometimes."

Bill pushed the letters at him across the table. "Take a look, Muff. I think you'll be surprised."

"I don't need no look," he said adamantly.

"Well, by God, I'll read them to you, then," exclaimed Bill in mounting anger. "Dear Santa... my name is Emily Brown. I don't need much this year, but I wonder if you could help my Pa find a job so that we can all be happy again. That is all that I want for Christmas, if it's not too much trouble." Bill looked at Muff, but his face was impassive, eyes vacant.

"Dear Santa," he continued from the other letter, "please bring my Pa a new coat and my Ma a pretty dress. And if there's any leftover, a sled for me and Em." Muff's eyes were still vacant and unseeing, the eyes of a man looking within.

"I'd say they were pretty fine children you have, Mr. Brown. Pretty special, indeed." Muff coughed uncomfortably.

"But you didn't come here to listen to me rattle on about children and letters to Santa, did you. Why did you come to see me this morning, Muff?"

"I'm not sure," he said clearing his throat a little. "But I thought maybe if you... uh, I don't know, I guess. I just wanted to talk to you. I thought maybe you could use some help in the store or sumthin'. Firewood, maybe? I kin cut firewood, all that you'd need."

"I have all the firewood I need right now, Muff," returned Bill honestly.

"Oh, ya, I suppose you do."

"But we'll be cutting ice soon. Sure could use some help there, someone to drive a team and help with the sawing and loading. You interested?"

And so Emily Brown received her gift from Santa. At least in a way, thought Bill. And through this meager job perhaps the other things would come in time and the fragile string of hope would hold for a little while longer.

Leon was up early that Christmas morning, while the stars were still out and the moon and the darkness. He didn't look at his watch before he got dressed, being driven by a much higher feeling than time.

Outside, he watched his breath in vapory moonlight mists rise to the stars. And seeing the stars, he noticed, as if for the first time, how bright they were, how distant. Some clouds drifted past the moon suddenly, casting him into a darker night, and he shivered. But the clouds passed, and soon the snow-covered country about him was bathed in the blue gray of moonlight.

It was mildly cold in the still night air, encouraging him to move about. He wandered aimlessly at first, across the tracks toward the cook shanty, then back again until he found himself at the stable. It was warm inside, warmth from living things. He looked at the oxen, these massive beasts of burden so docile in their stalls. The cat curled up in a pile of straw in the corner, eyeing him curiously, stretching out a front paw and yawning.

And he drifted into thought as aimless as his wanderings had been. He thought of a stable, probably much like this one, so long ago, or so the story went. But it seemed more than a story to him this morning. Perhaps it was his loneliness, or the early hour. Perhaps he had been working too hard, or had worried too much about things seemingly out of control with his life. But suddenly he was invested with a sense of the spiritual, settling in about his shoulders like a warm shawl. It comforted him and saddened him. For the story was suddenly a very real event. A poor wandering couple gave birth to a child in a stable, a stable much like this one. And a tear found it's way down his cheek. And he was glad that he was alone.

K. Wallin

The Twenty Ninth Chapter

ᴄWinter ᴅoldrums

When Christmas was but a memory and the 1st of the year had gone by with nary a change to the lives of those in Northern Wisconsin, winter settled in about the countryside in frozen landscapes of wind and snow. And as the temperature plummeted to the 20 below zero mark and clung there for several days like a stubborn child, Leon began to lose his fondness and appreciation for the wilds of the north. A hoary frost had formed along the walls of the bunkhouse furthest from the stove, though he was forever hauling wood to feed its ravenous appetite.

The lunchtime journey with hot food for cold and hungry men had also lost it's magic for him. It was difficult at best, to cart the steaming kettles and pots to the distance the loggers had made, and more difficult still, to actually be able to keep the food hot long enough to please them. There was a growing restlessness and irritability that came with the cold. Fights in the bunkhouse were more common, more vicious and begun by the simplest of matters. The Christmas spirit truly had faded.

Men who had worked the camps for many years knew it for what it was; cabin fever aggravated by cold and dismal days of work; cutting wood with hands sometimes feeling as cold and wooden as the trees that were cut; families distant and sometimes suffering in the same manner as the woodsmen. Spring was a hundred years away. Only the dreary drudgery of the miserable life of a lumberman remained in their minds, a never-ending task.

Cooper noticed the change in mood and disposition on one of his few visits to Camp #9. Leon had stopped shaving... and bathing, for that matter.

Trips to town for a bath no longer seemed important to him and he was surly and sour with the causal conversation tossed his way. It was the same with the others, though some were more used to the conditions. But Cooper was a smart man of vast logging experience and an innate understanding of the common lumberman. He left them alone. He cautioned Ox Pete to rule with an iron hand, to drive the men hard, for in this cold and dismal life, idle time meant trouble pure and simple.

"Ya ya," agreed Pete, inserting a thumb full of snoose in his lip. "I tell Buck, vee vork hard. Den if Buck get ugly tu, I go to Spooner and drink vhiskey all day, far avay."

"Me too," said Cooper, "Me too." Each day, the "sign" readers and self styled weather forecasters predicted the cold spell would break, yet it clung to the land for a week or more and offered no respite. The men sat about the bunkhouse in the evening, telling a few tales or two and nursing cold feet and frozen fingers.

"I don't know if I want to thaw this one out," said Helge from near the stove. "It don't feel so bad, dead like that. If I give it back to warmth, it's gonna pain me something awful."

"Well, if'n you don't give it back to warmth, it'll rot by spring and they'll have to cut it off," said Emil Larson. "Might as well keep it on. A man needs all the fingers he can get."

"Why is it so cold. Is it always so cold up here? Damn it's cold!" said Leon in a grumbling voice to no one in particular.

"Well, now son," said Bull, "This ain't much for cold just now. Cold is cold... real cold. This is just nuisance cold."

"How cold is real cold?"

"You see these scratches?" said Bull pulling open his underwear and revealing dark purple marks along his back. "Them were caused by real cold, ya might say."

"Ya might say," said Helge, "or ya might not."

"You shut up yer mouth, Helge Johnson, this is my story," he answered, then looking back at Leon, "and it's true what I say. Them were scratches caused by the cold. By real cold."

"I don't understand," admitted Leon, only mildly curious.

"Well, it was a few years back... maybe '97 or '98... I don't know, and I was trapping along the White River over Drummond way. Them pelts were prime, I tell you... cause the thermometer hit 20 below zero on December 1st and never did go above that til Spring. Man, I thought it was cold. Almost lost a couple of fingers in a beaver trap, 'cept the fingers were so cold, I didn't even know they was in the trap 'till I come to the end of the chain. They didn't even start hurtin' 'till spring." A few men gave a snicker and sidled a little closer. Not even Leon pretended these stories had any truth to them anymore, but yet listened with all the faith of a child in spite.

"But about them scratches," reminded Leon.

"I'm getting to it, I'm getting to it. Ya see, I thought it was cold then, real cold, but nearly tolerable... like now. Then it got colder... maybe 30 or 40 below zero. There was five feet of ice on the White, ten feet on the lakes, and fifteen on the ponds. I couldn't trap beaver no more cause it would take me all day to chop through the ice so when I finally would get to water, it was dark and I had to stop cause I couldn't see what I was doing. And when morning come, there wasn't a sign I had chopped a lick... it was all froze up agin."

"And the scratches?" reminded Leon again.

"Well, as I said, I couldn't trap beaver no more, nor muskrat, nor mink... none of them. So I thought I would trap me some fox or wolf or panther. Yes, sir, got me some fine pelts that way, so prime the fur was 6 inches thick. Hard to skin, but warm to wear.

"Well, what about them damn scratches," yelled Leon, surprised at his own aggressiveness. The men all looked at him and smiled. He had the fever for sure.

"I was getting to that, if you'd stop interuptin'," snarled back Bull. "Now where was I?"

"Pelts near 6 inches thick," offered Smiley.

"Oh, ya. And prime as anything you'll ever see. But then the weather turned cold. That real cold like I was talking about, maybe a hunnert below. I was starting to get a little prime myself, growing a little fur around the edges. I figured I would go get my traps and go home, or go to hell whichever was warmer. So I piled on some skins and headed out."

"Well, sir," continued Bull, "near my last trap, not in it, mind you, but near it, was a big panther all crouched over and ready to pounce on the bait I had there. He had a snarl on his face and a paw outstretched like he was gonna strike at it... but he just stood there looking at it with a glassy stare. Well, I never brought my gun with cause I didn't exspect to see no panther out in the cold like that. Figured they'd all be curled up in their holes someplace, kinda warm."

"What happened?" someone asked, "He attack ya?"

"Nope," replied Bull, spitting into the brass spittoon near the stove. "I thought he was gonna, but when he didn't, I went up to him to check him out... and he was frozen solid. Just like a piece of wood, he was. So I carted him home, like carrying a statue, paw outstretched and all, like an armload of cord wood. By the time I got back to the shack, I was bushed...

used up all my heat and energy getting the traps. So I set the panther by the fire, figuring to get to him later. Seems, he started to thaw out some and fell into a heap afore long and I forgot about him. Come morning and I was gonna walk out a there, get back to Pratt and sit by a fire and drink whiskey. Good Irish whiskey, was my plan. I noticed this prime black pelt a lying there, so I put it on around me. The temperature had warmed up some, maybe only 80 or 90 degrees below zero that day... but I see'd the elephant and was bent on going back to Pratt. So's I did. I got to Pratt and feeling kinda cold still, I stopped right off at Charley's to add a little whiskey to my blood, cause whiskey don't freeze much when it's inside ya. It was warm inside Charley's cause he had a fire going all day and all night, some good white oak, too. I never thought much about it, being still some frozen myself. But after an hour or so, I suddenly hears a rattle and roar and a scream that just plumb scared me half to death. I says, 'what the hell was that, Charley? You got the devil in here for sure!' But Charley, he just says, that devil you hear is on your back, and sure it was... the panther come to life and still snatching at that bait. He scratched me something fierce, scrambling outa there, his back claws cutting up my back as he dug in. Then he jumped off, took a swipe at the whiskey sitting on the table, but I moved it sudden like, so he just scratched the table some, then he went screeching out the door. Old Ted McGumby was in there then... he seen it... it turned his dadburned hair all white... and it would be today, if he weren't dead."

There were a few guffaws all around and a lightening of the mood, as the story wound down. "Now that was cold, real cold," he added.

"Gosh!" exclaimed Smiley. And then the laughter really began, including Leon who several months earlier would have believed every word.

"Well, you go see... at Charley's them marks are still in the table where the panther swiped at the whiskey."

"The way I heard it," said Helge, "you was drunk one night and stumbled into some barbed wire."

"Why, that's downright insultin'" said Bull. And when he looked around and saw the smirks on the faces of the others, he tackled Helge in a rushing roar. The other men moved out of the way and let the two of them wrestle and fight near the door.

"Yep, some folks are believers," said Emil Larson, "and some are skeptics."

"I didn't believe it for a second," said Leon scratching his hairy chin. The growth was out of laziness, not a particular hirsute desire.

"Me neither," said Smiley. Meanwhile the fracas continued around them, a fist thrown and returned now and again, but mostly it was aggressive wrestling.

"I know'd this gal who was a believer," said Ole. "A pretty young gal, as nice as you please. From a good Christian family, too."

"What about her," asked Charlie Helgestrom.

"Well, she was apt to believe a person. A real believer, she was. If they told her it was raining outside, though the sun was shining and all the sky was blue, she would figure you was dead on and the sky was lying."

"That so?"

"Said so, didn't I?"

"Well, what about her," asked Charlie.

"Was one day she got word that there was a card for her at the post office, it being her 16th birthday and all, and her having a sweetie visiting down south, down Chippewa way. So she appeared at the window and asked for her card. Well, this clerk fella, he was a young buck himself and partial to beauty, which this gal was... so he asked her to read the card to him, knowing already what it said. But the gal was mightily pleased at the mail received and was glad to oblige." Ole stopped and puffed on his pipe, as if pondering the merits of the tale and the direction it would take.

"Well," asked Leon, "what was in the card?"

"Twas from her sweetie alright. And she read it plain out to the clerk as proud as could be: I am sending this happy birthday message to the sweetest girl in the world, along with a money order for $16 dollars and 16 kisses. Love, Mortimer."

"Mortimer?"

"Well, where is my money order, she asks the clerk, for 16 dollars? I have it here, he replies and hands it to her. Then he adds, 'and I spose you want them 16 kisses too. And she says, being a believer and all, that if they was sent to her, she was sure she should have them. And so the clerk obliged her. And when she got home she tells her ma, she says, 'why the post office is the most amazing place, for they can deliver anything and better. Mortimer sent me 16 kisses and 17 were delivered!"

The guffaws following that revelation nearly out noised the grunts and groans of the fracas. And then in a loud crash and midst the remnants of a small table, it came to an end. Both men sat with backs against the wall, bleeding and bruised but none the worse for the pummeling received.

"Maybe we can finish this tomorrow," says Helge to Bull.

"Ya, or maybe in the spring," replies Bull.

And so the winter wore on, with infrequent days of bright blue skies and sunny warmth to tease of spring. But for the most part, the men at Camp #9 as well as throughout the rest of the woods, attended to their weary work from dawn to dusk and let the thoughts of spring keep them sane. Cabin fever was not limited to the lumber camps, however. In town and all the farms about, the cold drove the people in doors where they sat near the stove and listened to the wind rattle the windows.

Martha was more than happy to volunteer for a trip to town to pick up a few necessities. Anything to break the monotony and talk to a few people, perhaps stop and see the Gustavel's at the farm on the way back, though she was adamant that her interest was merely neighborly in nature.

Hours later Andrea could see her shadowy form coming across the pasture, bundled up in her winter coat and stumbling through the snow, her shoulder turned against the north wind. She watched as Martha let herself in through the gate, then pause as she closed it behind her. She stood still for a moment at the gate, staring back across the windswept pasture as if there was something new to be seen there. Had Andrea been closer and more in front, she would have seen blank eyes in a wooden face no longer bothered by the chill in the air. And then the packages fell from her arms as if she didn't know it or no longer cared. She remained that way for a few minutes more, until Andrea came from the barn and touched her on the shoulder.

"Oh! Oh, Andrea, you startled me. I was just... just thinking about things... that's all." She suddenly realized then that she no longer held the packages in her arms. "See what you made me do? Oh, these things will be ruined!"

Andrea stooped to help her gather up the parcels but Martha pulled them from her hands, saying nothing but giving a weak smile. "Good as new," she said finally and strode off quickly for the house.

"Oh, Mart" Andrea said to herself sadly, wondering what had suddenly taken hold of her mind. But then at supper it was as if everything was wonderful again, Martha in good spirits and everything as it should be. And so, too, Andrea put the moment out of her mind.

And then just as the cold spell broke, more despair set in. Diphtheria was about, robbing babies from cradles and cutting a swath of despair through the populace, young and old alike from Eau Claire to Ashland along the Chicago & Northwestern line. The Helegstrom's lost little Pat, and Gustav Nelson succumbed as did Elmer Anderson and the elderly Henrietta Fielding. The very young and the very old seemed the most vulnerable to it's death grip, but it sickened most everyone it came into contact with, making for some miserable weeks of recovery and quarantine. People were afraid to be out, to mingle with their brethren, to chance breathing in the disease. It increased the isolation and misery.

In the first week of February, the school was closed, for there were so many out sick or in fear of being sick, that Miss Fenton had nearly no one to teach. Alma watched her family closely, for sign of illness. She reacted in horror and sympathy at the tales of death that befell the Pratt citizens, but secretly she thanked the Lord that her family was spared.

And then word came of the Walden family. Robert was stricken, and Rebecca and mother, Anna. Doctor Parker was busy day in and day out attending to the sick as best he could, consoling those he could not help while the winter dragged on, long and dark.

The Johnson's arranged with John Cooper to get their supplies via the Pratt & Southeastern, Emil meeting the engine where it passed the north pasture. Here he would hear the latest tales of who was sick, who had passed into glory, and who was saved. These he would pass on to Alma, when they were alone in the dark of the night, as if speaking of this in daylight would somehow bring it closer. This too, they kept from the children, even Andrea and Martha, if they could. And in that darkness, they would pray.

At first, Joe thought it was 'glorious' that there was no school to burden him. Until he found that he was restricted to the limits of the farm. Ol' dynamite, his ski/sled was parked up against the barn, ready for use, but the use it saw these days was that of water and wood hauler, hardly the use of choice. Joe, his school record aside, was no dummy. He noticed the whispered conversations stopping abruptly whenever he came near, for the plight of Robert Walden was deliberately kept from him. And so, he arranged to be near, but out of sight, the next time Andrea and Martha whispered the horrible thoughts that plagued them.

"It's God's wrath," said Martha, "God's wrath for the unchristian way we have lived."

"Nonsense," returned Andrea. "What is unchristian in the way the Helegstrom baby lived? He wasn't more than 2 years old when the Lord took him."

"Well, all the same, it wouldn't hurt to examine our lives and make sure we have pure thoughts. Why, I haven't hardly thought of Bill in two weeks and I feel the better for it."

"Oh, Mart, sometimes you slay me."

"Well, it's true!" she insisted.

"How about the dream you had the other night? When I woke up you were hugging me so tight I could hardly breathe!"

"A person can't control their dreams, can they?"

"Mart, you are a stitch. But that's ok, that's the warmest I've slept since the first of the year." And they giggled, as they often did when sharing this type of revelation. But it was a nervous laugh that attended them now, and it stopped as suddenly as it started. Joe was about to come out of hiding, bored at the discussion at hand, when they lowered their voices some and continued in hushed whispers.

"Oh, Andrea, I'm so worried. What if Papa or Mama, what if you or Joe or Em... oh Andrea, what if Emma... I couldn't stand it, Andrea, I just couldn't!"

"Mart, it's ok... we'll be alright. None of us have even come in contact with anyone who's sick. Papa has Alfred just throw the supplies down and keep on going."

"I feel so sorry for the Helegstrom's. And the Nelsons. Oh, and the Walden's, Andrea, how terrible that must be... three of them sick, and who knows how many before it's through."

"Has Papa heard any more now, is... is the boy going to be alright?"

"I heard them whispering this morning, just after the train came by. It doesn't look good, he's very sick. Becky is getting along now, and Mrs. Walden too. But the boy... the doctor is very worried. He says maybe only a miracle can save Robert Walden."

And in the darkness of his hiding place, Joe felt his heart rise to his throat and make it difficult to breathe.

The Thirtieth Chapter

New life

In the evening, at the supper table, an extra prayer was added to the Grace before the meal at the Johnson house, to pray for those less fortunate. But though they usually did not come right out and mention specific individuals nor their personal misfortune, Emil felt so strongly for the Walden's that he implored God to watch over them in particular.

"And help the poor boy recover from that awful sickness," he finished, then looked up and around nervously. He didn't think the children knew what he was talking about exactly, until he saw the looks on their faces at the table... somber, subdued, even pale in the kerosene light. But no one said a word for a few moments, staring at their plates with their hands still clasped.

"God's vill be done, Papa," added Alma softly patting his arm, "God's vill be done."

"Ya ya," he replied. He removed his glasses and cleaned them with a corner of the tablecloth. When he had them on his head again, he looked at his children.

"Eat," he said, "Eat this fine food mama fix for us. Keep yew strong! Like horse!"

"Oh, great," said Martha, "that's just what a girl wants to be like... a horse for heaven's sakes." It was enough to bring laughter in these hard times, nervous laughter, lacking its usual release from tension, but music all the same.

"Have you heard any thing about the lumber camps, Papa?" Asked Andrea. "Is the sickness there?"

"Alfred says camps are doing vell, but for cold. No sickness... except for case of pneumonia. James Pell, I tink it vas. He vas taken home."

"But no sickness, right Papa? Buck and... and the others, they..."

"No sickness," said Papa again a little stronger. "Oh and Jim Curry lost a finger. It got pinched off in the Jammer chain. Nothing serious."

"Too bad it wasn't his toe," said Joe. "I heard Mr. Cooper say he's got six toes on each foot."

"Ya ya," laughed Emil, "I heard dat tu! Six toes on each foot."

"How does he play piggy or the Strawberry game?" asked Emma.

"Piggy?"

"Yes... he would have one piggy left over," added Andrea to more laughter.

"Papa?" said Joe soberly. "Can I go visit Robert Walden tonight? It's sorta important."

"No!" said Emil rather forcefully. "No, no visits. Soon it vill be spring and things vill be good. Yew play lots, then."

"Maybe school will start up again soon," suggested Andrea.

"Oh, great," moaned Joe.

"Yoseph, Robert is sick boy... very sick right now. He cannot play," explained Alma.

"But..."

"But nothing," said Emil. "Yew stay on farm. Plenty to do right here, lots of vork in barn."

"Yes, Papa."

"I heard Mrs. Hatch is going to have her baby pretty soon," said Martha in an effort to change the subject. "It's a wonder she doesn't just burst wide open with what she eats... or so I've heard. It's obvious she hasn't read the book by Dr. Aldrich."

"A book? On having babies? Vhere yew read such things, Marta?" asked Alma.

"Well... I haven't actually read the book... but Amy told me all about it. If Mrs. Hatch had read it she wouldn't have any trouble at all. She certainly wouldn't need Mrs. Muggsley coming over and filling her head full of notions."

"Mrs. Muggsley is gude midwife," countered Alma, "she knows..."

"No more talk about babies," interrupted Emil, "Vee eat now."

After dinner when the dishes had been washed and put away, the Johnson's settled about the living room stove in various activities. Emil reading the paper, though days old; Alma with more knitting, socks for Buck this time. Andrea was reading one of her favorite books, Martha writing a note to Bill. Emma was on the floor near the stove, setting her dolly's up in a little box and pretending it was a carriage and they were going to a dance. Joe was restless, sitting on the floor at Andrea's feet.

"I gotta," he whispered to himself.

"What's that, Joe?"

"Nothin'." He stood up and looked toward Emil, who had fallen asleep in his chair, the newspaper on his chest. "I'm going out in the barn for awhile. There's nothing to do in here."

"Yew dress warm, Yoseph," instructed Alma. "Is cold in barn, still. And yew check on that Molly cow, tu. She's not making milk so much, anymore."

"Well, it's been so cold lately, it's a wonder she hasn't been giving ice cream instead of milk," said Martha. An involuntary shiver passed through her at the thought.

Joe bundled up and went out the door quickly before any other orders or thoughts could be added.

Several days later, Emil was taken aback when the Pratt & Southeastern stopped along the north pasture and Doc Parker's face peered out at him. It was a careworn and weary face, pale in the glare of the white scenery and missing it's usual jolliness and color. Emil rubbed his eyes, thinking he had been mistaken, what with all that had been on his mind.

"Hello there, Emil," greeted the doctor with barely enough energy to cast his voice over the hissing noise of the idling train.

"Doctor, vhat is this?"

"A little sickness at the camps. Influenza mostly, from what Cooper says, but could be another case of pneumonia. I'd give anything just to treat a broken leg for a change, though even influenza is a vacation, now." He smiled wearily.

"Doctor... dat Valden boy... any news?"

"All bad, I'm afraid," replied Doc Parker in a grimace. It's in his larynx now... he can hardly talk... or breathe for that matter. There is nothing more I can do."

"Larex? Is dat his belly?"

"Larynx... his voice box." The doctor brought his hand up to his throat to illustrate. Emil nodded somberly, not quite understanding.

"Say, Emil, could you do me a favor? Mrs. Hatch is pretty close to her time... could be any day now. And I just don't have the time to spend on a normal childbirth, the way things are... and I've been exposed to all that diphtheria, anyway... could you send one of your daughters over to help? I've sent for Mrs. Muggsley who's a splendid midwife, but I'm not sure if she's in town just now. And Mrs. Wheeler has the fever at her place. I tried to get Doc Devine to come over from Mason, but he's got his hands full with his own people."

"Vell, yew betcha," said Emil, happy to be talking about birth instead of death. Vee send Mama and girls to help. Dat Martha, she know all about babies. She help out gude, I tink."

"Fine then, I won't worry about it anymore," he said looking a bit relieved. "But if there's trouble... you tell them to send word. Cooper will probably know where I am."

Emil nodded. Alfred had already dropped off the mail and a box of groceries while the two men had talked and was now anxious to go... as if he stayed in one place too long, the sickness would catch up to him. As the conversation between the Doc and Emil wound down, he gave a pull on the whistle. It startled everyone... including Alfred. And slowly the engine and the empty cars of the Pratt & Southeastern rumbled on to pick up the harvest of wood waiting for it in the camps.

"Any news, Papa?" the girls inquired as soon as he returned to the house. He was still stamping the snow off his boots and unwrapping his scarf when he told them about Mrs. Hatch.

"Of course vee vill go," said Alma immediately.

"And yew have a letter, Alma, from sister Anna in Vashburn." He handed her the envelope, the ink smeared from the moisture of the snow. "And Marta, tu," he added with a big smile.

"Nothing for me, Papa?" asked Andrea sadly. "No letter... no note... not even a sears catalog?"

"Vell, let me see. No letter... no catalog.... but vait, vhat is this?" He reached into his coat pocket retrieving a crumpled piece of folded paper. "Alfred said this vas for yew, Andrea, from one of the camps." He held it out to her, but she didn't take it right away. She was staring at it, trying to imagine what it could say, afraid to read it lest it not live up to her imagination.

"Maybe yew don't vant it, then. Maybe is for fire?" She gave him the smile he wanted and took the note, slipping it into her pocket for later when she was alone.

"Thank's Papa," she said hugging him. "You are a good postman, today. Now everyone is happy."

Wisely, Emil said nothing about the Walden boy or Doc Parker's concerns. And when asked directly, he dodged artfully around the subject, often exiting the discussion through a sudden fit of anger directed at something so inconsequential that Alma thought him going quite mad.

As nonchalantly as possible, Andrea retreated up the stairs to her bedroom, hoping to find a quiet secluded place to read her note. It could only be from Leon... Buck was not prone to writing and no others could possibly have a reason to correspond with her. It must be from Leon, then, she reasoned. Already Martha was by the window in the bedroom, reading the long flowing lines that Bill had so carefully penned. She was so absorbed in the letter she didn't even hear Andrea come in.

"Oh...Bill," she said sadly and barely out loud.

"What is it, Mart?"

"Oh! Oh, when did you come in? It's nothing... he's such a sweetheart." But a tear found it's way down her cheek in spite.

"Mart?"

"It's nothing!" she replied firmly. Then noticing the folded paper in Andrea's hand she maneuvered to change the subject. "Sooo... you have a note, what does it say? Is it from Mr. Mancheski?"

"I...I don't know, yet. I suppose."

"Well, read it you ninny!" Martha made room for her at the window where Andrea joined her, sitting on the chest of books and little treasures. Carefully she unfolded the paper, noting it's coarse and worn appearance, smoothing it out with her hands. It was a lined sheet apparently torn out of a ledger (and not too carefully). And it read:

Miss Andrea Johnson,

Forgive me for being so forward as to presume that you would look kindly on this correspondence. I am a man of few words, and those so seemingly clumsy and crude as to not warrant reading by eyes so lovely as yours. For it was those blue jewels of captured summer sky that have taken hold of my heart and invested it with a mind of it's own. It is my heart writing these words to you now, these few words. And though my courage is not as strong as I should want, it is enough to allow me to say that your beauty and character are without equal in this wide world. I held you only too briefly while we danced at Christmas time, but the memory of it will forever be the fuel of my dreams. For without those lovely thoughts of you, my dreams lack color and may as well be the barren drudgery of my daily life.

Forgive this intrusion, but my heart was most insistent that I share these feelings with you, that I may foolishly imagine that you feel them too.

That I might continue to feed this fire of tender warmth I have for you in my heart, I must for now remain, to you and to others, only,

Your most devout admirer

"Ohhhh Andrea.... a secret admirer! How thrilling! How romantic."

"How ridiculous," said Andrea.

"How can you say that?"

"Well... it must be from Leon... why is he being so... so... contrary, so secretive. I swear, Mart, that boy doesn't know what he's going to do next and neither do I. It's silly." She crumpled up the paper and threw it across the room.

"I wish Bill could write like that," said Martha demurely. "I wish Bill..."

They were interrupted by their mother calling for them from downstairs. But Andrea dawdled, waiting until Martha had started down and then she retrieved the note, smoothing it, scanning the words quickly once more then holding it to her bosom. Before she left she folded it once and put it in one of her books, the one about knights in shining armor, and returned the book to her cedar chest.

As it happened Alma could not go to be with Mrs. Hatch as promised. Anna had requested her and Emma to come to Washburn for a birthday party for Anna's little Agnes, to spend the night and return the next day. It was an opportunity for Emma that Alma could not bring herself to decline in spite of Mrs. Hatch. Besides, Martha knew of childbirth. She had been there, mother's little helper, when Emma was born. And now, so grown up, talking about books on babies and the right way to do things. Martha will be a good midwife for Mrs. Hatch, with Andrea's help.

Martha was not too thrilled at the news that she had been volunteered as a midwife, thinking perhaps she had talked a bit too much about things she knew very little about. But Andrea was delighted with having something to do... something of joy and happiness in the bleak and cold world that was winter.

"It is gude, yew go help Mrs. Hatch," said Alma after Emil had retreated to the sanctity of the barn. "Yew stay as long as yew need to. Papa and Joe vill be fine here vith lots of things to eat, and I vill be back the day after tomorrow."

"Yes, Mama," replied Andrea pulling on her boots.

"Well, I don't know why we have to go at all. If she had read the book by Dr. Aldrich, she probably wouldn't even need any help."

"Mart, I doubt Mrs. Hatch is the reading kind," said Andrea, though she didn't mean it unkindly.

"Well there are plenty of others that could help. Mrs. Wheeler, for instance. She helped you with Emma, Mama. Why not get Mrs. Wheeler?"

"Martha!" exclaimed Andrea.

"Well, I just don't see why..."

"Is because," interrupted Alma sternly. "Is because yew vere asked to help. Vee help our neighbors and friends, as they help us. Like in old country. Like it should be."

Martha grew silent then and just a bit sulky, characteristics far from her normally sunny behavior. While Alma was concerned about this attitude, she supposed it, too, was due to the winter gloom and confinement. Spring could not find them too soon, she thought. She watched from the frost covered window as the two girls plodded down the trail toward the Hatch residence, a small farm much like their own on the eastern outskirts of town. She watched them until they faded into the gray of the woods at the other end of the pasture, proud of her girls. And then it was time to gather together clothes for her and Emma, and perhaps a jar of preserves for Anna. There was a train to catch.

Mrs. Hatch already had a number of children about her and with Mr. Hatch working in one of Cooper's camp for the winter, it was work enough without being pregnant. And so very pregnant she was, huge and uncomfortable with feet swollen and sore. She often had fits of weeping melancholy in these long winter months and periods of great strength and fortitude.

The eldest Hatch child was Mary, a bright and cheerful girl of 8 years, woefully dressed in cast off and homemade clothes. Her hair was long and stringy, but she tried to tie it up in braids when she could manage. Mrs. Hatch depended on her... depended on her to accomplish things well beyond her years. And she tried. She tried hard. She tried so hard that her little girl days of childhood were slipping from her, thrusting her into an adult world of care and worry far before her time.

Two other Hatch children there were. Susan, a quiet and mournful child... the opposite of Mary and now just 6 years old. And Martin, a boy of 3 years, fat and jolly like his father.

The three of them stood gathered in the doorway of the bedroom watching their mother squirm in pain, when the Johnson girls entered the Hatch residence. Only Mary turned and smiled at them as they removed their coats. When Mrs. Hatch let out a moan growing into a squeal, Martha sat down heavily on the couch and stared at the opposite wall.

"You see to Mrs. Hatch, Martha," suggested Andrea, "and I'll mind the kids and get to cleaning up this place some. She looked about the small room, cluttered with debris and indicating at least recent neglect. "Martha?"

"I can't Andrea... that's it. I just can't." As Mrs. Hatch emitted another cry, Martha burst into tears.

Andrea was suddenly dazed, caught between the moans and squeals of Mrs. Hatch and the useless despair of her sister, sitting on the couch with her head in her hands. But before she could decide what to do, there was a knock on the door... a soft quick rap and then the door creaked open. It was Mary Muggsley.

"Well, what the hell is going on in here?" she asked, her blue eyes drawn wide by the squalor & commotion.

"Mrs. Hatch is having a baby," exclaimed Andrea.

"Well, I know that. Why isn't someone in there with her? Landsakes, get those kids out of the doorway and give her room to breathe." Mary removed her coat quickly and moved to get the children out of the way, pushing them toward Andrea. "Shoo, now... I'll let you know when you can visit with your mother," she said.

Mary moved with a heartfelt confidence, fixing the blankets around Mrs. Hatch, adjusting her pillow, feeling her forehead and brushing the hair out of her eyes.

"How soon?" she asked Mrs. Hatch.

"The... pains... are... very close... soon... ohhhhh," moaned Mrs. Hatch. "Doc Parker... he said it was a big... ohhhh... baby."

"Well, I suppose," said Mary putting her hand on Mrs. Hatch's abdomen, "judging by the size of Mr. Hatch, what else could it be?"

"Andrea!" she yelled. And Andrea came quickly to the door. "We need some boiling water and something to clean things up with... towels or rags... but clean ones... if you can find any. And something to wrap the baby in... it's kinda cool in here. Get Martha or the kids to stoke up the fire some... and clean up that mess out there."

"I'm glad you're here, Mary... we've never done this before," said Andrea.

"Well, neither have I" admitted Mary excitedly. But then seeing the look of fear creeping up on Andrea she added, "But how hard can it be?

Mrs. Hatch and the baby do most of the work. Now git... we're gonna need the water real soon!"

Andrea disappeared quickly, happy to be removed from the pain of Mrs. Hatch. Martha hadn't moved from the couch, though the kids had gathered around her in a curious half circle. Andrea found a large kettle and filled it with water, stoking up the stove before putting it on. With Mary Hatch's help, she found a clean white sheet. When the water began to boil, she scooped out a pot full and brought that and the sheet back to the bedroom.

"Just in time," cried Mary wiping her brow. Mrs. Hatch had her knees drawn up and her abdomen exposed. There was a reddish wetness on the bedsheets. Andrea looked at Mrs. Hatch... sweat soaked, hair in stringy wisps, her teeth gritted tightly together. And out of her clenched mouth came a variety of wails and moans that unsettled Andrea's nerves. And then she saw it; a little head crowning the opening.

"It's time to push, Mrs. Hatch," said Mary, nearly in tears. Andrea clasped Mrs. Hatch's hand and winced when the grip became painful. Mary situated herself in front of Mrs. Hatch, ready to ease the infant out into part of the clean sheet that had been torn off.

"What's this?" cried Martha from the bedroom doorway. "You get away from there Mary Muggsley! We are supposed to be the midwife!"

"Oh, would you just get the hell out of here!" grunted Mary between clenched teeth. There was a pause, where no one spoke and only the grunt and groans of Mrs. Hatch were heard. Martha was waiting for support from Andrea, but Andrea avoided looking at her, concentrating instead on comforting Mrs. Hatch. Seconds later, Martha stamped her dainty foot and retreated back to the living room.

"One more push, Mrs. Hatch... that's it... almost, almost... why it's a boy," she gasped, "a big boy!" And one final groan from Mrs. Hatch and it was squirming in Mary's hands. All three of them burst into tears of relief, tears of joy. And leaving the umbilical cord attached, Mary laid the baby, lightly wrapped, on the woman's chest and covered them.

Mary dragged a bloody hand across her forehead to brush a strand of hair out of her eyes and suddenly afforded Andrea a weak smile. Andrea, to her surprise, smiled back sincerely. An affinity for Miss Muggsley? Who would have believed?

"A beautiful baby," whispered Mrs. Hatch somewhat hoarse. "Thank you girls sooo much!"

A half hour later, Mr. Hatch showed up at the door, slightly out of breath and red faced. He had run, somewhat, from Camp #11 at the suggestion of Doc Parker, once it was determined that there had been no contagious sickness present. He lumbered in to Ellen Hatch and stroked her hair lightly.

"I come as soon as Doc Parker told me I could," he said, smiling broadly. "I run nearly all the way."

"I know ya did, Martin. Look," she lifted up the light blankets that covered her to reveal the baby on her bosom, "it's another boy!"

"A boy? Well, I'll be... a boy!" He took another long look at his new offspring, eyes wide in wonder and his breathing slowly returning to normal. "Looks kinda like a skinned rabbit now, don't he?"

"Martin!" she scolded. But Martin was a kind man who loved his children. He smiled until Andrea thought he would burst. He reached his chubby calloused fingers in under the blanket and gently stroked the fine hair on the baby's head.

"A boy!" he said again, this time looking up at Andrea and Mary and sharing his smile.

"Well," said Mary, "there's still much to be done." She turned to leave, grabbing Andrea by the elbow as she did, and together they retreated from the bedroom, closing the door. Mary stopped then and looked about the room.

The place had taken on a new appearance in the last hour or so that they had been there. While Andrea and Mary had tended Mrs. Hatch, Martha had cleaned up the house, finding places for things and dusting through layers of settled debris. She was in the kitchen tackling the stack of dishes and kettles when the other two found her. Her hair was as bedraggled as the two midwives's and hanging in her face, the kids gathered around her. She was singing to them, softly and sweetly and they were content for the time being.

"Why don't you take a break, Mart?" interrupted Andrea. Martha paused and threw the other girls a weary look. To add to the effect, which she was making overly dramatic, she removed a sudsy hand from the washtub and brushed back the strands of hair in her face.

"Why do I suddenly feel like the ugly stepsister?" asked Mary Muggsley to no one.

"Huh?" grunted Martha weakly. It generated a much needed giggle in both the other girls and even Martha had to smile then.

"C'mon kids," offered Mary. "I'll tell you a story in the other room. And in a little while you can go visit your new baby brother."

"What kinda story?" asked Mary Hatch.

"Well, just you wait and see," replied Mary hustling them out.

When the kids were shuffled off into the other room, Andrea joined Martha at the washtub, sticking her hands into the warm water and finding a nice china plate.

"It's a boy," said Andrea softly.

"I know," replied Martha, "I know. And Mary Muggsley was marvelous and Martha Johnson is a big fool." She had tears welled up in her eyes, ready to begin the rivers that would crisscross her face with the next good blink. Andrea was silent for a few moments, carefully selecting the words she would say.

"Someday, Mart... when I get married... and I am nine months pregnant and as big as a house, and my ankles are all swollen and bags under my eyes... and I feel that first pain that I know is the life inside me ready to be born... it's you, Martha Johnson, that I would want by my side... for my baby to take it's first breath in your arms... for you to brush aside the hair from my eyes and tell me it's alright... to tell me that it's a healthy baby that will grow up strong and happy. You Mart... no one else."

"Well, maybe," said Martha stemming the flow of tears with the back of her hand, "if I'm not too busy with my own little darlings." She smiled through the tears. "And only if you have someone else on hand to do the dishes."

Andrea, while putting some dishes away, came near the living room entrance and paused to hear the soothing tones of a fairy tale story being told by Miss Mary Muggsley. She was sitting on the couch with Susan on one side and little Martin Jr. on the other. In front of her was Mary Hatch and Mary was braiding her hair nicely while she told the story.

"... and a very hard working girl she was. Worked from dawn until dusk, until her hands were raw and sore. She had none of the comforts that they have in the city, like electricity and telephones and big bathtubs with plenty of hot water and fragrant soaps. No, she was stuck in the place of many miseries, where there were no comforts, and nobody liked her... and nobody treated her very nice."

"That's so sad," said Susan.

"Yes, it was. But..." she paused and looked at the children one by one, "there was a prince... a very handsome and very rich prince. He lived in the city and was looking for a beautiful maid... but he couldn't find her anywhere. Then one day he took the train to the country... to a little lumber town... and there he found her."

"What did he do then?" asked little Martin.

"Why, he kissed her. He kissed her sore fingers and he brushed her hair until it was shiny... and so pretty. And he was taking her away from all her misery... he was taking her to the big city..."

"So she could have lectricity," added Susan.

Andrea's heart warmed at the scene. Who was this young woman sitting in the parlor? Certainly not Miss Mary Muggsley. But just then Martha brought her back to the duties of the kitchen... so she pondered and worked. Pondered at many things... one of which was not pleasant; the obvious pain and discomfort of giving birth. As if the pain could be isolated from all the glorious feelings that a birth brings... and banished.

It was near dusk when the girls figured that they had done all that was humanly possible to restore some semblance of order and dignity to the small Hatch residence. Mr. Hatch would stay a day or two... but then he needed to return to the camp for work... for there was no other source of income in the winter months. So the girls promised to check in on the Hatch family from time to time... until the sickness time passed and other neighbors and friends could help attend to things.

At the door, in the midst of goodbyes, Mr. Hatch suddenly insisted that they each take a jar of pickles for their efforts. Seeing the importance of this gesture to the Hatch dignity, they gratefully accepted.

The girls walked together part of the way... until nearing the Chicago & Northwestern main track line. There Mary would be heading west into town while the Johnson girls would be taking the Pratt & Southeastern spur back to the farm. As they paused at this juncture for a second suddenly the old Mary Muggsley returned.

"Ugh! Pickles!" she grunted "Of all things". Then she heaved the jar down in the gully off the tracks onto snow-covered rocks where it burst. "Mama says Mrs. Hatch's pickles taste like they have been soaked in kerosene."

"Why, Mary Muggsley, how cruel!" scolded Martha. But Andrea's face was placid... hiding an emotion she was not sure of. She confronted Mary then, face to face and up close.

"You can do what ever you please, Mary Muggsley, and say what ever mean thought pops into your head. But I know who you are now, who you really are..." and then on sudden impulse, she kissed her cheek. Mary's face reddened, but she could not speak. She felt exposed and uncomfortable and just a little bit angry. She slapped Andrea's face with a hit that stung despite her gloved hands and then stormed off, tripping and cursing along the tracks to town.

"Andrea, what will you do next," commented Martha shaking her head in bewilderment.

K. Wallin

The Thirty First Chapter

The Green Dress

Daylight was beginning to wan as the Johnson girls found the Pratt and Southeastern track line and began the journey home. Both girls were unusually quiet as they walked the rails, though they were certainly tired enough to deserve some peace. As they came to the bridge over Twenty Mile creek, Martha suddenly hooked her arm in Andrea's and smiled at her. It was barely light enough to see the gaps in the ties as they crossed. A full moon was out, illuminating the white countryside in a pale blue glow. Hoary rings circled the bright orb, with color seeming to dance through the rings, depending on how you looked at it. Martha was pretty much content, until she heard a wolf howl in the distant hills to the south of them.

"Dorothy Riggs says she was almost eaten by a wolf once," said Martha.

"Oh, Mart!"

"Well it's true. I heard they follow your tracks in the snow... they know if you are a woman or child by the smell some say... and if you are a woman or a child... they follow you closer and closer, keeping to the shadows until you stumble and fall. Then they pounce on you!"

"Wolves don't eat people. They don't even like people," countered Andrea.

"Well, that's not what I heard. If you fall... you are doomed for sure." And in coincidence, she stumbled on a tie and nearly lost her balance but for Andrea. Cautiously she looked around and behind her. "That was close," she said.

It was a welcome sight when the lights of the Johnson farm came into view, never a sight so comforting as the lights of home. They left the track line at the path Emil had made to pick up the mail each day. The snow along the track had been dirtied by cinders from the engine's puffing smokestack, making a gray and ugly swatch through the countryside. But the field they were walking in now was an unbroken blanket of white, with swirls and drifts formed by the wind.

"Seems like it's getting colder again," observed Martha, closing her scarf tightly around her throat. "And Spring only 6 weeks away."

"With all the snow we've gotten this year, we'll be having snowball fights in June," retorted Andrea. "Oh, just to feel a warm wind on my face again..."

"A cold wind is better for the face," replied Martha, "gives it a healthy pink glow."

"I don't want to glow," mused Andrea, "I just want to be warm."

They both felt some relief when Andrea's hand touched the door and began to open it. But Martha pulled her back momentarily and looked into her eyes with a wounded expression. Still, she did not have to say the words.

"I won't say anything, Mart. Mrs. Hatch has a healthy baby boy and that's all that matters."

Martha gave her a quick hug saying nothing, and then edged by her into the warmth of the house.

She hated the dress. It was green, it was too business-like and it was a hand-me-down from Aunt Anna, who everybody knew had no taste in clothes. Andrea studied it carefully... perhaps a way to make it better... some lace, some trim, change the cuffs? No. It was a miserable dress and nothing could be done with it.

"Yew vill look nice in this dress, Andrea," said Alma.

"I'm only working one day at the store, Mama. Just one day. Mrs. Burke will be back the day after tomorrow. Can't I just wear one of my old dresses?"

"Ohh, Andrea. Yew must look so gude tomorrow. Who knows who vill come to store and see yew. This dress is gude for yew, make yew stand straight and pretty behind counter. Anna vill be so proud!"

"But Mama... it's so... so green," sighed Andrea.

"Yaa, green... like summer," nodded Alma smiling.

It was a dead issue then, the dress would be worn and Andrea would merely pray tonight that no one would come to the store tomorrow. She had to smile a bit though, at her luck in getting this chance to work. She had been standing in the store listening to Mrs. Burke talk about her aches and pains for awhile, trying desperately to find a polite way to retreat, when Mrs. Pell walked in. The thin, pinch-faced older woman was Mrs. Burke's next door neighbor and confidant.

"You'll have to cancel your trip tomorrow, Edna," she said in a high-pitched nasal voice. "I've just come to tell you that Trina has a cold and fever, almost like she done it on purpose, knowing you needed her to work. Not a lot of ambition, that Working Girl of yours." It was a treat to the ears when Mrs. Pell stopped talking, thought Andrea. Such a sound to come from a throat.

"Oh, my," said Mrs. Burke. "Is she alright?"

"I wouldn't be surprised at how fine she would be the minute you didn't need her," sniffed Mrs. Pell. "But Mrs. Smith brought over some medicine Dr. Parker had given her for the liver... said it should work as well for a cold, she shouldn't wonder."

"I guess going to Duluth is out of the question now," sighed Mrs. Burke. "And I was so looking forward to seeing my Laurel again... it's been near two months now."

"Well, perhaps you should try my Grandmother Lilly's cure for such things. A little horseradish, steeped in a gill of vinegar and add a little honey. Take that in a teaspoon every twenty minutes and I wouldn't doubt she should be on her feet in a few days," offered Mrs. Pell. The voice was annoying, plain and simple. It didn't seem to matter what the words were, thought Andrea. The words could be made of honey, but the voice was certainly steeped in vinegar like the proffered cure.

"A few days? Oh, my. I just couldn't close up the store for even one day with so many people needing things this time of the year... and everyone so sick. I'll just have to telegram Laurel that... well, unless you, Mrs. Pell, would consider... I mean...

"Mrs. Burke," interrupted Andrea suddenly. "I would be happy to take Trina's place for awhile. I've watched her... I know what to do."

"Oh, dear... do you think?" Mrs. Burke said weakly looking at Mrs. Pell.

It seemed to Andrea that the store was awfully cold in the morning. She had worked hard at stoking up the stove but now, an hour later it was just beginning to get comfortable standing behind the counter without her shawl. And still no customers on this cold brisk morning. She had watched the wind outside whipping by, had seen a few people pass down the street cold and hurried, but no one had bothered to stop. She almost wished that she had brought a book to read, though that was not the best thing to have passed to Mrs. Burke upon her return. So it was a heavy sigh and a little dusting to pass the time.

This store was a little different than the Straddle Creek Mercantile. While carrying many of the same items, it was directed more towards the homes, the people and personal needs where the Mercantile stock was aimed more for farm and camp life.

Later on Mrs. Pell came in to check on her... her vinegar voice biting into the silence like a buzzsaw and making Andrea awkward and nervous. And then a few others came in as the morning wore on, marveling at what a fine job she was doing, how nice she looked in the pretty green dress, but buying nothing. By noon she had sold perhaps $5 worth of goods, but at least it was comfortably warm throughout the store.

When Mrs. Gillis came in that afternoon on her usual rounds Andrea was inclined to stay out of her way, hoping that when she saw Mrs. Burke wasn't there she would pass on. Not so! Mrs. Gillis needed to know; where was Mrs. Burke? What was wrong with Trina? Had they tried Cayenne pepper tea or snake-root? When would Mrs. Burke return?

When Mrs. Gillis was satisfied that she had learned all that she could about that situation, she prattled on about business closer to home.

"That Walden boy isn't long for this earth, if you want my opinion. Deathly sick... deathly sick." She clicked her mouth while she paused between words, thinking. "Of course Dr. Parker don't know half of what he thinks he knows, has to check those books of his every time someone sneezes. You'd think he'd have treated everything at least once by now and wouldn't need those books anymore." Her eyes were always light and lively when she warmed to someone else's problems.

"Well..." said Andrea weakly, trying to think of something to say. She needn't have bothered.

"There's still something about that Mancheski fellow I can't put my finger on," mused Mrs. Gillis suddenly. "I told you about his writing career didn't I? Harper's Weekly? Well, the oddest thing... he has shown no interest at all in my Mister's experiences. Strange indeed, for a man who's supposed to be writing about logging hereabouts. Appears he may be sweet on someone too. Mrs. Hugdale says she seen him kissing someone over by the north road one Sunday. Kissing for no reason, neither and in broad daylight!"

Andrea blushed from her toes to the top of her head, hoping against hope, that Mrs. Gillis didn't notice. No chance.

"Say, dear... you had better let that stove cool down a bit in here, it has you all pink with the heat."

Just then the little bell above the door jingled, announcing another customer. Andrea was relieved even when she noticed it was Mary Muggsley. Anyone, just anyone, to steer Mrs. Gillis onto a new path of conversation. Mary daintily shook the snow from her dress and wandered toward the stove with obvious intent. The wind had painted rose in her cheeks, the warm rich color such a contrast to the cold porcelain white of her skin. It made Andrea think of a China doll.

"Hmmmm... Mary Muggsley," mused Mrs. Gillis. "My, but she's a pretty one, isn't she? The stories I've heard... well... mind you I'm not one for idle gossip but..."

"Excuse me, Mrs. Gillis," interrupted Andrea. "I have to tend to my customers." And she abandoned Mrs. Gillis mid-gossip, electing instead to move down the aisle to where Mary was fluffing the wetness out of her dress, looking like a partridge settling in on a nest.

"Well, well, well," clucked Mary as Andrea approached her. "What do we have here? A new storekeeper?"

"Trina is ill and I'm helping out Mrs. Burke," explained Andrea curtly. "Is there something I can do for you perhaps?"

Just then the bell above the door sounded, distracting Andrea momentarily as she watched Mrs. Gillis edge out the door into the cold wind.

"My what an interesting dress, Andrea. I don't think I could wear a dress like that myself. But hmmmm," she put her hand to her chin as if in deep ponderance, "I think it suits you perfectly... so... so sensible. And so green! I don't know if I've ever seen that shade of green before... or have I? Why, yes, I think I have. The day after the summer picnic, in church. It was Mr. Andrews in a tight necktie and still reeking of Bibon Brandy from the night before. His face..."

"Is there something I can help you with," interrupted Andrea, tiring of the slander.

"Andrea! How rude." she gushed in mock effrontery. Then seeing the whole effort had taken its measure of flesh, she changed the subject. "Well... I will need some gloves, I suppose. Some 'traveling' gloves, I think. Nice ones... white and soft. Could be I'll be traveling in a month or two... sooner if I'm any judge of my own affairs." Mary strolled smugly over to the counter where the gloves were laid out in neat rows. "I have such delicate and fine hands, the gloves must be of quality."

"There are a lot of nice things here, I'm sure you'll find something to your liking," replied Andrea. She was wondering to herself if talking to Mrs. Gillis was more calming.

"No... I don't think so. Nothing to suit me... nothing of quality. He would expect me to have only the finest, I'm sure," she said, nose slightly in the air. She dropped the bait, then scampered away from it with talk of other things... waiting for Andrea to snatch at it's meaning, pleading to be informed of who this 'he' must be. She was disappointed, however, as Andrea neatly sidestepped the trap.

"Well, if you think of anything suitable," she said, "I will be over behind the pay counter." And with that, she retreated.

A few moments later Mary approached and throwing a lace handkerchief on the counter she said, "this will have to do."

"Gloves and other 'quality' merchandise will just have to be purchased along the way I suppose. Perhaps in Minneapolis or Chicago... or New York."

"You're leaving?" Andrea asked while feigning disinterest.

"Well, certainly," she replied, delighted now that Andrea was tugging on the bait. "I could hardly expect Mr. Mancheski to put his budding career on hold, now could I? Once we're married there will be no other choice but for me to follow him back to civilization. A townhouse in New York will have to do for awhile, I suppose... but I'll soon have him on the right track. If he had me managing his career from the start, he never would have had to take this assignment in the wilderness anyway."

"He asked you to marry him?" Andrea said quietly.

"Well... not exactly, but he will," she replied. "A woman knows about such things... if she knows anything at all about romance. You know I usually get my way with men. It's a simple matter of being... well... agreeable to any idle notion a man might have about other unimportant things. About politics for instance or religion... or more delicate matters. If a woman is simply agreeable to these... delicate matters... why there's no telling what she can do." Her cheeks became redder as she prattled on. Her words were of conviction, a mind conditioned to believe what it needed to believe. But her movements betrayed her; nervous and restless as she talked, looking around and over her shoulder for any other listening ears that may have found their way unannounced into the store.

"That's disgusting," said Andrea much to her own surprise. But it felt so good to finally say it, she found the strength to say more. "You can make any excuse you want for having an 'agreeable' nature, Mary Muggsley, but the truth of the matter is that you are a spoiled little brat who wants to get her own way no matter what it takes and no matter who it hurts." She was surging with emotion unbridled, bringing the blood rushing to her face and making her own heart sound loud in her ears. "You don't know anything at all about romance... or love... or about men really, for that matter. All you know is what is in your own selfish heart. You're a mean...

Mary didn't let her finish. Her eyes flashing, she turned in a huff and stomped away out the door slamming it as she went. Then seconds later the door opened again and she stomped back in, again slamming the door and this time the little bell was blown off the frame and went dingling across the floor. Andrea was actually a little afraid as she strode up the counter with sudden conviction.

"Just who in the hell do you think you are, Andrea Johnson! Just what do you think you know about me, about how I feel, or what I want, or what I would do to get it. You seem to think your sanctimonious airs will ensure you a long and happy life, free from drudgery, free from misery, free from the boring everyday life that paints tired lines on your face, puts calluses on your hands and wears away at your spirit. Well, you're wrong, you're dead wrong. Just look at the pitiful lives around you; the dismal wretchedness of the 'nice' people, of the 'good' Christian people. Death stalks all of us, whether we are 'agreeable' or disgusting or just plain wonderful. Death doesn't care. Misery doesn't care. Maybe no one else cares, but I care." She paused to suck in a breath.

"Mary...I...I"

"Look, I am leaving this stinking little town... one way or another. And I am going to live my life. Live it! Do you understand? I am going to live it fast and careless and full of wonderful things." She paused a moment, thinking over the words Andrea had said. "And if there is a little meanness in my heart," she sniffed, "it's this miserable little town that put it there!"

She turned to leave then, her nose in the air and her calm returning. But suddenly she looked back, seeing for the first time the flush in Andrea's face, the moistness in her eyes, her trembling hands. For a moment confusion engulfed her and the two young women stared at each other, wordless, hearts pounding in fury. Mary gathered her wits first, hardening her gaze, with a mean little sneer on her lips.

"And heaven help the person that gets in my way," she said softly but with gritty determination. And in moments she was out the door.

It was fate, perhaps, that she ran into Mr. Cooper at the top of the path leading down to the depot. He graciously tipped his hat to her and greeted her cheerfully.

"Mary... I was just thinking about you," he said between the bite on his cigar.

"Why, Mr. Cooper, really! A man of your age," she teased. It was the usual Mary Muggsley approach to men; any man. But a little spent from her conversation with Andrea, she was already growing tired of it.

"No...no... I mean... I wanted to talk to you," he said uneasily.

"Ohhh Mr. Cooper," she replied wearily. "I would love to talk to you... but perhaps another time. I have some business to attend to just now." She was about to start down the perilous snowy path.

"This won't take long... we can talk as we walk. I think you may be laboring under a misunderstanding regarding..."

"Please, Mr. Cooper. This is not the time. I must get down the hill and..."

"Let me take your arm," he offered, slipping his big hand around her elbow, "and we can talk..."

"No," she said, violently pulling away from him. The sudden movement caused her to step too close to the bank and begin to slip. He tried to rescue her, but only managed to send them both sliding on down the hill tumbling through the snow midst a chorus of grunts and shrieks.

They landed side by side on their bottoms, sitting there dazed for a few moments. Finally she turned to him, her gracious facade lost somewhere in the fall.

"Now what the hell could have been so important?" she said trying to catch her breath.

He was a bit flustered at the whole matter and while trying to think of something to say, he noticed her dress had moved up and her legs were showing a bit more than what was modestly acceptable. Weakly, he pointed toward her limbs.

"Ohhhh, never mind the damn dress," she said in barely disguised anger. Never-the-less she smoothed out her dress so that it covered her again but remained sitting in the wet snow, so utterly dejected.

"It can wait," he said apologetically.

"Oh, no!" she cried. "I've already paid the price, you may as well give me the ticket."

"Well... it's just that I was thinking you may have misunderstood some things about Mr. Mancheski. He is not exactly who he seems."

"Well, who the hell is he, then, the King of Norway? I've never heard such balderdash. Help me up... help me up." She struggled to her feet with a little help from him, slapping at her dress to shake the snow off of it. Then suddenly more sensitive to the situation she looked around to see who could have seen this unfortunate affair. Seeing only a few railroad hands nearby she thought for a moment no damage was done to her dignity. It smoothed out her temper some and she resolved to bring forth the public Mary once more.

"Why, Mr. Cooper, whatever do you mean?"

"Well... Hrrmph," he stammered, unsure if this was still such a good idea. "Well, for one thing, he's not exactly my nephew. In fact, he's not a bit related."

"Oh, Mr. Cooper! And the resemblance was so strong!" She joshed. "But surely even you don't think that anyone believed that old poppycock. Those that know anything, know about Mr. Mancheski's real reason for being here."

"Well... that's not exactly true either," he said weakly. "I don't think he's even read a copy of Harper's Weekly let alone written for it. I'm afraid the whole thing is a sham, from start to finish." He felt better for having said it, if only to Mary Muggsley.

"Www...what do you mean? Surely... he... surely... you... what... " She paused, pondering, thinking fast, anger creeping up her spine and grand plans beginning to disintegrate. She suddenly reached out and gripped Mr. Cooper's arm tightly, almost painfully.

"What is going on?" she said between gritted teeth, her demure manner forgotten once more.

"He had a bit of trouble... needed a place to stay for awhile. I was trying to keep it quiet to save him some pride, but I didn't count on this." Mr. Cooper suddenly felt a bit foolish.

"What kind of trouble," she asked.

"Well, I don't know that exactly... but the truth of the matter, the whole truth, is that he doesn't have a penny to his name. Showed up here with his hat and one valise and that was it, all wet and bedraggled. A person couldn't help but feel sorry for him or want to help him. So I put him to work, take his mind off things, make a little money." As he talked he watched the anger in Mary's face being replaced by numbness, a vacant stare.

"And that's the whole of it," he continued. "I didn't count on you... on anyone... you know... taking an interest."

"I don't know what you are talking about," replied Mary huffily. "You... are a foolish old man." And with that she stalked off more ladylike than she felt.

K. Wallin

The Thirty Second Chapter

Joe is not well!

The rest of the day had been pretty much uneventful for Andrea. Not that the little affair with Mary hadn't clouded her mind while she rung up small purchases and engaged in small chatter with the few customers that bothered to be about. And it was still on her mind during the cold walk home, allowing her to ignore the stinging wind on her cheeks, keeping her feet moving at such a vigorous pace they actually felt rather hot and stuffy by the time she got to the house.

From the smells emanating out of the kitchen she knew her mother was busy... a chance to avoid her until she could find a way to rid herself of the foul mood that had followed her home. For Alma would know... Alma always knew... and it would make Andrea feel rather silly and childlike to try to explain her feelings right now. So it was upstairs to the bedroom she went, to rid herself of the green dress... to rid herself of the troubled thoughts on her mind, though surely not as easy as removing clothes. Martha was there, standing solemnly at the window, pressing her fingers against the icy pane and staring out over the bleak fields in the direction of Pratt.

"Ohhhh, the day I've had!" grunted Andrea as she tugged on the dress. In moments it was on the floor. She hugged the bare flesh of her arms where goose pimples were already setting up and briefly re-lived the days events. It made her grunt again..."Ohhhhhh".

"Well, what's wrong with you," asked Martha softly.

"Mary Muggsley! That girl! On and on she goes... about Leon and traveling gloves and... and... what she would do or wouldn't do to get her way. She always gets her way... somehow!" She emphasized the word to make it sound like immorality itself.

"Being agreeable she calls it. Agreeable! Of all the gall... acting like a St. Paul trollop in order to get her way. It's disgusting. Maybe what they say about her mother is true."

"Her mother?" asked Martha still calmly facing the window. Andrea barely heard the words. She paused from her rant long enough to draw her shawl about her bare shoulders and sit up on the bed.

"Her mother. Some say she actually was a St. Paul trollop. That she got into trouble and pregnant and needed a way out of town. How else do you explain Mr. Muggsley?"

"Oh, Andrea, don't be mean."

"Me? Mean? Well... I'm not so agreeable, that's for sure. And any girl that is, is no better than a St. Paul trollop at any length."

The room was quiet for the next few moments, while Andrea finally took note of Martha's somber mood. She still faced the window and a soft sniffle could be heard now and then, shaking her body slightly.

"I would like to think you are wrong, Andrea." She said. Andrea noticed that a handkerchief was in her hand... that it dabbled at her face. "There is love, you know. There is that. Love makes a difference." Andrea didn't answer. She was beginning to sense something was wrong, to feel it. Flashes of scenes, bits and pieces of conversation filtered through her mind and suddenly she felt she was choking on the answer.

"Oh no, Mart, not you!" She breathed.

"It was the day I dropped the packages in the snow," Martha said calmly, finally turning toward the room. Her cheeks were flushed, eyes moist. She didn't look at Andrea directly, but continued almost as if she was talking to herself.

"I guess I was still thinking about it. The packages just slipped from my arms."

"Oh, Mart... I..."

"I went to town that day, remember? Mamma needed some sugar and some yarn for socks and mittens. It wasn't that cold out... a nice walk... on the way back I decided to stop at the Gustevel's... to see about Gramma Lundstrom, you know she hasn't been feeling that well. Of course, she is nearly ninety years old now."

"Mart... you don't have to..."

"Shut up, Andrea... just Shut up!" Anger flared then immediately subsided. It put the vacant look back in Martha's eyes as she remembered the day.

"Bill was out working in the barn. No one was there, Andrea, just Bill. Everyone else had taken Gramma Lundstrom on the train to Ashland to visit her sister. Bill is rather handsome, don't you think? I thought so that day. And we talked and we... we did things. I didn't think I wanted to... I tried to tell him... but he said women don't know their own mind. But I did. At least I thought I did."

"He forced you?"

"No... of course not. Don't be silly. It's just that, I didn't *know* that I wanted to. But I must have, really. I must have. But I didn't like it much. Bill did. He said... he said..." But she could go on no further. The truth was out, naked and bare at last... but the burden on her heart seemed all the more. She broke down and cried, both hands over her face, her shoulders hunched and shaking lightly. Andrea pulled her up on the bed with her, cradling her in her arms, laying her own head across her back and stroking her hair, not knowing what to say and feeling the idiot for her careless words not long before.

"He'll have to marry you," Andrea said matter-of-factly. "I'll see to that. He'll marry you in the spring."

It was two days after the birth of baby Hatch, newly christened, "Elmer" after his grandpa, that the good news came; Robert Walden was on the mend. He would live. There were many that were pleased at the news, though somewhat surprised since he had sunk so low. But Joe was not surprised. He could have told you that he would be getting better a fortnight ago. And yet, he was strangely lethargic and quiet that night. Alma saw the change at supper through his lackluster appetite, and shortly thereafter discovered that his forehead was warm.

"Are yew getting a cold, Yoseph?" she wondered aloud while feeling his forehead with her cheek. Then she looked him in the face and saw the dull glaze in his eyes.

"My throat is kinda sore," he admitted reluctantly in a somewhat hoarse voice. Alma said, "Open," and he opened wide his mouth for inspection. She looked carefully, moving him near the light. Then she felt his neck with her fingers, probing softly, pushing lightly.

"Oww" he said. "Take it easy."

"Ok, Yoseph." She hugged him gently. "Yew get on up to bed, now. Yew rest."

"But Mama, its only 6:00 o'clock," he whined.

"Yew go," she said sternly. "I vill bring some medicine for the throat. Yew rest, now go." She pushed him toward the stairwell.

329

Emil had been watching her from over the top of his paper, feeling some uneasiness at even the mention of illness. "Vhat yew think?" he asked when Joe was up the stairs. "Mumps? I heard the Campbell girls have mumps. Could be the mumps?"

"I don't know, papa," she replied soberly. "I don't know," she echoed as she left Emil sitting in the parlor and entered the kitchen, where Andrea and Martha were finishing up the dishes. Emma was at the table talking to her doll.

"Vhere is syrup?" Alma muttered to herself while flinging open cupboards and moving the contents around. As she went on and could not find what she was looking for, she became more frantic, nearly irrational... until the girls suddenly stopped what they were doing and stared at her.

"What is it, Mama," asked Martha.

"Nothing, I tink. Nothing. He is a little sick. Nothing so much," she rambled.

"Who Mama? Buck?" asked Andrea.

"No...not Buck. Yoseph... is... is yust a little sick. A little varm and throat is sore... it is cold I think." The girls sensed the unspoken worry in her voice.

"Oh, mama!" exclaimed Andrea and tears welled up in her eyes.

"Is Joe sick?" asked Emma suddenly. They had forgotten she was in the room.

"A little sick," said Martha. "He has a sore throat."

"Oh. Well he can sleep with my dolly if he wants. But he can't pull her head off like the last time."

"That's nice, Emma. I will tell Joe."

"I'll go give him my dolly right now," she added starting to get down from the table.

"No!" said all the older ones in unison. It had the effect of frightening them all, including Emma who quickly jumped back up on her chair. The last month of cold weather and the dreadful days of illness and death of people they knew were beginning to play on them. Diphtheria was in the neighborhood and not a pleasant companion, the symptoms in the beginning, not unlike that of a common cold.

"He vill be fine," said Alma regaining her composure. She straightened out her dress and re-pinned a few strands of hair that had escaped. "I have seen... I know... it vill be ok vith Yoseph. Don't tell Papa, though. Yew know how he feels about...vell... yew know how he feels."

"Ok, Mama," nodded Andrea. "The syrup is in the pantry, I'll get it for you."

Late in the evening, Alma noted that Andrea was missing from the family gathering around the stove in the living room. Martha was reading to Emma, while Emil mulled over the newspaper several days old, smoking his pipe thoughtfully, but Andrea had slipped away somewhere. Fearing that she may have gone to Joe, sequestered to his bedroom until the nature of his illness could be determined, Alma, too, slipped away unnoticed to creep up the stairs. To her relief, Andrea sat alone in her bedroom, near the window on the chest that held her books. She was staring out over the frozen landscape while a dozen thoughts mingled in her mind, confusing her, making her pensive and sad.

"Yew vorry about Yoseph... I know... I know..." said Alma softly as she joined her by the window. "This is bad ting... this sickness. It is God's vay... but vee don't alvays like vhat God does in our lives sometimes."

Andrea nodded. "Will he be alright, Mama?" Are you sure... you have seen..." she wanted to ask again if Alma had had a vision, but was afraid to. Unable to finish the sentence, she turned back to the window.

"I... I do not alvays see so much... I do not alvays know vhat I see sometimes," replied Alma to the unfinished query. "It is God's vill, God loves all his children. Vhatever happens, vee do all vee can... and then it is up to Him."

"Ohh, Mama, I couldn't stand it if anything happened to Joe. I just couldn't." Alma hugged her then, the only response to such feelings.

"Soooo, yew get note from somevun? Papa tells me yew have note."

Andrea sniffed a little and nodded, looking up into Alma's wise grey eyes. "It's from Mr. Mancheski... I think. But it's not signed. Ohhh Mama, that's another thing... how do you know when you are in love... how do you know if you are in love with the right person?"

"The heart knows," she said softly.

"What if the heart is all wrong... I mean... what if you feel... what if you love... a person that is so wrong... that you know is wrong. That can't be right, can it?"

"The heart knows," said Alma again, "the heart knows vhat the mind does not. The heart knows vhat no one can tell you. And if the heart is so sure... then it cannot be wrong."

"I think it can still be wrong," said Andrea. "But sometimes... sometimes, I imagine that it isn't wrong, and it doesn't seem so bad."

"Yew tink tu much, Andrea. It is vhat yew du. Vhat is right or wrong about love, I don't know. But Mr. Mancheski is nice young man. He is troubled, perhaps. There is much heavy on his mind, like Andrea. Maybe he does not listen to his heart either, but he is nice young man."

"I suppose," allowed Andrea. And then they embraced once more, a tear forming in Andrea's eye as she hugged her mother and drank in the smell of baking bread, feeling the warmness, the kindness of her nature. She didn't want to let go. But she couldn't bring herself to tell her mother... that her confused thoughts were not about Mr. Mancheski.

Doc Parker stopped by after Alma had ascertained, at least to herself, that it was Diphtheria after all and not some other winter ailment. He listened to Joe's wheezy voice, listened to his heart and lungs. He had him open his mouth to observe the graying of the throat lining and the putrid smell so common to the illness. He did this while holding a handkerchief to his own nose, although aware that it was sending a message of concern to the patient. The doctor, himself, looked long worn and weary, with bags under his eyes and a weakness to his voice. He tried to smile at Joe and kid him just a little, but the pale little face beneath the sheets did not respond as he would have hoped, obviously aware of the seriousness of the situation.

"There is nothing else to be done," he said when he returned downstairs to the parlor. I'll have to add you to the quarantine list though. People need to stay away for awhile... and you should try not to get too close... but keep washing the bedclothes and sheets in boiling water when you can... and just... just keep doing what you are doing," he sighed.

"Vhat vee are doing?" exclaimed Emil, "vhat are vee doing? Vee vatch and vee vait and vee vorry and vee pray. This is not much dat vee are doing."

"Papa, lower your voice... do yew vant him to hear?" admonished Alma. "Vee do all that vee can in such tings."

"Hah! Vee do nothing... nothing... but vait, the hardest ting of all to do. Hah!" With that Emil retrieved his coat from the rack, and without saying another word, departed to the outside to smoke a pipe and wait some more.

"You have done all that you can," said the doctor again to Alma. "These things... well, they choose their own time and course. Some...uh, many... they suffer for a little while and then they get better and are bothered no more. For some... well, for some it is worse. That Walden boy now... worst case I have seen in many years... and he is better now. We'll watch him for a long while yet, but there is no doubt that he will live."

"And Yoseph?" asked Alma, though she knew the answer.

"Well, I... I don't know, Alma. He's a strong boy... but...he has it bad too. Almost like the Walden boy... up here," he indicated his throat, "in his voice box. For some reason that is the worst place. It swells up and makes it tough to breathe."

Alma was facing the doctor, but a blank stare was on her face. She was wringing her hands over and over and no longer heard the doctor. But she heard a voice... from inside... a voice that had spoken to her many times. Suddenly she groaned and started to collapse right in front of the doctor.

"Alma! Andrea? Martha?" called the doctor. Martha came running into the parlor from the kitchen and helped get Alma to the sofa. In a minute she was lucid once more, and looking very tired and just a little bit sheepish. Andrea caught her eyes only briefly, before Alma turned suddenly away from her, but it was a look she had seen before, a look that did not bode well.

"I didn't mean to scare you, Alma," said the doctor, almost as flustered himself. "I just thought you should know all the facts about it. You see, don't you? I didn't mean to frighten you."

"It's okay, doctor. I know yew are kind and caring man. Yew help so many people... and sometimes do not get paid for your vork." Turning to Martha she said, "yew go get the doctor some lefsa that I made last night, and a loaf of bread and a jar of preserves."

"Alma," he said, "you don't have to..."

But Alma held up her hand abruptly, silencing him. "It is not much, perhaps" she said, "but it is given in good faith. Vee are grateful to yew."

The doctor stood and smiled. "If Joe has half of your fortitude, he will be just fine," he said. He donned his coat and hat and put his hand on the doorknob. When Martha slipped a small box of goods under his arm he nodded a thanks to her.

"I have to run out to Camp 7 tomorrow," he said. "On the way back I'll stop in and see how you are doing. You get some rest, now Alma. I should think your little spell just now was due to being just plumb wore out more than anything."

He thanked them once more for the goods and left, hoping to avoid Emil in the yard, if he could. Emil saw him leave at once and started to come towards him, but the doctor kept walking and Emil realized the futility of further discussion anyway and threw up his hands and paced in the other direction, smoke puffing from his pipe in blue-gray bursts.

K. Wallin

The Thirty Third Chapter

ℒeon pays a Visit

The work was hard, the weather cold, and the men were bored and weary. Some of them reacted to this condition by getting mean and cranky. Some just withdrew inside themselves. The family men were worried about the diphtheria and influenza and thought daily of their family members and wondered how they were. Those without families wanted the winter to end, wanted the camp to breakup, wanted a fistful of money and a lively saloon.

It was the winter blues, hastened and intensified by the sickness and the cold. Ox Pete's solution was to work the men even harder, making them more tired and leaving them little time to think about such things. He watched them carefully... at meals, in the woods... stopping at the bunkhouse at night on some feigned excuse to sample their mood and dampen the fires of frustration and worry.

It being an early Sunday morning and a day of rest, the men gathered around after breakfast to share some stories, play cards and wash out a few things. For a change of pace, and upon Muggsley's approval, a good bunch of the men were in the dining hall where there was a little more room and a little more light.

"Alfred said the Sanderson girl got it," said Bull Finnigan. "The little one, with the curly hair. But not bad... not as bad as that Walden boy."

"Say," began Ox Pete, his foot up on a crate and his pipe in his mouth. "Dat reminds me... dat Valden boy... he's on da mend. Gonna be alright according to Doc Parker." He puffed thoughtfully on the pipe letting that news sink in.

"You ain't talked to Parker," objected Helge.

"Vell now, I did. I talked to 'em the day the Martin Hatch baby vas born. He tol' me den."

"Hah!" spit Helge. "Doc Parker weren't never here... and you never went down to Camp #11 when Parker was there."

"Vhat! Yew call me liar? Yew veasel of a... Vell now... " said Ox Pete changing course and mood suddenly. It struck him that Helge was trying to goad him... no reason... just because it was his way of coping with boredom.

"It could be dat I heard it from somevun who vas dere vhen the Doc said it," allowed Pete. "Now dat yew mention it, Helge, I don't remember exactly talking to Doc Parker hisself. But the Valden boy's gonna be alright... dat's for sure."

"Well that's good news," said Smiley. "I mean, I don't know the Waldens and all... but... that's good news, I'd say."

"In Chicago," added Leon, "when the diphtheria comes, they quarantine the whole house... sometimes the whole block. Kinda like fencing it in. You can't get it unless you been with someone who has it."

"Well that don't make no sense," said Bull. "Who gave it to the first guy who had it?"

"I heard it came from sheep," said someone from near the stove.

"Sheep?!?" exclaimed Helge with a grin. "No, I think that was something else." Everyone laughed though Smiley was unsure of the joke.

"So you ban to Chicago, eh?" Said one of the Canadians.

"I... I've been to lots of cities."

"So I know a fellow in Chicago... he good man... maybe you know him? He work on the waterfront... name of Blackie... you know eh?"

"Well..." Leon stammered. Ox Pete didn't like the look in the Canadian's eyes... mischief to be sure.

"I seen yew vhipping dat Ox today, Yohnnie," interrupted Pete. "I don't like it. I don't like it at all. Yust plumb mean. Dem oxes vorking hard... yew gotta vater dat road more... not vhip them oxes."

"I whip dumb ox to teach... he pull or get whip. Simple lesson, eh? Dey learn."

"Vell, maybe I give yew same lesson... maybe right now!"

"Maybe you try!" goaded the Canadian.

"I knew a man that had awful trouble with horses once," said Ole suddenly. "Awful trouble." The Canadian and Ox Pete still maintained direct eye contact, but slowed their mounting anger temporarily. "He lost one or two of them horses to sickness... they were so sick they just fell down and couldn't get up. No siree. But that's not the strange part."

"Strange part?" asked Bull. It was enough to interest most of the men now.

"Awful strange," continued Ole. "He had terrible luck with his horses. They wouldn't do as he'd say... kinda had a mind of their own, if you know what I mean. He'd try to get 'em to drive across rotten ice... but they wouldn't... they wouldn't mind at all. And he'd try to get 'em to eat dirt... cause it's so cheap and available and he didn't like making hay... but they wouldn't."

"Dirt, for cries sakes," said Bull.

"Nope, they wouldn't mind at all. Made him mad as hell, too, so he wouldn't feed 'em, to punish 'em. Didn't feed 'em at all for awhile, and they got sick. Some died. And he figured they did it on purpose just cause he told 'em they better not die."

"Well, he didn't feed 'em, what'd he expect?" injected Smiley. "Horses gotta eat, same as people."

"So he was down to one sickly horse, this guy," continued Ole. "One horse and sick at that. So he decides he might as well put it out of his misery. He was gonna shoot the horse to teach it a lesson.

"But...." started Smiley.

"Don't interrupt," cautioned Bull with a hand on the lad's shoulder.

"He was gonna shoot it, plain and simple... led it down by the pond and dug a grave for it. But then he sees... he forgot his gun. He has to run up and get his gun. Well the horse ain't dumb like he thinks. He sees the grave, he knows what's gonna happen. Well, the man runs back to the house and gets his gun... gonna teach that horse a lesson for sure... but when he gets back, what do you suppose the horse gone and done?"

"What?" said a number of the men engrossed in the story.

"The horse committed suicide! As soon as the man ran to get the gun, the horse used up the rest of his strength to gallop down to the pond and swam out to the deepest part... and drowned hisself. Yessiree... that man had the worse trouble with horses.

"The horse committed suicide?" asked Smiley. "I never heard of that." And the men guffawed... they laughed long and hard... mostly at the story and the obvious moral... but a little at Smiley, though he never knew it. Even Ox Pete found it amusing. And more to the point... the Canadian must have understood its meaning for he laughed the hardest of all.

"Suicide, py golly, dat vas gude one, Ole," mused Pete. Ole though maintained a straight face now, as he did through the story, as if the story were true and lacked humor.

Suddenly Joe Kinder poked his head in the door, a sober look upon his face. He scanned the faces of the men until he found Buck on the bench about to put a chaw in his mouth.

"Vell, vhat is it?" grunted Pete.

"Buck's got a visitor, Mr. Pete."

"Vell, bring him in, Yoe."

"Uh... well, it's a she, Mr. Pete. Maybe Buck should come out here and talk to her... do ya think?"

"Vell, of course I tink." Turning to Buck he said "Yew go talk... in my office if yew vant."

Buck shrugged and went outside without saying a word. Ox Pete went with him, figuring on hearing some news, any news. And the men crowded around the doorway to see who would be visiting the camp on a Sunday morning when it was barely light out. Leon noticed, even in the dismal daylight, that it was Andrea and he marveled at her courage... that she would come to visit so far into the woods like this, on her own and alone. It did not take the others long to figure out that the form standing down the trail was definitely female.

"Hey," mused Bull. "That's a gal. A good lookin' one too. And lookit that, from here I'd say she has a ..."

That was as far as he got. Leon pulled him back and landed a punch on his chin filled with a sudden frenzy of emotion and power. It knocked the man over and sent him sprawling.

"What the hell!" he snorted. "Why you..."

Helge put his hand on Bull's shoulder holding him down on the floor momentarily. "That's Buck's sister," said Helge calmly.

"Oh," said Bull. Then pondering it further, he said, "Ohhhh." He rubbed his chin thoughtfully and then stood up. Leon was in a boxing stance near the door, ready for anything. But Bull approached him with his hand outstretched.

"Thanks," he said. "I could've got into some real trouble there." Leon shook the proffered hand suspiciously.

When the men at the door observed Ox Pete turn around and return, they scattered back to some semblance of their original places. Pete entered the room soberly and looked around. "Yoe Yohnson's got the diphtheria," he said. Buck's gonna go home a bit... help out some. Ya know Emil's got dat bad leg." The men all looked at their hands or turned away, the foul mood of winter and work returning.

"And yew, Bull... yew take over for Buck. Helge can vork vithout yew for avhile.

Leon wanted to run out and talk with Andrea then, comfort her, perhaps. But when he could maneuver past Ox Pete to the door, Buck and Andrea were already gone, heading down the railway back to the Johnson farm in long strides. The urgency of their pace and the seriousness of the matter made him think better of intruding just now, in spite of modestly good intentions. Andrea explained the situation to Buck during the walk home, trying to make it sound hopeful, something she didn't really feel in her heavy heart. But mostly it was for Emil that she had retrieved Buck. Emil was beside himself with helplessness. He paced nervously in the kitchen, the parlor... stood at the bottom of the stairway, staring up the steps, listening to a hoarse cough and moan.

Alma kept herself busy. Constantly there was linen to wash, and bed clothes and washcloths. A pot of water was kept simmering on the stove at near all hours. It was important to wash everything that came into contact with Joe. To further minimize the possibility of spreading the disease, Alma would not let anyone into Joe's room, though on occasion they were allowed to stand at the doorway and offer comfort that they could not truly bring.

Buck and Andrea said little during the walk back to the Johnson farm, Buck not particularly conversational to begin with. They got back before noon and found Emil shoveling snow around the chicken coop, the finishing strokes to a job already completed some time ago. When Emil caught sight of them coming down the path, he paused from his labor and rested his chin on his mittened hand on top of the shovel handle. Buck thought he suddenly looked rather old and crooked, aware that he didn't come home and help as often as he could, as often as he should.

Emil stayed in his resting position until they had come up to the yard proper. "Py golly, Buck, it is gude to haf yew home," said Emil straightening a little. "Vhy don't yew come home to us more often? Vhy you not visit on Sundays like vee alvays do?"

"Sorry, Pa." was all Buck managed to say.

"Ahhh... is gude to see yew," smiled Emil. He moved closer and put his hand on Buck's arm, squeezing lightly.

The house was warm, thought Buck, too warm for someone who has been working in the woods. And it somehow had the smell of sickness about it, stuffy and stifling, with a faint odor of minty chest balm. It made him uneasy. He hemmed and hawed when Alma and Martha addressed him and hugged him. And but for Andrea standing between him and the door, would have chanced to run from the whole affair.

But the others were so overwhelmingly happy to see him that they would not let go. Before long he found himself at the door to the bedroom he once shared with Joe... and Joe laying there flushed and quiet... so unlike the pirate he had known. Alma, Martha and Andrea had crowded up behind, giving him courage but not much room.

"He's sleeping," whispered Buck to Alma.

But suddenly the puffy face moved, and sleepy lids revealed rather dull eyes. "No I'm not, Buck," said Joe weakly. Buck couldn't recognize the voice. It was that of an ailing old man, it seemed.

"Hello-du Yoeseph," said Buck a little louder. "Yew got a little sick?"

"Yeah... I didn't mean to... but...golly, Buck... I can hardly talk," he said hoarsely.

"Vell, vee don't need to stand here," observed Alma. "Vee go... and Buck vill come down vhen he's trough." And the girls retreated in mass, clunking down the stairs. Before she left, however, Alma warned Buck to get no closer than the doorframe, lest he catch the dreadful disease. To everyone's surprise, a half-hour later Buck was still up there talking now and again.

Andrea decided she had to get out of the house again. The day had brightened up gaily, a boost to the spirit. The sun was bright and unhindered in the early afternoon sky, the wind asleep in the west, the temperature crowding 30 degrees, one of the nicest days that Andrea could remember from the foul winter that had swallowed up their souls. She strolled out into the yard, taking note of the winter birds feeding around the chicken coop... the grosbeaks, the pine martins, the ever present chickadees. They scattered as she approached then regrouped behind her to continue their scrounging for seeds. Emil was back outside, too. It made him feel healthier, though he could not tell you why. Andrea found him staring down the well-worn path to town to the west. She put her arm around his shoulder and hugged him gently. He gave her a weak smile and turned back to stare down the trail. The sun was blinding off the white of the snow, a brightness they were not used to in these last several weeks.

"Py golly, another visitor, I tink," observed Emil, shading his eyes with his hand.

"Doc Parker, Papa?"

"I tink not," he replied. Then turning to her he said, "Andrea, yew tell me now. Yew tell me true."

"What, Papa?"

"Yew tell me...if mama...did mama see...did mama see in her mind of Yoseph? Did mama see Yoseph ... vill not do so gude? Emil did not believe in these visions that Alma experienced. Did not even like to have them mentioned, as if it was witchcraft and evil. But he understood some things about them. He understood that she only had visions when something bad happened. And if he was forced to admit it, he would say that she had seldome been wrong in all the time they had been together. Still... he normally refused to even talk about it.

"Did she see, papa?"

"Did she see... up here," Emil pointed at his temple. "Yew know vhat I am talking about... did she see someting about Yoseph?"

"Yes, I know what you are talking about, Papa. Mama saw nothing that I know of. Nothing since the tree fell on Buck last Thanksgiving." She wouldn't look at him though. She did not want him to see the doubt in her own eyes.

"Yaas... yaas, dat is gude," nodded Emil. It made him feel better and he let out a nervous sigh. "Yaas... dat is gude." He looked around at his farm... the buildings, the chickens scratching in the snow covered ground, the wind lightly brushing snow off of the trees. Something in the distance caught his eye. "I think that it is somevun yew know, Andrea," said Emil relieved from his thoughts for awhile. For he had suddenly recognized the young man coming down the trail. And when Andrea followed suit and shaded her eyes and studied the distant form, her heart leapt. Leon Mancheski it was, a sheepish look on his wind worn face.

K. Wallin

The Thirty Fourth Chapter

They All Fall

Leon was still trying to figure out how he got this far without figuring out a reason for the visit. All that he knew was what he felt in his heart, that young Joe Johnson was terribly ill and Andrea was hurting, a hurt he would hope to ease a bit, though he had no idea how.

He saw them standing at the gate up ahead, Andrea and her father, doubly awkward now that they could see him as well. There was no way to back out, to retrace his path and go back to town. So he bucked up his fortitude and met them with a restrained smile, noticing for the first time the quarantine sign on the gate.

"Hello... uh Mr. Johnson, Andrea."

"Hello-du," said Emil. "Yew come for visit?"

"Well, yes...I ...I hope that's ok. I forgot about the quarantine."

"Yew come to visit anyvun special?" pried Emil with a weary smile.

"Ah..." stumbled Leon.

"Oh, Papa..." joined in Andrea, "he probably heard about Joe and came to see if there was anything he could do."

"Yes, "said Leon gratefully, "I am sorry to hear that Joe is sick... and if there's anything I can do... anything at all... I would be most happy to. Whatever I could do."

"Ya ya...it is gude yew come. Yew can do something," said Emil.

"I can? Well, good... I would be... uh .. what is it I could do for you?"

"Yew take dis girl to town, for visit... she vork tu hard."

"Oh, papa! Don't listen to him, Mr. Mancheski, it is him that needs a break."

"But I would be happy to do that, to escort you to town, I mean. I'll buy you a soda or something! Will you come, Andrea?" Leon's enthusiasm was unmistakable.

"Yew go," said Emil, nudging her forward. "Yew go for awhile." And she did.

They took the wagon trail, where they could walk side by side and talk along the way. She overlooked the camp smell of smoke and sweat, having gotten somewhat used to it from Buck, something he was aware of. There was not even a wind to carry it away from them. When she was not looking, he studied her... the rosy cheeks of fresh air, the soft chestnut hair falling loosely about her shoulders. When she would turn to look at him, her blue eyes fairly danced and glistened. No makeup was needed on this pretty face.

"What are you staring at?" she asked.

"Oh... you... mostly," he replied, dragging his foot in the snow. "If I had a little more courage, I would tell you just how pretty you are out here in the sunshine."

"Oh, really? Funny how that courage seems to come and go with you. You never know where it will turn up," she said gamely.

"You kissed me first," he said defensively.

"Why, Mr. Mancheski, I did no such thing." she stopped along the road and faced him, hands on her hips and a trace of anger on her pretty face.

"In the cloakroom, at the hall," he explained. "You kissed me right on the lips as pretty as you please."

"Oh, oh," she stuttered unable to think of a reply. She continued down the road in frustration, stomping in long strides and he fought to catch up with her. Then she stopped and turned to him again, though he nearly passed her by in the suddenness of it.

"Well, there was mistletoe... and I thought maybe you hadn't been kissed for a long time... and ... and...well, I'm sorry it bothered you so much." And she stomped off again, with him following the best he could.

"It didn't bother me," he called to her, "I really liked it. That's why I kissed you when we were in the snow bank."

She stopped suddenly again and he nearly ran into her. "But there was no mistletoe in the snow bank," she said.

"I know," he admitted. "I kissed you then, because I wanted to. That's why, that's the only reason why. Because I wanted to. I'm sorry if it bothered you."

"It...it didn't bother me," she said feeling her face start to flush. "But you can't go around kissing people just because you want to." They stared at each other for a few minutes without saying a word. Then Leon broke the uncomforting silence.

"Andrea...I... well..." and thinking of nothing more to say, stood close to her, putting his rough and calloused hand upon her cheek. She didn't withdraw, her heart racing, her face burning. His thumb rubbed her cheek softly until slowly he brought his face close to hers, where she could feel his light breath upon her lips. And then he kissed her. Lightly it was at first, a soft caress. He was conscious of the feel of her nose, cold against his cheek, the warmth and lively feeling of her lips.

Suddenly she broke away, a shocked look on her face. She struggled out of his embrace and ran down the trail toward town, coat tails flying.

"Wait!" he called after her, a little puzzled. "Wait for me!" It was an effort to catch up to her on the snowy trail turning icy under the warming sun. She slowed some when the fury had been released and the embarrassment had taken over, and soon he was striding again by her side.

"What's the matter," he asked curiously, completely oblivious to her state of mind.

"See... there you go again, kissing me for no reason. Don't you listen? I have half a mind to turn Buck loose on you. Or Joe, when he gets better."

"No reason? I suppose a fella has to carry some mistletoe around in his pocket all the time if he ever wants to kiss his girl."

"I'm not your girl! For heaven's sakes, I barely know you. You might think you're some kind of smooth operator with the fancy notes and city ideas, but that doesn't mean a girl's gonna put up with being kissed any time you please." Her face was flushed with a healthy pink glow, her hair coming undone and flying in her face as she stamped along the trail.

"You kissed me back," he said rather softly. Then as he thought about it, he said it louder. "You kissed me back!"

"Why, Mr. Mancheski, I did no such thing. Of all the nerve!"

"That's why you're so upset... you liked it. You liked it and that makes you feel guilty."

She stopped on the trail and faced him square, trying to think of words to express the anger and disgust that she really didn't feel. But she couldn't talk. Her mouth opened several times, but no words came forth all the while her blue eyes fairly shone in the winter light, and he stood staring at her, a stupid smile on his face. When she had composed herself somewhat, she smiled a sheepish smile, suddenly feeling awkward and just a little bit out of control of the situation.

"Well," she started calmly, "you must fashion yourself a most charming and experienced young fellow to think that I would be that impressed with the whole affair. I've been kissed before, and better, I can assure you." She started walking again, before he could react... before he could wonder who else she may have kissed. She walked slower than before now, in a graceful and feminine manner, her change in moods a puzzle to him.

As he matched her step for step, she pursed her lips and smiled to herself as his words came back to her. His girl!

"Sooooo..." she said demurely.

"So?" he replied innocently.

"Sooooo... you think of me as your girl?"

"Well... I ...I..."

"Your courage has gone again, I guess," she sighed. "Just as well... so has mine. Today would be a good day to talk a little though, wouldn't you say? There's not much harm in talking, and there's so much I don't know about you. You may even have some questions about me you'd like to ask, if it's not too personal of course. There are just some things a girl won't talk about with a man... so don't ask those kind of things."

"Well... I... I guess talking's a good idea," he said.

"Good. Is there something you'd like to know about me? You've met my family."

"Well... what about this note thing you were talking about?"

Talk they did. While the snow melted from the branches and the chickadees chittered at them from stump to stump along the trail, they walked and they talked of many things. To Leon's amazement, nearly the whole Chicago business came tumbling out of his mouth on its own accord, depressing him and shocking her.

But even that revelation could not put a shadow on the day. If anything it brought them closer... closer in spirit as well as physically closer, their arms locking, their bodies bumping together as they walked. She felt his pain, he felt her heartfelt sympathy and concern. And together they both felt better. What healing power talk can be to two kindred souls.

They stayed in town only an hour or so, getting a soda at Hackett's confectionery, and strolling about. And though they curtailed the hand-holding when they reached the limits of the town, people still eyed them curiously and marked them down for further gossip when the occasion arose.

On the way back to the Johnson farm, though the warm and happy feelings persisted, Leon couldn't seem to get back to hand-holding again. Instead, their new relationship reached the playful stage. It was near Twenty Mile creek that Andrea challenged him to a race. He at once agreed, and almost before the words had left his mouth, she was off at a run, lifting her skirts slightly, while he struggled after her as best he could. When she turned to see how close he was at her heels, she stumbled and fell ungracefully into the snow. He stopped short, bent at the waist laughing so hard he could not continue.

"Laugh at a lady in distress, will you?" she chuckled in spite of herself. Then she grabbed up a handful of snow, quickly formed a snowball and hit him with it right in the chest."

"Oh ho!" he cried, "a war is it?"

"Ohhhhh," she uttered scrambling to run. Girlish laughter followed her path down the road with Leon close behind. He caught her at the wagon bridge and clung to her waist as she fought him half-heartedly all the while.

"I guess I'll have to cast you off the bridge to the icy waters, unless you pay the ransom" he cried gaily.

"And what is the ransom?" she asked.

"A kiss, fair lady... maybe two... maybe three!" he replied.

"Then, cast away... I'd rather kiss Twenty Mile creek," she laughed. So he pretended to thrust her to the edge and over, while she struggled and giggled. He held her by the waist and leaned her over the rail.

"No, no," she cried. "I'll pay."

He brought her back up straight and in his fond embrace, her blue eyes following his. His expression sobered at her look of quiet submission, her lips gently parted and moist.

"I'll pay," she said again almost in a whisper. He kissed her soft and quick, then withdrew to study her face once more, wrestling with feelings unfamiliar to him.

"Hey!" shouted a gruff voice from a distance. "Yew turn her loose." It was Buck in not such a pleasant mood. "Py golly I'll strike yew silly, I'll poke yew into next week!"

"No! Buck. It's alright," said Andrea. "It's ok, really. Mr. Mancheski and I are ... good friends."

"Mama says yew should come home," said Buck with a degree of concern in his voice.

"Is it Joe," asked Andrea, her hand coming up to her mouth in horror."

"He doesn't feel so gude," admitted Buck. "Mama says yew should come now!" The words were no sooner out of his mouth when Andrea started running down the trail. Buck started to go, then turned back to Leon. "Maybe I should hit yew, now, but maybe I vait til later. Yew vatch vhat yew do," he warned. "Yew vatch vhat yew do." Then he was off, Leon following at a distance, emotions flooding from his heart to his brain and getting all mixed up.

By the time Leon knocked quietly on the door and was admitted, Andrea was upstairs with Joe. Joe had asked for her specifically and ignoring her mother's warnings, she entered and sat on the bed near him, brushing his hair aside and trying to smile as sweetly as she could. Alma stood at the doorway, to allow them space, her hand at her throat and her eyes shiny. She would not yet give way to the breakdown of control, fighting back the tears, trying hard to keep the fear from her voice.

"Are you being a good patient?" Andrea asked, not knowing what else to say.

"Andrea," he hoarsely whispered, then coughed weakly. She leaned closer to him, so he didn't have to try so hard. Alma could no longer hear, so she moved back downstairs with the others.

"Andy...I...I...seen Ed Simms. He was standing over there in the corner smiling at me. How come Mama let him in, Andy? Why did he want to visit me?"

"Ed Simms died last Thanksgiving, Joe," said Andrea in a shaky voice.

"Andy... I feel so bad... I feel so... weak," said Joe. "I just..."

"Joe don't speak. You don't have to... save your strength until you're better."

"No..." he said. "I need ...to know... Do you think I am being punished for something?"

"Punished?"

"Is God mad at me?"

"No, Joe... of course not, nothing like that."

"I ain't been so good... I got in trouble... pretty much,"

"Joe, you haven't been so bad. You just got character, that's all. Character. It's a part of growing up. Like Huckleberry Finn. You know, that story I read you.

"Maybe I got too much character," said Joe. Andrea wanted desperately to break down and cry and hug him, but restrained herself.

"No, Joe... you... why, your character is just glorious. Glorious, I tell you." He smiled then. Barely... but a smile.

"Well, I'm sorry I ever been bad. I wouldn't be bad anymore. I'd be better to Mama, too. I know she worries bout me lots. I'd even give up being a pirate. But I had to go, Andy. I had to go."

"Go? Go where Joe?"

"Bob's gonna get better now ain't he?"

"Oh, Joe!" Andrea could take no more and started to cry. Tears streaked down her face uncontrollably while she put her head down beside his wheezy chest. He looked of death, pale and worn and deep inside her she knew. She knew what Alma had known since the day the doctor had come.

Joe ran his hand over her hair, gently. "Don't... cry... Andrea," he said in a hoarse whisper. "It ain't so bad."

Some time later Andrea came down the stairs, barely composed. Emil was distressed at how she looked, drawn and weary, drained of spirit. Alma immediately went upstairs to be with Joe.

"Papa," said Andrea, "Joe wondered if you would play the fiddle for him. He wondered if you would play the swallow song."

"Fiddle?" said Emil, "Fiddle? Yew see, Buck, he is feeling better, he vants the music. Py golly, vheres my fiddle...I'll play fiddle like yew von't believe me."

"Papa," said Andrea, "he wants the swallow song, Halsa dem darhemma, ok?"

"Vell, sure. I play swallow song for Yoseph. I vill play best I ever play, yew see."

In her distress, Andrea hadn't noticed Leon sitting in a corner chair near the stove. She eyed him now, his sheepish awkward look returning, and loved him dearly, if only for the moment. She wanted to find comfort in his arms, but merely nodded in his direction, he returning the nod politely. Martha followed this exchange somewhat curiously.

Soon, the mournful beauty of the swallow song, played expertly on the violin, filled the Johnson house. Emil stood at the foot of the stairs and put his heart into his music, drawing from the inner strength of love and family. Andrea would long remember that it was the best she ever heard him play; magical, spiritual. She sat down near Leon, mildly amused at the expression on Buck's face... and figuring she would have to straighten him out on a few things.

Martha sat with Emma in her lap, Emma's shoes and socks removed, her toes wiggling in anticipation and delight. Martha sometimes played the "strawberry game" with her before dressing for bed. So as the others listened to the music, Martha quietly pinched her toes, one at a time with her fingers and recited the Strawberry game:

Five little strawberries,
Purchased at the store;
One of them was rotten,
Then there were but four.

She pinched Emma's big toe when she got to the part about one being rotten, and screwed up her face as if there was a bad smell, much to Emma's delight.

Four little Strawberries,
Sour as can be;
One of them was wormy
Then there were but three.

Three little strawberries,
Looking mighty blue;
One of them was sandy,
Then there were but two.

The music played on, the melody sweeping everyone into a pensive mood, each lost in their own thoughts and loathe to speak, reluctant, even, to move.

Two little strawberries,
Never saw the sun;
One of them was sandy,
Then there was but one.

One little strawberry,
One and only one;
Made into a shortcake,
Now of course, there's none.

At the last of the strawberry game, Martha made as if she was going to eat Emma's toes, the shortcake, and Emma squealed in delight, only to receive a shhhhhh, immediately from Martha. But when Martha looked up, it was as if no one had heard. There was a broad smile on Emil's face, a contented smile. The music, played with such feeling, was warming him, reaching into his heart and lifting the veil of melancholy that so long had enveloped his spirit.

Andrea sang the last two verses of the song, beautifully and with as much feeling as the music itself bore.

> *Greet all those at home still*
> *Greet my dad and mother*
> *Greet the pretty green hillside*
> *Greet my little kid brother*

> *If I had wings, like the swallow*
> *I'd fly back home to thee*
> *Swallow, fly on homeward*
> *And greet them all for me.*

And when the last notes of the song were played, as the words and tune faded gracefully from the room together, a stifled shriek was heard from upstairs. It was like a dagger to Andrea's heart, for she knew... she had known. And ignoring all else she went to Leon and buried her head in his chest and wept.

"Vhat!" cried Emil. "But she doesn't see... Mama doesn't see, yew said!" He stared at Andrea's shaking form. He looked at his violin and bow in either hand, then to the ceiling, looking for God. He cast the violin and bow to the floor in a crash that startled everyone, making Buck jump to his feet. With a rare show of compassion he gave Emil a hug and escorted him to the door. They would cope with their grief outside, in private, the way men feel they ought to do sometimes. But those they left in the room, were all in tears, even Leon. And Emma too, though she didn't understand.

"Why are we crying, Martha," she asked.

"Because... Emma... because Joe went away." She hugged the child tightly.

"Isn't he coming back?" she asked.

"No," sniffed Martha... " No, he's not coming back, Emm." And she hugged her even tighter. Emma wept as the rest, though still not completely understanding. She snuggled her face into Martha's warm neck and cried.

"And he didn't even say goodbye," she sobbed.

K. Wallin

The Thirty Fifth Chapter

Winter Passes

As with most of the horrors that befall man, the dreary winter, the sickness and its dreadfull harvest, would slowly fade into the past, cast in shadowy memories of loved ones lost which would linger for eternity.

That Sunday at the Johnson farm in late February was a turning point for many things. The weather relented from the harshness of days past, giving in to the promise of Spring, though still some time away. It was enough to lighten the heart, for some.

The relationship between Andrea and Leon prospered on the grief that had befallen the Johnson's. Andrea found his arms a place of solace, his lips a haven for forgetfulness. His Sunday visits were an opportunity to get away from the house, away from the somber mood of Alma, the hollow look of Emil sitting in his favorite chair, pipe in hand but unlit. He would sit there thinking instead of reading his newspaper as was his custom, until finally he would slowly rise and walk outside... sometimes without even remembering his coat. And he would not play the violin. He would not even pick it up off the floor where he had thrown it that day. The violin would forever be tied to that dark day in February.

Several weeks had passed. There was already talk of the camps breaking up for the season, for as the snow began to disappear into the bright days of early spring, the logging roads became increasingly more difficult to navigate, the sleigh loads of logs harder for the oxen and horses to pull.

"Alfred says that Cooper is thinking about calling it quits for the year pretty soon," said Leon. "As nice as this weather seems, it sure is hard on the Oxen."

"I suppose," mumbled Andrea. "And what will you do?" They were walking from town back to the Johnson farm on a lovely Sunday afternoon coming up the last of the trail to the house.

"Do? Well, I don't know exactly. Up until a couple of weeks ago, I never gave it much thought."

"You'll be leaving probably. Getting out of these dreadful woods and back to civilization, back to a finer form of sanity."

"I don't know. I... I don't want to leave, really. I like it here. I feel safer here."

"Safer? How dare you!" she said angrily. "Don't you see... death can find you anywhere... misery lies in wait...in the streets of Chicago, in a lumber camp, in your own bed for heaven's sakes". She didn't realize it at the time but she was echoing Mary's sentiments, though for a different reason. "Safe? Why, there is no such thing." She began to cry then, choking on the feelings that worked their way up into her throat and strangled the words she was trying to say. Feeling helpless, Leon tried to embrace her but she pushed him gently away and strode off toward the house.

Leon called to her, softly at first, then louder until he saw Buck standing in the yard. Buck eyed him carefully then, and observed Andrea continuing into the house, tears still clinging to the corners of her eyes. On another day, another time... it would have been enough. He would have given this young man a thrashing, even not knowing or understanding the circumstances. But Joe's death had worn on him, as the others but perhaps more on the inside. He made a mental note of this brief affair... then turned his attentions to the woodpile and smote the hardwood chunks with all the energy that frustration and anger could muster. He worked harder and harder at it, striking forcefully, sometimes blindly...and broke the ax handle about the same time he broke his own spirit. Then somewhat subdued he carried in the fruits of his labor to stack inside the kitchen wood box.

Leon knew that Andrea's anger was not directed at him, but at the uncertainty of life and the fate that had claimed "her" Joe. And it would pass. But she was right about one thing. He would have to decide what he was doing and where he was going. And he wondered to himself if those plans included Andrea.

The men at camp had a restless look about them too, a thirsty look, a craven look... craving whiskey, women and song, no doubt. Bull Finigan smacked his lips every now and again looking for that burning taste and found them lacking. But it had found a place to occupy in his mind. The others were not much better, if not following Bull's course of thoughts, then thinking of home and loved ones.

For many, the arduous work that had consumed their efforts these last months would take a new direction, but continue just the same, for they were farmers that worked the land. Spring planting was not far off. There was land to clear, to increase the yield and the profit, and the labor. Spring merely announced a change of occupations for these hardy souls.

Ox Pete rode with Leon bringing the lunch to the men, now far distant from the camp. Little spurs of the railroad had been strung off in all directions, attempting to follow the tree harvesting, bringing the landings as close as possible to the work. But there was a limit to these efforts too, and now the sleighs were hauling long and difficult to reach the nearest siding. Ox Pete was preparing to make a decision.

The sleigh of hot soup and sandwiches hauled hard on the rutted trail, bogging down occasionally in the slimy mud of spring. When they were able to crest the last hill and see the work of the men spread out before them, they stopped. Ox Pete watched them at this distance for a while, puffing on his pipe. He could see a general lack of energy in their work, the struggle it was for the oxen to move the logs. And he noted, with displeasure, the way the French Canadian, Johnnie Sweet, whipped at the oxen as they strained in their traces.

"Dat man," he said mostly to himself, "need lesson about oxes."

"What'd ya say, Pete?" inquired Leon.

"Never yew mind," replied Pete, "yew move along now vhile soup is almost hot and feed dese men."

Leon goaded the oxen onward, down the slope to the main log landing. While the men gorged themselves on the hearty, if somewhat cool meal, Ox Pete wandered around looking at the various stages of the work at hand, and then back again, to smoke silently near the circle of woodsmen.

Finally, he said, "Vee quit today... I tink, ya Buck?" Buck nodded. "Yew men...yew finish up vhat is there... finish up gude. But I need Buck and Helge. Cooper come today to look over new timber for next year. Yew men finish gude, ok?"

"Ok," said Ole. And with that short communication, smiles began to break out over the bedraggled crew. And the friendly banter that was theirs and once so free, began to babble like a spring-fed brook finally free from the icy grip of winter.

"Was up Escanaba way, last year," began Helge suddenly. "Met this gal was so bowlegged she could get on a horse without lifting her leg." And so it went, the ending to a fine season of lumbering, the prelude to the next season. When Leon started the team back toward camp, Buck and Helge were riding in the wagon trying to keep the cans and kettles from banging together.

The train was in camp when they got back, Cooper sitting in the sunshine on a stump near the cook shanty, puffing on a cigar and looking just a bit impatient.

"Ox Pete," he said as the men came up, "I have been waiting!"

"Don't call me Ox," said Pete scowling.

"Well, I'll call you anything I damn well please as long as you are in my employ. Now let's get going. I haven't got all day." Pete didn't move, standing with his arms crossed and his pipe, long gone out, in his mouth. "Well?" said Cooper.

"Sometimes I hit peoples dat call me Ox," said Pete. "Sometimes they don't get up for long time. And today... today vee are done in this voods."

"I see," said Cooper putting two and two together. "Yes, I certainly see. Well... and you have a point there to be sure. You've done a fine job up here, Ox... I mean, Mr. Swenson. Now if you would accompany me for a little jaunt, perhaps we could find some work for next year. Do you think that would be possible, Mr. Swenson?"

"Yah," grunted Pete. But the smile Cooper expected to see didn't materialize.

"Might as well bring that new guy along, if that's all right with you, Mr. Mancheski. You might as well learn a little bit about this business." Leon was a little hurt by that "new" guy crack, but nodded. Cooper was not strengthening friendships this day. "Buck, I thought we'd head south... southwest... I know there are some pretty big hills... but there's fine timber that way too and we might be able to get a track up there somehow. Have you ever been up that way?"

"Yah," said Buck. "To Porkypine one spring. Fine timber."

"Porkypine?" inquired Leon.

"A little spring fed lake up there... good fishing... good place to go to be alone," offered Helge quietly.

"Good. You've been that way too, Helge, good. Now let's get started for heavens sake before the light goes. It ain't quite spring yet."

This odd troop, Cooper, Buck, Helge, Ox Pete and Leon trudged off single file to the southwest, with Cooper trudging along in the middle. It was some time before they hit untouched timber country, for the reach of the camp was far in all timbered directions. When they reached the front range of the rocky hills Buck was able to find a wide cleft that led more gradually upward until they were on top of the range into fine wooded stands. White Pine and Hemlock were still available here, and hardwoods when that gave out. Cooper, when he wasn't making plans in his head, now wore the friendly smile of a contented man.

They stopped to rest near a little brook that coursed north in a zig-zag path down the range and into the swamp near Camp #9. Those that smoked lit pipes and cigars thinking that this act helped the thinking process, and perhaps replaced their expended energy. Buck and Helge slipped new loads of snoose into their lips, spitting carefully toward selected spots in the snow. Leon just rested and took in the country about him. The woods were tall and majestic here... towering pines more than 100 feet high and as big around as two men could reach. It was a magical place, he thought, nearly expecting a wood elf to come and chase them away.

"How much farther to Porkypine?" asked Cooper after he had sat awhile.

"Coupla miles," answered Helge.

"Whats the country like, Buck? Like this pretty much?" continued Cooper, looking past Helge. He had a special affinity for Buck, though he would never admit it to anyone. Buck was more the type of man, that he wished he was; strong, no-nonsense... not bogged down in politics and business, and brimming with common sense and natural ability for physical things.

"Yah," said Buck, "pretty much."

"Well, no need to go any further, then. We'll rest here awhile and then head back before dark." He looked at the men and saw them more clearly for once. Haggard they were, bewhiskered (save for Leon), sweaty, stinking, hardy men, iron strong and sound. Perhaps it was the time, this ending of the season, but his affinity for these simple lumbermen was strengthening. He reached into his vest pocket and pulled out a full pint bottle of whiskey.

"Damn that Jake! He knows I don't drink during the day. Must've slipped this into my pocket when I wasn't looking, figuring it would bog me down some to carry it. Say, you boys wouldn't do me a favor and empty this thing would ya? I'd hate to waste it, but I'll be damned if I'll tote this thing all the way back to camp." It was a done deal.

Leon, not too interested in the whiskey, stood next to one of the largest white pines and looked up the trunk reaching far into the sky. The rest of the group quietly ignored him at first, concentrating on getting an equal share of the bottle. But Leon was in awe. Most of his woods experience had been from the edges, observing the cutting operations from a distance and marveling at the skill and endurance of the human factor, always amazed at the degree of destruction and its aftermath of slashed limbs and debri.

But here, in the midst of untouched forest, a new perspective gripped him. And he tried to put it into words. "How many years this tree has stood... weathering storms and snows of all ages. So tall and strong and majestic, roots so deep and sturdy. Makes a guy feel kinda puny, if you know what I mean." He was talking to no one in particular and expected no answer. On impulse he tried reaching his arms around the base, succeeding a little less than half way.

"Vell, Yah," said Ox Pete. "But they all fall, don't they." The others looked at Pete, amazed at the profound statement he had just made. And struck by the truth of it, a sadness enveloped them all.

They reached camp with the sun still well above the Southwest horizon. Buck discovered that another bottle of whiskey had mysteriously appeared and there was time to have a go at it before the other men returned from the days work. And so they gathered round and partook of the evil fruit. Leon lost track of them then, as his work was not quite over and he had to labor steadily to catch up. The evening meal was being prepared, and this was a most important chore that could not be ignored.

When he chanced to go outside, he found the men to be getting a little more animated each time, including Ox Pete and Cooper. It amused him and he actually thought well of the idea, this being the breakup of the camp and all that had happened. So he was somewhat surprised when he went outside to get some more firewood, that Buck suddenly stood before him, glaring in a suspiciously unfriendly manner.

"'Lo, Buck" said Leon.

"Yew!" exclaimed Buck. "Yew are trouble for sure. I should teach yew sum tings." Leon was taken totally aback. He didn't know what to say. He noted the others gathering around in interest.

"I fix yew. I told yew I fix yew vhen yew monkey around vith Andrea. She don't need yew to make her cry."

The image of Buck standing in the yard when Andrea went crying into the house suddenly struck him, and words of a threat uttered now and again. Leon's face reddened. He knew that Buck had been drinking... but he also knew that he was not drunk.

"Yew fight me now. I'll give yew chance to fight too. Yew hit me first, right here," he said pointing to his chin. "Yew hit hard, if yew can."

"I don't want to fight you, Buck. I didn't do anything," said Leon, hoping that not too much fear showed in his voice. Joe Kinder and Muggsley came out of the shanty, hearing the noise, but offered no words of support or defense.

"Py golly, yew fight or yew get knocked silly anyvay," insisted Buck. Leon started to panic now...looking for Cooper...Cooper would stop this nonsense. Buck had the sleeves of his shirt and underwear rolled up and his fists up in a fighting stance.

"Mr. Cooper... I ... I didn't do anything. Would you tell him to leave me alone?"

"Must've done something," mused Cooper.

"Buck, I...I didn't do anything."

"Vee see bout dat," said Buck spitting his snoose into the snow. "Vee see bout dat. I give yew one more chance to hit me here," he said pointing once again at his solid chin, "then I poke yew anyway. I poke yew into next week, maybe." The men were gathered around them, none offering Leon any support, all curious as to what he would do, none doubting the outcome of a fight, fair or otherwise.

Buck stood with his chin outstretched and Leon's options for avoiding a fight just about spent. So he resolved to himself that he would go down fighting, and hope his face would not look too badly when he woke up... maybe several days later. It was almost a comical thought, if the look on Buck's face had any kindness to it. Instead it was a frozen mask of anger and pentup frustration. So Leon took off his apron and rolled up his sleeves, and reluctantly advanced into the ring.

"Yew hit first... so everyvun know, it vas fair fight." said Buck thrusting out his chin yet again. And with quiet resolve, Leon swung.

Though hard, it was a glancing blow and Leon at once knew it would have little effect, so he braced himself for the storm. Instead, Buck fell flat on his face, out cold, his falling form revealing Helge standing behind him, a chunk of firewood in his hand.

"Hey," said Cooper, "you hit him from behind."

"Yep," agreed Helge, "and hard, too. Guess he'll be out for awhile."

"Vell, vhat'd yew do that for?" exclaimed Ox Pete.

"Didn't feel like another funeral today," he answered. "Besides, Buck wasn't mad at him," he pointed to Leon, still somewhat in shock at his narrow escape, "and what he was mad at, ya just can't fight."

"That's probably true," nodded Cooper. "But I suspect that Buck isn't gonna feel too kindly toward you by the time he comes to."

"Well, ya, I guess that's true. I figure on getting back over to Michigan or someplace. They must've forgot about me by now over there." He started walking down the tracks toward town. "I'll see Jake about my pay when I get to town," he shouted back to Cooper.

"Thanks, Helge," shouted Leon. "Thanks!"

"Well, I wouldn't stand around there waiting for him to come to," he yelled back. "Maybe I'll see ya next season," he waved and then picked up his pace.

The others looked at Buck's prostrate form on the ground, blood matted in his hair where a large bump protruded. Not a movement did he make, at peace with himself and the rest of the world in this unconscious state.

"Guess you better head back to town with me," suggested Cooper. "I think your job here is pretty well finished."

The Thirty Sixth Chapter

Spring at last!

If one paid no attention to the calendar, nor the days of warmth and sunshine, one could still tell that spring had arrived by the influx of woodsmen into the towns and cities of the northland. Into Ashland they came, and Cable and Drummond and Mason and Pratt, worn, haggard, thirsty men. Men with pay script in their pockets and desire to reap the rewards of their hard work in the saloons and bordellos that so welcomed them.

Sitting in the Straddle Creek Office, Leon and John Cooper could hear the shouts and laughter from down along the trackway, at the depot and across at Charley's Saloon. Most men opted for the more lively environment of Ashland, or Hurley or Hayward, and so their stop in Pratt was perfunctory, a whistlestop on the way to the excitement of the cities.

But for some, it was the last stop, last chance for whiskey and song, before going home to the bosom of their families. And it was these men that Pratt would have to contend with for a while, a fact that Sam Hacket had well in hand. The town had assigned a few constables and the jail cell was ready, in the schoolhouse.

"I guess I would stay away from Buck, for awhile," said Cooper. "Odds are he is madder at Helge than you, but I wouldn't think you'd want to face him again any time soon."

"Yeah," mused Leon deep in thought, rubbing his chin.

"In fact, you may want to move on, considering that Buck ain't apt to forget nor forgive, nor move on his self. Could be it's just a matter of time before he finds you to finish what he started."

"Yeah," mumured Leon.

"Well, on the other hand, he was drunk at the time. Maybe he doesn't remember, maybe he'll think it was your punch that sent him flying to the ground."

"He wasn't drunk," admitted Leon. "And I doubt if he would attribute that bump on the back of his head to a punch on the chin."

"Yes, that's true, I suppose. Well, what are you going to do, then?"

"Why does everyone keep asking me that? How the hell do I know what I'm gonna do."

"Right," said Cooper.

"I gotta see Andrea... talk it over and see... I guess."

"Well, if it was me, I would say stay clear of the Johnson farm. Ya never know if Buck'll be there, or in town or where he will be."

"Yeah," said Leon thoughtfully.

Later he went for walk. Not east toward the Johnson farm, but west along the tracks to Eighteen Mile Creek Bridge. He had pondered some there before, and now there was more pondering to do. He sat on the bridge, his feet dangling, staring north over the Bibon marsh that stretched along White River in the valley below. The marsh looked barren still, brown and gray without the greening of summer, but beautiful in its starkness and thought provoking in its grandeur.

He didn't know how long he had been sitting there, but he was suddenly conscious of someone staring at him from behind. When he turned, he discovered it was Billy Brown, a lumpy handkerchief in his hand full of childish possessions.

"I didn't mean to bother ya none," said the boy, "I was just wondering who ya was. Mr. Mancheski, ain't ya?"

"And aren't you that Brown boy?"

"Yeah," he replied forlornly. Leon noticed now, that there were bruises on the boys face along his chin and his right eye was fairly swollen.

"Where are you headed? Shouldn't you be in school or something?"

"Yeah, I suppose. But Pa... he...well... if you must know, I'm running away again. Emily said I shouldn't, but I gotta."

"You've run away before?"

The boy nodded slowly. "But he always caught me. They always brought me back. Guess I gotta run farther this time. I ain't never going back. Pa don't care nothing bout us anyway, why...whys he got to hit me? I wish Joe was here. You know he hit Pa with a snowball once? Gosh that was glorious." Then he paused while another thought entered his mind.

"I wish it were me that got sick and died, instead of Joe." It made Leon swallow hard.

"Sit down, Billy, would ya. I need someone to talk to." And Billy sat down, grateful for the kind word and the chance to delay his departure to places unknown. Leon and Billy talked for an hour or so, about many things. But in the end, it was about running away from trouble. He may not have been aware of it at first, but he was also talking about himself.

"Running away doesn't solve anything," explained Leon thoughtfully. "Even if your Pa doesn't find you right away, you will always wonder where you are going to run into him. Not tomorrow, or the next... but maybe next week. And even if he never finds you, you will still wonder... and be afraid that he may be around the corner. And what about your sister? And your mother? Won't they worry about you and wonder about you, and miss you? Wouldn't it be better to face your troubles head on? Perhaps someone can help you. Someone in the County or maybe someone right here in Pratt."

"Would you help me? Mr. Mancheski?" asked the boy hopefully.

"Me? Why I don't even... I can't even seem to help myself. I...well... I guess we both need to learn something here." And he told him a little bit about Chicago and about running away. And somehow this little affair with Buck didn't seem so serious or menacing. And in the frightened eyes of a young boy, he saw himself from nearly six months ago. In Billy Brown's fear and trouble, he found his own courage and strength.

The boy walked with him back to town, though still quite unsure about what was to come. Leon felt the same way. Billy's mother was in the depot looking for him when they arrived there, a ragged thin scrap of a woman, herself somewhat bruised, though not as evident on her bluish skin. She said not a word to Leon, but whisked Billy away down the tracks toward the east end of town, Billy turning now and again to see Leon standing helpless on the train platform. It rattled him and he started to lose the courage he had borrowed from the lad... started to doubt his own words of wisdom of only a half hour before.

So into Charley's saloon he went to seek another form of courage, hoping to get from a bottle, what he lacked from mere conviction. When he entered, his eyes searched nervously through the jostling throng of woodsmen for Buck. Not finding him, he elbowed his way to the bar and ordered a drink from a very busy Charley Halverson.

And another drink. And another. And when Bull Finigan and crew came in, there were more drinks, some free for the taking. And in the comradeship of his woods crew Leon's spirits were buoyed, though he knew from experience, when fighting one of their own...they would not interfere. With the intrusion of Elmer Rose's crew from camp #7, most still sober men were sure a fight would ensue before long. And in truth, the crowd did get more rowdy, with more shoving, more shouting, and more drinking. But Leon was a minor cog in this wheel of confusion, and all but ignored while he drank copious amounts of draught beer, until... until he crossed the line from what was once a sober man.

"Ok," he shouted above the din. "Ok, ok... bring on Buck Johnson then. If he wants to fight... I'll fight'em. Bring him here... is he here? Where is he?" He staggered in among the crowd looking for Buck. "Where is he... you bring him right here... he can't tell me who to kiss... I don't care if she is his sister... why...I...I...what you laughing at, you ugly skunk?"

It was the man named George, one of the poker players from Camp #7 with a whiskey grin lighting up his face in innocent splendor. But the grin faded when he recognized the poker crew that had visited from Camp #9 and especially Bull Finnigan.

"I asked you what you were laughing at, you mangy son of a... hey ain't you from Camp #7."

"Well, yah," replied George, quietly shifting his weight and reaching for the neck end of the bottle.

"Boy we kicked your asses in poker that day, didn't we Bull. Say, you haven't seen Buck have ya? I gotta talk to 'em." But George just shook his head and Leon stumbled on towards the door. George's eyes followed him across the room, a low sigh escaping his lips thinking he had just escaped a dangerous situation and wasn't that a most peculiar fellow. Leon wouldn't know for some time to come, but he had just started one of the worst affrays in the history of Pratt. Only the arrival of the late train going on to Ashland saved the saloons from total despair and destruction. Somehow the constables managed to herd the woodsmen onto the train, hoping they soon would be Ashland's problem.

But in the meanwhile, Leon was on his way out the door, when who should he meet but Muff Brown. It was not a good time for Muff Brown to run into Mr. Mancheski, especially while his senses were soaked in beer.

When Leon woke up the next morning, he was not sure exactly where he was, except that he had slept on the floor. Then, in a blur, he noticed school desks... and a chalkboard, which only added to his confusion. It took several minutes before he could focus through his headache to realize there were bars around his bedroom. And he was not alone, a form moved beside him.

Leon stood up and stretched somewhat painfully. His head was pounding from the hangover, the dry and putrid taste in his mouth disgusted him and he had to urinate badly. Luckily he found a chamber pot within the cell, and made quick use of it. When he turned around feeling somewhat relieved the other man was in the sitting position staring at him. To his horror he suddenly realized it was Buck Johnson!

"Say, vhat yew do in here, py golly. Yew are in yail? Vhy that beats all hell, yew being in yail. Vhat kind a man are yew, anyvay? No sister of mine is going to marry a yailbird, I tell yew."

"Well, you're in jail," countered Leon.

"Don't yew change the subject, vee talking about your unlawfulness. How can yew marry my sister? Yew are no better dan common thief to end up in yail."

"Marry your sister?" repeated Leon not comprehending.

"Yah, my Andrea. I think it might not be so bad... but not now...now yew in yail." Buck stood up and scratched the back of his head... lingering softly over the small scab he found there. Then he was at the chamber pot to relieve himself as well. Leon thought he would never finish.

"Vhat yew do, anyvay?" he asked as he turned around.

"W...well," stuttered Leon, "near as I can figure... I hit Muff Brown."

"Yew hit Muff Brown?"

"Well, yah... several times, I think," admitted Leon, vaguely remembering the altercation.

"Vhy, dat ain't no crime!" laughed Buck. "They should make a medal for someting like dat. I voulda hit him myself, if I vasn't so busy." He came closer to Leon and looked down to him, assessing him in a new manner. Leon stood his ground and subconsciously doubled his fists at his sides. Suddenly Buck slapped him on his back, hard, but in good humor. And though it jostled him and aggravated his hangover... it was the most heartfelt slap he had ever known.

He was let out of jail the next day along with Buck, it being Sunday and school resuming on Monday. Enough citizens of Pratt had advised Muff that pressing charges against Leon was not in his best interest, that the whole matter was dropped as quickly as it started. But Leon never forgot the look on young Billy Brown's face that day at the bridge, nor his comment regarding taking Joe's place in death.

The time spent in the cell was not wasted. He gave a lot of thought to the direction his life was taking, and the direction from which it came. There was no doubt about it, there were matters unsettled, which had to be settled, before he could settle down and consider a new direction... possibly with Andrea. If she still was interested in him.

She was interested in him. And worried about him. She had heard about the fight with Muff, through the gossip circle, and found it so unlike him it scared her a little. Not a fear for Muff certainly, but a fear that Leon no longer knew his own mind and would soon leave Pratt altogether, forever. Without her.

These thoughts played on her mind as she walked back from town along the tracks, occasionally stumbling on the ties so lost in the moment was she. And suddenly there was Robert Walden in front of her, standing meekly in the middle of the bridge over Twenty Mile creek, his hands in his pockects and a furtive look in his eyes. His face was pale from weeks being bedridden and he was shaking slightly as if from cold. But it was a bright sunny day and Andrea knew it was not the cold that was shaking Robert Walden.

Oddly, she had a hard time looking at him… he reminded her too much of Joe and the loss they all felt. So she said nothing and started to move past him, not wanting to talk, not wanting to remember. But as she sidestepped him along the bridge she heard him sniffle. Not a loud complaining sound, just a small leak of emotion. The thought of it broke her stride on the ties and she stumbled, catching herself quickly and regaining her balance. Carefully she turned around and looked at the boy, him looking back at her with a hollow glance. He needed something from her, she thought. Some comfort. But then, they could all use a bit of comfort. She wasn't sure whose spirit needed comfort the most. So what could she offer?

"I'm sorry about Joe," he said, sniffling lightly once again.

"I know," she replied. "You're looking better. I'm glad you were able to recover from…

"Joe did it," he interrupted.

"Joe did what?" she asked confused. She was getting a shadow over her heart and a lump in her throat. "Joe did what" she repeated.

"Joe saved me," he said on the verge of tears. He held out his hand, slowly opening it to reveal a flattened silver quarter. She felt faint and had to kneel down next to the outstrecthed hand. There was no mistaking Joe's lucky quarter.

"My brother told me… he came one night when I was near gone. Henry let him in through the window. He snuck up to my room and put it in my hand. I don't remember it… but I was holding it all night long. And in the morning… Mama told me I was getting better."

Andrea's face was as white as the snow. She couldn't find any words to respond. She couldn't bring herself to move, frozen in the kneeling position at the outstretched hand of a tormented soul.

"Why did he have to do that? He knew I was cantagerous... he knew I could make him sick. Why did he have to do that? It ain't fair, him being dead... and me being alive. It ain't fair. I... I...

She saw finally what he needed from her. He needed to be forgiven for a sin that was not his own. And strangely she felt the same guilt... that somehow she had let Joe down, that Joe had been taken because of something she did or didn't do, or something she said or didn't say, or something she felt. None of it was rational, yet all so real. It felt real... in the heart where it counted the most.

She reached for his hand and closed his fingers over the silver charm, holding his fist tightly together. "Joe did what he had to do," she said. "He felt you needed something... needed him and he was willing to take that risk. Imagine how he would have felt if you would have died and him wondering if he could have made a difference. Its what he had to do, Robert. Neither of us could have stopped Joe from doing what he had to do. Do you understand that?"

He nodded. But the feeling in the pit of his stomach would not go away. He felt as if he was going to die of guilt and a broken heart. He couldn't know that Andrea felt the same way.

"Thank you, Robert," she said. "I see now that Joe died a glorious death. He wouldn't have wanted it any other way. He was a hero! He couldn't have been any braver if ...

Robert flung himself into her arms sobbing nearly knocking them both off the bridge. Awkwardly she was able to sit herself down and they stayed that way, gently rocking back and forth for a few minutes. She didn't know what else to say, so she just cooed to him softly that everything was ok. Finally he backed out of her embrace and stood up. He sniffed once and rubbed the palm of his hand over his runny nose.

"Joe is a hero, ain't he," he said. "He'd like that."

"We all need help now and again," she replied standing up now. "And sometimes the cost is a little high, but that doesn't diminish the need. Joe did what he thought was best. And regardless of the end, I will always love him for it."

It was the words he needed to hear. The burden on his spirit was starting to lift, though the sorrow would never pass. "What should I do with this?" he asked, holding out his hand again.

"You keep it," she said. "You never know when you're going to need a bit of luck." And he smiled back at her, the first smile in many long weeks. "Glorious," he said. Andrea couldn't know it then, but their meeting that day had a profound impact on the rest of his life.

As she trudged back home she wondered about her own life, today and in the days to come. The Johnson farm was different now. Joe was gone, and now it was known that Martha and Bill would marry in the coming summer. Her father could not talk to her anymore... could not look at her for long. What had she done, she wondered. What had she done?

Emil was in the barn taking care of the endless amount of chores that seemed to multiply around a small farm. He always took time to pat the cows on the nose however, each one in turn, and offer some comforting words, usually in Swedish. He thought it made a difference in the amount of milk they produced, if they were happy or not. Andrea found him talking to the Molly cow and he looked somewhat embarrassed when he found her leaning over the stall and watching him.

"It makes dem vant to give us more milk, I tink," he said, sighing heavily. "Or maybe not. I don't know." He gave the cow another pat on the flank and picked up the pitchfork, and started to move manure, ignoring Andrea.

"Papa?"

"Yas," he replied not looking up.

"I've just come from town and... there is a dance on Saturday, at the Modern Woodmen hall. Most of the camps have broken up for the winter."

"Vell, dat is gude, a dance. The men have so much energy to spend... they should dance, they should all dance," he said continuing with his chores.

"Papa, they want you to play."

"Vhat?" He paused and looked at her over his glasses. But he could not look at her long and suddenly found something interesting at the end of the fork.

"They want you to play the violin, Papa, at the dance. Everyone will be there... and Mr. Walden with his mandolin... and everybody. They need you, Papa."

Emil took out his red handkerchief and cleaned his glasses, blowing hot breath on them and rubbing earnestly. He checked them once or twice, but it seemed he could not find them clean enough and continued with this little operation, much to Andrea's frustration.

"Papa?"

"I hear vhat yew say... about dance. A dance is gude, but I cannot play. I yust cannot play."

"But Papa..."

"I said I yust cannot play, Andrea!" he repeated forcefully, his face coloring slightly. He put the glasses back on and started with the fork again.

"Will we go?"

He nodded ever slightly in the affirmative, but conversation was certainly ended. And Andrea walked off with head bent low, the burden of Joe's death once again heavy upon her heart.

"Well, you made it through winter and woods," said Cooper sitting behind his desk with his feet propped up, cigar planted firmly in his jaws. He was speaking to Leon sitting in the "short" chair before him. "And I must say, you did marvelous. Ox...uh... Mr. Swenson and Muggsley said they found you almost tolerable and would probably put up with you again if they had to. That's a pretty strong recommendation coming from the likes of them."

"Well, I've heard prettier words, that's for sure," allowed Leon. "But I'll take that the way I think it's meant."

"Good! You learn fast, when you've a mind to," smiled Cooper. "Say, I'm leaving the day after tomorrow. I expect I'll be gone a couple of months or more... business, family and things... you know. You are welcome to use the back room of the office if you can't afford the hotel."

Leon nodded casually. Something was still on his mind... not Chicago or Andrea or Muff Brown... something he was having trouble putting into words. It was a feeling about trees. He wasn't sure if he should mention it to a Lumber baron, but he knew that he had to, just as well.

"Mr. Cooper... does it ever bother you? About the business, I mean."

"I'm not sure I follow you."

"Well... the trees... you... we are cutting all the trees." Cooper sat in silence, trying to grasp the point. "I mean, you come in here to Pratt... and build a railroad into the hinterlands of the woods... and men work for you... hard work from dawn to dusk and then some... for $26.00 dollars a month while you sell the fruits of the labor for God knows how much money lumber goes for in St. Paul...and when the trees are all gone... then you'll be gone."

"So?"

"So? So? My God, take a look around you. The forests are devastated... there's not much left but slash and trash. It's a wasteland where we've been."

"Makes you uncomfortable, does it?" replied Cooper calmly.

"Your damn right it does!" said Leon strongly.

"Well good! You are just the type of man this country up here needs," said Cooper.

"What?"

"You heard me. I have been talking reforestation for years. Why, don't you see? If it was handled right, the lumber industry up here would last indefinitely... would build thousands of houses all over this great country. But you know what they want instead? Farms! You see, all that land that you say is now slash and trash...will make some of the best farmland in the country, rich soil, unspent for thousands of years. We could be planting and harvesting hardwood and pulp for years to come on that land. But no, they want to plant potatoes."

"But the pines, Mr. Cooper. They took hundreds of years to grow... hundreds of years standing tall...you can't wait a hundred years to cut a pine again."

"I didn't say pine... I said hardwood and pulp. The era of white pine in this part of the country will dwindle out in the next few years, sadly, I suppose. But better that pine wood goes into a good frame house for a family than stand to rot over the years, or perish in a fire. I'll miss the pines, son... really I will." Leon didn't look too convinced. He sat there staring at the man, assessing him, wondering if this was another story to sell.

"Look, son, I know it seems rather harsh to you now, just another big business deal to line the pockets of republican industrialists and all that... but things are not always what they seem. There is a part of me that is out there every day, sweating with the woodsmen, feeling their pain, sharing their ills. There is a part of me that cries over every tree cut, knowing its a living thing... one of God's creatures in a way. There is a part of me lost with every White Pine cut, knowing that in a few years they will all be gone... and worse... that they will never be again as they are now. Many woodsmen feel that way, though most would be unable to tell you that. Why do you think I spend so much time up here in the woods? As Jake often reminds me, certain people are good at certain things. I could no more chop down trees than Ox Pete could run the organization. But I am here...I am close... I am a part of it... this great enterprise, this chapter in history. That is why I am here, in Pratt, that is why I get up in the morning."

Leon sat there thoughtfully, saying nothing. Somehow it made him feel a little better, but did nothing to shatter the image of the wasteland left behind by the loggers work. Still, if it was not Cooper, it would be some other company, and there were those that were not nearly as good to work for, according to Helge and a few others.

"You should see my brother, George, when he comes up here," added Cooper. "He actually thinks he can drive the 2-Spot engine. You should see Alfred in a panic." Cooper chuckled lightly at the thought. Leon had to admit that the vision of a well-dressed businessman driving the Pratt & Southeastern engine through the hinterlands deserved at least a grin.

"That's better," said Cooper seeing the lines of Leon's face lighten into a smile. "Say there's a dance on Saturday night, could be just the thing to shake the winter gloom from our shoes. I would expect that you'd be there?"

"Wouldn't miss it," agreed Leon heartily. "Wouldn't miss it for the world."

K. Wallin

The Thirty Seventh Chapter

The Season Ends

Saturday came none too soon for most residents of Pratt. Indeed, it was a time to shake the gloom of winter from their muddy feet and celebrate another successful season of timber harvesting in the northland. It was the talk of the town for the day. That and the budding romance between Leon and Andrea.

Leon spent Friday night in a room at the hotel, which was full to capacity, most rooms doubling up temporarily due to the influx of loggers in town. Leon thought it appropriate that he roomed with Smiley Birch, seeing as how he had spent most of the winter with him... not to mention the night of the Christmas dance. And he especially enjoyed the bath the next day... knowing his smell would have improved 100% compared to how he usually showed up at the Johnson farm. He even borrowed some good smelling stuff from Sam Hacket. He had a new set of clothes to slip into, charged the day before at the store. They were nothing fancy, he thought, but it beat the sodden wool of his winter clothes.

Looking in the mirror after dressing, he saw a new man. A lean and wind worn face greeted him, clean shaven and handsome in a more mature way than he remembered. His body felt more solid, more strong. And hell, he thought... it wasn't even me that was chopping trees. He was ready to dance... and it was only noon!

Strolling out of the hotel he decided to go visiting. But who to visit? It was already arranged for Andrea to meet him around 4 pm. It just wouldn't do to run into Mary Muggsley... nor spend any time at the saloon.

Whiskey did not always give good advice, he remembered. But there was Jake. He was always amused by Mr. Jacobs, and hadn't seen him most of the winter.

"Hi Jake," he greeted the Straddle Creek bookkeeper upon entering the office. Jake was sitting back looking through the mail.

"Well, who's this? It couldn't be our little Chicago ruffian? What a fine figure you are cutting these days, Mr, Mancheski." Leon's face immediately darkened. "What's the matter with you? You look like you got a bad piece of sour candy."

"Did Mr. Cooper...did he tell you...about Chicago? It was supposed to be a secret."

Jake suddenly colored. He tried to think of something to say to cover... anything... but the most he could do was drop some of the mail and fumble around for it on the floor.

"Did he tell you about Chicago?" Leon prodded again and Jake was forced to confess.

"Yes, he told me. He told me lots of things...but mostly things that would help me, help him look after you. He was just trying to help... and so was I."

"Help? How," pushed Leon. "By spreading the word about me? By telling people the kind of trouble I'm in? Suppose word got back to Chicago... suppose..." and he stopped talking to ponder this possibility himself, and it made an involuntary shiver pass through his body.

"Nothing like that," said Jake. "Nobody else knows but Cooper and me as far as I know. And we've been watching for you, watching to see if anybody came looking for you. Especially dudes... you know, fancy dressed people from the cities. He's had Julias keeping an eye out... and Charley and a few of the others, not telling them why, mind you, just asking them to be on the lookout."

"How long has this been going on?"

"Oh, I don't know. How long you been in the woods?"

"That long, eh?" And Jake nodded.

"Thought they had somebody too. Had me and Mr. Cooper all excited once with a report of a dude come in on the train. But it turns out it was just Mr. Hines."

"Mr. Hines? The lumber baron?"

"Well, yes. But Julias didn't know who he was at the time, and there was a few rough looking characters with him, all duded up too, though you could see their roughness right through their finery. Seems he was headed for Mason and the White River operation."

"Good thing you recognized him before you made a fool out of yourself," said Leon.

"Well...yeah... that would have been nice."

"Does...Mr. Halprin know now... and Charley? About me, I mean?"

"Well, not much. Not more than the fact that you needed their help some. In fact I think you'd be surprised at how many people are looking after you... for no other reason than you needed help."

Leon suddenly felt uncomfortable. The "little child" feeling came back to sit on his shoulders again. Needing help in your life was bad enough, but getting it from practically strangers was mortifying. It made him at once happy and sad, and propped up his pride to harmful proportions.

"Well, I don't need anybody's help," he said defensively, "and I want this whole thing to stop. I would appreciate it if you would notify all those do-gooders that think they need to look after me and tell them I am quite able to take care of myself."

"As you say, Mr. Mancheski, as you say. I certainly will. Maybe you are right about all this. Besides, those guys in Chicago have probably forgot all about you by now."

"Well, where's Cooper?" said Leon grumpily.

"Mr. Cooper is down at the company store just now. You should go see him and try out your new attitude on him," chided Jake. "He'll be really pleased."

Leon fled the Straddle Creek office, his good mood and cherry optimism somewhat dampened. He had it in his head to walk away from it now... to walk these feelings out... perhaps to the bridge on Eighteen Mile creek... but found he was heading, instead, to the company store to have a few words with his benefactor.

The store was fairly quiet for a Saturday. Bill Farley was trying to inventory the stock, now that the camps were broke up and establish a baseline for re-ordering the summer goods. Mr. Cooper was behind the counter at a large desk going through ledgers to see what the winter camp expenditures were. There were a few customers in the store, Mr. Gillis, Mrs. Stone and a few boys eyeing up the candy jar, Elmer Rose checking out the fishing poles. Occasionally Bill's inventory would be set aside to service a customer or answer a question, but mostly folks were just looking.

Leon had lost some of his steam by the time he had walked the block or more to the store. He hesitated at the door for a few seconds, then seeing John Cooper behind the counter reviewing ledgers and smiling.

That did it. That smile. Leon entered and proceeded to his confrontation, not having the slightest clue what he was going to say.

"Well, don't you look spiffy," observed Cooper looking up. "My my my my. I'd hardly recognize you, and certainly no longer by the smell." Mrs. Gillis and Mrs. Stone were close enough to hear that comment and chuckled sweetly. It angered Leon all the more.

"Don't change the subject!" said Leon rudely.

"What subject?"

"I don't need every Tom, Dick and Harry from Pratt to Mason looking after my welfare!" said Leon fairly shouting.

"Well, that's good to know," mused Cooper rubbing his chin and wondering what all this was about. "Because I am sure that Tom, Dick and Harry have much better things to do. Now what the hell are you talking about?" At Cooper's minor slip into vulgarity, the ladies mocked a look of shock and disgust and moved a little farther away from the men, but certainly not so far as they wouldn't hear every word.

Before Leon could answer, two more customers entered the store, woodsy looking characters appearing to have just come from a camp. Not recognizing them, Bill went to offer assistance but it was declined. They had just come into town from the woods, they said, and wanted to pick out a few nice clothes for the dance tonight.

"You know damn well what I'm talking about. You told Jake... everything. And who knows how many he told. You had these people... people that I barely know, trying to look out for me. Well I don't need it. I can take care of myself."

"Yes, I see that. Yes, indeed. But I wonder if that was so, six months ago when a wet and bedraggled lad showed up at my office like a frightened cat on a stormy night afraid even to give me his name. I wonder if that was so then... or if this is a recent development."

"It was different then, I admit," said Leon softening at the remembrance of that evening. "And its not that I don't appreciate your help...I mean I really do... but a man has to stand on his own two feet. He can't always depend on others to look out for him."

"Well, I suppose that's true," nodded Cooper secretly pleased at the changes he had seen in this young man. He could feel his own fatherly pride starting to inflate. "And you certainly seem capable of managing your own affairs."

"Thank you for that," said Leon.

"Yes, I would say that Mr. Leon Mancheski has his life well in hand." And he reached up and offered his own hand to the young man. It was gratefully accepted with a warm smile.

"Say... now that you're here... I've been going over these accounts," said Cooper back to business. "By the time I subtract all these charges on account that you've made over the winter, I'm afraid your pay voucher is going to be a little light. In fact..."

"Escuse me," interupted a voice from behind. It was one of the woodsmen. "Mr. Mancheski is it?"

"Yes?"

The man suddenly grabbed Leon, brutally pushing his arm behind his back, while the other pulled a revolver from underneath his coat and pointed it at Cooper. "We've been looking for you for a long time, son," said the man holding Leon. "A long time. Seems you have something that belongs to our boss. You think he was gonna forget about you just cause you was hiding in the woods? Guess you don't know how the business works and the boss ain't that generous."

"You can have the money and the book, just let me go," exclaimed Leon. "I'll show you where it is."

"Well that's fine. That'll make things easier. The boss will appreciate that. In fact, I think the boss would like to thank you in person. He likes cooperation. Suppose we go for a little ride after."

"You boys figuring on holding him like that all the way to Chicago," asked Cooper calmly. But neither man answered, just slowly backing up toward the door.

"This ain't a pea shooter gramps," said the one with the gun. "Now you just sit tight and let us worry about our own travel arrangements." All of the people in the store heard this chatter plainly, and in spite of the danger, in spite of the warnings, crowded forward as the men retreated, even the ladies.

"Stay back!" shouted one of the dudes, waving the gun in the air. They were just in front of the door and Leon had pretty much stopped struggling and given in temporarily to his plight, his mind trying to think of other opportunities that may arise. And then it dawned on him... they had no intention of taking him to Chicago... after they had what they wanted, he was expendable. And in this case, expendable was another word for dead. The thought of it made his blood run cold!

Just as they had backed up to the threshold the door opened. It was only Old John Morgan, but the door bumped the man holding Leon, and in the surprise and fluster, Leon managed to break his grip and struggle with him, knowing now what was at stake. He was fighting for his life! In that instance, the man with the gun took his eyes off the rest of the people to see what was going on and Bill Farley rushed him. He grabbed the gun arm and a struggle ensued.

"Where the hell's Buck when you need him," muttered Cooper and then rushed forward to help. Elmer Rose went to Leon's aid, but being a slight built man added little to the affair, the struggling men just stumbling around him.

Seconds later a shot rang out and Cooper slumped ungracefully to the floor. It caught Leon's eyes and enraged him, empowering him with a greater strength, and shortly he was able to overcome the man, with a little of Elmer's help. But then looking up, he was in time to see Bill get hit with the butt end of the revolver and bleeding from the right side of his forehead, slowly weaken and fall. Then turning to face the door where his partner lay quietly groaning, the man aimed the revolver at Leon.

"Kinda foolish, aint' ya," he said. "Ok if that's the way it is, then that's the way it is. It don't matter to me when or where. In a little bugtit of a town like this, daylight or dark is all the same. And in a few seconds, it won't matter to you either," he said grittily. Cocking the revolver, his lips curled up in a sneer.

But before he could pull the trigger or think about an escape, a sudden loud "thwack" was heard coming from behind him sounding of breaking wood. When the man collapsed on the floor Leon could see Mrs. Gillis standing over him, ax handle in her hands.

"Oh, my" was all she said.

Leon stood there stunned for a bit, unable to comprehend the reason for his narrow escape. Suddenly he was alive with energy and effort. He sent Elmer for Doc Parker while he and John Morgran tied up the supposed woodsmen, and then with the ladies help, he tended to his wounded friends.

Bill was dazed but conscious, and held a bandage to his own head, while sitting and leaning against the wall. "I shoulda known," he would say now and again. "They weren't woodsmen. They smelled too clean! I shoulda known."

Cooper was conscious too. A splotch of blood started high on the left side of his chest and moved down until his shirt was fairly matted. Mrs. Stone had found some bandages and gave Leon one to slip under Cooper's shirt to press on the wound and try to stop the blood. Mrs. Gillis, though calm, still had a grip on that ax handle.

"Coulda been worse, eh?" said Cooper from his reclining position. A couple of folded up shirts from the shelves were slipped under his head for comfort. Some blood had already found the floor where it smeared under the feet and knees.

"Coulda been worse, Mr. Mancheski," he said again. "Damn, got blood all over these cigars. Say, break off the wet part and light one for me, will ya?" Leon did so, lighting the stubby end puffing on it briefly to ensure a good start. When it was glowing, he allowed Cooper the weedy end of it.

He puffed on it contentedly for a second, then removed it from his mouth and said, "Could have been worse if a man hadn't any friends." And Leon looked about him at these people; Mrs. Gillis chatting with Mrs. Stone, saying she knew they weren't woodsmen from the first, and how she could tell; Bill Farley already up and cleaning the blood that had spattered on the floor; Cooper lying with a bullet wound, still bleeding, still grimacing with the pain.

"If it hadn't been for me, this wouldn't have happened," he murmured, his eyes slightly moist. "I'm so sorry, Mr. Cooper. I'm sorry, Bill."

"For what, son," said Cooper after another puff on his short cigar. "If you're going to be sorry about anything, be sorry that you didn't understand us better. Be sorry that you didn't understand... the nature of friends." And with that, the cigar slipped from his fingers and his eyes closed.

And only the soft sound of a grown man with his life well in hand, crying, could be heard in the Straddle Creek company store.

K. Wallin

The Thirty Eighth Chapter

The Medicine of Dance

Things were well in hand as the time for the dance approached. The dudes posing as "woodsmen" were in the custody of the Bayfield County Sheriff, charged with a number of things that would keep them behind bars for some time to come. It worked to Leon's advantage that they wouldn't talk about the "whys & wherefore" of their actions. A code of silence, somewhat enhanced by the fear of failure that they would have to report to their boss, served to render them mute. The Sheriff got little more from Leon, yet knew there was a story there when Leon's eyes could not hold his gaze for long... the hang-dog look of someone with something to hide, but he let it pass for now. Leon was aware that their silence had bought him some time... but not much, and soon his world of deception was going to cave-in on top of him.

John Cooper, to Leon's surprise, was alive and well and adamant about attending the dance. The bullet had missed his lung, lodging just above it, and other than the general loss of blood causing him to be dizzy and weak, he prospered well. The stain of blood on the company store floor would be an attraction for years to come, with many a young man marveling about the "shoot out", the facts of which had all but been obscured by legend.

Mrs. Gillis was overwhelmed with the thought of being present for the most awe inspiring gossipy event in the history of Pratt. Not a word uttered that morning had escaped her attention, not the least of which was the word "money". The fact that she was a participant in the event made her the center of attention and neatly brought all those that would listen, right to her doorstep. But the most significant effect of the affair on Mrs. Margaret Gillis was one that she was not even aware. Henceforth when someone offered to drink to her health in Charley's saloon, all patrons would stand, remove their hats and drink heartily to the lady with the ax handle. And is wont to happen, from then on if you landed a particularly good chop into wood, it was from wielding "Maggie's Ax", a colloquialism that would endure through the ages long after people had forgotten its origin.

And so the citizens of Pratt, having heard about and thoroughly discussed the shootout, the players, the sordid story, looked forward to the dance with even more excitement and energy, a major celebration of life.

Sam Hackett was beside himself. No amount of cajoling could convince Emil Johnson to pick up his violin and play. Emil had left it deliberately behind on the farm, but discovered that it had been smuggled aboard the wagon by Andrea and was indeed present. Sam held it out to him expectantly.

"We need you, Emil," he said sincerely, "the music is lacking... everyone says so."

"The music is fine," replied Emil. "Everyvun dance yust fine. Py golly, you could make music with a squeaky vheel and they still dance yust fine, I tell yew."

"But..." Sam started again, to no avail. Emil rudely walked away from him toward the food table.

But Emil did not think the music was fine. It needed a good fiddle and everyone knew it. He watched Bob Walden picking away at his mandolin, Mrs. Humphreys fingers dancing over the piano keys, and all the others pulling music up from the deep reaches of their souls...yet he could not play. Not today, not ever. And so he sighed. And tapped his foot the best he could without moving his arm as if to play.

"You might have been killed," said Andrea, her delicate fingers brushing through the hair above Leon's ear. He hugged her tight, reveling in the warmth he felt from her.

"But I wasn't," he said. They had walked away from the dance, down Cudworth street south past Burke's store to be away from the frenzy of the dancers and alone with themselves. Though spring was at hand, it was still cool, making their embrace seem all the more warm.

He held her face in his hands, marveling how her eyes looked so large and bright in the dusky light, her cheeks so pale. She forced herself to set aside the worry and smile at him... for he needed it, she knew.

And he kissed her, meaningfully and long while deep in embrace in the shadows of the street. It made the world around him twirl into nothingness and all other thoughts fade from his mind, the nicest form of refuge. But it wouldn't last. He had to come up for air sooner or later and always discovered that the world was still there.

"You're leaving aren't you?" She said suddenly, her eyes penetrating deep within his. It caught him by surprise. He had been trying to think of a way to tell her.

"I've got to, Andrea, for a little while, anyway. You know I've got to settle things down in Chicago. I thought it would just go away," he said, looking off in the distance, looking for words... "but... I guess its not going to. Maybe if they had the ledger... the book might be enough to change things. Or maybe if the police had it... it would be enough. I have to settle this... I have to... you know that, don't you?"

"I know," she admitted.

"I wish there was some other way," he said softly, almost under his breath. There's got to be another way." They hugged briefly for comfort and then hand in hand they started to walk back to the revelry of the hall. When they were on the edge of the circle of light cast by the kerosene lamps posted outside, she stopped suddenly. He turned to face her wondering what was wrong, trying to read the expression on her face. She was nervously playing with a button on her coat, both hands twisting and turning it until he was sure it would come off.

"You won't forget me?" she stammered in the darkness. "When you leave us and see the lights of Chicago... will you remember me at all?"

"Oh Andrea," he said rushing to her and taking her in his arms. "Forget you?" he murmured softly, his hand lightly upon her cheek. "Forget the touch of your nose cold against my face when we kiss? Forget the lovely scent of violets in your hair?" He brushed his hand through its curls about her shoulders. "Forget the warmth of your embrace," he whispered close, "why it would be easier to forget my own name." And they kissed once more, aware that it may be the last for awhile... that it may be the last.

When they re-entered the hall, the dancing was at fever pitch, a happy energetic throng. To Andrea's chagrin, Emil though actively clapping and tapping, was still no closer to playing the violin than before. It saddened her and she clung close to Leon's arm.

"May I have a dance, Mr. Mancheski?" It was sweet voiced Mary Muggsley in pink lace and curls. A vision of loveliness that for a moment made Leon's heart jump just a little.

"Well, I uhh..."

"Oh go dance with her," urged Andrea with a laugh. "I want to talk to Papa." Had she known what was on Mary's mind, she might not have been so willing to cooperate.

While Leon stepped lightly on the pretty little feet of Mary Muggsley, Andrea approached Emil and curtsied formally in front of him. "May I have this dance, young man?" she said with a smile upon her face.

"Why, certally, young lady." And he took her arm and led her to the dance floor joining in the happy crowd. And the music played on.

As soon as she was able to, Mary maneuvered Leon out the door and into the night. Leon thought perhaps it was because she was tired of his clumsy feet, but she held his hand tightly and led him in back of one of the wagons that was parked along the street to the side of the Woodsmen's hall.

"Andrea will be looking for me," he said, still clueless as to why he was being dragged out of earshot of the other guests cooling themselves in the night air.

"Forget Andrea," she said turning to him and suddenly thrusting her body forward into his. It caught him off guard and he smiled sheepishly as they stood there. She looked at him with her most wanton look, but she feared he was too stupid to respond. So she kissed him… a hot passionate kiss that made him forget for a moment just who he was kissing. It made him forget everything except the moment and the tender warm lips embracing his. When the kissing stopped and he opened his eyes he found her smiling sweetly, her minted breath and light perfume still intoxicating his senses.

"I knew there was more to you than anybody knew," she said, softly staring into his startled brown eyes, her hand absentmindedly reaching up to finger his lapel. "A touch of larceny, perhaps," she continued. "I like that."

"You don't understand," he uttered, a bit confused himself.

She put her finger softly on his lips, saying "shhhhh". "Oh I understand," she said. "Thugs from Chicago wouldn't come all this way if a few dollars were at stake. You've a little fortune stashed away don't you, you clever darling." She caressed his cheek with delicate fingers and he felt himself beginning to perspire.

"Well…", was all he could stammer.

"Well…", she mocked him. "How much is our little fortune?"

He was intoxicated by her touch on his face, by the smell of her breath, by the moonlight on her blonde hair, by the warmth of her body still pressed firmly against his own. So he answered without thinking, "Nine thousand". And regretted it as soon as he said it. "But no one knows... not Cooper, not even Andrea. I shouldn't have told you," he sighed heavily.

She comtemplated it quickly and then smiled and kissed his cheek. "I think you will find me a most agreeable traveling companion," she said. "You just leave the arrangements to me, I'll take care of everything." When she saw the weak look in his eyes, she trailed soft kisses across his cheek and whispered softly in his ear. He was nodding, sighing. She was sure any doubt was erased from his mind by the time they returned to the dance. She smiled as he stumbled away into the crowd. Monday would be her last day in this drab little town. It made her feel like dancing!

Little Emma was sitting on a chair in the corner near the food table watching the dancing and milling crowds with disinterest. Now and again she tried to see through the milling bodies to where the boys were running about, then would sigh and sit back. She declined many offers of food and dance from concerned adults, including both Andrea and Martha... resolved to sit and watch. She caught the attention of Robert Walden, however, and when he could escape momentarily from the Pirates without their seeing, he came and sat down next to her.

"Joe went away," she said to him, near tears. The sight of Robert brought the memory of Joe back vividly into her mind and weighed heavily on her heart.

"I know," he whispered to her. He put his arm around her lightly. "I'll take care of you now, Emma. If anyone bothers you at all, I'll take care of them, you just see if I don't. I don't care how big they are." It brought a smile to her shiny face.

"You hear that music?" said Cooper from his bed. "I'm going, I tell you. Now hand me my shoes."

"The doc says no," replied Jake, "and no it is. No dance."

"Jake, you're fired!" said Cooper, wincing a little at the motion his anger brought.

"Again? That's the third time today."

"Well, if you were nicer to me, I wouldn't have to fire you so much. Damn it, Jake, hand me my shoes."

"Now listen you old fart, we came just a little too close to losing your fool hide today...and we aren't going to take any more chances. Its not that we really care what happens to you... but if something does happen to you, we're liable to have your brother George up here running the train and scaring hell out of the engineers."

"Jake?"

"I know, I know...I'm fired."

"Jake, thanks, ok? I mean it... you've been very good to me and I appreciate it. Ok?"

"Ok" said Jake. "Now you got a couple of days of mending and you may still make your train on Monday. If you cooperate, that is. So lay back there, now and I might let you suck on a cigar, providing you don't light it."

"Jake, you are just too nice to me, you know that? I know I don't deserve it, but... Jake would you do me one little favor?"

"What?"

"Hand me my shoes?"

Most of the people, looking back on the dance, thought it was the best one they ever had. Of course they said that about nearly every one. There were fewer drunks than usual, owing to the fact that most had gotten the initial rush out of their system in the last few days, and those that hadn't were pursuing their interests in Ashland or Hayward or places a little farther from home. Those that remained were ready to get into the dancing and went at it most energetically. Even Buck was seen to give it a whirl once or twice, though safely on the arm of Andrea and Martha. And for a while some of the men thought it was quite a novelty to give Mrs. Gillis a tumble or two. She later confided to Mrs. Stone, that had she known an ax handle would provide her with so much attention, she would have whacked somebody a long time ago, there being plenty of men that could use it.

All in all it was a fine night, lasting long and marred only by the lack of a good violin player in the orchestra.

The Thirty Ninth Chapter

Here that whistle blow!

Sunday was rather quiet in Pratt, the dancers just a little bit mellowed from the activities of the night. The churches were packed, with families reunited with their woodsmen, all thanking the Lord for safe passage through the winter's work and the bounty of its labors.

The midday meal at the Johnson farm was jarred from its usual subdued dignity by Martha's burst of excitement regarding her matrimonial affairs. It seems a date had been set... following adequate discussion about the matter with Bill Gustavel at the dance, and now plans could be made. And what plans, for she had many ideas all crowding her head at once and they came out of her mouth the same way.

"We could do it here at the farm, in the pasture perhaps, it's so pretty in June. Or at the church of course...but that's so traditional. I heard Sally Potts say that her sister got married right on the train...on the train for heavens sakes," she gushed. "We could wear lavender dresses...that would go so well with the broach aunte Ester gave me... and Bill in his best suit. Harry Wellstone is going to be his best man, you know. Harry's bringing his girl up from Chippewa Falls to be with him for this. Who knows who else might get married, now that we have shown how easy it is to make plans and all. I heard Sally Potts is just waiting for Mr. Jacobs to say the word... and he will say it too, if I am any judge. Who else? Well that Smiley Birch that Buck worked with this last winter is kinda sweet on somebody, though no one is exactly sure who. And Mary Muggsley of course"... but her voice trailed off as she looked up at Buck's troubled face.

387

"I vonder vhere Helge vent to," he said softly.

"I heard he was in Michigan again," said Martha. "But I think he might want to come to my wedding in June. Do you think so, Mama? Helge would cut quite a handsome figure in a suit, don't you think?"

"Ya, Ya all men look so nice ven they dress up. But is so hard to get them dressed sometimes. Helge vill come if he hears yu are getting married."

"Voman alvays vant a man to look like Sunday, no matter how hard he vorks," added Emil. "It makes no sense at all. A man should look like vhat he is...a farmer, a logger, a businessman."

"Ya," joined in Buck. "I don't have a suit to fit no more. It chokes me."

"Well, you'll both be dressed proper for my wedding or I'll choke you myself," replied Martha. "Really!" And both men smiled at her.

"You know what would be just glorious, Andrea? If you and Leon were inclined to marry... and for goodness sakes, everyone thinks so... maybe we could have a double wedding! Imagine, both of us...in beautiful lavender dresses...your brown hair setting off my blonde... white flowers all around us. Emma as the flower girl... looking just like a miniature bride. Ohhhhhh!" exclaimed Martha in barely suppressed excitement.

But the similar excitement she expected to see rise in Andrea was missing, her demeanor downright subdued, considering the subject.

"Andrea?"

"He's leaving, Mart. Tomorrow. Going to Chicago to see to some things... some important things, he said." Her face was sober, her eyes shiny. "I don't know when he will be back or...or if he will be back."

"Andrea! What are you going to do? How can you let him go like that. How can he leave?"

"How? By train, Martha Johnson. He's leaving by train."

"Well, I know, but I meant..."

"I know what you meant...I just don't know anything. He has to go, that's all."

"Its all right Andrea," said Alma softly patting Andrea's hand.

"Ya, ya," said Emil. "He might come back and vork in voods again, vee see, for sure. He's not much a logger, but a pretty gude chore boy, I tink, ya Buck?"

"Well, you can't take that chance, Andrea," said Martha. "You just can't take that chance. You gotta go with him! You got to go to Chicago with him! Doesn't she Mama?"

"No!" said Emil forcefully. "No," he said softer when he saw that everyone was suddenly looking at him, "yew cannot go to Chicago. Vhat vill yu do? Yust leave me... yust leave us like that?"

"Well, she's just got to go, papa." said Martha. "Right Mama? She could stay with Aunte Ester."

"I think..." started Alma, then glanced quickly at Emil, who glared back. "I tink if there is vay, Andrea should go. But she cannot...vee have no money for such a trip."

"But mama, there's a little we've been saving...it's almost enough," pushed Martha.

Mama shook her head no. "That money," she said in a low trembling voice, "is for stone marker...for yoseph. No, if there vas vay, maybe she go. But there is no vay."

Andrea couldn't help herself. Tears rolled down her cheeks and dropped from her chin to her plate of food. But she wasn't sure if it was because the trip was out of the question, or if it was thoughts of Joe.

"I am sorry Andrea, dat your fellow is going avay," said Emil sincerely. "But it is not very gude time. I could not vork this venter... and vee use all Buck's money even... and he get not much for himself. Maybe next year... vee sell more potatoes...maybe I vork in voods again...maybe..."

"Maybe it will be too late," said Martha cruelly.

"Martha!" scolded Alma. "Yu don't talk to your Papa like that. Papa has given so much... and Buck too."

"I'm sorry, Papa." she said contritely.

"It's ok Papa. I want to stay here, anyway," said Andrea, wiping the wetness from her cheek. "Mrs. Burke says I can start work in the store next month. She needs help with the confectionary during the summer months. And then...well there's other jobs I could do to help."

"Do we get strawberry sodas for free, Andrea?" asked Emma. It was easy to forget she was there sometimes, when the conversation turned to more adult topics.

"For you, sweetheart...if you are a real good girl."

"Oh, goody." said Emma clapping her hands in glee. "That's a good job!"

"Yas dat is gude, Andrea," soothed Alma. I have a feeling dat fellow vill come back tu...and yu vill be very happy."

"Well, I don't..." started Martha, but then wisely let the matter drop. "Maybe it won't be so bad."

In bed that night, Emil was restless. He tossed and turned and pulled at his mustache. From time to time he would reach for his watch on the bed table, opening it and trying to stifle its little song while lighting a match and once more taking note of the time. It was hours of this before Alma said anything.

"You vorry about vhat?" she whispered.

"Everyting," he said. "Yust everyting, py golly, but mostly I vorry about Andrea. She is such a good girl. She knows vhy she cannot go."

"She knows," agreed Alma. And gave him the kiss on the forehead he so strongly needed but could never ask for. "She knows."

By Monday, Cooper was well enough to travel. He walked slowly and gingerly to the Depot giving himself plenty of time, Jake following behind, watching the older man and expressing concern over every exertion. Cooper ignored him for the most part.

They stood on the platform in the morning light, the sunshine feeling good against their skin in the cool Spring air. Julias came out of the storeroom wheeling some cargo on the cart, checking tags, and nodding, mumbling to himself. Looking up he noticed Cooper and Jake standing near the express mail pole.

"Say, that was some doings at the store, Mr. Cooper," he yelled over to them. "I'm glad things turned out alright... it just wouldn't be the same around here without you."

"Well, thanks Julias."

"Yep... it would get kinda quiet around here, that's for sure," he said.

"Am I that noisy, Julias".

"Yep," said Julias, continuing to bustle about the cargo. When he was satisfied things were in order he went over to stand beside the men, pulling his watch out of his pocket and squinting at the dial. "Should be about Tank Lake about now..." and they listened for a whistle, marveling when it sounded in the distance as if on cue. "Beautiful morning, ain't it? Even the train is on time this morning. But not many passengers, looks like."

"Has Mr. Mancheski been by here yet?," asked Cooper casually.

"Not that I seen," replied Julias.

"Some kids got into my woodpile behind the office last night," said Cooper. "Tore it all up. Beats me how a guy can sleep through something like that... but then... that fellow kinda surprises me now and again."

"Night Owl Bill ain't left yet... I'll askem if he seen 'em," offered Julias jaunting off before Cooper could reply.

"I wish I had his energy," commented Cooper as the door slammed behind Julias. "That man reminds me of a bumble bee... always buzzing around everything, yet to look at him, you'd never think he could fly."

As quick as he went in, Julias came out again, whisking over to the men, lifting his hat and scratching behind his ear as if deep in thought. "Bill says he left late last night when the express came through. Almost got run over flagging her down," he says. "Then him and her gets on while the engineer screams and cusses and they're gone. Peculiar ain't it?"

"There was woman with him?" asked Jake

"That's what Bill says."

Jake looked at Cooper's impassive face and mistakenly took the look for bewilderment.

"Ya know, Mr. Cooper," he said. "I used to think you were a pretty good judge of character." Cooper smiled weakly. "Gone without a goodbye. Gone without a thank you very much, hate to leave. So she got him after all. The wonderous charms of Miss Mary Muggsley have finally ensnared a prey worthy of her attention. And Mr. Cooper is as surprised as every one," mused Jake smugly.

Cooper's smile broadened. Without a word he nodded to the area of the platform that was in shadows, where Mary Muggsley had just arrived and stood waiting, nervously primping and preening, traveling gloves gracing the fine features of her soft hands. She found the men staring at her and so she gave them a charming Miss Mary smile.

"Have you seen Mr. Mancheski," she asked gaily. "We're leaving today."

The train coming from the west was on time, its whistle sounding nearly a mile before Eighteen Mile creek bridge and several times thereafter until its chugging sound could be heard coming down the rail. They stood on the platform in a rush of mist from the engine as it passed and watched the huge machine finally squeak to a stop with the first coach car lined up expertly with the platform. Nightowl Bill came out of the depot then, to add another package to the mail pouch, a book sized parcel wrapped in brown paper and addressed with a childish scrawl. He waved at the men, doffed his hat to Miss Muggsley, then went to find his buggy. His shift was over, now that the day had begun.

Fifteen minutes later when the train pulled out, there were still three men on the platform and one red-faced female building up a head of steam of her own. Mary looked once more at the rear end of the train heading east toward Ashland, where the Wisconsin Central was waiting to take her to Chicago, then strode over to Cooper. There was no smile this time.

"It appears," she said between gritted teeth, "that if some people knew better how to point a revolver, I'd be out of this burg by now." Then she stormed away, mud flinging off her heals as she strode down the path.

"She sure is pretty," sighed Jake as the men watched her form dwindling in the distance, still animated, arms swinging left and right as she walked. "Even when she's mad." Then turning to Mr. Cooper, "you knew about this?"

"Not everything," admitted Cooper. "I came this morning to see if there was going to be any fireworks. Never dawned on me he'd get away from Miss Muggsley entirely. That's the human spirit for ya. Appears there's still a lot about that boy we don't know."

"Think he'll be back?"

"Hard to tell, Jake, even for me. If he took the Express to St. Paul, odds are he's headed west. That caught me by surprise. I thought for sure he would he would be heading to Chicago to straighten things out. Maybe there are more reasons for not going to Chicago than he's mentioned. Maybe we don't know this boy at all."

Cooper leaned against the depot wall and pulled out his watch. Jake noticed that it wasn't Cooper's watch at all, not the big dull chrome one that never seemed to work. This one played a little song. "I got a couple of hours before my train to St. Paul," he said casually. "But you know, I really don't mind the wait."

As he leaned there against the rough boards of the depot, appreciating the bright sunshine in a cloudless blue sky, Cooper would allow his gaze to pan over the White River valley to the north, his appreciation for its beauty obvious upon his face. He reached into his inside coat pocket for a cigar, but came out with a twig of maple instead, courtesy of Jake. He smiled and stuck it in his mouth, absently trying to puff on it now and again. Just down the tracks Mrs. Williams was sweeping the porch and the men could hear her swatting at the dogs on her stoop good-naturedly and calling them fool names. In the distance could be heard the soft tinkling of the bell around Wheeler's bull as it ambled slowly out to pasture. And the lightness in the heart and mind of John Cooper was not from the loss of blood.

The winds of March blow cool and indifferent through the winter fields and barren woods of the Northland. They bluster and push at the windows and doors, chasing smoke from the chimneys and causing passersby to hide behind woolen scarves as they wind their way around frozen puddles and rutted roads. Those that know of such things can still feel the hand of winter on these March winds, and see snow yet in the northern sky. There are others, however, that refuse to entertain such gloomy thoughts, thinking fondly of early summers they have known, sure that the weather will spring soon to sunshine, warm rain and pretty flowers. March, she just laughs and Summer comes when it will.

The End

About the Author

K. Wallin was raised in a small town in Northern Wisconsin, once a whistle stop along the Chicago, Minneapolis, St. Paul & Omaha railroad and a shipping point for logging operations in the vicinity. As a child he played in the remnants of the logging era, building a fort in the old lumber train roundhouse and hunting along the old railroad grades and logging trails. While performing research for the town's centennial book in 1984, he became enamored of the story of the people; the loggers, the farmers and tradesmen that had carved this village out of the wilderness. In "A Lumbertown Tale" he brings this story to life; the drama, the hardships, the joys and the sorrows.